Exploring
Social Insurance

Can a Dose of
Europe Cure Canadian
Health Care Finance?

Exploring
Social Insurance

Can a Dose of
Europe Cure Canadian
Health Care Finance?

Edited by
Colleen M. Flood, Mark Stabile, and Carolyn Hughes Tuohy

School of Policy Studies, Queen's University
McGill-Queen's University Press
Montreal & Kingston • London • Ithaca

SCHOOL OF
Policy Studies

Publications Unit
Policy Studies Building
138 Union Street
Kingston, ON, Canada
K7L 3N6
www.queensu.ca/sps/

Library and Archives Canada Cataloguing in Publication

Exploring social insurance : can a dose of Europe cure Canadian health care finance? / edited by Colleen M. Flood, Mark Stabile and Carolyn Hughes Tuohy.

Includes bibliographical references and index.
ISBN 978-1-55339-213-2 (bound).—ISBN 978-1-55339-136-4 (pbk.)

1. Medical care—Canada. 2. Medical care—Europe. 3. Medical economics—Canada. 4. Medical economics—Europe. I. Flood, Colleen M. (Colleen Marion), 1966- II. Stabile, Mark III. Tuohy, Carolyn J., 1945- IV. Queen's University (Kingston, Ont.). School of Policy Studies

RA410.55.C35E7929 2008   362.10971   C2008-900110-9

Contents

List of Tables and Figures   vii

Foreword   xi
Hugh Segal

Acknowledgements   xiii

1. Introduction: Seeking the Grail: Financing for Quality,
   Accessibility, and Sustainability in the Health Care System   1
   Colleen M. Flood, Mark Stabile, and Carolyn Hughes Tuohy

2. Health Care Financing, Efficiency, and Equity   37
   Sherry Glied

3. Efficient and Fair Financing of the Public Share of Canadian
   Health Care Insurance with Greater Reliance on the User-Pay
   Approach   59
   Jack M. Mintz and Andrey Tarasov

4. Payroll-Tax Financed Health Insurance: A Way for the Future?   91
   Morley Gunderson and Douglas Hyatt

5. Social Insurance versus Tax Financing in Health Care:
   Reflections from Germany   115
   Stefan Greß, Stephanie Maas, and Jürgen Wasem

6. A Competitive Market for Social Health Insurance in
   Five Countries: Is There a Relation between Funding and
   Organizing Health Care?   139
   Wynand P.M.M. van de Ven

7. Funding Health Care Services: The Optimal Balance   163
    Timothy Stoltzfus Jost

8. The Comparative Dimension of Policy Analysis:
    Rules of the Game?   185
    Ted Marmor

9. Challenges and Changes in Pharmacare: Could Social Insurance
    Be the Answer?   199
    Steve Morgan

10. Between the Dream and Sleepwalking: Pragmatic Possibilities
    for Canada   221
    Terrence Sullivan

11. Policy and Politics: A Commentary on the Conference on
    Social Insurance for Health Care: Economic, Legal, and
    Political Considerations   233
    Joseph White

12. Conclusion   251
    Colleen M. Flood, Mark Stabile, and Carolyn Hughes Tuohy

    Index   277

    Contributors   285

List of Tables and Figures

TABLES

CHAPTER 1

A2.1 Relationship between financing type and health care expenditure   35

CHAPTER 2

1 Relationship between spending composition and spending growth   45

2 Lifetime spending by quintile and redistributive effect of health care spending   51

CHAPTER 3

1 Health care spending in developed OECD countries   65

2 Sources of health care funding and out-of-pocket payments in developed OECD countries   67

3 User-fee rates in the simulated policy options   77

4 Expected decrease in total demand for physician and hospital services in response to the implementation of user-fee policy options 1–6, Canadian average   79

5 Expected reductions in provincial public spending on physician services by policy option and by province   80

6 Average per household premium caps by province-specific household income distribution quintiles   81

7 Average per household premium caps, by family size   82

8 Total expected annual user-fee premium payments per person, after premium allowances and caps are taken into account   82

9 Total expected annual user-fee premium payments per family, after premium allowances and caps are taken into account   83

10 Expected health premium revenues, by policy option and
    by province   84
11 Expected total provincial public revenues/savings from
    the proposed user-fee program   84

CHAPTER 5
1 Taxes vs. social insurance: fairness   119
2 Taxes vs. social insurance: financial sustainability   121
3 Taxes vs. social insurance: employment   123
4 Income, morbidity, and consumption of health care
   services of enrollees in social health insurance and
   private health insurance   126
5 Employment consequences of a substition of social
   insurance funding   133

CHAPTER 6
1 Risk Equalization System 2006   147
2 Level of competition on the social health insurance market
   in 2006   152
3 Tools for an individual health insurer to influence its health
   care expenses for mandatory social health insurance, 2006   156

CHAPTER 11
1 Canadian health care expenditure   234

FIGURES

CHAPTER 1

1 The menu of policy responses   10
2 Health expenditure in the OECD as a share of GDP, 2003   14
A1.1 Public confidence: Canadian attitudes toward needed
      changes in health care system, 1988–2004   28
A1.2 Public confidence in international perspective:
      percent responding "System needs to be entirely rebuilt,"
      six nations, 2004, 2005   28
A1.3 Public confidence – sustainability: percent very or
      somewhat confident quality care will be available when
      needed, five nations, 2004   29
A1.4 Provider satisfaction: hospital executives very or
      somewhat satisfied with health care system, five nations, 2004   29
A1.5 Provider concern – sustainability: hospital executives
      reporting own institution funding insufficient to maintain
      current service levels, five nations, 2004   30
A1.6 Public health expenditures as a percentage of GDP,
      two scenarios, 11 nations, 2005 and 2050   30
A2.1 Average growth in public health spending by funding type   31
A2.2 Changes in social insurance and tax funding:
      social insurance countries   32
A2.3 Changes in social insurance and tax funding: tax financed
      countries   33

CHAPTER 2

1 Composition of financing, 2000   40
2 PPP adjusted health care spending per capita,
   1960 and 1990   44
3 Cohort survival by quintile: Canadian men   48
4 Cohort survival by quintile: Canadian women   48
5 Annual spending by quintile, men   49
6 Annual spending by quintile, women   50
7 Change in tax share and health share of GDP, 1975–2003   55
8 Change in tax share and in public health expenditure share
   of GDP   55

CHAPTER 5

1 Sources of health care financing in Germany 2004   124
2 Sources of health insurance premiums of employees
   as a percentage of pre-tax income   125

3 Income tax as a percentage of taxable income   128
4 Federal sales tax as a percentage of disposable income   128
5 Health care expenditure and premium income in social
   health insurance   130
6 Tax funding of social health insurance in Germany,
   2003–2010   131

CHAPTER 6
1 The financing system in the Netherlands, 2006   142
2 Three modalities of a subsidy system   145

CHAPTER 8
1 Total health care expenditure and public share of
   total health care financing in 1970   190
2 Total health care expenditure and public share of
   total health care financing in 2000   191
3 Public health care financing as a percentage of total
   health care financing in 1970 and change of total health
   expenditue as a percentage of GDP from 1970 to 2000   191
4 Comparative health care costs: US, UK, Germany, and
   OECD average   193

CHAPTER 9
1 Health care financing as the flow of funds between pools   201
2 The financing of medically necessary physician and
   hospital services in Canada   202
3 The financing of pharmaceuticals in Canada   204
4 Canadian expenditure on physicians services, hospitals, and
   pharmaceuticals, 1975 to 2005, with projections to 2017   207
5 Canada's 2006 population pyramid and the public liability
   of age-based pharmacare   210

CHAPTER 10
1 Public and private sector shares of total health expenditure 222
2 Provincial/territorial government health expenditure
   proportion of Gross Domestic Product, Canada, 1974–1975
   to 2006–2007, in current dollars   223
3 Provincial/territorial government expenditure as a
   proportion of provincial/territorial Gross Domestic
   Product, Canada, 1992–1993 to 2005–2006   224
4 Top priorities for health care spending   226

Foreword

Hugh Segal

The theory of path dependency in public policy and political science emerges from an economic theorem that posits that continuing in an existing path is always easier and more likely than radically shifting from a path's established direction. In terms of policy areas like the administration of justice, international affairs, or the sacred trust of public health care funding, this core rule seems to apply with great consistency. Indeed, even the so-called debates between the left and right on health care funding in Canada seem to be more centred on what kind of footwear to deploy walking or running along the established path as opposed to any radical departure to build a path in an entirely new direction.

Wherever one might find oneself on the Canadian political spectrum – the left, the right, or the centrist versions of either preference, or as a patient, health provider, or political or public service actor responsible for aspects of our health care system – it has become quite clear that however inspired or humane the premises underlying the Canadian public health care and insurance system, the fiscal capacity to continue in an uninterrupted straight path from where we are now is severely threatened by demographic, fiscal, personnel, and technological factors. In a free society, doctors and nurses cannot be compelled to work more, or even stay in their profession. Whatever strategies for health maintenance and illness prevention are deployed today, whatever professional preparation or immigration solutions are tried to increase provider supply, these will not produce short-term results. And, most importantly, in fiscal terms, with most provinces at or above the 50 percent mark in healthcare expenditures, and many hospitals experiencing huge financial pressures across Canada, there is no reason whatever for any complacency on the core financing challenge itself.

In our debates about health care policy choices, our proximity to the United States often unfairly produces a sense that our only choices are the Canadian model status quo versus the U.S. private/HMO/seniors Medicaid and Medicare options. The great and enduring value of the ideas, empirical insights, and analysis in the 12 chapters of this book is the outreach to European experiences, where there has been more innovation on the financing issue by both social democratic and Christian democratic governments. And these are governments that, along with their social insurance model, also share more broadly the Canadian value of health care for all without regard to financial capacity.

If there was ever a time to open the windows wide for a conceptual and structural debate around financing options consistent with both the premises of social solidarity and fiscal responsibility, that time has arrived. And the debate must be about more than just private versus state options. It must be a debate that explores models that have been used elsewhere to sustain both quality health care and financial management of growth pressures and the ensuing fiscal risks. *Exploring Social Insurance* is a thoughtful, multi-variant, and carefully articulated primer for just such a debate. It is not only useful for governments and planners to look ahead at future options but particularly helpful in removing North American blinkers and encouraging us to benefit from experiences driven by similar values but different popular financing models elsewhere. These social insurance models appear very much to yield both flexibility and sustainability in ways not always achievable within a unique tax-based financing regime. Now that Ottawa has begun to pass on both the health reinvestment dollars of Prime Ministers Chretien and Martin and the fiscal disequilibrium transfers into provincial fiscal bases launched by the Harper administration, and provinces and health providers are still short of financial sustainability, this book could not come at a better or more necessary time.

HUGH SEGAL is Senior Fellow at the Queen's School of Policy Studies, and the junior Senator (Conservative) from Ontario in the Canadian Senate. He is a former President of the Institute for Research on Public Policy.

Acknowledgements

We would like to acknowledge generous financial support from the Government of Ontario and particularly the Ministry of Health and Long-Term Care for both this volume and the two-day conference in November 2006 to workshop the papers in the volume. We are grateful to all the commentators at the conference whose contributions influenced both the final papers and our own thinking. We thank Sujith Xavier and Oscar Cabrera for their hard work and assistance at every step of the project. We thank Anita Srinivasan and Zora Anaya at the School of Public Policy and Governance at the University of Toronto for their help in organizing the conference workshop. Finally, we are grateful to the publishing division at the Queen's School of Policy Studies and the McGill-Queen's University Press for their assistance in producing this volume.

Chapter 1

Introduction: Seeking the Grail: Financing for Quality, Accessibility, and Sustainability in the Health Care System

Colleen M. Flood, Mark Stabile, and Carolyn Hughes Tuohy

Sustainability, quality, accessibility – is it possible to obtain a balance of all three – a holy grail – in any health care system?

Circa 2006, sustainability, quality, and accessibility are front and centre questions in Canadian health care. With respect to sustainability, all Canadian provincial governments are concerned about the growing share of public budget absorbed by health care and are questioning the sustainability of the present system. In Ontario, 45 percent of total provincial spending is devoted to health care, and this is predicted to increase into the future; in Alberta, that percentage is lower at 38 percent but undoubtedly still of concern (CIHI 2005). Apart from questions of sustainability, hard questions are being asked by the public and by providers about issues of quality and accessibility. In particular, the public is very concerned about wait times, and the 2005 *Chaoulli* decision – in which the Supreme Court ruled that the *Quebec Health Insurance Act* and *Hospital Insurance Act* prohibiting private medical insurance in the face of long wait times violated the *Quebec Charter of Human Rights and Freedoms* – has sprung open the debate about private insurance for financing more timely treatment in the private sector. There are also concerns, raised by every recent commission charged with investigating the future of medicare, over the breadth of services covered. The "system" presently leaves important non-hospital and non-physician services outside the universal single-payer model, in a realm of mixed finance and with various limitations on coverage and eligibility. In the Ontario context, for example, there are concerns about access to prescription drugs on the part of the working poor.

Pressures on the public system are only likely to increase as technological change exacerbates existing schisms. Increasingly, the locus of care is shifting out of the realm of medically necessary hospital and physician services for which universal first-dollar coverage is provided under the current Cana-dian model. Expensive drugs are being developed, often of questionable benefit or alternatively offering significant benefits to a relatively small number of individuals. Pressure is put upon provincial governments to publicly fund these drugs, raising sustainability issues. Yet if the same drugs are *not* publicly funded, questions are raised about quality and accessibility of the public sys-tem. Furthermore, the increasing capacity of health care to improve the quality of life is creating a grey zone of services, devices, and drugs that are not strictly "medically necessary" in the sense of prolonging life or sustaining a practical level of functioning but nonetheless can enhance individuals' en-joyment of life. Cultural change, coupled with technological innovation, is also a source of pressure. Modern consumer society replete with cable-on-demand, iPods, blogs, etc., is a society where wants are both met "on demand" and tailored to individual preferences. Unsurprisingly, people in these socie-ties are increasingly unwilling to tolerate the prospect of waiting for care when they need it or want it, or with other limitations on access. Given that the current scope of public coverage appears difficult to sustain, how can health care beyond that scope and more timely care be financed? As Lester Thurow wrote: "Being egalitarians, we have to give the treatment to everyone or deny it to everyone; being capitalists, we cannot deny it to those who can afford it. But since resources are limited, we cannot afford to give it to everyone either" (1984).

DEFINING FINANCING OPTIONS

In order to help us frame the questions and to provide further and better under-standing of the models of public/social/private financing that exist, we begin by defining the basic financing models used across most OECD countries. The first two of these models represent forms of public financing. That is, they entail mandatory contributions, and the funds are collected and managed by either a state agency or by a not-for-profit agency regulated by the state. The latter two are private financing models. The four models are as follows:

1. Public systems funded through *general tax revenues*. This form of financ-ing is usually progressive so that there is both income solidarity and risk solidarity; in other words the rich redistribute to the poor and the healthy redistribute to the sick. Countries with these systems include Australia, Canada, Denmark, Finland, Ireland, Italy, Norway, New Zealand, Portu-gal, Spain, Sweden, and the UK.
2. *Social insurance systems* funded through mandatory contributions (a per-centage of income often contributed to by employers and employees), administered by a state agency or a not-for-profit agency delegated by the

state, exercising power (sometimes monopoly power).[1] This form of financing can be funded on a progressive basis, although benefits beyond a basic package may vary somewhat by occupational status. Countries that are described as forms of social health insurance countries include Austria, Belgium, Czech Republic, France, Germany, Greece, Hungary, Iceland, Japan, Korea, Luxembourg, Mexico, the Netherlands, Poland, Slovak Republic, Switzerland, and Turkey (Colombo and Tapay 2004, 11-12). We are interested in those countries that through mandates use social health insurance to effectively provide for universal health insurance coverage for all citizens and achieve a measure of both income and risk distribution. Thus we are particularly interested in countries like France, Germany, and the Netherlands.

3. *Private not-for-profit* insurance funded through voluntary contributions in a competitive market, administered by private corporations that do not distribute profits. This kind of insurance *may* voluntarily pool risks to ensure some cross-subsidization from the healthy to the sick, and/or regulation may require such cross-subsidization in the form of preventing risk-rating premiums and/or preventing cream-skimming (requiring insurers to take all who apply irrespective of pre-existing conditions). Heavily regulated private not-for-profit insurers can to all intents and purposes mimic public insurance. Proposals being implemented in the Netherlands are moving that country from a social insurance country to a heavily regulated insurance market with mandates for coverage for all.

4. *Private for-profit ("commercial")* insurance, funded through voluntary contributions in a competitive market, administered by private corporations that distribute profits to owners of share capital. This kind of insurance generally does not pool risks from the healthy to the sick. The US system bases a significant proportion of its system on this model, although it still has very large public program for the poor and the elderly. One should also note that government may regulate private commercial insurers (as it does in Australia and to some degree in many US states) to prevent risk-rating and cream-skimming.

Jurisdictions vary in the extent and the ways that they combine these funding models and in the regulatory frameworks that they establish to govern them and thus the extent to which access is assured on the basis of need and not ability to pay. The OECD, categorizing the various roles of public and private financing across different countries, includes with "public" both taxation revenues and social insurance. This volume considers the consequences of funding health care services through taxation revenues versus funding them through social insurance, and what applicability, if any, these consequences have for the future of Canadian health care finance.

If there is one consolation to Canadian governments as they wrestle with the future of medicare, it is that sustainability concerns are not unique to Canada. Indeed, one clear lesson to arise from cross-jurisdictional comparison is that, counterintuitively, there is no obvious solution to be had to broader sustainability concerns from moving to greater degrees of private financing. *All* countries, regardless of the level of private financing in a system, appear to wrestle with the issue of sustainability and with similar pressures on public spending. Some jurisdictions, however, seem to have fewer difficulties with managing waiting lists. Some countries – like the US – achieve this by leaving many citizens under-insured or uninsured – an approach unlikely ever to be embraced here, given Canadian values. But other countries, particularly social insurance countries in Northern Europe such as Germany and France, manage to achieve universal access without long waiting lists, while bringing a wider range of services (including pharmaceuticals, home care, long-term care) into their universal plans. Social insurance countries in Western Europe seem to achieve largely the same redistributional objectives as countries funded by taxation revenues, but they do so by sourcing a much greater percentage of financing through employer and employee contributions. Noting these apparent advantages of social insurance countries, a number of countries with predominantly tax financed systems are considering increasing the role for social insurance funding in their financing schemes. At the same time, however, many of the social insurance countries are seeking to shift more of the burden of health care financing onto the general tax base. It appears that given the advantages of different modes of finance, a diversification of the funding base for health care is an increasingly attractive option cross-nationally.

In judging the appropriate mix of social insurance and general taxation, various considerations come to bear. We analyzed spending patterns across several OECD countries and make the following observations (see appendix 2 for detailed results). First, social insurance countries do not skimp in terms of the amount of funding distributed on a progressive basis (what we will call public funding) for health care, relative to countries that rely predominantly on tax financing – nor are they in general more generous. We find no significant difference between social insurance and tax financed countries in the level of public health care spending, controlling for GDP. These results are similar to those found by Sherry Glied in her chapter in this volume. Social insurance countries spend slightly more on total health care spending (between 70 and 100 public-private partnership dollars more per capita, according to our calculations), a difference that must be attributable to higher levels of private spending. Furthermore, the dynamics of social insurance systems seem to be slightly more sensitive to feedback effects between public and private finance – we find, for example, that increases in private financing are associated with somewhat larger subsequent declines in public spending (and vice versa) than is the case in tax financed countries, although the differences are not large. It may be that in these employment-based systems, the boundary between public and private finance is somewhat more permeable than it is in tax financed systems, but understanding this relationship would require getting underneath these gross aggregate correlations to the finer details of system design, both fiscal and regulatory.

What does appear to be the case is that the social insurance systems are *prima facie* not to be marked by the level of concern about waiting times and other dimensions of quality as are experienced in Canada. Whilst the Netherlands does report problems with wait times, most social insurance countries in Western Europe, including France and Germany, do not report a significant problem (Siciliani and Hurst 2004, 4). It may be that these highly regulated employment-based systems are better able to incorporate their somewhat higher levels of private spending without deleterious effects on the public system. It may also be that when both workers and employers are engaged in the management of the sickness funds and in negotiating with providers, the result is a better alignment of supply and demand than is the case when central government executives perform these roles. These are, however, conjectures at this point and beg to be further explored.

Social insurance countries have their own mélange of concerns and issues – including concerns about the impact of employment-based levies on employment levels and investment. These systems are also products of a long history of institutions and accommodations that are not readily transportable in part or in whole to the Canadian context. And it must be noted that each of these countries includes a component of tax-based financing in its funding mix for health care, just as a number of predominantly tax financed countries include some social insurance components. In the quest for sustainable modes of financing that maintain and improve quality and accessibility, more diversified sources of public funding may well represent the way forward. In this light, the potential of social insurance as one of the components of public finance for health care in Canada is a subject deserving of intense and rigorous exploration.

In the first section of this introduction, we sketch out in more detail the nature of the problems in Canada and clarify our definitions of quality, accessibility, and sustainability. We then explore the policy options that are likely to move us towards an optimal balance of quality, accessibility, and sustainability. Of the three policy options – spending smarter, creating informed demand, and sustainable funding arrangements – we choose to focus on the last of these, not because it is any more important than the other two but because in the Canadian context it has been relatively under-studied. We then frame our discussion of possible funding arrangements by setting out the possibilities in terms of, first, the primary type of funding source for health care systems and, second, a categorization of how systems draw the boundaries between the public and private divide. The second section raises the research question we need to address to determine whether social insurance, as a component of health care financing, may or may not contribute to finding the optimal balance – the grail – in Canadian medicare.

SECTION I: DEFINING THE PROBLEM

THE CANADIAN PERSPECTIVE

Sustainability and the Budget Squeeze. For the past several years, provincial health care budgets have been growing at a rate faster than provincial revenues, with the result that health accounts for a larger and larger share of provincial expenditures. Although projections forward based on past experience depend upon the particular time period chosen as the historical base, it is clear that under any likely scenario, health care in the future is going to grow faster than GDP. Unless government revenues grow faster than GDP, therefore, the gap between the rate of increase in health care costs and the rate of increase in government revenues will continue to grow.

In the Ontario context, there is a concern about crowd-out of other critical areas of spending (education for one) in favour of the ever-yawning abyss of health care spending. Between 1989 and 2003, for example, real per-capita health care spending in Ontario increased by 20 percent, while real per-capita spending on post-secondary education fell by more than 20 percent (Tuohy 2006). If health care is not to crowd out the capacity of governments to respond to the needs of their populations, methods must be found to keep public expenditures on health care within legitimate boundaries. Is it still possible to do this and achieve access and quality goals?

Quality and the Connection with Wait-Times. Meanwhile, as governments wrestle with the sustainability issue, the public health care system appears to be under increasing strain. The bellwether indicator may well be high rates of utilization of emergency rooms (ERs) and associated waiting periods for ER service (Canadian Association of Emergency Physicians 2005).[2] Of more political salience, however, are concerns about waiting times for certain other services, notably elective procedures such as joint replacements and cataract surgery but also for diagnostic imaging and some cancer therapies. Numerous waiting time initiatives are underway, and some are demonstrating results (Alberta Health and Wellness 2006, 14; Cardiac Care Network of Ontario 2006, 12).[3] These improvements have involved both reorganization and increased public spending within the existing hospital and physician sector; further progress is likely to require continued investment, putting further pressure on sustainability.

Building on public concern regarding waiting times, the decision of the Supreme Court of Canada in the *Chaoulli* case thrust into the spotlight a long-simmering issue: the formal or effective bans on private insurance for publicly covered physician and hospital services in most provinces under the prevailing Canadian model (Flood, Roach, and Sossin 2005). *Chaoulli* has clearly stirred public debate about the appropriate role of private insurance in the health care sector and provided momentum to privatization advocates. We address below whether in fact greater reliance on private funding would alleviate broad sustainability concerns.

Access and Issues of Coverage. Under Canada's financing model as established by the *Canada Health Act*, only "medically necessary" physician and hospital services qualify for universal, first-dollar coverage. All other health services are either privately financed or are covered under varying provincial public plans with age- or income-based limitations on eligibility and co-payment requirements. The shift of many services out of hospital raises issues of entitlement to out-of-hospital pharmaceuticals, home care, and long-term care, and questions of the capacity of the health care system to manage the transitions from hospital care to home care or long-term care. Demand for these services is likely to increase with the aging of the population, and the health care system must be able to respond, not only through the provision of personnel and facilities but with a financing mechanism that maintains and improves access.

Neither pharmaceuticals nor home care or long-term care are provided for under the *Canada Health Act*; yet from a health perspective and from a justice perspective, access to these services can be just as critical as access to hospital and physician services. Increasing coverage in these areas in the present Canadian model would require one of two approaches. The first approach would be to reallocate public investments from hospital and physician services to prescription drugs, home care, or long-term care. Undoubtedly, this would be difficult politically and inadvisable as a matter of public policy, given the existing interests that benefit from public funding and the extent that the "core" is already viewed as in stress. The second option is to raise additional funds. This will test the electorate's tolerance for tax increases. Another approach is to consider other avenues of financing to achieve access goals: for example, through social insurance or mandates for and regulation of private insurance. An important question to address is whether collecting a portion of funding through social health insurance is more politically palatable than through general taxation revenues.

Sustainability in Collision with Access: The Case of Pharmaceuticals. The fastest growing sector in cost terms is the pharmaceutical sector. The continual development of new, more targeted, and extremely expensive drugs raises fundamental questions about the capacity and the responsibility of publicly funded programs to absorb the resulting costs. Moreover, since out-of-hospital pharmaceuticals do not fall under the ambit of the *Canada Health Act,* private insurance is already well established in the pharmaceutical sector, and debates about inclusion of new drugs will inevitably entail a consideration of the appropriate role of private insurance.

Across Canada, provinces take different approaches to financing prescription drugs. In Nova Scotia, seniors may contribute to a Pharmacare plan but must play a flat-rate premium ($400); there are some exceptions for those on very low incomes. In other words, Nova Scotia's plan pools risk for the over 65s but achieves a limited amount of income redistribution. In contrast, Ontario achieves some measure of income redistribution by funding pharmaceuticals through taxation revenues for all those over 65 and those on social assistance and provides catastrophic coverage through the Trillium Drug Benefit (coverage for those who spend 4 percent of their net household income on prescription drugs.) Employers provide private insurance coverage for many, but there are still serious gaps in insurance amongst the self-employed and working poor while even higher-income seniors retain public coverage (Montague and Cavanaugh 2004, 52).[4] Quebec ensures a universal drug plan through mandates for the purchase of private insurance, subsidies for the poor, and regulation to prevent risk-shifting. The larger copayment requirements for the elderly and the poor which were introduced as part of the the universal scheme, however, have given rise to concern (Tamblyn et al. 2001)

Apart from considerations of fairness and equity, lack of pharmaceutical coverage can affect overall health outcomes and is tied to willingness to access other publicly funded health care such as physician services (Stabile 2001) Fair access to pharmaceuticals is also a particularly important issue for people with chronic illnesses, and limitations on access impair their ability to manage those illnesses.

Access to new drug therapies *within* hospitals is also becoming problematic. In particular, new and very expensive cancer therapies are being developed; and these developments are seriously out-pacing the ability of public revenues to keep up. Pressure on the public insurance system to cover these drugs is enormous, given that the alternatives are either that the patient must pay for this out of pocket or rely (if the service is covered) on unregulated private health insurance. Ontario has made a decision not to fund new cancer drugs like Velcade, Alimta, and Zevalin as they are not viewed as cost effective. However, individual patients still wish to purchase the drugs, viewing even a small extension of life-expectancy as being worthwhile. Indeed, many new treatments may not be justifiable from a population perspective (enough benefit for enough people) but still hold the promise of benefit for certain individuals. The cancer drugs in question are not over-the-counter prescriptions and must be infused. As a result, the Ontario government is presently considering whether patients should be able to buy these cancer drugs in public hospitals rather than requiring that they find a private clinic or go to the United States to receive infusions. Difficult issues like these at the public-private divide are likely to increase.

Such difficulties raise the question of the sustainability of the distinctive Canadian model of health care financing, under which a core of services is exclusively publicly funded from taxation revenues, other services are partially publicly funded, with limitations on eligibility, and yet others are exclusively privately funded. This model has many advantages in terms of equity of access and the economies associated with the monopsony power of a single payer for core services; but it does imply a large and growing claim on the health share of public budgets, or a growth in the size of the public fisc itself. Moreover, aside from the question of how sustainable growing health care costs may be for the economy as a whole, the *political* sustainability of the Canadian model is in question as provincial governments stare down the barrel of galloping growth rates in provincial public spending while simultaneously patients and public clamour for new investments to meet their concerns about access and sustainability.

DEFINING THE TERMS, EXPLORING THE TRADE-OFFS

A word on terminology before we begin our exploration of different financial integration options – in particular combining or substituting some elements of our tax financed system with social insurance. In particular, we wish to clarify what we mean by "quality," "access" and "sustainability." These terms each connote a spectrum of possibilities. For example, "access" to "quality" care may, in the eyes of some, mean first-dollar coverage to the latest cancer drug, regardless of the relative cost of benefit of the drug. Such demands on the terms "access" and "quality" will inevitably mean that sustainability is unobtainable. In other words, if providing quality care means doing all that can conceivably be done in a given case up to the point at which no further clinical benefit can be gained, if providing accessibility means that this must be done for everyone in all cases without financial barriers, and if sustainability means finding ways to fund this all from the public purse, then we have an intractable problem.

We suggest that extreme definitions of access and quality – in essence, definitions that assume individuals have unlimited and insatiable desire for medical care of any therapeutic benefit – are straw arguments. If by the goals of quality and access we mean that a system should provide efficacious and cost-effective care for a comprehensive range of patient needs, that there should be no undue financial barriers to accessing critical care (which we stress does not necessarily imply first-dollar public funding on a universal basis), and that the structures of health care financing and delivery overall do not under-mine the ability to ensure a robust standard of care for all, then there is the possibility that the grail – the balance of access, quality and sustainability – is within reach.

SECTION 2: POLICY OPTIONS

The problem of finding the "right" balance of quality, accessibility, and sustainability is a public policy "elephant" – both in terms of size of the share of public budgets consumed by health care but also because the problem is perceived in different ways by those who, like the proverbial "blind men," approach it from different directions and with different perspectives. Because each nation is different in the way health care delivery is organized and fi-nanced, the balance of concern about the three policy goals also varies across nations. We will now turn to consider the menu of policy options available to policy-makers in the search for the grail.

The Menu of Policy Responses. There are basically three interrelated ap-proaches to attaining an optimal balance among the goals of quality, accessibility, and sustainability. We conceive of these approaches as forming the three points of a policy triangle (see figure 1) in which what is done at each point has implications for the other two.

FIGURE 1
The menu of policy responses

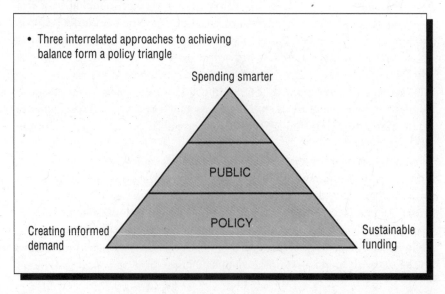

- Three interrelated approaches to achieving balance form a policy triangle

Spending smarter

PUBLIC

POLICY

Creating informed demand

Sustainable funding

1. *"Spending Smarter."* One way of closing the gap between the two trajec-
    tories of health costs and government revenues is to realize greater
    efficiencies (reducing the costs of achieving a given outcome, controlling
    for quality). Challenges here involve the organization of health care de-
    livery, the supply, regulation, and remuneration of health care practitioners,
    and the appropriate locus for governance and managerial decisions. Be-
    hind each of these challenges lies the root problem in health care – the
    substantial information asymmetry that exists between providers and pa-
    tients and between managers/regulators and providers. In the latter regard,
    it is difficult for managers and/or regulators to efficiently manage/regu-
    late when they do not have good information about the correlation between
    inputs into the system and health care outcomes.
2. *"Informed Demand."* Another way of closing the gap is to manage rising
    expectations and create informed demand on the part of the public and
    patients for care. The problem in part is that patients don't know what
    they need – and they are accustomed to the availability of certain practi-
    tioners or procedures. Patients are not focused on or provided with
    information about obtaining effective responses to particular health-related
    conditions – or, in other words, evidence that demonstrates the impact of
    treatment on their health. Instead patients and the public are preoccupied
    with inputs and processes (the numbers of tests and/or drugs provided, the
    speed with which they are provided) rather than measurable outputs. The
    dual challenge here is to put in place effective arrangements that are respon-
    sive to demand (see *"Spending Smarter,"* above), while ensuring that the public
    has adequate information on which to base expectations about health care.
3. *"Designing Sustainable Funding."* Even with more efficient and effec-
    tive organization and a better alignment of expectations and available
    resources, it is likely, given technological development and population
    changes, that health care costs will grow at rates above the growth in GDP
    and hence above the growth in government revenues, for the foreseeable
    future. Accordingly, it is important to integrate the various current sources
    of finance for health care – public revenues, private out-of-pocket pay-
    ments and private insurance – in a way that preserves and enhances the
    quality and accessibility of health care.

We wish to stress that no point in the triangle can be addressed in isolation;
all are critical prongs in a strategic government response to managing and
governing a sector that absorbs 10 percent of the Canadian economy. Much
work and thought has been given to one point of the triangle, namely spending smarter initiatives. Reform initiatives have included regionalization,
devolution, integration, reform of scope of practice, primary care reform,
redesigning financial incentives, and much more. There has been less devotion

to creating informed demand and designing sustainable funding arrangements. Again, we emphasize that all three initiatives are important parts of an overall government strategy; however, here (and in the chapters that follow) we propose to concentrate primarily on the largely neglected area in Canada of the design of sustainable funding arrangements. What kind of integrated funding arrangements – tax based, social insurance, private insurance, out-of-pocket payments – best provide a sustainable revenue base for a health care system that meets quality and accessibility goals? More specifically, we wish to explore the disadvantages and advantages of funding health care primarily through social insurance (as in Germany, the Netherlands, France, etc.) as opposed to primarily through taxation revenues (as in Canada, the UK, New Zealand, and Australia).

SECTION 3: PUBLIC-PRIVATE FUNDING MIX

Turning to how countries define the *mix* of public and private finance for health care, we see that there are essentially four pure models for drawing the boundary between public (including both general tax financed and social health insurance) and private finance:

1. *Parallel or duplicate* public and private systems for all services. In these systems patients may purchase private health insurance to cover services that ostensibly are also provided in the public plan but for which there are concerns about quality or timeliness. Countries that have parallel or duplicate health care systems include New Zealand, the UK, Australia, Ireland, Spain, and Italy. In such systems, physicians generally are allowed to work in both the public and private sectors on an unrestricted basis.
2. *Group-based* systems with public or social insurance coverage for certain population groups and private coverage (publicly regulated to various degrees) for others. Examples here are the Netherlands and Germany. In the Netherlands, until recent reforms, the top 30 percent of income-earners were excluded from the social insurance scheme and as a consequence had to purchase private health insurance or self-insure. In Germany, top income earners can opt out of the social health insurance scheme and buy private health insurance. However, having opted out, a German citizen may return only if his or her income falls below a certain level. Moreover, in contrast to duplicate or parallel insurance systems, there are strict limits on the extent to which having private coverage secures preferential treatment.
3. *Copayment* systems in which public funds cover a portion of the charge for services and private funds finance the remainder. The best example is

the French social health insurance system where patients must pay a 30 percent copayment fee for every service received. However, 92 percent of the population hold private insurance through their employment group or purchased individually, to cover the *ticket modérateur*, significantly dampening any possible effect of the copayment on utilization.

4. *Sectorally based* systems in which certain services are publicly financed and others are privately financed. The strongest example is the Canadian model; full public funding for "medically necessary" hospital and physician services, and a mix of private and public funding for other services. In this system, physicians are prevented from billing the public insurance system for medically necessary services if they bill privately for medically necessary care; however, physicians may opt out of the public system and practice privately. Private health insurance for medically necessary care is very limited, and queue-jumping is not condoned (Flood and Archibald, 2001)

Each of these four models has different dynamics, with different implications as to the impact of changes in the public/private balance for the public system. Most nations exhibit a mix of these financial models, with a centre of gravity in one or the other.

As mentioned, the centre of gravity in the Canadian system is first, with respect to forms of financing, from taxation revenues, and second, with respect to drawing lines between the public/private divide, in a sectorally based system. The "single-payer" model of public finance on a universal, first-dollar basis, for which Canada is best known, applies almost entirely to physician and hospital services and encompasses the great preponderance of those services. Through various fiscal and regulatory measures, this single-payer model not only provides universal public coverage but protects the public system against erosion by constraining and inhibiting the development of a parallel privately financed system seen in countries such as the UK, Australia, New Zealand, Ireland, Spain, and Italy.

SECTION 4: THE PRIVATIZATION SOLUTION?

In the Canadian context, while privatization is frequently put forward as a possible solution to the problems that bedevil medicare, particularly concerns about wait times, the exact form of privatization under debate and what its impact would be on sustainability, quality, and accessibility are frequently unclear (Day 2005; Walker and Wrona 2006). The debate about sustainable financing has largely been reduced to one of whether or not to allow a duplicate or parallel private health insurance tier and has ignored the wider funding questions to be researched and debated. Below we explain why allowing a parallel or duplicate private tier for physician and hospital services is not likely to help Canadian governments achieve a better balance of sustainability, quality, and accessibility.

Canada is unusual among tax funded systems in taking a sectoral approach rather than allowing a parallel or duplicate system. Other countries like the UK, New Zealand, Australia, Spain, Italy, and Ireland, with systems funded through taxation revenues, allow a duplicate or parallel private tier. Advocates of privatization in Canada frequently argue that allowing a duplicate or parallel system would reduce stress on the public system and thus reduce waiting times for all – both for those able to purchase private care and those left in the public system. However, as the graph below illustrates, many countries with parallel or duplicate private health insurance report significant problems with wait times (e.g., Australia, the UK, New Zealand, Ireland, Italy).

As figure 2 clearly demonstrates, given the problems of wait times in many parallel/duplicate two-tier systems, one cannot conclude that enabling a parallel or duplicate insurance will address concerns of timeliness in the Canadian system. (It may do so for those with private health insurance but not for the rest of the citizenry). Advocates of privatization in Canada often employ

FIGURE 2
Health expenditure in the OECD as a share of GDP, 2003

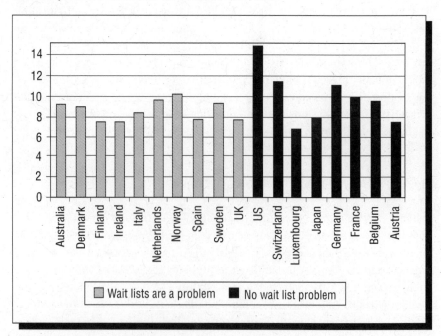

Source: Based on OECD Health Data 2005.

examples of northern European countries, such as Germany, to bolster their claim that a duplicate or parallel private tier will improve access and quality in the Canadian system. However, as we have pointed out, Germany is not a duplicate or parallel private system but a group-based system. Few privatization advocates in Canada argue in favour of a German social insurance system with the possibility of opt-out for the very wealthy. Nor do they argue that we should shift the basis of funding from taxation revenues to social insurance, as is the case in France, with large copayments required at point-of-service (30 percent) and then subsidize the purchase of private insurance to help cover the cost of the copayment. In truth, most proponents of privatization in Canada effectively argue for a UK system: with universal coverage funded from taxation revenues but with the option for those with private health insurance to queue jump. Proponents of privatization in Canada rarely *explicitly* refer to the UK or New Zealand as systems that best reflect the model they are advocating for – because these systems have long and difficult histories with wait times.

Maintaining an exclusively publicly funded core of services for the broad spectrum of complex and chronic health needs, as in the Canadian system, serves to ensure the quality and accessibility of those services. The weight of the evidence suggests that there are both short-term and longer-term effects of a duplicate privately financed tier on the ability of the public tier to meet its objectives. Competing private and public tiers can alter the incentives faced by providers, the risk pool in the public system, the cost of delivering services in the public system, and overall demand for health care services (Flood 2006; Stabile 2006).

All systems have boundaries, however, and as discussed earlier, access and quality cannot mean universal first-dollar access to all services, regardless of cost-effectiveness. But accepting such a definition leaves open the possibility that individuals should be free to purchase in private markets services that are not included in the public system. This may result in negative fiscal consequences for the public system (Glied 2006). Patients may be willing to pay for, and providers to supply, services beyond those limits – beyond the range of conditions that are cost-effective (e.g., a second MRI – "just to make sure"), or at levels of enhanced quality that do not meet cost-effectiveness criteria (e.g., higher-quality prosthetic joints), or faster than the time limit offered by the public system. Allowing such enhancements to listed services to be provided privately does risk eroding the public system primarily by diverting limited capacity from the public sector to the private sector.

In theory, it may be possible to address these risks through regulatory and tax measures. Indeed, it is important to note that, similar to Canada, many countries take a range of regulatory measures to limit the extent to which physicians devote their attentions to private-pay as opposed to public patients (or patients covered by social insurance.) Many countries that *prima facie* allow top-up or duplicate private health insurance (i.e., do not have a law explicitly prohibiting it) take other measures to stop the deleterious effects of the private tier on the public system. For example, Swedish physicians are largely employed on a salaried basis and are not permitted to treat private patients during working hours; this severely limits the incentive they have to maintain private practices. Some countries such as Luxembourg, Greece, and Italy take measures to prohibit or limit the extent to which physicians can bill the public system and also receive private payment (Colombo and Tapay 2004, 24). Other countries use price regulation and other measures to reduce the detrimental impacts of draining capacity from the public to the private tier. We have deep reservations on the extent to which Canada could liberalize existing regulation of the public-private divide without adverse consequences for the public system. Certainly, further cross-national research is warranted to evaluate the effects of more liberal regulatory regimes. For example, it will be important to evaluate recent attempts in the UK to regulate the amount of time that consultants spend treating private patients as opposed to public patients in public hospitals.

Physician or hospital services are characterized by inherent limits in terms of capacity, and increasing capacity requires injection of significant public funds in terms of training costs and infrastructure. In contrast, the private provision of drugs does not necessarily impose a resource drain on the public provision of identical services. It may thus be possible to improve overall welfare and equity, and moderate the rate of growth in public health care costs, by allowing for a mix of public and private finance in the drug sector. One could envisage, for example, a system that had mandatory social insurance for the poor to ensure access to prescription drugs and either left wealthier individuals to purchase care in private insurance markets or included them within the social health insurance mandate. Such a financing regime for drugs would not have the same negative flow-back consequences to the public system as a similar system of financing would have for physician services.

As discussed, advocates for privatization in the Canadian context often try to attribute the absence of waiting time problems in social insurance countries such as Germany and France to the fact that that they have duplicate or parallel private insurance. As we have demonstrated, this is a false attribution. However, although in our view solutions for Canada probably do not lie in duplicate or parallel private insurance, it is certainly worth exploring with greater rigour the benefits and costs from a Canadian perspective of social health insurance and whether and to what extent adopting this mode of financing could assist Canada with finding the right balance of sustainability, accessibility, and quality.

SECTION 5: SUSTAINABILITY, QUALITY, AND ACCESS ACROSS JURISDICTIONS

Returning to our public policy elephant, to add to the complexity, not only do different nations have different approaches to the right balance of sustainability, quality, and access but providers, patients, the general public, and government within each nation are also likely to have different takes on the problem.

These different perspectives are evident in cross-national survey work undertaken by the Commonwealth Fund. The fund regularly surveys public opinion regarding various aspects of the health care system in Australia, New Zealand, the UK (tax financed and parallel/duplicate systems), Canada (tax financed and sectoral), the US (commercial private insurers and group based) and Germany (social health insurance and group based). The fund has also surveyed patients[5] and providers (hospital executives) in each nation. These surveys show Canadians as remaining relatively satisfied with the design of the system, although public confidence declined dramatically after the fiscal constraint of the 1990s (figures A1.1 and A1.2 in appendix 1). In terms of quality and access, Canadians report relatively few financial barriers to access (except with respect to prescription drugs outside hospital) but relatively long waiting times for elective surgery. Concerns about the sustainability of the system, however, do not appear to be as salient for the general public as they are for providers and governments: a substantial majority of Canadians report that they are "very" or "somewhat" confident that quality medical care will be there when they or their family members need it – indeed, they are marginally more likely to report such confidence than those in the other nations surveyed, although the differences across nations are small (figure A1.3). It can nonetheless be argued that the category of "somewhat confident" does not amount to a rousing vote of confidence in the sustainability of the system.

As for providers (hospital executives), we see that levels of satisfaction with the overall health system are relatively high in all nations except the US, although the majority in each nation (again except the US) is only "somewhat" satisfied (figure A1.4). And finally, Canadian hospital executives appear least confident in the sustainability of the system, in that they are most likely to report that levels of funding are insufficient to maintain the current quality of service into the future (figure A1.5).

While there are national variations (and a major exception in the case of the US), this limited evidence suggests that governments generally face public and provider populations that are relatively satisfied with the overall design of their respective systems, although the levels of satisfaction are such that some change is desired. The different designs of the respective systems have generated different problems – waiting times in the UK, Canada, and New

Zealand; financial barriers to care in Australia, New Zealand, and most especially the US. A majority of providers across nations (except the US) worry about their ability to sustain existing levels of quality at current levels of funding.

Meanwhile, as touched on earlier in our discussion of privatization, *all* governments are looking at projections into the future of the costs of their current systems with great trepidation. A 2006 working paper from the Organization for Economic Cooperation and Development (OECD) projected that public health spending in OECD nations would increase on average from 6.7 percent of GDP to 12.8 percent by 2050, taking into account demographic change and assuming that, over and above demographic effects, health costs increase at an annual rate 1 percent faster than income. If the rate of utilization increase were to be progressively constrained so that health costs grew only in line with income by 2050, public health spending would grow to 10.1 percent of GDP. (In Canada, public health expenditures would grow from 7.3 percent of GDP in 2005 to 13.5 percent (under the "cost pressure" scenario) or 10.8 percent (under the "cost containment" scenario) by 2050 (figure A1.6). Thus, every country, regardless of the public-private mix and regardless of the extent to which the system is privately financed, *all* face questions about the sustainability of public financing. The US system, which of all systems relies to the greatest extent on private financing, already spends more public dollars per capita than Canada does, while leaving 48 million citizens without the security of health insurance.

So what solutions are feasible in terms of sustainable financing? It is important to note that the Commonwealth Fund survey described above has only recently included Germany and does not include France, the Netherlands, and other northern European jurisdictions with social insurance systems or regulated private insurance (regulated to achieve access goals). Also as mentioned earlier in discussion, many agencies treat taxation funded and social insurance funded systems as effectively equivalent. We think that in the Canadian context it is important to begin to explore the differences, advantages, and disadvantages of funding through a mix of taxation revenues and social health insurance. While, as we note above, there are significant advantages to a universal single-payer tax financed model in preserving a robust public system, it must be funded adequately if those advantages are to be realized – otherwise quality and accessibility will suffer. As health care grows as a share of the economy across advanced nations, the ability of a single mode of public finance to keep pace is diminishing, and other mechanisms such as social insurance deserve close consideration.

In the search for the holy grail there seem to be some positive outcomes in social insurance jurisdictions: the primary source of funding comes not from taxation revenues but can still be progressive (if it is income based); waiting times are often not a problem; and there is universal access to a broader range of services. How is this achieved? What are the costs and consequences of a social insurance model? Would social insurance be a path forward in Canada for expanding universal access to pharmaceuticals, a particular problem of sustainability, access, and quality? What about for home care, long-term care?

SECTION 6: DEVELOPING A WORKING MODEL OF SUSTAINABLE FINANCING: CAN A DOSE OF EUROPE CURE CANADIAN HEALTH CARE FINANCE?

The papers in this volume address and debate the merits of diversifying the Canadian funding base for health care to include a component of social insurance. In chapter 2, Sherry Glied places the health care financing mix within the broader context of policy goals and instruments. She maintais that both tax financed and social insurance systems can achieve equal efficiency goals, depending on the program design. She notes that the overall efficiency of the system will depend heavily on how providers are paid and how care is delivered, and that perhaps these features are greater drivers of efficiency than the choices over how revenue is raised. With regards to equity, she insists that equity must be considered over the full life cycle, and must include both the financial contributions to the health care system and use of care. Finally, Glied makes an important but perhaps startling point that if the goal of social spending is to achieve greater progressivity through the redistribution of resources, other areas of government expenditure, namely education, are more likely to achieve this goal than health care.

In chapter 3, Jack Mintz and Andrey Tarasov re-examine the principles underlying health insurance programs, noting that while insurance contracts aim to provide as complete coverage as possible, program designs also must work to offset both moral hazard and adverse selection problems. This trade-off generally results in insurance programs that provide less than complete coverage. The authors note the dual objectives of efficiency and equity in seeking the optimal tax structure to finance public programs. They note that all public finance should strive to minimize the impact on the allocation of resources in the economy. In addition they point out that accountability is an important component of publicly financed programs and that the current Canadian tax structure offers little opportunity for taxpayers to compare the true costs and benefits in the health insurance system. The authors also note that an equitable tax structure will strive for both horizontal and vertical equity and that this implies that there be some link between contributions to the insurance pool and the use of services.

Employing the above principles, Mintz and Tarasov find that relying completely on general tax revenues to fund the health insurance system is problematic. They note that payroll taxes (effectively the way that social insurance systems are funded) may offer more transparency and accountability than general taxation, but that they too have limitations. In particular, payroll taxes rely heavily on the working age population and impose a burden on employment and production, and can create perverse incentives for employers. The authors offer an alternative, complementary financing structure, proposed by Aba, Goodman, and Mintz (2002), which would use the tax system to collect limited amounts of user payments based on the yearly use of health care services. The authors argue that imposing such payments would help align the public financing of health care services with the financing objectives outlined above.

In chapter 4, Gunderson and Hyatt continue to test the benefits of relying more heavily on social insurance payments, and on payroll taxes in particular, to finance public health care expenditures. They examine the existing payroll taxes in Canada used to fund other public programs: employment insurance, workers compensation, and the Canada/Quebec Pension Plans. In each case they judge the financing structure of these programs against the criteria of efficiency, equity, sustainability, administrative ease, compliance, and political acceptability. The authors argue that, based on these criteria, payroll taxes are indeed the appropriate financing structure for the programs listed above, although not without some limitations. However, they are sceptical about using payroll taxes for increased health care financing. While payroll taxes offer substantial advantages for the programs they currently finance, the authors argue that they offer little advantage over alternate forms of financing such as general revenue or consumption taxes in the case of health care finance. The primary reason for this conclusion is that the benefits, users, and incentives inherent in the publicly financed health care system are not directly linked to employment the way that employment insurance, workers compensation, and pensions are. The authors conclude by noting that while payroll taxes do have some advantages, such as the ability to earmark contributions, the political attractiveness of imposing taxes on employers rather than individuals, and the fact that payroll taxes do not tax savings and investment the way that general revenue taxation does, they still remain unconvinced of the benefits of moving a substantial portion of health care financing to a payroll tax base.

The focus of the contributors then turns from examining the principles and objectives of health care financing to the experience of social insurance countries in Europe. In chapter 5, Stefan Greß explores social insurance funding in Germany and the trade-offs faced by German policy-makers dealing with increasing health care costs. He begins by exploring the objectives of health care financing in Germany – fairness and solidarity, sustainability, and efficiency – noting the similarity between these objectives and the objectives of most tax financed systems including the Canadian system. Greß reviews some key lessons from the German social insurance system, including the importance of universality and risk solidarity/subsidization (a topic taken up in greater detail by Wynand van de Ven in chapter 6). Greß notes that the German system, while predominantly funded through social insurance, is in reality a mixed funding system, relying heavily on social insurance (which covers approximately 56 percent of expenditures) but also maintaining a diverse mix of revenue sources. General taxation, however, plays a relatively small role in the German financing structure (approximately 6 percent) and in Greß's view, Germans will need to contemplate relying more on general tax revenues to further diversify the *public* revenue sources.

In chapter 6, Wynand van de Ven examines developments in five countries with competitive social insurance markets: Belgium, Germany, Israel, the Netherlands, and Switzerland. He examines how each country works to keep health insurance affordable in the context of competitive insurance markets. In particular, he examines mechanisms for risk adjustment and premium subsidization. In all the countries examined, citizens have some choice among health insurers and in all five countries there is imperfect risk equalization, and patients may suffer from risk selection. Two important points with particular reference to considering financing reform emerge from this cross-country analysis. First, van de Ven shows that there does not need to be a relation between the funding of health insurance and the organization or structure of the health care system. All governments strive to improve the efficiency of their health care systems, and using government planning or competition and markets to achieve greater efficiencies does not necessarily hinge on whether insurance is funded through general tax revenues or social insurance premiums (or vice versa). Second, he makes the point that the two key objectives of any health care financing structure – cross-subsidizing from higher income to lower income individuals and cross-subsidizing from lower risk patients to higher risk patients – can be achieved under either a social insurance system or a general tax revenue system.

Following these reviews of experience with social insurance in a largely European context, Tim Jost in chapter 7 extends the international sweep with a broad overview of available options for health care financing, both public and private, drawing upon experience in the United States, Canada, Australia, and Israel as well as Europe. Briefly but comprehensively, he traces the historical evolution of social insurance and general taxation-based options, and highlights the apparent merits of each model. From this review he draws four or possibly five principles to undergird a system of financing for health care. First, extraordinarily expensive services should be funded from sources that provide the widest possible risk spreading – notably general revenue tax funding. Second, non-essential products or services, such as cosmetic surgery or products or procedures that are scientifically regarded as ineffective, are candidates for private finance, although this principle raises the devilishly difficult question of defining medically necessary or essential services. Third, population-based public health services with their very broad risk pool implication should be tax financed. Fourth, considerations of political economy would dictate that the most powerful providers (physicians, hospitals, and suppliers of pharmaceutical) be paid for by public funds, on the argument that the countervailing power of large provider groups and public authorities will generate a more optimal allocation of resources than competitive private markets. A fifth and final principle might be that frequently purchased, low cost items be purchased on an out-of-pocket basis, although this raises concerns about underutilization by low-income individuals. On balance, Jost finds little reason "other than political expediency" for Canada to consider introducing a social insurance component into its health care financing mix. The full institutional traditional infrastructure of social insurance, he argues, would hardly be warranted for a single slice of the system such as drugs, and more likely the result would be simply another form of general taxation.

Concluding the set of commentaries on the international experience, Ted Marmor begins his contribution in chapter 8 on a note of caution. He warns that comparisons with other nations can be misleading as a base for policy decisions, unless the comparative analysis is judiciously framed and carefully executed. In the context of the topic of the current volume, he draws several limited but relevant observations from the international sphere. First, he notes that governments in all nations, regardless of the particular funding mix for health care, are concerned about projected rates of increase in health care costs. Like Glied, he emphasizes that the mode of finance is only one of several influences on the level and rate of increase in health expenditure. Second, he notes that there are few if any international examples of the sort of policy shift under consideration in this volume: namely, a shift from a funding base for health care drawn primarily from general taxation toward a more diversified funding base incorporating elements of social insurance. While such a shift has been debated in a number of nations, it has not in fact occurred to any substantial extent. Finally, he argues that while the fiscal rationale for such a shift may be weak, it may nonetheless have political merit in providing a firmer base of legitimacy for public contributions to health care finance than does general taxation (an observation supported by historical and cross-national experience). Marmor suggests that this may indeed be the case in Canada if this nation is experiencing a weakening of a sense of citizenship and a strengthening of "worker-saver solidarity." This is a key and provocative question for the issues under review here, but within the scope of the present volume, it is one that Marmor of necessity leaves open.

Chapters 9 and 10 focus primarily on pharmaceutical coverage within Canada. Steve Morgan in chapter 9 advocates a mix of tax financing and social insurance to finance universal coverage for out-of-hospital pharmaceuticals –

a mix that he argues is best able to promote the twin goals of equity and efficiency. He provides an overview of the current patchwork of coverage across Canada, as well as the alarming recent and projected rates of increase in expenditures on pharmaceuticals, to argue that there is currently a window of opportunity for policy change in this area. He proposes the establishment of a segregated fund for pharmaceutical coverage, funded either solely through social insurance levies on employees and employers or through a mix of social insurance and tax mechanisms. Such a fund would not simply be a passive insurer but would manage the pharmaceutical budget on the model of New Zealand's PHARMAC.

Terry Sullivan in chapter 10 addresses a specific and particularly pressing issue of drug coverage in Canada – namely, coverage for newly developed and very expensive cancer medications. In this arena he sees the challenge as broader than determining the appropriate mix of public financing. In his view the more fundamental challenge is to deal with the trade-offs inherent in a framework that combines a dominant system of taxed based finance with a large market based system of finance. He argues that the *Canada Health Act* framework, although it does not apply to out-of-hospital pharmaceuticals, nonetheless affects our expectations of how pharmaceuticals *should* be covered – that is, on a comprehensive, universal, first-dollar basis. Given in particular the technological and economic realities of cancer treatment, he maintains that Canadians are experiencing a rude awakening from that "dream." Cancer, he point out, is "increasingly being managed by a complex multimodal approach to treatment, including increasingly expensive drugs, many of which confer some survival advantage," and bluntly concludes that the "increasing costs of new biologically active agents mean that, if more stringent cost effectiveness considerations are applied to public coverage, more of these drugs will have to be managed by private expenditure."

Within the Canadian framework, the case of cancer drugs requiring intravenous infusion presents a particularly thorny problem. The regulatory framework requires that these drugs be infused in hospital; yet barring additional dedicated public funding, hospitals can rarely afford to provide such treatments from within their own budgets. Thus patients have faced a Catch-22: the drugs are not available in-hospital and cannot be obtained outside hospitals, even on a privately financed basis, without travelling out of the country. In response, a small number of private infusion clinics have arisen (some adjacent to public hospitals) and are tolerated by public authorities. Sullivan argues that public policy should not involve mere passive toleration of these developments but rather should deliberately incorporate and regulate them within a new policy framework. This framework could also include a federal program of coverage for "catastrophic" drug costs, but such a program cannot, on cost-effectiveness grounds, cover all drugs. The framework should also incorporate funding, possibly on a social insurance model, for community-based care, including some areas of drug coverage.

In chapter 11, the last chapter before the editors' conclusion, Joe White presents an overview of some of the key issues raised in this volume and engages with several of the contributions. He astutely notes that the interest in social insurance as a component of a more diversified funding base for health care in Canada stems from a sense that this is a bulwark against the easiest alternative – capitulation (principally through passive toleration) to the growing pressures for an increasing role for private finance. In this light, he situates Canada's unique model of public finance for health care within the international context in a way that bears repetition here:

> While it may seem obvious and logical to Canadians, Canada's method of health care financing, in which the government directly operates insurance for both medical and hospital care, is unique. Most other rich democracies either rely mainly on separate social insurance funds, or provide most services directly, without an explicit insurance mechanism. Germany, France, and Japan are examples of social insurance countries. The United Kingdom, Norway, and Sweden are examples of direct provision. A few countries provide insurance funded from general revenues for a portion of the population (Parts B and D of the US Medicare program for the elderly and disabled) or a portion of services (medical services in Australia; "extraordinary" expenses in the Netherlands).

In considering how Canada might move from this unique position to a more diversified funding base including some elements of social insurance, White goes on to address some of the fundamental questions considered throughout this volume: the merits and demerits of payroll-based levies (their relative progressivity/regressivity and their effects on the macroeconomy); the functioning of earmarked taxes within public budgets; and the governance issues raised by separate management of a portion of the public budget for health care. With regard to payroll taxation, he agrees with Glied that its relative progressivity/regressivity needs to be considered in life cycle and system wide contexts, and that social insurance and general taxation modes have no inherent advantage in this respect depending on their design. As to macroeconomic effects, his view is that the effects on employment of introducing payroll levies within the limited scope contemplated for Canada (potentially for out-of-hospital pharmaceuticals) are likely to be marginal, especially if these levies replace in large part the arrangement currently in place through private labour-management agreements. With regard to the question of earmarked taxation within public budgets, White reviews the dynamics of what he terms "entitlement" (social insurance) and "bureau" (general taxation-based) budgeting and concludes that "some form of dedicated funding, especially for services that are not covered under the *Canada Health Act*, is at least no less appropriate than general revenue finance, and may be superior." White is more sceptical about the merits of the third dimension of social insurance, separate management. He believes the governance issues to be quite problematic, but nonetheless concludes that since these issues have been addressed to a greater or lesser extent in other jurisdictions, they should not pose an insuperable barrier, should Canada decide to embark on this route.

However, White argues that regardless of all these considerations, the political feasibility of introducing a component of social insurance into the Canadian health care funding mix will ultimately be definitive. He points out the political obstacles to the introduction of social insurance for pharmaceuticals (including the fact that a large proportion of Canadians already have employer-based coverage and could resist change as Americans have done in the broader health insurance context). Nonetheless, he agrees with Morgan that the sheer demographic weight of the aging of the baby boomers may threaten the stability of the existing framework of employer-based plans, coupled with public coverage for the bulk of those not in the workforce. While the threat creates a window of opportunity for policy change, what will happen within this window is unpredictable and will depend on political circumstances and political entrepreneurship.

In the concluding chapter, we address the themes that run through these various commentaries and suggest directions for financing reform in Canada. Clearly there are no obvious cures, and all financing proposals are replete with their own sets of advantages and disadvantages. Moreover, a particular reform, even if theoretically a good option, may simply not be feasible politically. We are cognizant of these political realities but are also conscious that the dangers of passivity in the face of complexity may mean that the only solution will increasingly become a greater role for private financing.

NOTES

[1] Social insurance has historically been administered on a not-for-profit basis. In 2006, the Netherlands introduced major reforms to its social insurance system to bring both not-for-profit social insurers ("sickness funds") and for-profit private insurers under a single framework. In Switzerland, the health insurance framework adopted in 1996 mandates a basic package to be offered by competing not-for-profit sickness funds and also provides for private insurers to be authorized to offer the compulsory basic package, although authorizations of private insurers have been slow to develop. These attempts to incorporate for-profit insurers within a social insurance framework are new and untested, and bear close watching to assess the feasibility of this variant of the social insurance model.

[2] In a news release dated 7 February 2007 (Ottawa), the Canadian Association of Emergency Physicians note that 14 million Canadians use the emergency department and that 74 percent are concerned about prolonged waiting times.

[3] For example, Alberta's strategy aimed at hip and knee replacements reports a decrease in wait time for first orthopedic consult from 35 to 6 weeks, a decreased wait time between first consult and surgery from 47 to 4.7 weeks, and decreased length of hospital stay from 6.2 to 4.3 days. Ontario's Cardiac Care Network reported that between March 2005 and April 2006, 91 percent of all bypass patients received treatment within their recommended wait time (compared to 84 percent in 2004–05) and there was a 42 percent reduction in the number of days waited for bypass and catheterization procedures.

[4] Montague and Cavanaugh note that while 80 percent of Canadians have adequate drug coverage, 10 percent are underinsured, and 10 percent have no coverage at all.

[5] "Patients" were defined as those who answered "yes" to one of following: rated their health fair or poor; reported a serious chronic illness or disability; had been hospitalized or had major surgery in the last two years.

REFERENCES

Aba, S., W.D. Goodman, and J.M. Mintz. 2002. "Funding Public Provision of Private Health: The Case for a Copayment Contribution through the Tax System." C.D. Howe Institute Health Papers Series 163. www.cdhowe.org.

Alberta Health and Wellness.2006. *Annual Report 2005/2006*. www.health.gov.ab.ca/resources/publications/AR06_sec1.pdf.

Blendon, R.J., C. Schoen, C.M. DesRoches, R. Osborne, and K.L. Scoles. 2002. "Trends: Inequities in Health Care: A Five-Country Survey," *Health Affairs* 21 (3): 182-91.

Blendon, R.J., C. Schoen, C.M. DesRoches, R. Osborne, K. Zapert, and E. Raleigh. 2004. "Confronting Competing Demands to Improve Quality: A Five-Country Hospital Survey." *Health Affairs* 23 (3): 119-35.

Canada Health Act. 1980. RSC c. C-6.

Canadian Association of Emergency Physicians. 2005. "Canadian Association of Emergency Physicians Calls for Emergency Department Wait Times and Overcrowding to Be Made a Priority within Government Wait Time Strategy." News release, 12 December. www.caep.ca/002.policies/002-05.communications/2005/051212-media-release.overcrowding.pdf.

Cardiac Care Network of Ontario. 2006. *Monitoring Performance, Managing Access, Moving Wait Times: Annual Report 2006*. www.ccn.on.ca/memberpdfs/ar-2005-2006.pdf.

Chaoulli v. Quebec (Attorney General). [2005]. 1 SCR 791.

Canadian Institute for Health Information. 2005. *National Health Expenditure Trends 1975-2005*. www.cihi.ca.

Colombo, F., and N. Tapay. 2004. "Private Health Insurance in OECD Countries: The Benefits and Costs for Individuals and Health Systems." Working paper, OECD.

Day, B. 2005. "It's a Realistic Medical Goal: Let's Eliminate Waiting Lists, Not Study Them." *Vancouver Sun*, 9 November.

Flood, C.M. 2006. "Chaoulli's Legacy for the Future of Canadian Health Care Policy." *Osgoode Hall Law Journal* 44 (22): 273-310.

Flood C.M., and T. Archibald. 2001. "The Illegality of Private Health Care in Canada." *CMAJ* 164 (6): 825.

Flood, C.M., K. Roach, and L. Sossin. 2006. *Access to Care, Access to Justice: The Legal Debate over Private Health Insurance*. Toronto: University of Toronto Press.

Glied, S. 2006. "Inequalities and Externalities in Health Care Consumption." Working paper, Columbia University.

Montague, T., and S. Cavanaugh. 2004. "Seeking Value in Pharmaceutical Care: Balancing Quality, Access and Efficiency." *Healthcare Papers* 4 (3): 51.

Organization for Economic Cooperation and Development. 2001. "OECD Health at a Glance: How Canada Compares." Policy brief, OECD. www.oecd.org/dataoecd/5/25/2465559.pdf.

– 2006. "Projecting OECD Health and Long-Term Care Expenditures: What Are the Main Drivers?" Economic Department Working Paper 477. Paris: OECD.

Schoen, C., R. Osborne, P.T. Huynh, M. Doty, K. Davis, K. Zapert, and J. Peugh, 2004. "Primary Care and Health System Performance: Adults' Experiences in Five Countries," *Health Affairs Web Exclusive* (July-December): 487-503. http://content.healthaffairs.org/cgi/reprint/hlthaff.w4.487vl.

Schoen, C., R. Osborne, P.T. Huynh, M. Doty, K. Zapert, J. Peugh, and K. Davis. 2005. "Taking the Pulse of Health Care Systems: Experiences of Patients with Health Problems in Six Countries," *Health Affairs Web Exclusive* (Nov. 3): 509-25. http://content.healthaffairs.org/cgi/reprint/hlthaff.w5.509v3.

Siciliani, L., and J. Hurst. 2004. "Explaining Waiting Times Variations for Elective Surgery across OECD Countries." *OECD Economic Studies* 38(1).

Stabile, M. 2001. "Private Insurance Subsidies and Public Health Care Systems." *Canadian Journal of Economics* 34 (4): 921.

– 2006. "Private Financing outside the Publicly Funded System." Mimeo, University of Toronto.

Tamblyn, R., R. Laprise, J.A Hanley, M. Abrahamowicz, S. Scott, N. Mayo, J. Hurley, R. Grad, R., E. Latimer, R. Perreault, P. McLeod, A. Huang, P. Larochelle, and L. Mallet. 2001. "Adverse Events Associated with Prescription Drug Cost-Sharing among Poor and Elderly Persons." *Journal of the American Medical Association* 285 (4): 421.

Thurow, L.C. 1984. "Learning to Say 'No,'" *New England Journal of Medicine* 311: 1569-72.

Tuohy, C. 2006. "Quality, Sustainability and Accessibility in Health Care." Mimeo, University of Toronto.

Tuohy, C., C. Flood, and M. Stabile. 2004. "How Does Private Finance Affect Public Health Care Systems? Marshalling the Evidence from OECD Nations." *Journal of Health Politics, Policy, and Law* 29 (3): 359-96.

Walker, M., and D. Wrona. 2006. *Waiting Your Turn: Hospital Waiting Lists in Canada*. 16th ed. Vancouver: Fraser Institute.

APPENDIX 1
Cross-National Surveys of Public, Patient and Provider Opinion

FIGURE A1.1
Public confidence: Canadian attitudes toward needed changes in health care system, 1988–2004

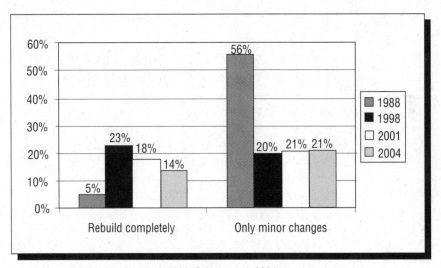

Sources: OECD 2006; Blendon et al. 2002; Schoen et al. 2004.

FIGURE A1.2
Public confidence in international perspective: percent responding "System needs to be entirely rebuilt," six nations, 2004, 2005

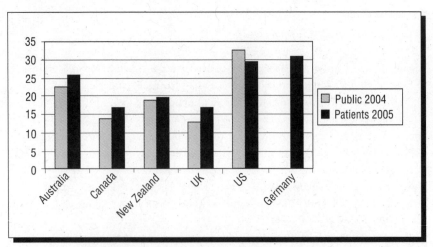

Sources: OECD 2006; Schoen et al. 2004; Schoen et al. 2005.

FIGURE A1.3
Public confidence – sustainability: percent very or somewhat confident quality care will be available when needed, five nations, 2004

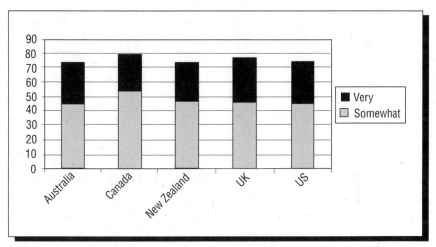

Sources: OECD 2006; Schoen et al. 2004.

FIGURE A1.4
Provider satisfaction: hospital executives very or somewhat satisfied with health care system, five nations, 2004

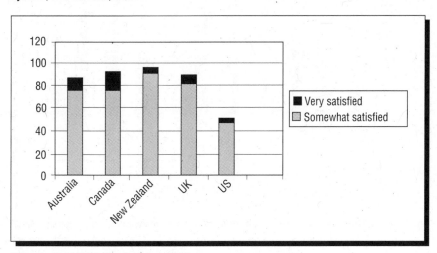

Sources: OECD 2006; Blendon et al. 2004.

FIGURE A1.5
Provider concern – sustainability: hospital executives reporting own institution funding insufficient to maintain current service levels, five nations, 2004

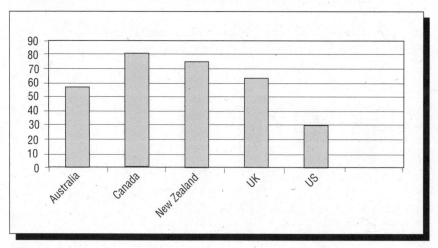

Sources: OECD 2006; Blendon et al. 2004.

FIGURE A1.6
Public health expenditures as a percentage of GDP, two scenarios, 11 nations, 2005 and 2050

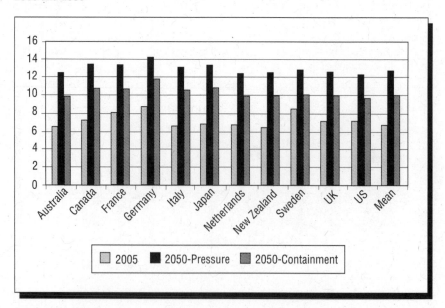

Source: OECD 2006.

APPENDIX 2
Spending Patterns across Tax Financed and Social Insurance Countries in the OECD

We investigate whether countries that raise public health care revenues predominantly from social insurance premiums have higher levels of spending than those that raise public health care revenues through general taxation.

We use a sample of 20 countries from the OECD and data on health care spending between 1980 and 2004. We categorize countries into two groups: social insurance countries (Austria, Belgium, France, Germany, the Netherlands) and tax financed countries (Australia, Canada, Denmark, Finland, Greece, Ireland, Italy, Japan, New Zealand, Norway, Portugal, Spain, Sweden, the UK).

We begin by graphing the relationship between the growth in health care spending and the financing type.

FIGURE A2.1
Average growth in public health spending by funding type

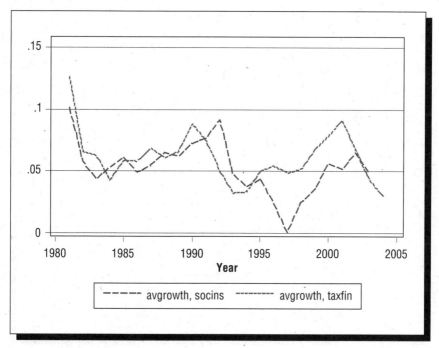

Source: OECD Health Database, 1980–2004.

Between 1980 and 1995 there appears to be very little difference in public health care spending by financing type. There is a significant dip in growth rates for social insurance countries in the late 1990s relative to tax financed countries, but spending patterns begin to realign by the early 2000s.

Many countries use a mix of financing methods to raise revenue for public health care expenditures. OECD data contain information on revenues by financing source. We use these data to plot the change in revenue mix for both social insurance countries and tax financed countries. We hold the type of country fixed according to the categories outlined above.

It is difficult to pick out any particular pattern between the country types, but it appears as though tax financed countries experience a significant increase in social insurance funding in the mid-1990s after holding social insurance revenues quite flat for a long period of time. However, this is driven entirely by OECD data collection. There is little data for Japan pre-1995, and the inclusion of Japan post-1995 drives up the social insurance funding numbers. (A similar data problem with Austria accounts for the smaller increase we observe in the social insurance countries.)

FIGURE A2.2
Changes in social insurance and tax funding: social insurance countries

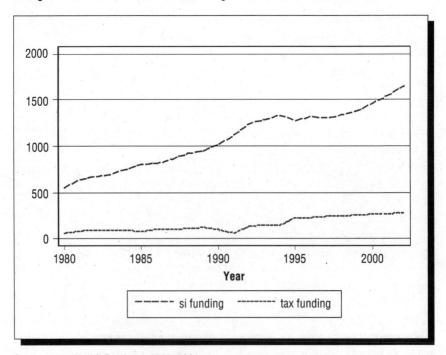

Source: OECD Health Database, 1980–2004.

FIGURE A2.3
Changes in social insurance and tax funding: tax financed countries

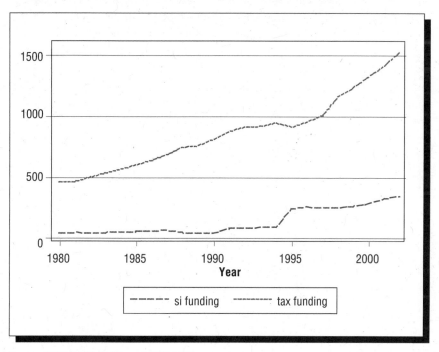

Source: OECD Health Database, 1980–2004.

We then model public and total health care spending as a function of whether a country is a social insurance country, the country's GDP, fixed year effects, lagged log private health care spending, lagged log total health care spending, and log public spending on non-health related areas. We examine public health care spending over time (logs and levels), total health care spending over time (logs and levels), and the growth rate of public health care spending over time (logs and levels).

The findings are summarized in the attached table. We find no significant difference between social insurance and tax financed countries on the level or log of public health care spending. We find that social insurance countries spend slightly more on total health care spending – between 70 and 100 public-private partnership (PPP) dollars more. Since there is no difference in public spending, this difference must therefore be driven by private spending. We find no significant difference in the growth rate of public health care spending between social insurance countries and tax financed countries.

34   COLLEEN M. FLOOD, MARK STABILE, AND CAROLYN HUGHES TUOHY

Finally, we explore whether the models in Tuohy, Flood, and Stabile (2004) are sensitive to financing structure. That is, we examine whether the relationship lagged private health care spending and public health care spending differs by the predominant financing type in a country. The results (not shown here) suggest that increases in lagged private spending remain negatively correlated with a changes in public spending, and that these correlations are slightly larger for social insurance countries. That is, while we find an elasticity of approximately -0.23 for tax financed countries, we find an elasticity of approximately -0.29 for social insurance countries.

TABLE A2.1
Relationship between financing type and health care expenditure

	-1 Public exp. on health/capita PPP	-2 Public exp. on health/capita PPP	-3 Log public exp. on health	-4 Log public exp. on health	-5 Total exp. on health/capita PPP	-6 Total exp. on health/capita PPP
Social insurance country	16.097 [0.62]	39.855 [1.87]	-0.002 [0.12]	0.008 [0.99]	122.91 [5.07]**	70.46 [2.36]*
GDP/capita PPP	1,318.15 [24.07]**	161.39 [1.93]	1.561 [37.12]**	0.307 [10.18]**	1,306.01 [23.23]**	982.501 [10.63]**
Log priv health care spending		-308.988 [11.97]**		-0.279 [30.05]**		178.736 [5.65]**
Lagged log total health spending		1,160.77 [17.11]**		1.134 [46.53]**		
Log other public spending		-86.618 [2.10]*		-0.023 [1.53]		241.467 [4.64]**
Observations	403	381	403	381	427	381
R-squared	0.85	0.92	0.91	0.99	0.9	0.9

... continued

TABLE A2.1
(Continued)

	-7 Log total exp. on health	-8 Log total exp. on health	-9 Growth in pub. health exp.	-10 Growth in pub. health exp.	-11 Growth in log pub. health exp.	-12 Growth in log pub. health exp.
Social insurance country	0.072 [4.81]**	0.002 [0.11]	-0.009 [1.43]	0.021 [1.19]	-0.001 [1.25]	0.003 [1.26]
GDP /capita PPP	1.15 [33.33]**	0.788 [15.91]**	0.13 [5.05]**	0.262 [6.17]**	0.018 [4.67]**	0.036 [5.65]**
Log priv. health care spending		0.18 [10.61]**		0.046 [2.66]**		0.007 [2.62]**
Lagged log total health spending				-0.178 [5.18]**		-0.027 [5.32]**
Log other public spending		0.241 [8.65]**		0.01 [0.32]		0.001 [0.29]
Observations	427	381	381	381	381	381
R-squared	0.93	0.95	0.24	0.32	0.25	0.32

Notes: Absolute value of t statistics in brackets.
* significant at 5 percent; ** significant at 1 percent.
Source: Authors' calculations using OECD Health Database, 1980–2004.

Chapter 2

Health Care Financing, Efficiency, and Equity

Sherry Glied

The most appropriate generalization of the financing of developed county health care systems is that they share no general characteristic. Few systems fall squarely into any single box, and even systems that more or less do have evolved in their financing over time. In 1960, the cost of health care in the OECD countries consumed just under 4 percent of their collective GDP. By 2000, it consumed twice as high a share of the GDP. This escalation in spending is nowhere accommodated without debate or modification.

The goal of a financing system is clear: a health care system – and its several components – should be financed in a manner that is both efficient and progressive. An efficient system minimizes the dead-weight losses associated with raising and disbursing revenue. A progressive system redistributes resources from the rich toward the poor. This chapter examines how alternative financing systems perform with respect to these two goals.

I focus here on choices among general revenue, social insurance, private insurance, and private out-of-pocket financing in all or portions of a health care system. These choices have efficiency and equity implications, both in the collection and the disbursal of funds. These implications arise at three levels. First, financing choices affect the efficiency with which the health care system produces and supplies health care services. Second, these choices have redistributive implications within the health sector. Finally, the choice of how to collect funds cannot be disentangled from the functioning of the social service sector and the economy as a whole. Together they have implications for the general efficiency and equity of society broadly.

DEFINING TERMS

The principal choices for financing a health care system are general revenues, social insurance financing, private insurance financing, and out-of-pocket payments. General revenue financing here refers to a system of revenue collection through a broad-based tax. All or a portion of this tax may be dedicated to the health care system (although this is generally just an accounting convention). General revenues may be raised at the federal, provincial/state, or local levels. Although often associated with progressive financing, general revenues can be raised through tax vehicles that are also more or less progressive – from a progressive income tax to a relatively regressive sales tax (or a highly regressive sin tax). General revenues are used to finance a portion of the health care system almost everywhere. In countries that rely primarily on social insurance, general revenue funds are often used to cover the costs of non-workers. General revenue financing usually refers to a pay-as-you-go arrangement, where current revenues are used to finance current expenditures.

There is no clear definition of social insurance financing. I use the term here to refer to a system in which some group of people, usually workers, is mandated to make contributions to a health care financing (or, for example, retirement) program.[1] Social insurance contributions are usually either regressive (a flat per capita mandate) or proportional (a flat payroll tax rate). Social insurance financing based on payroll taxation faces the problem that the tax base, which excludes non-labour income, may be narrower than under broader scope general revenue financing (Amelung, Glied, and Topan 2003). Moreover, some social insurance systems cap the maximum contribution, reducing the progressivity of this financing mechanism. Contributions collected through the social insurance system should finance the full insured cost of the health program (or a pre-specified proportion of that cost). Thus, the contribution level or rate is tied to the cost of providing health insurance. Social insurance payments may vary with the choice of plan in a multi-plan system (as in Germany), or they may be fixed (as in the US Medicare program). Social insurance systems can employ pre-funding, i.e., building up "trust funds" to account for future expenses, but meaningful trust funds (that cannot be readily encroached) are rare.

Private insurance financing may be individual (although this too is rare except in highly regulated contexts) or operate through employers or other purchasing organizations. Except in highly regulated contexts or in employer-sponsored groups, the price of coverage is related to expected health expenditures – older, sicker people pay more for coverage and premiums rise as health expenditures rise. The concept of progressivity does not have a clear analogue in the private pay case. Under private coverage, people choose both how much to purchase and, by extension, how much to pay as a share of their income. Even in a situation without health insurance, however, health care utilization rises less than proportionately with income (the income elasticity of health care utilization is, at the micro level, less than one). The premiums paid by lower income people are only slightly lower than those charged to higher income people, a situation that would be viewed as regressive if the premiums were taxes. A special (and particularly regressive) complication of private financing occurs through the favourable tax treatment of private employer-sponsored health insurance premiums, which exists in many countries including Canada (in all provinces except Quebec), the United States, the UK, Denmark, France, and Australia. In this situation, a tax subsidy is regressively distributed in the context of otherwise privately financed health insurance. Finally, virtually all observed private health insurance contracts are of short duration – almost always only one year. This makes it difficult to pre-fund care, except through savings mechanisms outside the health system.

Out-of-pocket payments are those payments into the health care system that are made directly at the point of service. In this category I include full payments (as in the case of pharmaceuticals or nursing home care for those without insurance coverage) as well as copayments and deductibles. A system with only out-of-pocket payment would (in a tax sense) finance health care regressively, since health service use rises less than proportionately with income.

Note that the revenue raising and benefit disbursing components of these systems work differently over the life cycle than they do at a point in time. At a point in time, income taxes tend to be more progressive than social insurance taxes which, in turn, are generally more progressive than consumption and value-added taxes (VAT). When costs and benefits are computed over the life cycle, however, relative progressivity can change because higher income people generally live longer than those with lower incomes. Consumption taxes are paid throughout life and reflect consumption (which generally exceeds income among older people). This means that survivors (who have higher lifetime incomes, on average) will pay more in lifetime consumption taxes than decedents (who have lower lifetime incomes), making this tax more progressive. Conversely, income and particularly social insurance taxes appear less progressive in the life cycle context. Younger people pay relatively higher taxes, but those with lower incomes may disproportionately fail to survive and collect benefits at older ages.

Figure 1 illustrates the composition of health care financing across the OECD countries. In most countries, insurance covers about 80 percent of health care costs, with out-of-pocket spending accounting for the remainder. The structure of out-of-pocket spending, however, varies substantially among countries. In the United States, which lacks universal insurance coverage for those under 65, a small number of individuals account for a large share of out-of-pocket costs. In some countries, certain services are excluded from public insurance

FIGURE 1
Composition of financing, 2000

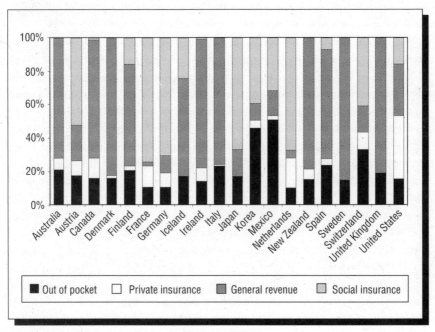

Source: SourceOECD, online. Downloaded October 2006.

coverage, and out-of-pocket spending accounts for a large share of costs for these particular services. In other countries, a broader range of services is included in the health insurance package, but substantial copayments are required for all services.

Private insurance accounts for a substantial share of health care costs only in the United States, and even in the United States, private insurance accounts for only about one third of health spending. Outside the United States, the private insurance share varies between 0 and 16 percent (Canada ranks fourth at 11.5 percent). In some countries, private insurance plays a large role in the health care market, even though it finances only a small proportion of care. Indeed, the prevalence of private insurance (that is, the proportion of the population covered by some private insurance) is greater in France, Switzerland, and the Netherlands than in the United States (OECD 2006).

Countries differ markedly in their use of general revenues and social insurance funds to finance the public share of expenditures. In the English-speaking countries, as well as in Italy, Sweden, and Denmark, general revenues finance virtually all public health expenditures. At the other extreme, in France and the Netherlands, general revenues play an insignificant role, and social insurance pays the bulk of health expenditures.

Various combinations of general revenue and social insurance sources present different efficiency and equity trade-offs. An assessment of the overall efficiency and progressivity of tax systems usually requires complex modelling. Kessleman and Cheung summarize evidence on the progressivity of the Canadian tax system (2004). Unfortunately, the studies they cite are somewhat dated and do not reflect recent changes in tax structure. Overall, Kesselman and Cheung find that in Canada, those in the lowest income quintile pay an average tax rate of about 17 percent (mainly through consumption, corporate, and payroll taxes), while those in the highest income quintile pay an average tax rate of about 43 percent, with personal income taxes accounting for the bulk of these taxes. Kesselman and Cheung also report average tax rates by age group and family status. Younger adults and single people pay much higher average taxes than do single parents, single earner families, or older people. Thus, the Canadian tax system is fairly progressive, but progressivity differs across groups.

Financing systems also differ in the efficiency with which they raise funds. In general, financing systems are more efficient the less they distort individuals' choices (around work, consumption, investment, etc.). In this sense, private insurance (without a tax subsidy) and out-of-pocket payments are fully efficient. Tax-based financing systems are less efficient, but their relative efficiency depends on the entire structure of the tax system. For my purposes here, I will focus on how financing affects efficiency in the operation of the health care system rather than on the efficiency of the financing system itself.

FINANCING CHOICES AND THE EFFICIENCY OF THE OPERATION OF THE HEALTH CARE SYSTEM

A health system operates in an economically efficient manner if health care resources cannot be reorganized in a way that would make all members of society better off. Technical efficiency occurs when health care system inputs are used optimally to address a particular health care need. As technical efficiency depends on the systems used to pay providers, any of the insurance financing systems is compatible with a range of provider payment mechanisms. For example, a general revenue financed system could pay providers using salaries (as in the UK), fee-for-service rates (as in Canada), case rates (DRGs), or capitated rates (as for primary care purchasers in the UK).

In market competition the invisible hand of the market determines optimal payment rates for goods and services providers. There are many reasons that this happy outcome may not occur in the health care system and the market may bid prices up too high. Provider monopoly power or other related payment inefficiencies, however, do not affect the choice of financing system.

Payment rates may also, in theory, be established independent of the form of financing, although this may be practically difficult to achieve. For example, by using regulation, systems with decentralized revenue collection can achieve the same monopsony payment rates that centralized payment systems can, as was the case in the all-payer rate setting systems that set uniform payment rates for all payers and all hospitals in several US states during the 1980s and early 1990s. Moreover, large private purchasers (as in the US, Germany, and the Netherlands) may have enough market power to exert appropriate countervailing pressure in the provider marketplace.

System efficiency begins to tie into financing when consumer choices enter the health care system. The first place this occurs is in the decision to use care. Multiple econometric analyses (and common sense) suggest that systems with copayments or co-insurance will tend to reduce the use of services. As countless commentators have argued, there is no particular reason to believe that the decisions of uninformed consumers/patients to reduce their service utilization will be medically appropriate. There are, however, situations where requiring the consumer to face some cost consequences of specific decisions would improve the efficiency of the system. For example, consumers might be asked to make choices between initiating treatment with a less costly drug or initiating treatment with a more costly alternative. Requiring out-of-pocket payments in this context is compatible with any of the insurance financing arrangements and may improve the efficiency of the system. The effects on equity depend on protections that are put in place for lower income people.

A connection between efficiency and financing may also arise in the context of system fragmentation. The difficulty of defining and measuring health care services, the complexity of services that need to be organized, and the problem of hand-offs among services suggest that more aggregated forms of payment – including payment to health plans or provider groups – may be preferable to provider-specific payment arrangements. Organizing care into multiple health plans (including plans with integrated delivery), paid risk-adjusted capitated rates may (in principle) improve the efficiency of care. Once a system is divided into multiple distinct delivery systems, however, consumers/patients must be compelled or provided with incentives to select an appropriate delivery system and stick with it.

Consumers can be induced to choose efficient plans by allowing (risk-adjusted) premiums to vary among plans and requiring higher payment for more costly plan choices (as in the Netherlands and Germany). Even in this case, however, any source of financing can be used to make the basic plan payment, and additional payments would be out-of-pocket. Moreover, efficient choice of plans can also be accomplished by paying plans risk-adjusted equivalent rates per capita, and then permitting plans to compete only on the scope of services included in the plan.

The options above suggest that achieving the goal of efficiency within the health care sector is fundamentally compatible with any form of general financing. Another element of efficiency, however, is choosing the appropriate size of the health care sector relative to spending on other goods and services. In pure general revenue systems, this can only be accomplished globally, through the political process. Within that process, providers and disease interest groups are likely to exert substantial political pressure to maintain or expand the size of the system. Moreover, since health care spending constitutes only one of many government services, it may be difficult for ordinary citizens to assess the efficiency of the system. The lack of transparency and political accountability of general revenue financed systems has led some analysts to prefer social insurance financing.

Under social insurance financing, the cost of health care is more transparently obvious to taxpayers, in the form of a tax rate or mandated premium payment.[2] Moreover, social insurance financed systems increasingly organize their systems into capitated health plans (paid risk-adjusted rates) so that consumers can adjust their consumption of health care and other goods at the margin. The basic social insurance payment to health plans can be set at a government-mandated minimum level, and consumers who wish to consume more health care may choose more generous plans, paying out-of-pocket for the incremental valuation.

Private insurance systems can also have transparent payment levels and permit consumers to choose more or less expensive health plans. In practice, the existence of employer-sponsored insurance, the preferential tax treatment of premiums, and the existence of substantial risk selection between plans may make it more difficult for private insurance systems to achieve efficiency in the delivery of services.

In sum, almost all financing choices are compatible with efficiency in the delivery of health care. Arrangements with transparent costs, such as social insurance models, may reduce the ability of providers to exploit their concentration within the system. Arrangements that require consumers to pay for more costly than average choices may, at the margin, improve the efficiency of the mix between health care spending and other sectors.

Empirical assessment of the effects of financing arrangements on health care spending is necessarily constrained by the limited number of similar countries available for study. The OECD routinely collects data on the costs and financing of health care systems (OECD 2006). Consistent data are available for about 20 health care systems in the 1990s, and somewhat fewer in the 1980s and 1970s. There is considerable persistence in the per capita cost of health care across countries over time (see figure 2), even as financing arrangements change. Thus, rather than examining the effect of financing on health care spending at a point in time, I use this extended time series to assess

FIGURE 2
PPP adjusted health care spending per capita, 1960 and 1990

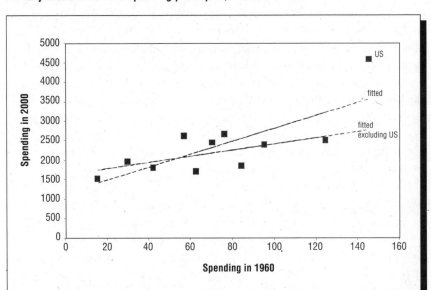

Source: SourceOECD, online. Downloaded October 2006.

the relationship between financing arrangements and the rate of growth of health care spending over time during each five-year period. I estimate (separately for each of 1975, 1980, 1985, 1990, 1995, and 2000) simple equations of the form:

$$\text{Total expenditure}_t = \alpha + \beta \text{general revenue share}_{t\text{-}5} + \chi \text{social insurance share}_{t\text{-}5} + \delta \text{out-of-pocket share}_{t\text{-}5} + \phi \text{total expenditure}_{t\text{-}5} + \varepsilon$$

I also estimate specifications that include controls for changes in the demographic composition of the population (aging) and repeat the analysis using financing composition at the end rather than the beginning of the period. These modifications do not substantively affect the results. Results of the main analysis are reported in table 1. I report results including and excluding the United States.

The main finding of table 1 is that there is no persistent and regular relationship between the structure of system financing and the rate of growth in per capita health expenditures in a health system. The results including the United States suggest that between 1990 and 1995, countries that began the period with a greater proportion of health care expenditures funded from general revenues, social insurance, or out-of-pocket financing experienced less cost escalation did those with more private insurance. Conversely, over the 1970–80 period, countries with more private insurance experienced less cost escalation. When the United States is excluded from the analysis, countries with more general revenue financing or more out-of-pocket financing (but not those with more social insurance financing) experienced less cost growth than did those with more private insurance financing over the 1990–95 period; there are no other statistically significant results. I also examine how the composition of public financing affected the rate of growth of public expenditures over time. The results are similarly variable over time, suggesting no clear pattern.

TABLE 1
Relationship between spending composition and spending growth

	1975	1980	1985	1990	1995	2000
Total expenditures						
Gen rev	+	+	0	0	-	0
Soc ins	+	+	0	0	-	0
OOP	NA	+	0	0	-	0
(N)	(6)	(11)	(8)	(11)	(16)	(20)
Total expenditures, no US						
Gen rev	0	+	0	0	-	0
Soc ins	0	+	0	0	0	0
OOP	NA	NA	0	0	-	0
(N)	(5)	(7)	(7)	(9)	(15)	(19)
Public expenditures						
Gen rev		+	0	0	-	0
Soc ins		+	-	-	-	-
OOP		+	-	-	-	-
(N)		(6)	(8)	(10)	(16)	(20)
Public expenditures, no US						
Gen rev			0	0	0	0
Soc ins			0	0	0	0
OOP			0	0	-	0
(N)			(7)	(9)	(15)	(19)

Data from SourceOECD, 2006 download. Results are from regressions of spending in column heading year regressed on expenditures (total or public, respectively) five years earlier, and on the composition of spending five years earlier. + indicates positive correlation, 0 indicates no significant correlation at 10 percent confidence level, - indicates negative correlation. Omitted category is private insurance.

The findings of these analyses are consistent with the theoretical discussion above. While taxes vary in the efficiency and progressivity with which they raise funds, the efficiency of operation of the health care system itself appears to depend much more on how providers are paid and how the delivery of care is organized than on the method used to raise these funds.

FINANCING CHOICES AND LIFE CYCLE EQUITY

In addition to measuring financing choices in terms of their impact on the efficiency of operation of the system, it is also important to judge these choices on how they contribute to the equity of the system. The standard metric of progressivity used in public finance assesses progressivity as the ratio of taxes paid to income. This makes sense if the funds collected through taxation are used to fund public goods that are equally available to all. In the case of cash or in-kind transfers, however, equity requires an assessment of both revenue collection and transfers made. Equity suggests that there should be *net* benefit transfers to lower income people. For any given level of national health spending, the degree of equity in a health care system depends both on how revenues for the system are raised and how spending in that system is disbursed among beneficiaries.[3]

In assessing the effect of system financing on system equity, I therefore follow the public finance literature and examine how the difference between payments made and benefits received from a health insurance program for higher income people compares with the difference for lower income people. In the case of a fully private system, this calculation is straightforward. Premiums paid each year reflect expected health care benefits for that person in that year. Premiums each year are, after a non-income related adjustment for loading, actuarially equal to benefits received that year. Lifetime premiums paid are actuarially equivalent to lifetime benefits received. Although the system generates ex-post redistribution between the healthy and the sick, the system is entirely non-redistributive ex-ante.

Social insurance and general revenue financed programs depart from this model in two ways. First, these programs pool all beneficiaries, so payments made in any given year reflect the average cost of all beneficiaries covered in that year, not individual-specific costs. Second, payments into the system each year are related to current income, according to the design of the tax system. This means that lifetime premiums need not reflect lifetime benefits.

To see the implications of these two features, imagine that income was unrelated to either health expenditures or health status. In a progressive financing system, this would imply that in each year, higher income people would pay more into the system than they would receive (and vice versa). The same pattern would hold over people's lifetimes. The system would be redistributive from high to low income.

In most universal publicly financed health care systems, including Canada's, however, income is related to both health expenditures at a point in time and to health status. This relationship has three components. First, at any given age, lower income people are usually in worse health than are higher income people. This leads them to use more health care services, generating a progressive distribution of benefits. Second, conditional on need, higher income people and lower income people may use care differently, even under universal free access to care. Van Doorslaer and Masseria (2004) find that in about half of OECD countries (including Canada), conditional on need, lower income people are more likely to use hospital services than are higher income people, and in most countries, they spend more days in hospital once hospitalized. Conversely, in all OECD countries, conditional on need, higher income people are more likely to see any doctor, to use specialist services, and to have more specialist visits than lower income people (see also Roos and Mustard 1997).[4] On average, conditional on health status, higher income people use the system more intensively and use more costly health services than do lower income people.

Third, income is closely related to mortality. In Canada, in 1996, life expectancy at birth was about five years longer for men in the highest income quintile than for men in the lowest income quintile. Life expectancy for women was about 1.6 years longer in the highest income quintiles than in the lowest (Wilkins, Berthelot, and Ng 2002).[5] Lower income people were much less likely to survive to age 75. While about 69 percent of higher income men survived to 75, only 53 percent of lower income men did (see figure 3). Among women, 80 percent of higher income but only 73 percent of lower income survived to age 75 (see figure 4). This pattern of differential survival, combined with similar spending at each age and increasing spending over the life cycle, reduces the lifetime spending benefits of a public health insurance system for lower income people.

This combination of factors means that the extent to which benefits under a universal health insurance system are distributed in a progressive fashion, and the net progressivity of the system, are empirical questions.

A small literature examines the net progressivity of social welfare systems in life cycle context. Several studies have examined this question in the context of pension systems in the United States and Canada (see, for example, Brown 1998, who concludes that both the US and Canadian pension systems remain progressive after accounting for longevity) and in the context of the US Medicare system, which provides universal health insurance to people 65 and over. Studies of the US Medicare system, a universal, social insurance financed health insurance program for people 65+, reach conflicting results

FIGURE 3
Cohort survival by quintile: Canadian men

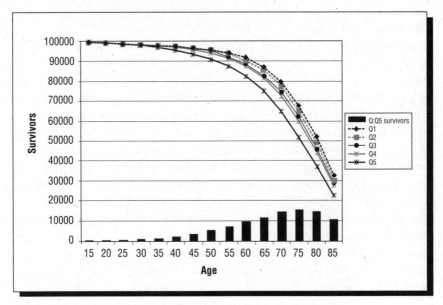

Source: Statistics Canada Life Table data, 1996. Provided by Russell Wilkins.

FIGURE 4
Cohort survival by quintile: Canadian women

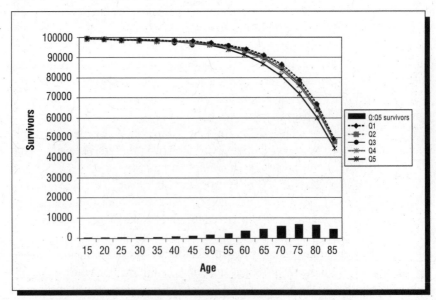

Source: Statistics Canada Life Table data, 1996. Provided by Russell Wilkins.

on progressivity. In their basic calculations (omitting the utility value of insurance), McClellan and Skinner (2006) conclude that Medicare generates modest dollar transfers toward higher income people. Bhattacharya and Lakdawalla (2005), using education rather than income as the measure of socioeconomic status, find that the hospital benefit in Medicare is somewhat progressive.

I examine this question in the Canadian context using data from the Canadian Community Health Survey 2000[6] (CCHS), data on mortality rates by income quintile in 1996 from Statistics Canada, and data on expenditures from OECD. I compute the average number of general practitioner visits, specialist visits, and hospital days by age group and gender and by income quintiles, using household-size adjusted income quintiles provided in the CCHS. I then assign a level of spending (intended to include associated ancillary services, diagnostic tests, etc.) to each general practitioner visit ($75), specialist visit ($375), and hospital day ($1000), so that total spending for physician service use and hospital use corresponds (roughly) to the OECD population totals for Canada. I use these data to compute spending levels by quintile throughout the life cycle. Figures 5 and 6 present these spending patterns for men and women.

FIGURE 5
Annual spending by quintile, men

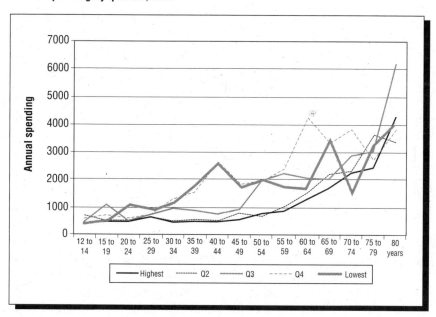

Source: Author's tabulations of the Canadian Community Health Survey, 2000, combined with 1996 life table data from Statistics Canada.

FIGURE 6
Annual spending by quintile, women

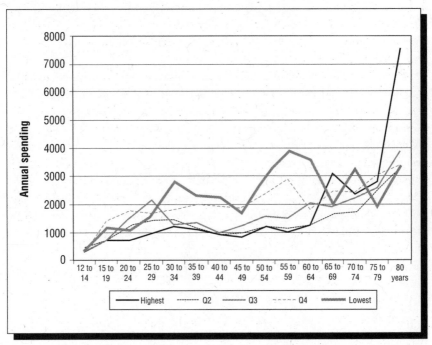

Source: Author's tabulations of the Canadian Community Health Survey, 2000, combined with 1996 life table data from Statistics Canada.

As expected, health care spending rises with age for both men and women. For both men and women, there is a pronounced difference in health spending between the three upper and two lower quintiles from ages 30 to about 55. After about age 55, spending patterns of the groups begin to converge. In late life, spending for the upper quintiles accelerates much more quickly than among the lower quintiles.

I next combine these data with the information on survival. Using these combined data, I compute lifetime public health care expenditures in Canada by quintile. I calculate these expenditures at age 12, at age 25 (not shown), and at age 65. These results are reported in table 2. In each set of results, the first column reports results that do not adjust for life expectancy and do not discount later spending. The second column reports results that adjust for life expectancy but do not discount later spending. The third column reports results adjusted for life expectancy and discounted at 5 percent.

Undiscounted, unadjusted lifetime health care spending measured at age 12 ranges from about $85,000 (high income men) to $170,000 (low income

TABLE 2
Lifetime spending by quintile and redistributive effect of health care spending

	At age 12				At age 65			
	No LE	0%	5%	Redistributive effect at 5%	No LE	0%	5%	Redistributive effect at 5%
MALE								
Highest	84953	66449	42332	0.13	52810	35521	19185	0.18
Q2	95603	74698	48218	0.15	57653	38430	20927	0.20
Q3	129646	99472	64762	0.21	70187	43042	23200	0.22
Q4	159807	129991	86414	0.28	68912	44595	24542	0.23
Lowest	138298	105591	72194	0.23	61943	34521	18959	0.18
Low: high	1.63	1.59	1.71		1.17	0.97	0.99	
Low: mid	1.07	1.06	1.11		0.88	0.80	0.82	
Mid: high	1.53	1.50	1.53		1.33	1.21	1.21	
FEMALE								
Highest	127961	108881	69488	0.17	78174	60134	32276	0.27
Q2	104700	92895	63603	0.16	45956	35450	19132	0.16
Q3	124467	110567	75552	0.18	52484	40296	21766	0.18
Q4	155599	139694	96697	0.24	57302	44085	23977	0.2
Lowest	170540	151924	104844	0.26	53090	39145	21331	0.18
Low: high	1.33	1.40	1.51		0.68	0.65	0.66	
Low: mid	1.37	1.37	1.39		1.01	0.97	0.98	
Mid: high	0.97	1.02	1.09		0.67	0.67	0.67	

Source: Author's tabulations of the Canadian Community Health Survey, 2000, combined with 1996 life table data from Statistics Canada and SourceOECD, October 2006. Spending computed as general practitioner visits at $75, specialist visits at $375, hospital days at $1000. Redistributive effect describes share received by group from $1 of health care spending, by gender.

women). Adjusting for differences in life expectancy reduces lifetime spending. For high income men, the effect of adjusting for life expectancy (without discounting) is to reduce expected lifetime spending by about 22 percent for men (slightly more for lower income men) and by about 11 percent for women (slightly more for higher income women). Discounting substantially reduces lifetime spending, particularly measured at earlier ages, because most health care costs occur in later life. Discounted lifetime health care costs are between 12 percent and 65 percent higher for women than for men in each quintile.

The three rows below the quintile estimates indicate the ratio of lifetime health spending between the highest and lowest quintiles (Q1:Q5), the middle and lowest quintile (Q3:Q5), and the highest and middle quintile (Q1:Q3).

The patterns are quite different for men and women. Using the discounted figures, among men, lifetime expenditures are about 10 percent higher for men in the lowest quintile men than for men in the middle quintile, while spending is about 50 percent higher for men in the middle quintile compared to those in the highest quintile. Among women, the differences are smaller. Spending for women in the middle quintile is about 9 percent higher than spending in the highest quintile, while spending in the lowest quintile is about 40 percent higher than spending in the middle quintile.

Measuring lifetime expenditures at age 25 rather than age 12 has little effect on the patterns (not shown). Consistent with prior studies in the United States, however, lifetime expenditures beginning at age 65 tend to be slightly higher for higher income groups than for lower income groups.

The final column in each of the panels describes the redistributive impact of putting $1 of tax funds into the health care system. The modest relationship between lifetime health care spending and income means that a universal health insurance system can only be slightly redistributive. Putting $1 of tax funds into the public health insurance system effectively channels between $0.23 and $0.26 toward the lowest income people, and about $0.50 to the bottom two income quintiles. For example, suppose all funds for a universal health insurance system were generated from the top three income quintiles. As these quintiles also use health care services, about half of the funds raised would be returned to them. The other half of the funds raised would be redistributed to the bottom two income quintiles.

The life cycle and cross-service patterns of health care spending also suggest that some forms of health care spending are more progressive than others. Lower income people are disproportionate users of hospital days, perhaps because arranging discharge is more complicated for those with fewer resources (Van Doorslaer and Masseria 2004). In most health care systems, low income people are less likely to initiate specialist care than are higher income people, despite their worse initial health status. In most countries, lower income people use more hospital days, conditional on hospitalization, than do higher income people. In Canada, higher income people also make disproportionate use of elective surgical procedures such as hip replacement and knee replacement (Roos and Mustard 1997). Finally, higher income people make more use of health care services at older ages, while lower income people have disproportionately higher use in mid-life.

These patterns suggest that focusing the marginal public health care dollar on skilled nursing days, access to general practitioners, and care associated with conditions that manifest in mid-life will have a more progressive effect than focusing additional tax dollars on elective surgical procedures or specialist care. At the margin, progressive financing sources should be devoted to progressive ends.

HEALTH CARE IN THE BIGGER PICTURE

The optimal design of health care system financing cannot be assessed in isolation from the rest of the components of the economy and the welfare state. Public funds used to finance health care cannot be used for other purposes. If health care spending rises, either taxes must increase or other services must be cut. This problem is acute in the case of health care spending because this sector is growing more rapidly than any other element of government budgets. Moreover, the relatively modest progressive impact of spending on health care raises the risk that rising health care spending is displacing more progressive cash or in-kind transfer programs.

A limited number of studies have examined the effect of in-kind transfer programs such as health insurance programs on the general progressivity of the welfare state. If non-cash benefits are very large relative to incomes, the inclusion of universal, uniformly distributed, non-cash benefits would significantly reduce measured inequality in a population. If non-cash benefits are progressively distributed, their inclusion will reduce measured inequality still further. Smeeding et al. (1993) use data from the early 1980s to examine the impact of including non-cash benefits in the measurement of economic inequality across countries. In that study, inclusion of non-cash in-kind benefits (including public health insurance) had little effect on the relative rankings of countries in terms of economic inequality.

In a recent paper, Garfinkel, Rainwater, and Smeeding (2006) revisit this issue. Their analysis incorporates the value of in-kind educational and health transfers (measured at the average cost across countries), and the distributive impact of the taxes used to finance these transfers. Note that Garfinkel, Rainwater, and Smeeding conduct their analysis at a point in time and do not incorporate the life cycle considerations described above. They find that the most important redistributive in-kind transfers are those that provide education to children. Inclusion of these benefits substantially alters the picture of relative well-being among children across countries.

Garfinkel, Rainwater, and Smeeding isolate the effects of health spending transfers by conducting analyses that focus only on the population 65 and over. In their analyses, health spending levels vary by age but not by income level. Empirically, health spending varies relatively little by income at older ages, suggesting that this assumption probably does not affect their results very much.

Garfinkel, Rainwater, and Smeeding report results for the population 65 and over using average values of health benefits across country.[7] As expected, they find that unadjusted income inequality tends to be higher in the English-speaking countries and lowest in the Scandinavian countries. Consistent with Smeeding's earlier study of the 1980s, however, the inclusion of the value of in-kind transfers (net of the impact on equity of the revenue collection to finance them) has very little effect on measured inequality, at least among older people. Inclusion of these benefits leads the inequality ratio for the low income vs. middle income population to fall slightly in most cases (by a maximum of 7 points, from 62 to 69 in Belgium) and actually generates a decline in equity in a few cases (by a maximum of 8 points, from 58 to 50, in Germany). The effects on inequality between the high and middle income population are slightly greater in magnitude, but equally inconsistent in direction.

These results suggest that public financing of the health care system has surprisingly little impact on overall economic equality. This implies that the value of health benefits received, net of taxes paid, by income quintile is small relative to income and other components of well-being and, consistent with our findings above, that health spending at a point in time does not vary greatly with income.

The final question of interest is the impact of *rising* health care expenditures on equity. No studies have examined this question directly. Instead, I examine the evolution of health care spending and tax revenue over time.

Figure 7 shows how the tax share of GPD and the health care share of GPD have evolved across the OECD over time. The tax shares of most economies have risen substantially since 1975, but there is considerable variation among countries in rates of growth of taxation. In most countries, the health share of GDP has also increased since 1975 but the health share of GDP has increased less than the tax share of GDP. In these countries, increases in taxation have more than accommodated rising health care spending. By contrast, in six countries – Canada, Germany, the Netherlands, Switzerland, the United Kingdom, and the United States – the rise in health care spending as a share of GDP has been greater than the rise in tax revenue. In most of these countries, this pattern reflects a relatively slow increase in tax revenue rather than a relatively rapid increase in health care costs. If all health care spending in these countries were public, other types of spending would have been displaced by health care expenditures.

Figure 8 repeats this analysis using the public health expenditure share of GDP. Although the six countries above differ substantially in the share of expenditures that are public, the pattern seen in figure 7 is repeated in figure 8. In these countries, tax policy has been constrained and has not accommodated increases in publicly financed health care expenditures. Rather, the effect of constraining taxes has been that publicly financed health care expenditures have displaced other forms of government spending. Without further information, however, it is not possible to ascertain the relative efficiency or equity of this displacement.

FIGURE 7
Change in tax share and health share of GDP, 1975–2003

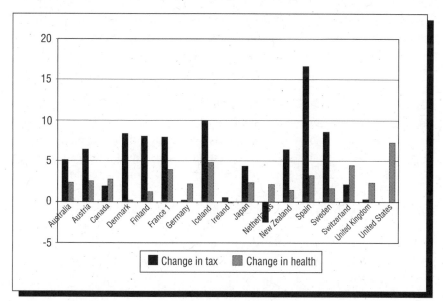

Source: Health data from SourceOECD, downloaded October 2006. Tax share data from OECD annual revenue statistics at http://www.oecd.org/dataoecd/18/23/35471773.pdf, table 2.

FIGURE 8
Change in tax share and in public health expenditure share of GDP

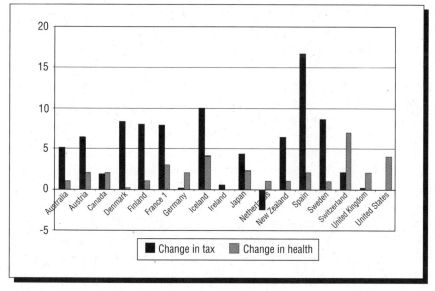

Source: Health data from SourceOECD, downloaded October 2006. Tax share data from OECD annual revenue statistics at http://www.oecd.org/dataoecd/18/23/35471773.pdf, table 2.

IMPLICATIONS FOR FINANCING

The analyses presented in this paper suggest, first, that the form of health care financing has no systematic relationship to the efficiency with which the health care system operates, at least to the extent that efficiency can be proxied by cost.[8] Second, over the life cycle, public expenditures on health care appear to be modestly progressive, with the main progressive impact of this spending occurring among middle-aged people. In Canada, $1 of tax money spent on health care generates about $0.50 worth of benefits to the lower two income quintiles and about $0.50 worth of benefits for the upper three income quintiles. Third, patterns of health service utilization in developed countries suggest that the marginal dollar of health care spending – money used to purchase high-tech equipment or specialist services – is less progressively spent than the average dollar. Depending on the form of financing, this marginal dollar may not be distributed progressively at all. Fourth, health care spending has little impact on the general distribution of well-being in society. Distributing progressively financed public funds through universal health insurance programs has limited impact on the distribution of total income. Finally, rising health expenditures threaten to displace other types of publicly financed transfers. This outcome has already occurred in many relatively low tax share economies, including in Canada.

This pattern of results has two implications for the form of financing of the health care system. In terms of public financing, the results suggest that forms of revenue collection that tax both older adults and young people are more equitable, over the life cycle, than those that tax younger people and cover older people. The greatest redistributive benefits of public health financing occur among middle-aged people who become seriously ill or disabled. Differential mortality and relatively equal health status among survivors make public financing of benefits to the elderly less redistributive.

In terms of the mix of public and private financing, the potential for public health insurance to crowd out other forms of redistributive benefits without generating significant redistribution themselves suggests that a mixed financing system may be the optimal way to balance efficiency and equity in health care. At the margin, increasing the level of public health expenditures to address ever-improving health care technologies will eventually – and, in some instances, may already – reduce the overall level of equity in society by moving scarce tax revenues from cash to less redistributive in-kind transfers. Progressive taxes are most effectively deployed to provide progressive benefits. Targeting these funds toward lower income groups is likely to enable the maximum level of redistribution at the lowest efficiency cost.

NOTES

Thanks to Courtney Ward, Mark Stabile, Colleen Tuohy, and participants at the November 2006 University of Toronto conference on Social Insurance for Health Care.

[1] According to the United Nations System of National Accounts, 1993, Annex IV, para. 4.111, an insurance program is designated as a social insurance program if at least one of the following three conditions are met: (i) participation in the program is compulsory either by law or by the conditions of employment; or (ii) the program is operated on behalf of a group and restricted to group members; or (iii) an employer makes a contribution to the program on behalf of an employee.

[2] Note that the transparency of the system may be obscured to the extent that the health care tax or premium payment for an individual also captures a redistributive component.

[3] Since health care costs have been rising more rapidly than financing, there are substantial intergenerational transfers in the health care system. I will treat these inter-cohort transfers as progressivity-neutral.

[4] These income-related patterns are partially attributable to differences in access to health facilities in (higher income) urban and (lower income) rural areas.

[5] I am grateful to Russell Wilkins for sharing the mortality data with me.

[6] Courtney Ward graciously provided me with these data.

[7] Garfinkel, Rainwater, and Smeeding also report results using the actual value of health care benefits in each country. Using the average value of health benefits (as I do here) has the effect of reducing the impact of high US health care costs on the extent of inequality reduction achieved through health benefit transfers in the US.

[8] As noted above, alternative sources of revenue themselves have efficiency implications, regardless of how the funding is used.

REFERENCES

Amelung, V., S. Glied, and A. Topan. 2003. "Health Insurance and the Labor Market: The German Experience." *Journal of Health Politics, Policy and Law* 28 (4): 693-714.

Bhattacharya, J., and D. Lakdawalla. 2006. "Does Medicare Benefit the Poor?" *Journal of Public Economics* 90 (1-2): 277-92.

Brown, R.L. 1998. "Social Security: Regressive or Progressive?" *North American Actuarial Journal* 2 (2): 1-33.

Garfinkel, I., L. Rainwater, and T.M. Smeeding. 2006. "A Re-Examination of Welfare States and Inequality in Rich Nations: How In-Kind Transfers and Indirect Taxes Change the Story." *Journal of Policy Analysis and Management* 25 (4): 897-919.

Kessleman, J.R., and R. Cheung. 2004. "Tax Incidence, Progressivity, and Inequality in Canada." *Canadian Tax Journal* 52 (3): 709-89.

McClellan, M., and J. Skinner. 2006. "The Incidence of Medicare." *Journal of Public Economics* 90 (1-2): 257-76

Organization for Economic Cooperation and Development. 2006. *Health Data*, 2006. Paris: OECD.

Roos, N.P., and C.A. Mustard. 1997. "Variation in Health and Health Care Use by Socioeconomic Status in Winnipeg, Canada: Does the System Work Well? Yes and No." *Milbank Quarterly* 75 (1): 84-110.

Smeeding, T.M., P. Saunders, J. Coder, S. Jenkins, J. Fritzell, A.J.M. Hagenaars, R. Hauser, and M. Wolfason. 1993. "Poverty, Inequality, and Family Living Standards Impacts across Seven Nations: The Effect of Noncash Subsidies for Health, Education, and Housing." *Review of Income and Wealth Series* 39 (3): 229-56.

van Doorslaer, E., C. Masseria, and the OECD Health Equity Research Group Members. 2004. "Income-Related Inequality in the Use of Medical Care in 21 OECD Countries." *OECD Health Care Working Papers* 14. Paris: OECD.

Wilkins, R., J.M. Berthelot, and E. Ng. 2002. "Trends in Mortality by Neighbourhood Income in Urban Canada from 1971 to 1996." *Health Reports* 13 (Suppl): 45-72.

Chapter 3

Efficient and Fair Financing of the Public Share of Canadian Health Care Insurance with Greater Reliance on the User-Pay Approach

Jack M. Mintz and Andrey Tarasov

Given the aging of Canada's society and the significant health care costs borne by the public sector, greater focus has been placed on financing alternatives for funding health care. This paper makes a case for greater use of user-pay related charges as an efficient and fair method of financing health care costs in Canada similar to methods in European countries, keeping in mind the need to relieve low income Canadians from health cost burdens.

A controversial issue in Canada is whether a user-pay approach, based on insurance principles, should be used to finance public spending on health insurance for Canadians. Currently, both the federal and provincial governments in Canada primarily use general revenues to finance health care expenditures, despite the fact that many jurisdictions might use some form of user-pay related tax or fees to finance at least part of their health care costs. From an insurance perspective, government funding partly related to usage of the system would be appropriate for at least two reasons. First, it would help engage Canadians in the proper provision of services. Second, it would mitigate the so-called "moral hazard" problems that arise from patients not taking preventive steps to reduce the incidence or cost of health care.

In our review of federal and provincial financing of health care in Canada, which is financed by general revenues or in part by fixed premiums related to income, we come to the conclusion that public funding of health care could be substantially improved if there were user-pay related charges raised to fund a share of health care costs using the current personal income tax system (see Aba, Goodman, and Mintz 2002), so that governments need not rely more heavily on distortionary taxes. This would improve not only the accountability and efficiency of the health care system but also the efficiency and fairness in the tax system, with those enjoying the benefits of public services paying for some of the cost. Alberta, Ontario, and British Columbia are in the best positions to revise their health premiums by converting them into usage-based premiums capped to ensure that low income Canadians are not hit with large fees. The extra revenue generated by these use-related premiums would fund more health care but also reduce some of the excessive demand for health services without compromising the objective of insuring catastrophic risks faced by Canadians.

Canada has a unique approach to financing health care insurance. In contrast to most countries, where most services have a mix of public and private spending to support health care needs, public funding is directed at funding hospital and physician services with no out-of-the-pocket spending for these expenditures except in very limited situations.[1] On the other hand, Canadians pay privately for many health services, including dental and optical services, pharmaceuticals, and long-term care, which are not covered by public health insurance plans for the majority of people in most provinces. Despite our "no user-pay" philosophy for certain services, Canadian governments cover a smaller portion of health services compared to the average industrialized OECD country. It is hard to see why Canada has taken a different approach from that of many European and other OECD countries, most of which have some form of user-pay system for hospital and physician services.

Below, we review the principles for funding health care insurance. We then compare funding for health care in Canada with that of other countries, and follow with an evaluation of the different sources of government tax funding. As a conclusion, we provide a reform measure that could be adopted by the provinces to fund health care with a more efficient and fair payment, using the income tax system for collection in order to relieve low income Canadians from paying user fees. We estimate that significant new revenues – up to $6 billion – could be raised to fund health care, with relatively low payments involved.

PRINCIPLES FOR FUNDING HEALTH CARE[2]

To understand the best approach for governments to finance health care insurance, it is important to lay out why they provide it. In practice, the role of any kind of insurance is to pool the risks faced by individuals, where the chance of each person's facing a contingent liability may be small but the costs incurred if that contingency occurs could be large – as in the case of fire insurance and other risk-related activities. An insurance agency pools risks across a population by collecting a premium from each insured member of a plan and covering the costs of those members who incur the liability.

The individual pays a premium that reflects the cost of benefits paid to the insured population. When risks are fully insured, individuals simply pay a premium to cover all potential risks. For example, under full insurance, implying that the rates are actuarially fair and that there are no transaction costs, if the chance of a person's becoming ill in a year is 2 percent and the average annual cost per illness is $15,000, the insurance premium set to cover insured risks would be $300 for each member of the plan, permitting the plan to operate without a loss.

Insurance is provided in many countries to cover a host of other contingencies that families and individuals face. Insurance rarely insures risks fully, however, since it could result in a greater incidence or higher claims being assessed. People may take less care to prevent risks: for example, they may fail to prevent fires with better electrical wiring. This problem is referred to as the *moral hazard* problem (Arrow 1970). To avoid the negative consequences of moral hazard, insurers adjust insurance policies to provide a break for those who are less likely to claim benefits. On the other hand, contract provisions are also adjusted so that people who impose greater liabilities on the insurer have to pay higher premiums or face higher deductibles.

Another source of inefficiency related to insurance markets is *adverse selection*, which arises when it is difficult to separate high risk and low risk insured persons (see Akerlof 1970). When insurance businesses cannot effectively distinguish between high and low risk insurees, they assess a premium that is based on the historical market information averaged across the insured population or its particular segments. Because this premium reflects a presence of high risk individuals and is therefore high, this could discourage low risk insurees from buying insurance and could leave them completely uninsured, with only high risk individuals willing to buy insurance. Insurers may try to separate the high risk from low risk insurees by using signals about their health – age, marital status, smoking and drinking habits, high blood pressure, and other attributes – and charge differential fees depending on the perceived risk. Nonetheless, the presence of high risk insurees increases the cost of insurance overall, even for the low risk individuals.

Insurance contracts therefore are aimed to provide insurance that is as complete as possible, but at the same time are also designed to mitigate moral hazard and adverse selection problems. To encourage better preventive care and avoid unnecessary costs, insurers use instruments that provide less than full insurance at a reasonable cost as a way of sorting the population by good and bad risks. These policies include deductibles (only expenditures greater than the deductible amount are covered), bonus payments (monetary rewards are provided for those who make few or no claims), and experience rated premiums that are adjusted according to a person's claims history.

PUBLICLY PROVIDED HEALTH INSURANCE AND THE NEED FOR INCENTIVES

Governments involve themselves in the provision of health insurance for two reasons. First, since health care is a significant cost for low income families, governments provide subsidies for the purchase of private insurance (often mandated for employers) or provide public insurance directly. Thus, one role of government mandated or publicly provided basic insurance programs is to provide access to health insurance for the whole population. Second, governments play a role in health insurance markets if high risk persons are unable to buy insurance and are thus unable to cope with high costs of major health problems or ill health. Governments may then mandate the provision of health insurance for the broad population, including high risk individuals.

Yet even though a government may provide funding for health insurance, full insurance of risks is inappropriate. The moral hazard and adverse selection problems result in higher losses incurred by a publicly operated insurance plan with uniform coverage, since individuals take less care to avoid health risks and tend to overuse the charge-free system. Thus, as in the case of privately provided insurance, it is appropriate that governments use cost and risk sharing incentives such as copayments to reduce the impact of moral hazard on the costs of the program (Breyer and Haufler 2000).

Canadian governments have used incentive mechanisms for social insurance programs in a number of contexts. Drug programs in most provinces have copayments or deductibles for insured claims. Canada/Quebec Pension Plan benefits and contributions are related to years of work and employee earnings. Most provincial governments provide workers' compensation using "experience rating" techniques: employer contributions are adjusted upward for those who make greater claims on the system. The United States uses experience rating for an employer's unemployment insurance contributions, which are based on claims by its employees.

PRINCIPLES FOR PUBLIC REVENUE-RAISING

In Canada, the current government practice is to fund health care from general revenues, payroll taxes, and income-tested premiums unrelated to the usage of health care services. Since tax burdens vary from one individual to another, the current financing method for health care is akin to a health insurance premium that varies across individuals according to their income, consumption, employment status, or other attributes, unrelated to health. A health funding system of this form offers no reward for those who avoid health care costs, as would be given under a bonus or deductible scheme. It also does not impose caps or provide reductions in the amounts claimed on by doctors on behalf of those patients who may intentionally engage in high health-risk behaviour or who may simply take less care in avoiding health care risks. Under the current public insurance system, payments and reimbursements are made irrespective of the individual's claims history.

For publicly provided health care services, Canadians should seek a financing approach that improves the overall objectives of both the tax system and public spending. The primary role of the tax system is to fund public expenditures, including public health insurance. Two important principles for optimal tax financing of public expenditures are well known: efficiency and equity.

Efficiency: An efficient tax system has a minimal impact on the allocation of resources in the economy. Further, a tax related to benefits received by taxpayers from public programs is efficient since users can compare the incremental costs of operating the program with the incremental gains that result from added expenditures on it. Under Canada's existing financing system, efficiency is impaired since neither medical service providers nor patients see any connection between the benefits received from public health care and the costs of providing the services, which can result in the excessive use of insured health care services. Empirical evidence shows that a 10 percent increase in prices directly charged for health services can reduce health care use by 1.7 to 7 percent.[3]

Accountability mechanisms could improve as well if health care providers and patients knew that the use of health care services meant that a patient would contribute more to the system. The current financing approach provides no opportunity for taxpayers to compare the true costs with the benefits of the system.

Equity: An equitable tax system recognizes that people in similar economic circumstances should pay similar amounts of tax (horizontal equity), and those in different economic circumstances should pay different amounts of tax (vertical equity). When consumption levels of public services vary among people in otherwise similar economic circumstances, equity is improved if contributions are related to the cost of those services. Equity is improved further if individuals who may assume health risks that result in greater health care expenditures contribute more to the costs of the health care system.

Some have argued that it is unfair to impose a "tax on the sick" (Lewis 1998), but this statement is based on the assumption that all health care needs are unrelated to a person's actions. Although it is often the case that luck or heredity affects a person's health, personal preventive actions also have some influence on health outcomes. For example, some individuals visit physicians and hospitals more often than they should since no direct monetary cost is incurred for the visit. This practice can lead to longer waiting times for all other users, including those who are in more urgent need of treatment. Additional incentives for eliminating unnecessary visits to physicians and hospitals would reduce waiting times and further ensure that those who need treatment the most receive it first. It would, therefore, be equitable to provide some incentives in a social insurance system to reduce the moral hazard and adverse selection problems. The incentive in a contribution (cost sharing) system is the portion of health care costs borne by the individuals who use the system, putting a limit on amounts paid so that those who incur catastrophic health expenditures would be immune from high payments. The scheme that we propose would not hurt those incurring high health costs, and yet like other Canadians, they would still make a contribution to the cost of public-provided health care services, enabling more services to be provided.

EXPERIENCE OF OECD COUNTRIES[4]

To compare the performance of the Canadian health care sector with that of other countries, we looked at the sample of 22 industrialized OECD countries. Tables 1 and 2 make use of the most recent available data and key statistics on structure and performance of health care sectors in these countries, including Canada.

At the provision stage, the countries in our sample can be divided into groups with mostly public provision of health care services (Austria, Denmark, Finland, Norway, Sweden, Italy, Greece, Spain, and Portugal); predominantly private provision (Belgium, Canada, France, Germany, Japan, New Zealand, Switzerland, and the United States); and a mix of the two types of provision.

At the funding stage, each country uses an individual mix of public and private funding sources, including general taxation revenues and social insurance contributions (payroll taxes) on the public side and out-of-pocket payments (user fees) and private health insurance premiums on the private side. However, several common funding patterns can be identified in our sample.

THE PUBLIC SECTOR IN HEALTH CARE

In almost all countries in our sample, health care systems provide statutory health insurance coverage to all or virtually all residents of that country. In the majority of these countries, the public sector plays a key role in health care financing. The average share of public funding in total health funding among the industrialized OECD countries in our sample was 72.6 percent in 2004. Canada's share of public funding was 69.8 percent in 2004 and 69.6 percent in 2005 and has been consistently below the sample's average since 1993. However, Canada's share of public health spending in total public expenditure has been consistently above the OECD sample average in each year between 1990 and 2004. Although the OECD sample average ratio of public health spending to total public spending has been growing since 1993 (it was equal to 12.1 percent in 1990, 14.2 percent in 2000, and 15.4 percent in 2005),

TABLE 1
Health care spending in developed OECD countries

#	Country/variable	Total health expenditure					Public health expenditure			
		Per capita	Average real per capita annual growth rate since 2000	As a share of GDP	Public expenditure as a share of total health spending	Private expenditure as a share of total health spending	Per capita	Average real per capita annual growth rate since 2000	As a share of GDP	As a share of total government spending
	Measurement units	PPD USD[a]	%	%	%	%	PPD USD[a]	%	%	%
	Observation period	2004	2000-2004	2004	2004	2004	2004	2000-2004	2004	2004
1	Australia	3,120	4.4	9.6	67.5	32.5	2,107	3.9	6.5	17.7[c]
2	Austria	3,124	1.8	9.6	70.7	29.3	2,207	2.0	6.8	13.6
3	Belgium	3,044[c]	6.7[c]	10.1[c]	71.1[c]	28.9[c]	2,165[c]	4.4[c]	7.2[c]	14.1[c]
4	**Canada**	**3,165**	**4.2**	**9.9**	**69.6**[d]	**30.4**[d]	**2,210**	**4.0**	**6.9**	**17.2**
5	Denmark	2,881	2.6	8.9	82.9[c]	17.1[c]	2,203[b]	3.6[b]	7.3[b]	13.2[b]
6	Finland	2,235	5.2	7.5	76.6	23.4	1,712	5.7	5.7	11.3
7	France	3,159	4.7	10.5	78.4	21.6	2,475	5.6	8.3	15.4
8	Germany	3,043	1.3	10.6	76.9	23.1	2,341	0.4	8.1	17.3
9	Greece	2,162	4.4	10.0	52.8	47.2	1,141	4.6	5.3	10.7
10	Ireland	2,596	7.1	7.1	79.5	20.5	2,063	9.3	5.7	16.8
11	Italy	2,467	2.5	8.7	75.8[d]	24.2[d]	1,852	3.6	6.5	13.7
12	Japan	2,249[c]	2.2[c]	8.0[c]	81.5[c]	18.5[c]	1,832[c]	2.3[c]	6.5[c]	16.8[c]
13	Luxembourg	5,089	10.7	8.0	90.4	9.6	4,603	11.0	7.3	16.8
14	Netherlands	3,041	4.1	9.2	62.3	37.7	1,894	3.6	5.7	12.3

... continued

TABLE 1
(Continued)

#	Country/variable	Total health expenditure					Public health expenditure			
		Per capita	Average real per capita annual growth rate since 2000	As a share of GDP	Public expenditure as a share of total health spending	Private expenditure as a share of total health spending	Per capita	Average real per capita annual growth rate since 2000	As a share of GDP	As a share of total government spending
	Measurement units	PPD USD^a	%	%	%	%	PPD USD^a	%	%	%
	Observation period	2004	2000–2004	2004	2004	2004	2004	2000–2004	2004	2004
15	New Zealand	2,083	4.9	8.4	77.4	22.6	1,611	4.7	6.5	17.3^b
16	Norway	3,966	5.1	9.7	77.9^d	22.1^d	3,311	5.4	8.1	17.8
17	Portugal	1,824	1.6	10.1	73.2	26.8	1,334	1.9	7.4	15.2
18	Spain	2,094	4.6	8.1	70.9	29.1	1,484	4.3	5.7	14.8
19	Sweden	2,825	3.9	9.1	84.9	15.1	2,399	3.9	7.7	13.6
20	Switzerland	4,077	2.8	11.6	58.4	41.6	2,382	4.1	6.8	18.3^c
21	United Kingdom	2,508	5.0	8.1	87.1^d	12.9^d	2,164	6.7	7.0	16.0
22	United States	6,102	5.1	15.3	44.7	55.3	2,727	5.5	6.9	18.9
	Simple average	3,039	4.3	9.5	73.2	26.8	2,192	4.6	6.8	15.4
	Population-weighted average	3,824	3.9	11.2	65.9	34.1	2,268	4.2	6.9	16.8

Notes: ^a Purchasing power parity adjusted U.S. dollars. ^b Year 2002 observation. ^c Year 2003 observation. ^d Year 2005 observation.

Source of data: OECD Health Data 2006 database (October 2006 version).

TABLE 2
Sources of health care funding and out-of-pocket payments in developed OECD countries

#	Country/variable	Sources of health care funding (as a share of total health care financing)					Out-of-pocket payments by household (OPP)			
		General government revenue	Social security funds (payroll taxes)	Out-of-pocket payments by households	Private health insurance premiums	Other private sources of health funding	Per capita OPP	Average real per capita annual growth rate since 2000	OPP as a share of private health funding	OPP as a share of final household consumption expenditure
Measurement units		%	%	%	%	%	PPP USD[a]	%	%	%
Observation period		2004	2000-2004	2004	2004	2004	2004	2000-2004	2004	2004
1	Australia	67.5	0.0	20.0	6.7	5.8	624	5.60	61.5	3.3
2	Austria	21.3	49.3	14.7	8.7	5.9	459	-0.28	50.2	2.6
3	Belgium	8.9[c]	62.2[c]	23.5[c]	3.4[c]	1.9[c]	717[c]		81.6[c]	4.5[c]
4	**Canada**	**68.2**[d]	**1.4**[d]	**14.9**[d]	**13.2**[d]	**2.3**[d]	**472**	**2.20**	**49.0**	**2.7**
5	Denmark	84.5	0.0	13.9	1.6	0.1	400	-0.64	89.1	2.6
6	Finland	59.6	17.0	18.9	2.3	2.1	423	3.02	81.1	2.9
7	France	3.3	75.0	7.6	12.4	1.7	239	-1.52	35.0	1.5
8	Germany	10.0	66.9	13.3	9.0	0.8	403	5.22	57.6	2.4
9	Greece	23.2	29.5	45.2	2.1	0.0	977	4.48	95.6	6.7
10	Ireland	75.2	0.7	13.5	6.7	3.9	351	6.98	56.0	2.3
11	Italy	75.7[d]	0.1[d]	20.3[d]	0.9[d]	3.0[d]	519	-0.74	83.9	3.1
12	Japan	17.5[c]	64.0[c]	17.3[c]	0.3[c]	0.9[c]	389[c]	3.00[c]	93.5[c]	2.5[c]
13	Luxembourg	18.0	72.4	6.7	1.7	1.2	340	8.12	69.8	1.4
14	Netherlands	3.0	59.3	7.8	19.1	6.0	238	0.76	23.7	1.5

... continued

TABLE 2
(Continued)

#	Country/variable	Sources of health care funding (as a share of total health care financing)					Out-of-pocket payments by household (OPP)			
		General government revenue	Social security funds (payroll taxes)	Out-of-pocket payments by households	Private health insurance premiums	Other private sources of health funding	Per capita OPP	Average real per capita annual growth rate since 2000	OPP as a share of private health funding	OPP as a share of final household consumption expenditure
Measurement units		%	%	%	%	%	PPP USD^a	%	%	%
Observation period		2004	2000-2004	2004	2004	2004	2004	2000-2004	2004	2004
15	New Zealand	77.4	0.0	17.2	5.1	0.3	359	6.46	76.1	2.5
16	Norway	70.2^d	13.4^d	15.7^d	0.0^d	0.8^d	623	1.38	95.2	3.6
17	Portugal	72.2	1.0	20.6	4.7	1.6	375	-0.18	76.6	3.4
18	Spain	65.6	5.2	23.6	4.7	0.8	494	4.52	81.1	3.4
19	Sweden	85.5	0.0							
20	Switzerland	17.0	41.4	31.9	8.7	0.9	1,301	1.94	76.9	6.3
21	United Kingdom	83.4^b	0.0^b							
22	United States	32.2	12.5	13.2	36.7	5.4	803	1.82	23.9	2.9
	Simple average	47.2	26.0	18.0	7.4	2.3	525	2.7	67.9	2.8
	Population-weighted average	37.1	28.6	14.3	15.7	2.9	529	2.0	49.1	2.6

Notes: ^{a} Purchasing power parity adjusted U.S. dollars. ^{b} Year 2002 observation. ^{c} Year 2003 observation. ^{d} Year 2005 observation.
Source of data: OECD Health Data 2006 database (October 2006 version).

Canada's ratio has been increasing even faster each year since 1999, ranging from 13.6 percent in 1990 to 15.1 percent in 2000 to 17.2 percent in 2004. This trend suggests that for the federal and provincial governments of Canada, health care expenditures and issues are an increasingly important current and future spending priority.

THE PRIVATE SECTOR IN HEALTH CARE

Private sector financing plays a very important role in health care financing in several countries, including the United States (55.3 percent of total financing in 2004), Greece (47.2 percent), and Switzerland (41.6 percent). Canada, with its 30.4 percent share of private funding, also belongs to a group of countries with a relatively strong financing role of the private sector (more than 25 percent in total funding). In 2004, in addition to the United States, Greece, Switzerland, and Canada, this group included Australia, Austria, Belgium, the Netherlands, Portugal, and Spain.

DOMINANT FUNDING SOURCES

The countries in our OECD sample differ in terms of their dominant funding methods. Members of one large group, which includes Australia, Canada, Denmark, Finland, Ireland, Italy, New Zealand, Norway, Portugal, Spain, Sweden, and the United Kingdom, finance more than 50 percent of their total health care expenditure with general taxation revenue sources. On the other hand, some countries, including France, Belgium, Germany, and the Netherlands, finance less than 10 percent of their health care spending with general taxes.

Members of another large group, which includes Austria, Belgium, France, Germany, Japan, Luxembourg, and the Netherlands, finance more than 50 percent of their total health expenditure with payroll taxes. However, for an even larger group of countries, including Australia, Canada, Denmark, Ireland, Italy, Japan, New Zealand, Portugal, Spain, Sweden, and the United Kingdom, payroll taxes represent a very insignificant (below 5 percent) share of health funding.

The out-of-pocket payments by households are a fairly significant private source of health care funding in most of the countries in the sample, except for France, Luxembourg, and the Netherlands, where out-of-pocket payments finance less than 10 percent of health care expenditure. Greece (45 percent) and Switzerland (32 percent) lead the list of countries that extensively rely on this source of funding.[5] Australia, Belgium, Italy, Portugal, and Spain follow with more than 20 percent of their funding coming from out-of-pocket payments. Canada, with its 15 percent share, is in the middle of the group of countries falling into the 10-20 percent range of financing from out-of-pocket payments. Canada also belongs to a large group of countries in which out-of-pocket payments represent the second largest source of health care financing; this group includes Australia, Belgium, Denmark, Finland, Germany, Ireland, Italy, New Zealand, Norway, Portugal, Spain, Switzerland, and Sweden. In the majority of countries using out-of-pocket payments, the latter are typically represented by cost-sharing arrangements (copayments, co-insurance, and deductibles) on certain health care services.

Private health insurance plays an important role as either a substitute or a complement to statutory health insurance in several countries, including the United States, Switzerland, the Netherlands, France, and Germany. In terms of a funding share of private health insurance premiums, Canada (at 13.2 percent) is in a relatively small group of developed OECD countries, including France, the Netherlands, and the United States, in which private health insurance premiums account for more than 10 percent of total health care financing.

Overall, several general conclusions can be made by looking at the OECD data:

- In almost all developed countries, public sources finance the major share of health care spending;
- Most countries rely on taxation revenues and social health insurance to finance health care;
- Taxation based financing is predominant among the northern countries (including Canada, Denmark, Finland, Sweden, and the United Kingdom) and in southern Europe (Italy, Spain, and Portugal);
- User-pay related contribution systems for health care funding are quite common across OECD countries but less so in Canada;
- The average share of user fees in the total mix of health care funding has been increasing over time across OECD members, with many countries recently introducing or planning to implement cost-sharing schemes to finance both primary and secondary health services.

ALTERNATIVE REVENUE SOURCES FOR FUNDING HEALTH CARE

Each source of health care funding generally has both pluses and minuses that need to be taken into account when deciding on the optimal mix in health care funding. The following section provides a summary of common pros and cons of different funding sources (see also Mossialos et al. 2002 for detailed discussion).

GENERAL GOVERNMENT REVENUES

Much of public health care funding comes from general revenues. In part this reflects a desire not to earmark taxes for specific purposes since governments have difficulty balancing budgets when rigid financing is put into place. Further, so long as the tax system is optimized in the sense of achieving efficiency and equity objectives, it would make sense to use general revenues to fund health care expenditures.

In theory, a tax financed system provides all residents of a country with the same access to equivalent care, irrelevant of their relative contributions. Tax financing detaches payment liability from the experience of poor health or the use of health services. It is also more flexible and adaptable than other sources of funding in matching changes and, in particular, large increases in health costs and spending. At least in theory, tax funded systems relying predominantly on locally collected taxes are associated with higher levels of revenue-expenditure matching, improved accountability, better responsiveness to local preferences, and stronger separation of health from other competing funding priorities.

Nonetheless, there are certain problems in relying solely on tax financed systems for a major public expenditure like health care. For example, in Canada, health care spending is almost one-quarter of total government spending and typically almost 40 percent of provincial spending. Thus, reliance on general revenues alone to finance health care increases tax rates substantially on existing tax bases, including taxes on mobile factors of production (labour and capital). Further, no direct link exists between the usage of health care services and the associated liability under taxation based funding; therefore, tax financed health care fails to deal with the moral hazard problems discussed above. Also, health care providers in tax financed systems are often said to be less responsive and accountable to their patients and customer concerns. This happens mostly because pricing and product choice decisions are not based on market competition and actual consumer demand but rather are largely dictated by results of negotiations between the government and health service providers.

Taxation funded health care systems are often prone to strong political influence and political pressures from various interest groups, including those representing the interests of health care providers and suppliers. The interest groups are marginally satisfied as long as health costs and expenditures are allowed to steadily increase, typically at the rates exceeding inflation. In such systems, any shortages in tax based funding, which come with poor economic conditions, result in active debates on inadequate funding patterns; however, at the same time it is usually very politically difficult, if not impossible, to implement cost containment reforms involving cost cutting and efficient pricing. Canada and the United Kingdom are good examples of such systems, where allegations of serious underfunding are very common yet cost containment reforms are very slow to be adopted.

Taxation based systems can also be susceptible to political issues at the resource allocation stage among different public ministries. In such systems, allocations to the health care sector greatly depend on political support of health care policies and reforms and on the relative political weight and the bargaining power of the health related authorities versus other government bodies. In most countries the Ministry of Health or other government agency responsible for the health care sector traditionally lacks authority in comparison with other ministries.

PAYROLL TAXES (SOCIAL INSURANCE CONTRIBUTIONS)

Many European countries have used payroll taxes to fund health care, as discussed above. Payroll-tax based funding offers several advantages to the countries that choose to use it. First, social insurance schemes do not discriminate against individuals with low income and poor health. Second, the revenue is earmarked and therefore is better protected from political interference, especially if budgetary and/or spending decisions are devolved to independent bodies. Third, payroll taxes are also a relatively transparent revenue source and therefore are highly acceptable to the general public.

Nonetheless, payroll taxes as a source of health care funding have their limitations, especially in industrial countries with an aging society, low fertility rates, and a work force that is no longer growing. First, payroll taxes represent a significant extra burden on employment, production, and economic growth during recession times. In highly competitive labour markets, the total cost of employment needs to be contained; therefore, increases in insurance contributions can substitute out wages in the total labour cost. In other words, employers can shift their share of payroll contributions to employees by reducing growth rates in nominal wages. Denmark's recent use of general revenues to fund social security and health care has been attributed to supporting a more flexible labour market.[6]

Second, if social insurance is not mandatory for the entire working population (only for full-time workers), it can create incentives for employers to offer part-time jobs that pay below the minimum threshold, to outsource employment to self-employed contractors, or to create jobs in the shadow sector of the economy. Larger domestic labour costs due to high payroll taxes give an extra incentive to employers to outsource many contracts and job positions to other countries.

Third, many systems of social health insurance use current employment income as the contribution base, which is becoming less satisfactory for several reasons. Because social health insurance relies on a relatively narrow revenue base linked to employment income and perhaps self-employed income, it may fail to generate sufficient revenue, especially in countries with aging population and low participation in the formal labour force. Wealth can significantly affect the ability to pay but is not taken into account under payroll taxation. Capital income, which accounts for an increasing proportion of individual income, is not charged under payroll-tax based funding.

Fourth, similar to health care systems funded through general government revenues, payroll-tax based systems may be prone to political pressures. For example, health care systems funded through social health insurance funds may be highly politicized if the independent social-insurance agencies that operate these funds are captured by interest groups. Also, in systems with uniform social health insurance coverage, provider job actions affect all or most of a country's population and thus have greater political effects.

In the case of a single social insurance fund, insured individuals typically have no choice over plans and/or providers and may be offered a health plan that lacks quality, comprehensiveness, and adequate responsiveness to needs. The Netherlands has tried to address this issue with several funds operating to provide insurance for the population.

Other European countries are debating whether they should eliminate or reduce payroll taxes as a source of revenue to fund social benefits. Given the significant "legacy" cost faced by businesses with payroll taxes on workers to fund benefits for the elderly, it is not surprising that many countries are looking to move away from payroll taxes as a source of revenue for health programs. The Danish experience is an important example of why payroll taxes should not be a source of revenue to fund health care.

OUT-OF-POCKET PAYMENTS (USER FEES)

Out-of-pocket payments are commonly used in many countries to reduce excessive pressures on health care systems by reducing incentives for overconsumption. This form of payment also improves access to health care services because some people will choose not to use the services when facing even a very small user-fee cost.

Further, user fees reduce the tax burden on taxpayers because the public health system is responsible for small health care payments. They also provide additional revenue when governments are having difficulty in funding health care by taxation or social insurance contributions; user fees can thus decrease budget deficits and improve fiscal sustainability of a health care system. With user fees imposed selectively on some health services, the government can reduce its spending on non-essential services and instead concentrate its funding on prioritized or more cost effective services. In particular, the extra revenues raised through user fees can be used to finance health services targeting low income individuals.

By coordinating prices among different categories of health services, user fees can enable better redistribution and control of service use. In other words, through a system of user fees, the government can affect the pattern of consumer utilization for some health services and can send the signals to the market about its priorities. For example, by not charging fees on HIV testing or meningitis vaccination, the government can encourage the public use of these services.

The system of out-of-pocket payments can encourage consumers to seek more cost efficient (yet not necessarily less effective) forms of health care services (for example, the use of phone-based or Internet-based professional assistance lines instead of actual physician visits in many less urgent cases). User fees make individuals more aware of health service costs and can indirectly affect service pricing by providers.

The usual concerns raised about user fees are that they may discourage lower income households from seeking health care services. Unless an accompanying system of exemptions and ceilings is introduced, user fees are usually regressive and are strongly biased toward single, high income, and healthy individuals. They discriminate against those individuals who have poor health or those who have to use health services relatively heavily due to circumstances beyond their control. On the other hand, the user-fee system does not have adverse effects on health service provision if low income and disabled individuals are fully or partially exempt.

Introduction of user fees increases the demand for private insurance, which is likely to increase the demand for employer based private insurance. In competitive labour markets, employers substitute from wages toward health care benefits and decrease a share of monetary compensation in the overall labour costs. The latter decreases the amount of disposable income available for consumption and reduces the overall consumer benefits (see also Stabile 2001).

Finally, the introduction of user charges typically involves additional administrative costs, especially if they are accompanied by a set of exemptions and ceilings.

A NEW DIRECTION FOR FUNDING HEALTH CARE INSURANCE: USER-PAY RELATED TAX BASED PAYMENTS

No financial source for health care is perfect, and different mixes of taxes and fees are required to the extent that they minimize distortions and achieve equity among taxpayers. As shown in table 3, Canada makes little use of payroll taxes to fund health care (less than 2 percent) but does rely on general revenues for two-thirds of funding. The balance is paid for by out-of-pocket expenses (15 percent) and private health insurance (13 percent). However, most of the out-of-pocket expenses and premiums are directed at services not covered by medicare. These amounts have been roughly stable in the past 15 years (table 3).

As discussed above, Canada is one of the few countries not to use more incentive based funding schemes for hospital and medical physician services. Certainly, user fees could be considered for primary health care services in Canada, although they are often criticized for hurting the poor the most.

There is another approach to introducing a cost-sharing mechanism, and that is to use the current personal tax system to collect a user-pay related charge on health care benefits. This would require governments to assess the public health care benefits received by individuals and report on a T-Health slip the value of the benefits. Aba, Goodman, and Mintz (2002) modelled a 40 percent charge on health care benefits subject to the income-based limit that the payment should be no more than 3 percent of household income in excess of $10,000.

The virtues of using a tax-paid approach compared to general revenues, payroll taxes, and user fees would be the following:[7]

1. As with user fees, governments would need to assess costs for services provided to the public. (This is not currently done for many hospital services.) Such pricing would encourage greater accountability and give scope to providers to compare the net benefits of different procedures.
2. Using the tax system to determine benefits and charges reduces some administrative costs that would be incurred, since it is tied to tax administration.
3. The income limitation and the exemption reduce the effect of the user-pay related charge on low income Canadians and those facing high costs due to illness.
4. Some reliance on a user-pay related charge reduces the need to raise distortionary marginal income tax rates or payroll taxes that are paid by a working population.
5. Such user-pay related charges encourage better engagement of the public with health care services; as well, they improve efficiency and equity in the tax system.

While the tax based user-pay related charge has many advantages, it has less impact on demand for health care compared to user charges that are assessed and paid at the time when the service is provided.

In Canada, three provinces currently have health care premiums, but none are related to actual usage of the system (such as in the case of a deductible).

Little justification can be given for the absence of a deductible or bonus that would tie the demand for health care with actual payments. Certainly, the proposed system above could be easy to implement by tying premiums to amounts used and limiting them to a percentage of income so families would not be unfairly burdened.

AN EXAMPLE OF A FAIR AND EFFICIENT USER-PAY APPROACH

The proposed user-fee program consists of the two components: a user-fee cost schedule and an income based premium schedule. The former specifies the basis to calculate each family's billable user-fee charges on physician and hospital services. The latter determines the actual share of these user-fee charges that is annually paid by each family through the income tax collection system.

The proposed user-fee program addresses only charges on primary care (physician) and hospital services, which are currently covered by provincially administered health insurance plans. Physician services are provided by general practitioners such as family doctors, and by specialists, including medical specialists (such as neurologists, dermatologists, and psychiatrists) and surgical specialists (such as urologists, gynecologists, and general surgeons). Hospital services to individuals include inpatient services (those involving overnight stays) and outpatient services, including ambulatory care service visits, day/night care visits, and emergency visits.

OPTIONS

The proposed user-fee program consists of the user-fee cost component and the income based premium component. The former specifies how each person's and household's spending on physician and hospital services is estimated. The later deals with how these incurred costs are paid for through the income based premiums.

We estimated the material effects of six different policy options, three strictly based on user fees in the form of copayments and the other three involving a combination of copayments and co-insurance. With copayments, a patient is charged a fixed dollar amount for each unit of service provided. With co-insurance, a patient pays a fixed percentage share of a health service cost. The policy options that we consider involve only user fees on physician and hospital services but can be easily expanded or modified to incorporate new charges on these as well as other health services. Table 3 below provides a summary of user-fee charges under each simulated policy option.

While it would be plausible to apply co-insurance rates to hospital services in policy options 4 to 6, we did not have reliable data on the exact nature and

TABLE 3
User-fee rates in the simulated policy options

Services	Policy 1 (P-L)	Policy 2 (P-M)	Policy 3 (P-H)	Policy 4 (I-L)	Policy 5 (I-M)	Policy 6 (I-H)
Family doctors (GPs)						
Per visit/consultation	$5	$10	$15	20%	30%	40%
Per procedure	$5	$10	$15	20%	30%	40%
Specialists (medical and surgical)						
Per visit/consultation	$5	$10	$15	20%	30%	40%
Per procedure	$10	$20	$30	20%	30%	40%
Hospitals						
Per outpatient visit/ consultation	$5	$5	$5	$5	$5	$5
Inpatient services						
Per each day of an overnight stay	$5	$10	$15	$5	$10	$15
Per inpatient stay	$10	$20	$30	$10	$20	$30

Note: P: copayment based program; I: co-insurance based program; L, M, and H refer to the low, medium, and high value options in copayments or co-insurance premiums of the simulated user-fee programs.

average costs of inpatient and outpatient visits and therefore chose to apply copayment fees to hospital services in all six policy options.

INCOME BASED HEALTH PREMIUMS

The income based premium component of the proposed policies includes a set of decisions on the choice of: (i) the income tax base for the health premiums, (ii) applicable personal allowance/deductions, and (iii) marginal premium rates. In all six policy options, we apply the same set of financing assumptions.

First, the tax base is set to equal the family (household) income from all sources.

Second, we assume that an income based allowance of $9,000 is given for each family member, including children and disabled individuals who require caretaking services by other family members. This ensures that larger families with one or more children, as well as those with disabled individuals, are sufficiently protected against naturally higher family expenditures on health care services. Under the proposed per person allowance, the actual average per person premiums are likely to be higher for single individuals and childless couples, which at least partially restores some inequity issues that exist under the current income tax system with respect to families with children. The size of the proposed per person allowance is chosen to roughly match the size of the federal basic personal allowance amount. The actual policy can use the exact federal personal amount to make the calculations of health care premiums easy and uniform among provinces and to blend this process into the existing federal-provincial income tax system.

Third, the marginal premium rate is set at 3 percent, which is applied to the household income after all applicable allowance deductions have been made. This premium rate is used to calculate the maximum amount, or cap, that can be charged against the family income for the health care costs incurred by family members during a calendar year. The actual total health care premium that is paid by a family is equal to the lesser of: (i) the maximum 3 percent premium cap and (ii) the user-fee cost of physician and hospital services charged to a family health care card over a calendar year.

Let's look at a simple example to see how this system would work in practice. Suppose we look at a married couple with two children, a combined annual income of $84,000, and a total health care user-fee bill of $600 charged to their family health card account. Applying the per capita allowance of $9,000, we get the taxable income of $60,000 = $87,000 − 4 x $9,000. The health premium cap size for this family is then equal to $1,800 = $60,000 x 0.03. Since this family's health care bill was assessed at $600, which is lower than the premium cap of $1,800, their tax liability will be equal to $600. If this family's annual health care bill were high at $3,000 (which is very unlikely but is still possible in the case of serious illness or injury sustained by any of the family members), the family's tax liability would only be limited to the size of the family's premium cap amount, that is, $1,800. If all family members were healthy during the year and, as a result, their billable user fees were only $50, then the actual tax liability for this family would be only $50, or only $12.50 per a family member.

In calculating the expected user-fee expenses and the expected payable health premiums, we need to take into account the negative impact of user fees on the demand for related health services. We are not aware of any comprehensive study that would estimate the long term effects of actually implemented user fees on primary health care services. Based on information from different sources, however, we can expect the short term price elasticity of demand for physician and hospital services to be approximately equal to -0.13 on a move from 0 percent to 10 percent in co-insurance rates, -0.19 on a move from 0 percent to 25 percent, and -0.25 on a move from 0 percent to 50 percent. Roughly the same conclusions can be applied to the effect of copayments if the latter are measured as a percentage of relevant service costs. The short run demand from physician and hospital services is relatively elastic in response to the initially introduced user fees, but it becomes increasingly inelastic as the size of these fees increases.

Since we are interested in longer term effects of user fees on the demand for physician and hospital services, we need to use some measure of a long run price elasticity. For the purposes of our simulation exercise, we assume that a very conservative estimate of such long term elasticity would be equal to 50 percent of the corresponding short term elasticity. It is safe to make these assumptions because the reported short term elasticity numbers are likely to be biased upwards for two reasons: first, the estimates of short term price elasticity mostly come from sources which cite the results of controlled policy experiments; second, our proposed user-fee schedule is combined with significant allowance amounts and premium caps, both of which greatly decrease the price sensitivity of demand for health care services. We believe that our estimate is very conservative on the safer side. It does not overestimate both the short term and long term effects of the proposed policy options on the applicable utilization rates and therefore does not overestimate the expected public savings and extra revenues from the implementation of these policies.

Making this assumption of the longer term price elasticity and taking into account the non-linearly decreasing relationship between the user-fee size and the price elasticity of demand for health services, we derive a function that approximates this relationship well and apply it to each of the six policies and the relevant user-fee-free utilization rates to estimate the expected changes in per capita demand for physician and hospital services. Table 4 reflects the expected longer term demand effects of policy options 1 to 6, in this case averaged across health service types and across the provinces.

TABLE 4
Expected decrease in total demand for physician and hospital services in response to the implementation of user-fee policy options 1–6, Canadian average

	Policy 1 (P-L)	Policy 2 (P-M)	Policy 3 (P-H)	Policy 4 (I-L)	Policy 5 (I-M)	Policy 6 (I-H)
Expected decrease in demand for health services (%)	-6.6	-8.2	-9.5	-7.9	-9.2	-10.2

Note: See table 3.

Unfortunately, we did not have reliable data on the actual hospital costs of inpatient and outpatient services and on the actual share of these costs in the total provincially funded hospital financing. Therefore, we conservatively assume that user fees on hospital related services will not affect the level of provincial public spending on hospitals. On the other hand, we assume that decreases in demand for physician services directly affect the level of physician billing against the provincially funded health insurance plans. Therefore, we can apply our estimates of expected changes in demand for physician services to calculate the effect of user fees on provincial public spending on physician services. Given lower utilization rates for physician services, we assume that the level of public spending will decrease proportionately to a fall in demand for the relevant services. Table 5 estimates the expected reductions in provincial expenditure on physician services due to lower utilization rates after the user-fee structure is implemented.

TABLE 5
Expected reductions in provincial public spending on physician services (CA$million), by policy option and by province

	Policy 1 (P-L)	Policy 2 (P-M)	Policy 3 (P-H)	Policy 4 (I-L)	Policy 5 (I-M)	Policy 6 (I-H)
Newfoundland and Labrador	22.7	28.9	33.1	23.9	27.9	31.1
Prince Edward Island	5.3	6.7	7.7	5.6	6.5	7.3
Nova Scotia	39.8	50.1	57.9	45.1	52.5	58.6
New Brunswick	30.7	38.7	44.8	35.0	40.7	45.4
Quebec	229.2	287.3	331.6	266.2	309.7	344.9
Ontario	668.3	846.4	969.1	722.5	840.1	935.5
Manitoba	57.1	72.4	83.7	62.8	73.2	81.7
Saskatchewan	46.0	58.4	67.4	50.2	58.5	65.3
Alberta	124.9	155.0	179.6	151.5	176.0	196.0
British Columbia	183.6	229.3	266.0	219.3	254.9	283.8
Canada (provincial total)	1,407.6	1,773.2	2,040.8	1,582.2	1,840.2	2,049.7

Note: See table 3.

To calculate the total expected public spending benefits from the proposed policy options, the expected savings from lower provincial public costs of physician services should be combined with user-fee premiums on physician and hospital services, which will be annually collected by either federal or provincial government within the existing personal income tax system. The sum of the public savings and the extra premium revenue gives us the total benefit to the provincial government in each province, should it decide to implement the proposed user-fee program.

ESTIMATION OF USER-FEE PREMIUM CAPS

The proposed income based premium structure calls for per capita $9,000 allow-ance and 3 percent premium caps on taxable family income. Tables 6 and 7 show the average maximum premium caps per household that can be charged under the proposed plan. Table 10 presents the distribution of average premium caps by province-specific household income quintiles, while table 11 shows the distribu-tion of average premium caps for different family sizes.

TABLE 6
Average per household premium caps by province-specific household income distribution quintiles

	1st quintile (0-20%) $	2nd quintile (20-40%) $	3rd quintile (40-60%) $	4th quintile (60-80%) $	5th quintile (80-100%) $	Total distribution $
Newfoundland and Labrador	10	211	629	1,217	2,033	818
Prince Edward Island	40	320	708	1,303	1,924	859
Nova Scotia	20	378	836	1,401	2,085	944
New Brunswick	16	316	759	1,352	2,026	894
Quebec	39	471	957	1,554	2,106	1,026
Ontario	49	685	1,352	1,796	2,298	1,236
Manitoba	40	510	976	1,551	2,106	1,037
Saskatchewan	34	462	983	1,592	2,257	1,066
Alberta	77	691	1,411	1,875	2,313	1,273
British Columbia	41	579	1,170	1,666	2,287	1,149
Canada (provincial average)	42	580	1,163	1,675	2,253	1,143

The size of average health premium caps as a percentage of total family income, with distributions by province specific household income quintiles, is relatively small – on average 1.5 percent of income, ranging from 0.3 per-cent of income for the lowest quintile to 2.1 percent for the highest.

ESTIMATION OF PAYABLE PREMIUMS

After the income-based premium allowances and caps are taken into account, families make actual health premium payments that do not exceed their user-fee billing charges. Tables 8 and 9 show the average expected per person and per household premium payments to be made under each of the policy options 1 to 6.

TABLE 7
Average per household premium caps, by family size

	1 person $	2 persons $	3 persons $	4 persons $	5+ persons $	All households $
Newfoundland and Labrador	821	821	828	805	752	818
Prince Edward Island	826	837	855	880	842	859
Nova Scotia	924	935	940	947	916	944
New Brunswick	869	888	897	897	848	894
Quebec	1,012	1,004	1,038	1,037	976	1,026
Ontario	1,193	1,207	1,232	1,270	1,198	1,236
Manitoba	990	988	1,053	1,065	979	1,037
Saskatchewan	1,023	1,034	1,050	1,128	1,022	1,066
Alberta	1,272	1,258	1,265	1,303	1,169	1,273
British Columbia	1,118	1,103	1,145	1,182	1,144	1,149
Canada (provincial average)	1,107	1,104	1,133	1,192	1,129	1,143

TABLE 8
**Total expected annual user-fee premium payments per person ($),
after premium allowances and caps are taken into account**

	Policy 1 (P-L)	Policy 2 (P-M)	Policy 3 (P-H)	Policy 4 (I-L)	Policy 5 (I-M)	Policy 6 (I-H)
Newfoundland and Labrador	32	58	80	39	56	72
Prince Edward Island	36	64	90	44	63	82
Nova Scotia	35	63	87	52	75	95
New Brunswick	37	65	90	53	76	97
Quebec	47	89	124	79	114	144
Ontario	47	86	124	61	89	117
Manitoba	39	73	104	52	77	100
Saskatchewan	42	78	110	55	81	105
Alberta	37	65	93	64	93	122
British Columbia	37	70	100	64	94	121
Canada (provincial average)	43	80	114	65	94	121

Note: See table 3.

TABLE 9
Total expected annual user-fee premium payments per family ($),
after premium allowances and caps are taken into account

	Policy 1 (P-L)	Policy 2 (P-M)	Policy 3 (P-H)	Policy 4 (I-L)	Policy 5 (I-M)	Policy 6 (I-H)
Newfoundland and Labrador	81	146	202	97	141	181
Prince Edward Island	86	152	212	105	150	193
Nova Scotia	83	153	211	126	183	230
New Brunswick	89	158	219	129	185	236
Quebec	110	205	289	184	264	335
Ontario	127	235	341	167	244	319
Manitoba	98	183	260	130	193	251
Saskatchewan	106	192	270	139	200	258
Alberta	93	168	241	166	241	315
British Columbia	94	174	252	161	236	305
Canada	110	204	292	164	239	309

Note: See table 3.

For the majority of families the expected premium payments will be significantly below their premium caps. However, even those families that will incur significant health costs on physician and hospital services will be securely protected by the proposed premium caps, which limit the maximum user-fee premium to a low range of 0 percent to 2.2 percent of household income.

Using the projected 2007 provincial population estimates, we can calculate the overall expected health premium collections for each of the policy options 1 to 6. Table 10 shows the expected total user-fee revenue that the provincial governments can generate by implementing the proposed user-fee program.

Combining these estimates of user-fee revenue with our conservative projections of provincial public savings from the lower utilization of physician services, we can estimate the total provincial public benefits from the proposed policy options 1 to 6. Table 11 presents these estimates.

Note that the estimates above do not take into account those savings that can accrue from possible decreases in utilization of hospital services after user fees on these services are introduced. While we took into account the impact of expected decreases in the use of hospital services when calculating user-fee revenues, we did not calculate the applicable impact on the existing provincial hospital spending, due to the relevant per service cost data limitations. However, since utilization rates for inpatient hospital services are

TABLE 10
Expected health premium revenues (CA$million), by policy option and by province

	Policy 1 (P-L)	Policy 2 (P-M)	Policy 3 (P-H)	Policy 4 (I-L)	Policy 5 (I-M)	Policy 6 (I-H)
Newfoundland and Labrador	16.2	29.4	40.6	19.5	28.4	36.6
Prince Edward Island	5.0	8.9	12.5	6.1	8.8	11.4
Nova Scotia	32.2	58.6	81.1	48.6	69.9	88.4
New Brunswick	27.6	48.4	67.4	39.8	56.6	72.3
Quebec	364.8	681.7	955.5	611.0	875.4	1,108.0
Ontario	598.4	1,104.8	1,593.0	786.8	1,145.3	1,497.3
Manitoba	46.6	86.5	122.6	61.7	91.4	118.4
Saskatchewan	41.6	76.8	108.2	54.4	79.7	102.9
Alberta	126.8	226.3	323.5	222.5	322.8	421.2
British Columbia	163.4	303.5	438.3	279.8	411.0	527.5
Canada (provincial total)	1,422.5	2,625.1	3,742.7	2,130.2	3,089.3	3,983.9

TABLE 11
Expected total provincial public revenues/savings from the proposed user-fee program (CA$million)

	Policy 1 (P-L)	Policy 2 (P-M)	Policy 3 (P-H)	Policy 4 (I-L)	Policy 5 (I-M)	Policy 6 (I-H)
Newfoundland and Labrador	38.9	58.3	73.7	43.4	56.3	67.7
Prince Edward Island	10.2	15.6	20.2	11.7	15.3	18.7
Nova Scotia	72.0	108.7	138.9	93.7	122.4	147.0
New Brunswick	58.3	87.1	112.1	74.7	97.4	117.7
Quebec	594.0	969.1	1,287.2	877.3	1,185.2	1,452.9
Ontario	1,266.7	1,951.2	2,562.1	1,509.3	1,985.4	2,432.9
Manitoba	103.7	159.0	206.3	124.5	164.6	200.1
Saskatchewan	87.6	135.2	175.6	104.7	138.2	168.1
Alberta	251.7	381.4	503.0	374.0	498.8	617.2
British Columbia	347.0	532.9	704.4	499.1	665.9	811.3
Canada (excluding territories)	2,830.1	4,398.3	5,783.5	3,712.4	4,929.5	6,033.6

Note: See table 3.

likely to fall after the proposed user fees are introduced, we can expect decreases in overall public hospital spending. Given very high per person public hospital costs incurred by provincial governments, one can expect that even small decreases in hospital utilization rates will result in significant per person and aggregate public savings, which should further increase our estimates of public benefits from implementing any of the proposed user-fee policy options.

CONCLUSIONS

Canada relies primarily on general revenues to finance health care. In our view, this is better than using payroll taxes that would create strains on labour markets with an aging society.

Nonetheless, the difficulty in relying solely on general revenues to finance health care is that it places most of the health care burden on those paying the most taxes. High marginal rates have an impact on work effort, savings, and investments and therefore discourage economic activity. Some reliance on user-pay related charges would be appropriate to improve both efficiency and equity in the tax system.

A user-pay related charge need not be user fees that impact more harshly on the poor. Instead, a health premium could be collected in part based on usage, with amounts paid subject to an income limitation. The collection could be done through the personal tax system, thereby alleviating Canadians from paying charges at the time they need the service. A user-pay related charge would raise significant revenues for health care and would improve transparency, accountability, and efficiency in health care funding and delivery.

It is hard to see why Canada is so reluctant to consider more charges requiring greater citizen engagement. Other countries have relied on user fees for many hospital and physician services without compromising the pubic support given to households for health care services. Some sort of charge for health care would be an appropriate step in the future.

NOTES

[1] In Canada, governments fund almost 99 percent of all expenditures on physicians' services and 92 percent of total hospital expenditures (Canadian Institute for Health Information 2006). As discussed below, many OECD countries provide greater public support as a share of health care costs than Canada even though they rely on some user-related charges to fund health care.

[2] This section follows the discussion in Aba, Goodman, and Mintz (2002).

[3] Estimates of demand elasticities for health care vary across type of service (Cameron et al. 1988) and income class (Tuohy, Flood, and Stabile 2001, 13). Ellis (1986) finds that ambulatory mental health care use falls by almost one-half when services are priced at full cost rather than provided free. Stabile (2001) suggests that the demand for private health care insurance would fall by 4 percent if prices rose by 10 percent. The current tax exemption given for employer-paid health insurance (recently extended to self-employed individuals) increases not only supplemental health insurance demand (by 20 percent) but also publicly funded health care costs (by 10 percent). Gruber (2001) provides a survey on the impact of prices on the demand for health insurance.

[4] The information presented in this section is based on the data from the 2006 version of the OECD Health Database, with a sample of 22 developed OECD countries including Canada.

[5] Mexico (51 percent) and Korea (37 percent) are the out-of-sample OECD countries with a very high share of out-of-pocket payments in total funding in 2004.

[6] Nonetheless, the incidence of employer payroll taxes tends to fall most heavily on worker salaries, which implies that the impact on employment is lessened. See Dahlby (1994) for discussion of incidence.

[7] Both the Mazankowski and Graydon reports (PACH 2001a, b and Graydon 2002) in Alberta recommended some form of user-pay related charge for health care premiums. Under both reports, individuals and families could receive a rebate of their health care premium if little was spent on services for them. Over and above the basic health care premium, a charge would assessed subject to an income limitation.

REFERENCES

Aba, S., W.D. Goodman, and J.M. Mintz. 2002. Funding Public Provision of Private Health: The Case for a Copayment Contribution through the Tax System. C.D. Howe Institute. Health Papers Series 163. www.cdhowe.org.

Akerlof, G.A. 1970. "The Market for Lemons: Qualitative Uncertainty and the Market Mechanism." *Quarterly Journal of Economics* 84 (November): 488-500.

Arrow, K.J. 1970. *Essays in the Theory of Risk Bearing*. Amsterdam: North Holland.

Breyer, F., and A. Haufler 2000 . "Health Care Reform: Separating Insurance from Income Redistribution." *International Tax and Public Finance* 7 (4/5): 445-62.

Cameron, A.C., P. Trivedi, F. Milne, and J. Piggott. 1988. "A Microeconomic Model of the Demand for Health Care and Health Insurance in Australia." *Review of Economic Studies* 55: 85-106.

Canadian Institute for Health Information (CIHI). 2006. "*Health Care in Canada*." Ottawa: CIHI.

Dahlby, B. 1994. "The Distortionary Effect of Rising Taxes." In *Deficit Reduction: What Pain, What Gain?*, edited by William B.P. Robson and William R. Scarth. Policy Study Series 34. Toronto: C.D. Howe Institute.

Docteur, E., and H. Oxley. 2003. "Health-Care Systems: Lesson from Reform Experience." OECD Economics Department Working Paper 374.

Docteur, E., H. Suppanz, and J. Woo. 2003. "The US Health System: An Assessment and Prospective Directions for Reform." OECD Economics Department Working Paper 350.

Duckett, S.J., and T.J. Jackson. 2000. "The New Health Insurance Rebate: An Inefficient Way of Assisting Public Hospitals." *Medical Journal of Australia* 172: 439-42.

Ellis, R.P. 1986. "Rational Behavior in the Presence of Coverage Ceilings and Deductibles." *Rand Journal of Economics* 17 (2): 158-75.

Graydon, G., et al. 2002. "A Sustainable Health System for Alberta: A Report of the M.LA. Task Force on Health Care Funding and Revenue Generation." Edmonton: Government of Alberta.

Gruber, J. 2001. "Taxes and Health Insurance." Mimeo, Massachusetts Institute of Technology, Cambridge, Mass.

Imai, Y. 2002. "Health Care Reform in Japan." OECD Economics Department Working Paper 321.

Lewis, S. 1998. "Still Here, Still Flawed, Still Wrong: The Case against the Case for Taxing the Sick." *Canadian Medical Association Journal* 159 (5): 497-99.

Madore, O. 1993. "Health Care Financing: User Participation." Economics Division Background Paper BP-340E. Ottawa: Government of Canada.

Mossialos, E., Dixon, A., Figueras, J., and J. Kutzin, eds. 2002. "Funding Health Care: Options for Europe." European Observatory on Health Care Systems Series. Buckingham, UK: Open University Press.

Organization for Economic Cooperation and Development. (OECD). 2004. "OECD Economic Surveys: Canada."

– 2005. "OECD Economic Surveys: Sweden."

– 2006a. "OECD Economic Surveys: Australia."

– 2006b. "OECD Economic Surveys: Switzerland."

Premier's Advisory Council on Health (PACH). 2001a. *A Framework for Reform: Main Report*. Edmonton: Government of Alberta.

– 2001b. *Is Alberta's Health System Sustainable? A Framework for Reform: Appendices*. Edmonton: Government of Alberta.

Stabile, M. 2001. "Private Insurance Subsidies and Public Health Care Markets: Evidence from Canada." *Canadian Journal of Economics* 34 (4): 921-42.

Tuohy, C.H., C. Flood, and M. Stabile. 2001. "How Does Private Finance Affect Public Health Care Systems? Marshalling the Evidence from OECD Nations." Mimeo, University of Toronto.

DATA SOURCES

Canadian Institute for Health Information (CIHI). 2005. *National Health Expenditure Database*.

Canadian Life and Health Insurance Association. 2005. *Facts and Figures: Provincial Reports*.

OECD. 2006. *Health Data 2006 database* (October version).

Statistics Canada. [2007.] *CANSIM database*.

Statistics Canada. 2006. *Canadian Community Health Survey, 2005, Cycle 3.1*.

APPENDIX
Data and Data Sources

For the purposes of calculating user fees, we needed to estimate the cost bases and utilization rates of physician and hospital services across ten Canadian provinces. Our calculations are based on the statistics from the Canadian Institute for Health Information (CIHI) and from Statistics Canada's 2005 Canadian Community Health Survey (CCHS).

Due to a very large number of different medical procedures and other services performed by physicians, we aggregated total physician services into two general categories: consultations/visits and procedures. We used CIHI's 2003–04 Canadian National Grouping System Categories Report to obtain the estimates of: (1) average public costs of consultations/visits and procedures performed by family doctors (general practitioners) and specialists and reimbursed by a provincial insurance plan in each province, and (2) average per resident counts of inpatient and outpatient hospital visits in each province. CIHI's 2004–05 Medical Care Database (MCBD) data were used to estimate the resident number of outpatient hospital visits and inpatient hospital stays, as well as the average duration of inpatient hospital stays and the average number of inpatient days per person.

We combined the data from CIHI sources with the micro-level data calculated based on the 2005 Canadian Community Health Survey (Statistics Canada 2006), which provided us with detailed per person and per household estimates of general practitioner and specialist visits/consultations and inpatient hospital stays. The availability of the person and per household data for province-specific family income distribution quintiles allowed us to calculate income-specific health care premiums and relate them to the micro data on physician and hospital services' utilization. In particular, the 2005 CCHS data were used to derive household-size based and family-income based distributions for each province and Canada.

To find the 2007 estimates of our statistics, we adjusted the 2003–05 data on household income levels and public costs of health care services by applying the annual 2 percent inflation rate factor. We obtained the 2007 projections of provincial population from Statistics Canada's population series. The 2007 estimates of provincial public health spending on physicians and hospitals were calculated based on the actual and estimated 2003–06 statistics from CIHI's National Health Expenditure database (NHEX).

Due to data limitations, we do not provide calculations for the Canadian territories; therefore, Canadian averages throughout our calculations represent averages across the ten provinces

CIHI's 2003–05 data on utilization rates for physician and hospital services are used as a proxy for our 2007 estimates of the per capita demand for these services.

Chapter 4

Payroll-Tax Financed Health Insurance: A Way for the Future?

Morley Gunderson and Douglas Hyatt

The financing of health care in Canada is drawing increased policy attention for a number of reasons. Health care budgets are the largest component of provincial government budgets, accounting for one-third of provincial spending in 2006, up from 27.6 percent in 1997.[1] Health expenditures are expected to grow even more in the future, given the aging population and its longer life expectancy combined with the fact that almost half of health care spending is on persons age 65 and over in spite of the fact that they (currently) constitute less than 13 percent of the population.[2] As a growing proportion of the baby boom population enters the elderly age bracket, health care spending will increase. Health care spending is also an area where *potential* expenditures are almost limitless, given the latent demand that exists in that area. This is especially the case for the elderly who tend to have more chronic conditions where some form of treatment is always possible (CIHI 2005a; 2005b). This trend is furthered by the fact that technological advances in that sector tend to be cost enhancing rather than cost saving. This occurs in part because improvements in technology expand new demand by allowing more patients to meet their latent demand, and this *expansion effect* outweighs the *substitution effect* – the latter associated with the fact that technology allows some cheaper procedures (e.g., drugs) to substitute for more expensive procedures (e.g., surgery) (Cutler and McClellan 2001). As well, many of the cost saving procedures (discussed subsequently) are often politically unpopular and give rise to other trade-offs that have negative consequences. The components of health care expenditures that are disproportionately used by the elderly (drugs and care facilities for seniors)[3] are also the expenditures that are increasing the most and are predicted to increase even more in the future.[4] Over the next 15 to 25 years in Canada, the pure aging of the population by itself is predicted[5] to add an average annual increase of about 1 percent to health care expenditures, over and above the expenditure increases that are occurring for other reasons.

For residential care facilities for the elderly and for prescription drugs, the increases are over 2 percent per year. Many of these trends are outlined in the chapter by Flood, Stabile, and Tuohy in this volume. Clearly, a looming funding crises is impending, which implies either expenditure cutbacks or additional sources of funding.

In such circumstances, it is not surprising that alternative or complementary forms of financing this large and growing beast with its insatiable appetite are being sought. This paper outlines the pros and cons of using employer-based, social insurance-type earmarked health-care payroll taxes, compared to the current practice in Canada of largely using income taxes.[6] As indicated in Wanless (2001, 46), approximately 70 percent of health care spending in Canada is publicly financed, with only about 1 percent financed from social insurance-type payroll taxes. Amongst OECD countries for which comparable data exists, a similar situation prevails in Australia and New Zealand. However, the reverse is the case for France, Germany, and the Netherlands where payroll taxes are used to finance the bulk of health care spending, with the income tax system financing only 3 percent in France, 4 percent in the Netherlands, and 6 percent in Germany. Payroll taxes for financing health care also exist in Austria, Belgium, Luxembourg, and Switzerland (Normand and Busse 2002, 62). As well, the United States finances its Medicare program for the elderly and its Medicaid program for the poor mainly out of payroll taxes. Four Canadian jurisdictions (Quebec, Manitoba, Ontario, and Newfoundland) have a payroll tax levied on employers that is *labelled* a health or education tax but goes into general revenues. The Northwest Territories does have a payroll tax levied on employees for the purpose of taxing non-residents who otherwise would pay their income tax in another jurisdiction. British Columbia and Alberta impose separate medicare premiums (Kesselman 1997, 120-1). In essence, payroll taxes are a common way of financing health care, raising the issue of whether Canada should go further in this direction.

That issue is the focus of this paper. A comprehensive analysis of the pros and cons of various tax systems is beyond the scope of this analysis; rather, the emphasis is on lessons that can be learned from the payroll taxes that are used in Canada to finance the existing social insurance programs of workers' compensation, unemployment insurance, and the Canada/Quebec Pension Plan (C/QPP). The emphasis is not on whether the whole system in Canada should be financed by a social insurance-type payroll tax but rather on whether *marginal expansions* in health care expenditures should be financed by such payroll taxes.

A number of criteria will be used to judge the alternative tax systems. These include:

- Allocative *efficiency* from creating minimal distortions and disincentives in other markets;

- *Vertical equity* in both *financing* (based on ability to pay and progressivity, so that wealthier persons disproportionately pay more than do poorer persons) and *access* (based on need);
- *Horizontal equity* in terms of the equal treatment of persons who are in equal situations;
- *Intergenerational equity* so that one generation does not substantially cross-subsidize another;
- *Guarantee of future funding* and sustainability;
- *Direct line of sight* between taxes and benefits so that there is transparency in the system;
- Minimized *administrative costs* of financing the system;
- A high degree of *compliance* in tax payments; and
- *Political acceptability*.

We begin with a discussion of the current financing of the main social insurance programs of workers' compensation, unemployment insurance and the C/QPP, emphasizing such features as incentive effects, experience rating, and intergenerational transfers. With this background in place, we provide a more general discussion of the pros and cons of financing through payroll taxes as opposed to general tax revenues and apply this to the health care area. We conclude with a summary and policy discussion. Our main conclusion is that there is little rationale for using payroll taxes to finance marginal increases in health care, and that the burden of proof should fall on those who want to make that case. As indicated previously, the exact nature of the tax that should be used is beyond the scope of this analysis, although treating some health care costs as taxable benefits or using consumption taxes have particular appeal (see footnote 6).

SOCIAL INSURANCE EARMARKED PAYROLL TAXES FOR WORKERS' COMPENSATION, UNEMPLOYMENT INSURANCE, AND CANADA/QUEBEC PENSION PLAN

The term "social insurance"[7] is used here to denote programs that are financed by *payroll* taxes that are *earmarked* to pay for specific benefits that provide insurance against negative outcomes. The main programs provide insurance against the loss of earnings arising from various circumstances: being injured at work (workers' compensation); being unemployed (unemployment insurance); and foregoing employment income by retiring (Canada/Quebec Pension Plan). All are financed by a payroll tax based on a percentage of earnings. The tax can be levied on employers, employees, or both, and all have a ceiling or cap beyond which premiums are not paid. The term "premium" is used to describe the payment since it is analogous to an insurance premium paid for a specific potential benefit. In the case of these payroll taxes, only those who contribute to the "insurance" fund are eligible to receive subsequent benefits; this would not be the case if earmarked payroll taxes were used to finance health care. Because the taxes are earmarked for specific insurance benefits and only those who contribute are eligible, there is a more direct line of sight between the premium and the potential benefit.

In contrast to such benefit-linked payroll taxes, revenues raised from *general* payroll taxes go into general tax revenues so that there is no direct link between taxes paid and benefits received. The general payroll taxes may be labelled as linked to a particular benefit like health or education, but because they go into general tax revenues and non-payers are eligible for benefits, they are not directly linked to the benefits. This is the case, for example, with the payroll taxes in four Canadian jurisdictions (Quebec, Manitoba, Ontario, and Newfoundland) that are labelled as health or education taxes and that are based on payroll. The remainder of this section discusses the three main benefit-linked payroll taxes, paying particular attention to their features that have implications for more funding of health care through such earmarked payroll taxes.

WORKERS' COMPENSATION (WC)

Workers' compensation provides no-fault insurance for injuries or diseases arising out of employment. In Canada, workers' compensation is under provincial jurisdiction. It is financed out of a payroll tax that is generally shared between employers and employees, currently averaging about 3 percent of payroll and subject to a ceiling beyond which taxes are not paid. There is some broad industry-level experience rating in that the premium varies in part depending upon the accident rate of the industry rate group, for example, ranging from slightly over 1 percent in government to slightly under 9 percent in construction in Ontario in the late 1990s (Gunderson and Hyatt 2000, 174). In spite of this substantial variation, safer industries generally cross-subsidize unsafe ones in that the premiums do not fully cover the expected payouts in the higher rate groups. In general, there is no firm-level experience rating in Canada although it is increasingly being introduced. Intergenerational transfers can also be involved since it is essentially a pay-as-you-go system with the current workforce paying the benefits of those who are injured and receiving compensation. The presence of sometimes very substantial unfunded liabilities – expected future obligations exceed the funds available to meet those obligations – means that redistribution is occurring so that the current generation of workers and firms are subsidizing the older generation of workers and firms who did not make sufficient contributions to cover the benefit obligations arising from their workplace accidents and diseases (Gunderson and Hyatt 2000). Income replacement benefits can be very high, typically in the neighbourhood of 85-90 percent of lost wages. Only those who pay into the system are eligible.

The empirical evidence indicates that WC has a wide range of incentive effects (Gunderson and Hyatt 2003):

- Higher income replacement rates generally are associated with negative health and safety outcomes including increased injuries and claims as well as reduced probabilities of returning to work.
- Because the economic incentives to return to work are reduced, more stringent administrative requirements are often utilized. These include: reducing support for those who are "deemed" to earn a certain level of income; vocational rehabilitation requirements; a duty for employers to accommodate the return to work of injured workers up to the point of "undue hardship" on the employer; and more stringent contesting of claims and detection of fraudulent claims.
- Experience rating of employers creates an incentive for them to provide a safer and healthier workplace, although it also induces them to engage in more stringent claims management and contesting of claims.
- Longer waiting periods before workers are eligible to receive compensation benefits (a form of deductible or co-insurance) provides incentives for a safer and healthier workplace, although there is some limited evidence suggesting that not claiming for short-term injuries can lead to longer-term injuries.
- "Forum shopping" occurs, whereby there is some substitution across disability and income maintenance programs (e.g., WC, UI, and CPP disability) depending upon the generosity of the programs.

UNEMPLOYMENT INSURANCE (UI)

Unemployment insurance is under federal jurisdiction in Canada. It is financed by a payroll tax with premiums currently of slightly under 2 percent of earnings on employees and slightly more on employers (1.4 times the employee contribution). The payroll tax is subject to a ceiling so that further taxes are not paid once the ceiling is reached. Premiums do not generally differ according to the usage by industry, firms, or individuals (i.e., there is no experience rating). This is in contrast to the United States, where firm-level experience rating prevails. In 1996, Canada experimented with experience rating applied to workers by reducing the benefits depending upon their repeat-use of UI. In spite of its success in reducing repeat use, it was eliminated in 2000 under political pressure from Atlantic Canada where it was having a disproportionate impact.

Premiums under UI are adjusted so that the system is self-financing, with government funding having ceased in 1990. The fact that the system is self-financing means that UI no longer acts as an automatic stabilizer, infusing more government funds into the system when unemployment is high. Workers in regions of high unemployment have shorter qualification periods and longer benefit periods. The earnings replacement rate is 55 percent, increasing to 60 percent for persons of low earnings with dependents.

The empirical evidence indicates that UI has a wide range of incentive effects:[8]

- Increasing the incidence and duration of unemployment;
- Fostering layoffs as opposed to other forms of downside adjusting such as labour hoarding or reduced hours or wages;
- Fostering seasonal work and persistent repeat use;
- Encouraging labour force participation to build eligibility for UI;
- Fostering large spikes in weeks of employment at the minimum weeks necessary to be eligible for UI; and
- Discouraging labour mobility in the direction of market forces – out of high unemployment regions and into low unemployment ones.

The experience rating of firms in the US has a strong effect on reducing layoffs and unemployment. Canada's limited experience with experience rating of individuals, through reductions of benefit for repeat use, did reduce repeat use.

CANADA/QUEBEC PENSION PLAN

The Canada/Quebec Pension Plan is a federal earnings-based program (with a separate program in Quebec) designed to replace a portion of earnings upon retirement. It is financed from a payroll tax imposed equally on employers and employees. Because it is, and has been, a pay-as-you go system, the rates have increased substantially in recent years (currently at around 10 percent of earnings divided equally between employers and employees) so as to ensure funding for the future retirement benefits of the large baby boom population, the leading edge of which is now approaching age 65 when normal retirement benefits commence. This effectively moves it toward a more contributory model to fund future liabilities. Without such rate increases, the increasing ratio of pensioners to active workers would have involved huge subsidies from the small tax base of active workers to the large and growing recipient base of pensioners. The pay-as-you go nature of the system, when combined with an aging and longer lived population and slower wage growth, has meant that extensive intergenerational subsidies have been involved, with Canadians born in 1920 receiving extensive subsidies, those born in 1960 (who will be 65 in

2025) receiving modest subsidies, and those born after 1980 receiving no subsidies and perhaps a modest penalty (Gunderson, Hyatt, and Pesando 2000, 395).

Since C/QPP does not have clawbacks for those who continue working, it does not have substantial incentive effects inducing retirement, except for the income effect from the fact that it facilitates the ability to afford to retire. As well, receiving early retirement benefits on an actuarially adjusted basis does require one to "substantially cease working." Clawbacks do exist, however, in other aspects of the public pension system such as Old Age Security, the Spouse's Allowance, the Guaranteed Income Supplement and provincial top-ups.

The empirical literature on retirement decisions[9] finds that retirement has been induced by features of public pension systems and especially the clawbacks in systems like US Social Security (Gruber and Wise 1999; Lazear 1986; Lumsdaine and Mitchell 1999). As indicated, C/QPP does not have such clawbacks, but it does have a requirement to cease working to receive early retirement benefits. As well, clawbacks of benefits exist in Old Age Survivor, Guaranteed Income, and Spouse Allowance. Baker, Gruber, and Milligan (2003) estimate that the retirement inducing effects of the income security system in Canada accounted for between 22 percent and 58 percent of the increase in the retirement rate over the period 1985 to 1995. Baker and Benjamin (1999) also estimate that the elimination of clawbacks in the C/QPP in the 1970s had a substantial effect on encouraging older workers to contribute more in the labour market in the form of more weeks per year.

ULTIMATE INCIDENCE OF THE PAYROLL TAX

As indicated, all three of these social insurance programs (WC, UI, and C/QPP) are financed by a payroll tax imposed on both the employer and employee. There is general agreement, however, that the ultimate incidence of the payroll tax is not where it is initially levied. More specifically, most (i.e., approximately 80 percent) of the payroll tax is shifted backwards to workers in the form of lower compensating wages for the benefits associated with the program (Abbott and Beach 1997; Dahlby 1993; Kesselman 1996, 2001; and Lin 1999). This reflects the fact that labour is generally the immobile factor of production that cannot "escape" the tax; that is, labour supply is generally inelastic so that the reduction in labour demand engendered by a payroll tax on employers gets shifted to workers through eventual wage reductions. In a world of mobile capital, where product prices are set by international competition, it is difficult to shift the cost to capital or forward to consumers. If employers benefited directly from the program, however, they would not reduce their demand for labour as a result of the payroll tax, which in turn means that they might not shift their portion of the tax back to workers. Workers might also regard the benefits as equal to the cost and hence have no behavioural responses (Summers 1989). This can be the case especially for workers' compensation, since workers give up their right to sue their employer in return for the no-fault benefits. Vaillancourt and Marceau (1990), for example, find that the employer portion of EI and QPP costs in Quebec were shifted back to workers in the form of lower compensating wages, while this was not the case for WC, presumably because employers directly benefited by the protection from tort liability provided by WC.

MACROECONOMIC IMPACTS OF PAYROLL TAXES

There is often a general perception that because payroll taxes are imposed on the labour input, they reduce the demand for labour and hence are "killers of jobs"; if the bulk of the costs were ultimately shifted back to workers, however, then this would have no long run effect on employment, though it would mean lower real wages for workers. While this may be the case in the long run, wage rigidities in the short run may lead to reductions in employment. As well, even in the long run, not all of the costs may get shifted back to labour, in which case the tax on labour may reduce employment. Dungan (2000) provides Canadian evidence from a macro-model indicating that payroll taxes can lead to substantial reductions in employment and output and increases in unemployment in the short run and that this may last for several (e.g., five or six) years until the longer run adjustments to wages occur. It is also possible that these effects may be more permanent to the extent that not all of the costs of the payroll tax are ultimately shifted back to labour as some studies suggest.

Dungan's simulations also suggest that the reductions in employment and output and increases in unemployment are likely to be smaller for *income tax increases* that would raise the same revenue as the workers' compensation payroll tax. This occurs because the WC increase leads to an immediate increase in prices and hence inflation, which spurs tight monetary policy, which in turn amplifies the multiplier reduction in output and employment. As well, the immediate increase in the real after-tax wage paid by employers sets off an immediate employment reduction and hence a reduction in labour income and a further reduction in consumption and hence output. As indicated, this would also occur for income tax increases, but Dungan's simulations indicate the reduction in output would be smaller for income tax increases.

LESSONS FOR A PAYROLL FINANCED HEALTH TAX

What lessons emerge from the above discussion of payroll taxes to finance WC, UI, and C/QPP for the potential to use a similar social insurance type of payroll tax to finance health care expenditures?

- Payroll taxes for WC, UI, and C/QPP create a fairly direct line of sight between the tax and the potential ultimate benefit of insurance against *losses of earnings* that would otherwise occur because of a work related injury or unemployment or retirement – hence the phrase "social *insurance*" applied to these programs. These payroll taxes on earnings are based on the protection of earnings or the replacement of lost earnings. This is not the case with a health payroll tax, however, since the health expenditures are not work related.

- The benefit payouts from such benefit-linked programs can create disincentives to work both because the additional income enables recipients to afford not to work and because benefits are often clawed back if the recipient works (hence reducing the net monetary returns from working). Because health benefits are not work related or clawed back if the person works, such incentive effects would not prevail. The fact that recipients do strongly respond to monetary incentives, however, highlights that they likely will respond to such incentives embedded in health care benefits; that is, they will use them more when the cost is low and paid by third parties, as is the case with Canadian health care.

- Experience rating, deductibles, and co-payments can reduce the use of the system compared to situations when the private parties do not pay any cost for using the system. This would also be the case with health care in whatever manner it is financed. Experience rating of individuals is not likely to be feasible in health care since it would entail restricting use by repeat users. Experience rating of employers depending upon the use of the health care system by their workers could be feasible, and this could encourage employers to use employee well-being programs and manage stress related factors at the workplace, although it would also discourage their hiring workers with health risks. More evidence on this trade-off would be needed to determine on balance whether this would be a desirable route; albeit experience rating in general appears a desirable policy. Certainly deductibles and copayments are feasible in health care no matter how it is financed, although this obviously raises the spectre of two-tier health care.

- The ultimate incidence of the payroll tax is largely shifted back to workers in the form of lower compensating wages in return for the benefits associated with the programs. Even if the payroll tax is initially imposed in part or in full on employers, most of it will ultimately be borne by workers for the benefits they receive. This would also be the case with a payroll tax on health care. This can occur either because of a relatively inelastic aggregate labour supply (unable to escape the tax) or because employees do not respond because they value the benefits as equal to the premium.

- To the extent that the tax is not shifted back to labour in the form of compensating wage reductions, employment and output will be reduced and unemployment increased. This can occur in the short run during the transition to the wage reductions, and it could occur in the long run if not all of the payroll tax were shifted back to labour.
- A limited amount of evidence suggests that payroll taxes give rise to larger reductions in employment and output and increases in unemployment when compared to income tax increases that would raise the same revenue.
- Payroll taxes can give rise to intergenerational transfers if they are based on a pay-as-you go system and are not fully funded. This is especially the case when an aging population gives rise to an increased ratio of recipients and a smaller tax-paying base. This is also an issue, however, for financing out of income taxes.

FEATURES OF PAYROLL TAXES AND IMPLICATIONS FOR HEALTH CARE

Payroll taxes have a number of features with important implications for their desirability as a form of tax. This is especially the case when, for example, they are compared to an income tax used to finance health care. While a formal analysis of the efficiency and equity implications of all of the different tax bases and options is beyond our scope here, the important features of payroll taxes are highlighted, with particular emphasis on their implications for financing health care through such earmarked payroll taxes.

COMPLIANCE AND ADMINISTRATIVE SIMPLICITY

Compliance and administrative simplicity are easy with a payroll tax since the taxes can be collected through the payroll system. This is one of their appeals in less developed countries where collection through the income tax system can be difficult. Complications can arise, however, given the growing component of non-standard employment in such forms as subcontracting, self-employment, limited-term contracts, internships, and temporary-help agencies, as well as the growing proportion of fringe benefits. As well, exemptions for small firms are common on the general grounds that they are creators of jobs. This raises the issue of how to define a small firm as well as the appropriateness of such an exemption since the bankruptcy of small firms also destroys jobs. Furthermore, mixed systems of funding health care can give rise to administrative costs. As stated by Kirby (2002, 23), "The existence in some countries of multiple funds and the lack of integration in purchasing health services often results in high administrative costs." Mixed systems can also give rise to muddled perceptions over the financing of the program and who is paying and how much.

In developed countries like Canada, however, income taxes are generally not difficult to administer. This is especially the case for extending taxes at the margin, given that income taxes are already in place. In fact, the general payroll taxes that exist in the four Canadian provinces indicated above are collected through the income tax system even though they are based on payroll.

PRE-COMMITMENT TO CONTINUING THE GOVERNMENT PROGRAM

Direct-benefit payroll taxes provide a strong incentive for governments to continue the program, given that those who financed it through a payroll tax consider that they have "paid for" the program. The direct line of sight between their payments of an "insurance premium" and the expectation of insurance coverage would make it difficult for governments to drastically alter such programs. The link is not direct, as evidenced by the fact that intergenerational transfers often occur as can cross-subsidies across payers. Nevertheless, such programs are not as susceptible to changes as programs financed out of general tax revenues can be (Mossialos and Dixon 2002, 285; Nooneman and van Doorslaer 1994). As F.D. Roosevelt stated when he established the US Social Security system, "Those [payroll] taxes were never a problem of economics. They are politics all the way through. We put those payroll contributions there so as to give the contributors a legal, moral, and political right to collect their pensions. With these taxes in there, no damn politician can ever scrap my Social Security Program" (cited in Rosen 1999, 189).

LINKING BENEFITS TO TAX COST

By linking benefits to the tax cost, payroll taxes also provide a more direct line of sight and visible connection between the benefits of the program and its costs. The costs are more overt. This in turn may help constrain costs, as taxpayers see more closely what they are paying for the program. They may be more likely to accept restraint on the benefit payouts knowing what such payouts cost or to accept tax increases that they know are directed toward health benefits they value. Arguments, however, have been made to the contrary. Kirby (2002, 23) states, "Another criticism of payroll taxes with respect to efficiency is that the various European Sickness Funds, which are responsible for collecting and managing the contributions made by employers and employees, have little incentive to control costs because they have the ability to raise contribution rates." Hinrichs (1995) also argues that persons making contributions through social insurance schemes may also increase their demand to maximize the return on their individual contribution. They see that they paid for the service, and hence they may be more inclined to use it.

It is the case that the more direct line of sight between payroll tax increases and health expenditures may reduce resistance to payroll tax increases to finance additional expenditures because individuals see that their payroll tax increase goes into health care, which they presumably value. In contrast, they may regard expenditure increases financed by an income tax as coming from a "black hole" where they do not see any direct link to benefits from their taxes. Because they do not directly see the cost associated with more health care expenditures, they may prefer more expenditures.[9]

Clearly, the more direct line of sight between taxes and benefits under a social insurance payroll tax compared to an income tax could increase or reduce resistance to higher expenditures. The evidence also seems to be mixed. Normand and Busse (2002, 75) claim "International comparisons show that social health insurance systems have higher expenditures than tax funded systems." OECD (2000) evidence indicates this relationship. However, causality is difficult to establish in this area, since higher expenditures in social insurance payroll tax systems can occur for a variety of reasons other than the effect of the transparency of the direct line of sight between taxes and benefits (Mossialos and Dixon 2002, 285). The evidence itself is controversial. For example, Flood, Stabile, and Tuohy (chapter 1, this volume) find that there is no significant difference between tax financed and social insurance systems with respect to levels of *public* spending on health care; rather, the latter are associated with higher levels of *private* spending, possibly because in a number of cases social insurance is paired with a highly regulated system of private insurance as a way of achieving universal coverage.

Earmarked payroll taxes may also facilitate ensuring that those who benefit from the program pay the cost. They may also confine the cost to those who are working, which may be important for programs like WC, UI, and C/QPP that generally replace lost earnings (respectively, from being injured, unemployed, or retired). In contrast, there may be resentment from taxpayers if general revenues are being used to support earning losses when such social insurance programs could have insured against the losses.

In the case of health care, however, these possible advantages of a payroll tax do not apply. There is no intent to restrict the health benefits only to those who are employed or who have paid into the social insurance fund. The linking of benefits to tax costs is not intended, at least at the individual level. At the aggregate level, however, this might be the case if we considered social insurance funding for a specific part of health care financing such as pharmaceuticals.

POLITICALLY ACCEPTABLE EARNINGS REPLACEMENT INSURANCE

The benefits paid out of benefit-specific payroll taxes are generally replacing a specific portion of lost earnings (e.g., 55 percent under unemployment insurance, and 85-90 percent under workers' compensation). As such, higher benefits are paid to persons of higher earnings, although caps can exist on the benefits, just as they do on the taxes. This is a natural result of their largely being insurance type programs rather than income maintenance or redistributive transfer programs. This form of insurance is politically acceptable because it is regarded as one in which the fixed proportion of earnings replaced is the *quid pro quo* for the fixed proportion of earnings paid as a premium.

If the program were financed out of an income tax system or even a general payroll tax that went into general revenues where there was no direct line of sight with the benefits, this would not likely be politically acceptable even if the income tax were progressive so that high earners paid a progressively higher tax. As Kesselman aptly stated (1997, 9), "Earnings replacement – where the benefits rise with the individual's accustomed (and "insured" earnings") – would probably be unacceptable in a program financed out of general revenue. Even if the tax system were substantially progressive, paying out larger benefits to higher earners would not likely pass the test of public acceptance." This would especially be the case with health benefits: it would not likely be politically acceptable if persons with high earnings received greater health benefits from a public system, even if they were taxed more for the service.

NON-DISTORTIONARY TAX

To the extent that the benefit-linked payroll taxes provide expected benefits that are equal to their tax costs, those who are taxed are essentially buying a service (insurance against earnings loss, in the case of WC, UI, and C/QPP). In such circumstances the tax is the equivalent of a private market price paid for the service, and it should therefore have no distortionary effect on decision margins such as the income-leisure margin and hence work incentives (Kesselman 1997, 38). The *benefit payouts* may have distortionary effects, as discussed previously, but the *taxes* should not.

Of course, the expected benefits are not necessarily equal to the tax costs since there are cross-subsidies by industry, individuals, and different generations. Furthermore, in the case of general payroll taxes that are not linked to specific benefits but go into general tax revenues, there is no direct link to the benefits. Hence the payroll tax would be like an income tax imposed only on the earnings base, and this would distort income-leisure choice decisions (leisure not being taxed) and hence have adverse effects on work incentives and hence efficiency effects. This form of tax also drives a wedge between what consumers are willing to pay for the goods or services produced by labour and the wage or price that labour is willing to accept to produce those goods or services (and hence gives rise to an efficiency loss). As well, payroll taxes can distort the decision margin between moving to covered and non-covered jobs. Although he does not provide evidence on the point, Kirby (2002, 23) states, "In contrast to general taxation, a payroll tax may also impede job mobility; employees may be unwilling to move to a non-covered job (such as self-employment) in some systems for fear of higher contribution payments or fewer benefits (as in the United States)."

INCENTIVES THROUGH EXPERIENCE RATING

As discussed previously, payroll taxes can be experience rated so as to minimize the moral hazard problem in insurance markets whereby paying a fixed insurance premium irrespective of the use of the system does not provide incentives to reduce risk. Experience rating can provide the proper incentive to reduce risk since there is a closer link between cost and use. In the case of workers' compensation, for example, experience rating led to safer work environments and reduced accidents. In the case of unemployment insurance, it reduced unemployment and its duration as well as seasonal unemployment.

This benefit of possible experience rating is not likely to be feasible in health care since it would entail restricting use by repeat users, and such users are likely to be in greater need of the insurance for catastrophic care. Experience rating of employers depending upon the use of the system by their workers could be feasible, and this could provide them with an incentive to provide employee well-being programs and manage stress related factors at the workplace; however, it could also discourage them from hiring workers with health risks.

TAXING OF NON-RESIDENTS

By being administered through payroll taxes at the individual's workplace, such payroll taxes can tax non-residents who otherwise may not pay taxes in the jurisdiction where they work as opposed to reside. This was one rationale for the greater use of payroll taxes in the North West Territories where non-residents often came and worked for short periods of time and then returned to their permanent residence elsewhere (Kesselman 1997, 136). This is not likely to be a major issue, however, for other jurisdictions.

APPEARANCE OF A TAX ON EMPLOYERS

Payroll taxes levied on employers give the appearance that employers are paying the tax. This may be regarded as vertically equitable in that employers, and especially large employers, may be regarded as better able to absorb the tax (international competition notwithstanding).

As discussed previously, however, this is largely an illusion, since the bulk of the tax initially imposed on employers is ultimately shifted to labour in the form of wages compensating for the expected insurance benefits. If the tax is not shifted to workers, then they will experience employment reductions as employers reduce their demand for the now more costly labour.

It is the case, however, that the appearance of the tax falling on employers may capture elements of reality. First, the evidence suggests that most, but not all, of the incidence is ultimately shifted back to labour. Second, the long run adjustment to wage reductions (realistically, slower wage growth) takes time, and in the meantime the employer is bearing at least some of the burden of the tax. Third, in a world of mobile capital, additional taxes imposed on business may deter business investment and the jobs associated with that investment. For these reasons, even the appearance of a tax on employers is likely to give rise to political resistance to such a tax, unless modifications in other taxes such as corporate taxes are made to compensate.

DOES NOT TAX SAVINGS

Income taxes "double tax" savings by taxing the income out of which savings are made and then taxing the returns to the investments from the savings. Payroll taxes do not tax the return to investment, and hence payroll taxes do not directly tax savings.[10] Consumption taxes also have this feature. These taxes thus do not distort the allocation of capital or the incentive to save or to allocate consumption over the life cycle (Kesselman 1997, 37, 51). To the extent that this is the case, however, it would seem sensible to move directly to a consumption tax, given its beneficial features (Mintz, cited in Kirby 2002, 19).

SMALLER TAX BASE

The tax base for payroll taxes (labour income) is obviously less than that of income taxes. This means that higher rates will have to be applied to compensate for the lower base. For purposes of financing government programs, broader tax bases are generally considered desirable because they do not distort decision margins across the different sources of income. Payroll taxes also disproportionately fall on labour intensive sectors. As stated by Kirby (2002, 23), "the negative impacts on certain labour-intensive sectors could be significant."

PROGRESSIVITY

Progressivity, whereby wealthier persons pay a larger proportion of income in taxes, is generally considered a desirable feature of tax structures to facilitate vertical equity, even though progressive rates can also reduce work incentives since the additional income moves people into higher marginal tax brackets. Income taxes have numerous features (especially higher marginal tax rates for higher income) that facilitate progressivity and hence vertical equity.

Payroll taxes, in contrast, have features that generally make them regressive or at least not progressive, and international evidence for health care financing bears this out (Wagstaff et al. 1999). This is the case when the tax rate is constant as is common in payroll taxes. The ceilings beyond which no further payroll taxes are made also make them regressive. Allowing higher income persons to opt out of public health insurance if they have their own private insurance (as occurs in Germany) would also impart an element of regressivity (Kirby 2002, 23). As White points out in chapter 11 of this volume, however, "Social insurance per se is not always less progressive than general revenue finance. General revenues can be proportional (the local income tax in Sweden) or regressive (almost all consumption taxes). The incidence of social insurance taxes depends not only on flat rates but on exclusions and discounts (whether high income people pay on a lower share of income, or low-income people have income excluded or taxed at lower rates)."

CEILINGS ON PAYROLL TAXES

The individual ceilings on payroll taxes can also induce employers to work their existing workforce longer hours rather than hiring new workers (Benjamin, Gunderson, and Riddell 2002, 176). This is because no further payroll taxes are paid for the existing workforce at the ceiling, while payroll taxes will be incurred for new hires. The longer hours can foster workplace stress and disrupt work-family balance.

AUTOMATIC STABILIZER

Payroll taxes like those for unemployment insurance can serve as automatic stabilizers if more funds are collected during the peak of a business cycle when employment is high (therefore dampening the peak) and spent during the trough when employment is low (therefore expanding the economy). The *spending* side of this mechanism would not be operative for health care since it is not spending that would generally be expected to increase in a downturn and subside in an upturn. *Revenues* from payroll taxes (being levied at a flat rate), however, are less counter-cyclical than progressive income taxes. Although he does not provide evidence, Kirby (2002, 23) also asserts: "Health care financing via a payroll tax is vulnerable to periods of economic downturn, since reduced revenues from lower employment and freezes in income levels would result in smaller contributions to the Sickness Funds."

INTERGENERATIONAL INEQUITIES

Intergenerational burdens can be involved in any pay-as-you-go tax system where current generations of taxpayers are paying for the benefits received by other generations. This will be an issue with the current income tax financing of health care in Canada as the population ages and older generations disproportionately use the health care system, although they do contribute some in taxes. It is even more of a concern, however, for payroll taxation since the burden is borne by an even smaller, younger working age population who pay the payroll tax. As Kirby points out (2002, 24), "A crucial factor with respect to payroll taxes is that, in terms of intergenerational fairness, a payroll tax has an impact similar to but worse than income taxation: the burden is borne entirely by the younger and working age population."

INCREASED BARGAINING POWER UNDER TAX FINANCED SYSTEMS

Health expenditures financed out of income taxes may provide governments with more bargaining power in negotiating payments with health care providers (Mossialos and Dixon 2002, 286). However, such monopsony purchasing power can also occur with social insurance systems organized around a fund that can have leveraging in its purchasing. As well, the welfare implications of such power are not obvious even if they keep expenditures lower in an income tax financed system.

CONCLUDING OBERVATIONS

Clearly there are pros and cons to the use of payroll taxes to finance health care. Our assessment, however, is that while payroll taxes have several significant potential advantages for public finance of particular types of social insurance programs, they appear to offer little advantage for financing public health care relative to the mainstay alternatives of personal and business income taxes and indirect consumption taxes.

Payroll taxes do have positive features such as ease of compliance and administration, but complications can arise with the growing components of non-standard employment and fringe benefits as well as integration in mixed financing systems. Furthermore, in developed countries like Canada, income taxes are generally not difficult to administer especially for extending taxes at the margin. Earmarked payroll taxes provide a direct line of sight with the tax and the benefits, and this can give taxpayers a degree of entitlement that provides a strong incentive for governments to continue the program. Seeing more directly that health care is "not free" may also help constrain costs or perhaps expand expenditures if taxpayers value the health care, although the government's ability to raise contribution rates may reduce the incentive to control costs (and international evidence suggests that expenditures are higher under payroll tax systems).

Earmarked payroll taxes may also facilitate ensuring that those who benefit from the program pay the cost and that the benefits are confined to those who pay the cost, albeit in the health care area this possible advantage of a payroll tax is not relevant since there would be no intention of restricting access to those who are employed and pay the taxes. Payroll taxes can also make it politically acceptable to provide high earnings replacements to higher paid persons, as is the case with WC, UI, and C/QPP. Again, however, this advantage is not relevant for health care since it would not likely be politically acceptable if persons with high earnings received greater health benefits from a public system even if they were taxed more for the service.

Payroll taxes may not distort decision margins if the expected benefits are equal to the tax costs, but such a condition does not generally prevail given the cross-subsidies by industry, individuals, and different generations. Payroll taxes can also distort the decision margin between moving to covered and non-covered jobs. The use of payroll taxes to essentially tax non-residents is not an issue for health care. The advantages of payroll taxes to have positive incentive effects through experience rating is also not relevant to health care, since frequent users are unlikely to be experience rated.

Payroll taxes may be politically attractive to the extent that they are imposed on large employers, although the ultimate incidence of the tax is shifted to labour through lower compensating wages. Until it is shifted (or if it is not ultimately shifted to labour), it will have negative impacts on employment and output, and the appearance of the tax on employers may deter investment and the jobs associated with that investment.

Unlike income taxes, payroll taxes do not tax the return to investment and hence savings. Consumption taxes, however, also have this feature as well as other desirable features, and provincial income taxes essentially turn out to be close to consumption-based taxes. Since the tax base for payroll taxes is less than the broader base for income taxes, higher payroll tax rates would have to be applied to raise the same revenue, and this would disproportionately fall on labour intensive sectors. Payroll taxes also tend to be regressive relative to income taxes, and the ceilings on payroll taxes can encourage employers to work their existing workforce long hours rather than hire new recruits. Any automatic stabilizing features of payroll taxes are not available to health care payroll taxes since expenditures would not be automatically increased in downturns. In fact, reductions in revenues during downturns could jeopardize the system. While any pay-as-you-go system can give rise to intergenerational inequities, these are likely to be especially severe for payroll taxes since the burden is borne on the subset of the younger and working age population.

Overall, our assessment is that payroll taxes do not have substantial advantages over the mainstay alternatives of personal and business income taxes and especially indirect consumption taxes for financing health care. Furthermore, many of the traditional advantages of payroll taxes are ones that would not apply to health care. As such, we conclude that the case for expanding payroll taxes to finance marginal increases in health care expenditure in Canada has not been made. The burden of proof should rest on those who want to make the case.

A reviewer of our paper commented that an important feature of the context in which payroll taxes would be implemented is through the widespread existence of employer health benefit plans. Social insurance for drug costs could potentially be of benefit in holding down the prices of pharmaceuticals for private as well as public purchasers. Furthermore, a "pay-or-pay" version of social insurance could establish a more level playing field and hence gain political support in some segments of the business community. Clearly, the design of the intersection between employer plans and social insurance is critical, and might be able to take account of some of the concerns that we raised.

As indicated previously, the focus of our paper has been to analyze payroll taxes as a way to finance marginal increases in health care expenditures and to analyze existing payroll taxes with that in mind. While we do not believe that the case has been made for payroll taxes, the preferred way to finance increases in health care expenditure is beyond the scope of this analysis. However, proposals to include some of the costs of the services received from health care as taxable benefits in income taxes merits more attention, as does an increased use of consumption taxes.

NOTES

[1] Calculations from Statistics Canada, CANSIM, table 385-0001, "Consolidated Federal, Provincial, Territorial and Local Government Revenue and Expenditures (Provincial and Territorial Component) for Fiscal Year Ending March 31, Annual (Dollars) (Data in Millions)." http://cansim2.statcan.ca/cgi-win/cnsmcgi.exe?Lang= E&C2Fmt=HTML2D&CIITpl=SNA___&ResultTemplate=THEMSNA4&CORCmd= GetWrap&CORId=104#HERE

[2] Calculations based on data contained in CIHI (2005a) B-1. Persons age 75 and over receive 33 percent of health care spending even though they make up slightly less than 6 percent of the population.

[3] In 2005, of the $142 billion spent on health care in Canada, 30 percent was for hospitals, 17 percent for prescription drugs, 13 percent for physicians, and 9 percent for other institutions, mainly residential care facilities for the elderly (CIHI 2006, 9). In 1997, expenditures on drugs overtook spending on physician services (CIHI 2005b, iii).

[4] Between 1990 and 2000, drug spending per capita increased by 93 percent, more than twice the average of 40 percent for health care spending in general. Drug costs are expected to increase even more rapidly in the future with some new, very effective but costly drugs coming on stream (Kirby 2002, 2).

[5] Such predictions have been made in CIHI (2005a, 25), the Conference Board of Canada (2004) and Pollock (2002).

[6] Modifications to the existing income tax system to finance health care are beyond the scope of this analysis and will be outlined in other chapters of this volume. Aba, Mintz, and Goodman (2002) and Mintz, Gordon, and Chen (1998), for example, have proposed having individuals include some of the costs of the services they received from health care as taxable benefits in their income taxes. Mintz (cited in Kirby 2002, 19) has also emphasized the desirable properties of consumption taxes.

[7] The terms "social insurance," "social security," and "welfare programs" are sometimes used synonymously (Grosseketler 2004, 324). In North America, however, "social security" is often used to refer to the specific US Social Security public pension system, and "welfare" is commonly referred to as "social assistance."

[8] Evidence on the effects of employment insurance is summarized in Benjamin, Gunderson, and Riddell (2002, 561–56).

[9] This could be one of the reasons why public satisfaction tends to be greater with systems financed out of payroll taxes compared to those financed out of income taxes and general revenues, although the dissatisfaction could reflect other factors associated with payroll taxes rather than being "caused" by payroll taxes. Based on European survey evidence, Mossialos (1998) finds that individuals in countries where health expenditures were financed from social-insurance payroll taxes thought that the amount of spending was just right. In contrast, those in countries where it was financed from income taxes at the national level felt that governments should spend more on health. Such comparisons of public satisfaction are difficult, however, since other factors come into play. As Mossialos and Dixon (2002, 285) indicate, the countries where health care is financed from income taxes tend to have low expenditure on health care, and this could be driving their preference for more care. Furthermore, they indicate that in general the public opinion survey evidence suggests that individuals are more willing to accept tax increases that are directly linked to specific expenditures.

[10] It is the case, however, that the provincial income tax (PIT) is close to a consumption-based (not income-based) tax for the great majority of taxpayers, on account of its treatment of tax-deferred savings (RPPs, RRSPs), zero capital gains on owner-

occupied housing equity, and reduced tax rates on most other forms of capital income except for interest. Hence, the effect on savings may not be that different between a general payroll tax and PIT, except for very high wage earners who max out their allowable contribution to tax-deferred savings plans.

REFERENCES

Aba, S., J. Mintz, and W. Goodman. 2002. "Funding Public Provision of Private Health: The Case for a Copayment Contribution through the Tax System." *C.D. Howe Institute Commentary 163.* Toronto: C.D. Howe Institute.

Abbott, M., and C. Beach. 1997. "The Impact of Employer Payroll Taxes on Employment and Wages: Evidence for Canada, 1970-93." In *Transition and Structural Change in the North American Labour Market*, edited by M. Abbott, C. Beach, and R. Chaykowski, 154-34. Kingston, ON: IRC Press.

Baker, M., and D. Benjamin. 1999. "How Do Retirement Tests Affect the Labor Supply of Older Men?" *Journal of Public Economics* 71: 27-51.

Baker, M., J. Gruber, and K. Milligan. 2003. "The Retirement Incentive Effects of Canada's Income Security Programs." *Canadian Journal of Economics* 36: 261-90.

Benjamin, D., M. Gunderson, and C. Riddell. 2002. *Labour Market Economics: Theory, Evidence and Policy in Canada.* 5th ed. Toronto: McGraw Hill.

CIHI. 2005a. *Provincial and Territorial Government Health Expenditures by Age Group, Sex and Major Category: Recent and Future Growth Rates.* Ottawa: Canadian Institute for Health Education.

CIHI. 2005b. *National Health Expenditure Trends.* Ottawa: Canadian Institute for Health Education.

CIHI. 2006. *Health Care in Canada.* Ottawa: Canadian Institute for Health Education.

Conference Board of Canada. 2004. "Understanding the Impact of Population Aging." In *Defining the Canadian Advantage: Performance and Potential, 2003-2004.* Ottawa.

Cutler, D., and M. McClellan. 2001. "Is Technological Change in Medicine Worth It?" *Health Affairs* (September/October): 11-12.

Dahlby, B. 1993. "Payroll Taxes." In *Business Taxation in Ontario*, edited by A. Maslove, 80-170. Toronto: University of Toronto Press.

Dungan, P. 2000. "The Effect of Workers' Compensation and Other Payroll Taxes on the Macro Economies of Canada and Ontario." In *Workers' Compensation: Foundations for Reform*, edited by M. Gunderson and D. Hyatt, 118-61. Toronto: University of Toronto Press.

Evans, R. 2002. Financing Health Care: Taxation and the Alternatives. In *Funding Health Care: Options for Europe*, edited by E. Mossialos, A. Dixon, J. Figueras, and J. Kutzin, 31-58. Buckingham: Open University Press.

Grossekettler, H. 2004. "Social Insurance." In *Handbook of Public Finance*, edited by J. Backhaus and R.Wagner, 323-83. New York: Kluwer Academic Publishers.

Gruber, J., and D. Wise, eds. 1999. *Social Security and Retirement around the World*. Chicago: University of Chicago Press.

Gunderson, M., and D. Hyatt. 2000. "Unfunded Liabilities under Workers' Compensation." In *Workers' Compensation: Foundations for Reform*, edited by M. Gunderson and D. Hyatt, 162-87. Toronto: University of Toronto Press.

– 2003. *Economic Incentive Strategies for Engendering Healthy Workplaces*. Ottawa: Health Canada.

Gunderson, M., D. Hyatt, and J. Pesando. 2000. "Public Pension Plans in the United States and Canada." In *Employee Benefits, Labour Costs and Labour Markets in Canada and the United States*, edited by R. Alpert and S. Woodbury, 381-412. Kalamazoo, MI: Upjohn.

Hinrichs, K. 1995. "The Impact of German Health Insurance Reforms on Redistribution and the Culture of Solidarity." *Journal of Health Politics, Policy and Law* 20 (3): 653-94.

Kesselman, J. 1996. "Payroll Taxes in the Finance of Social Security." *Canadian Public Policy* 22: 162-78.

– 1997. *Canadian Payroll Taxes: Economics, Politics and Design*. Toronto: Canadian Tax Foundation, 1997.

– 2001. "Payroll Taxes and the Financing of Social Security." In *Labour Market Policies in Canada and Latin America: Challenges of the New Millennium*, edited by A. Berry, 135-58. Boston: Kluwer Academic Publishers.

Kirby, M. 2002. *The Health of Canadians: The Federal Role*. Vol. 6, *Recommendations for Reform*. Ottawa: Standing Senate Committee in Social Affairs, Science and Technology.

Lazear, E. 1986. "Retirement from the Labor Force." In *Handbook of Labor Economics*, edited by O. Ashenfelter and R. Layard. New York: Elsevier.

Lin, Z. 1999. "Payroll Taxes in Canada Revisited: Structure, Policy Parameters and Recent Trends." Ottawa: Statistics Canada, Business and Labour Market Analysis Division.

Lumsdaine, R., and O. Mitchell. 1999. "New Developments in the Economic Analysis of Retirement." In *Handbook of Labor Economics*, edited by O. Ashenfelter and D. Card. New York: Elsevier.

Mintz, J., M. Gordon, and D. Chen. 1998. "Funding Canada's Health Care System: A Tax-Based Alternative to Privatization." *Canadian Medical Association Journal* 8: 493-6.

Mossialos, E. 1998. *Citizens and Health Systems: Main Results from a Eurobarometer Survey*. Brussels: European Commission, Director General for Employment, Industrial Relations and Social Affairs.

Mossialos, E., and A. Dixon. 2002. "Funding Health Care in Europe: Weighing up the Options." *Funding Health Care: Options for Europe*, edited by E. Mossialos, A. Dixon, J. Figueras, and J. Kutzin, 272-300. Buckingham: Open University Press.

Nonneman, W., and E. van Doorslaer. 1994. "The Role of the Sickness Funds in the Belgian Health Care Market." *Social Science and Medicine* 39 (1): 1483-95.

Normand, C., and R. Busse. 2002. "Social Health Insurance Funding." In *Funding Health Care: Options for Europe*, edited by E. Mossialos, A. Dixon, J. Figueras, and J. Kutzin, 59-79. Buckingham: Open University Press.

OECD. 2000. *OECD Health Data 2000: A Comparative Analysis of 29 Countries*. Paris: Organization for Economic Co-operation and Development.

Pollock, A. 2002. *Aging as a Health Care Driver*. Ottawa: Health Canada, Applied Research and Analysis Directorate.

Rosen, H. 1999. *Public Finance*. 5th ed. New York: McGraw-Hill.

Summers, L. 1989. "Some Simple Economics of Mandated Benefits." *American Economic Review* (May): 177-83.

Vaillancourt, F., and N. Marceau. 1990. "Do General and Firm-Specific Employer Payroll Taxes Have the Same Incidence?" *Economic Letters* 34: 175-81.

Wagstaff, A., E. van Doorslaer, and H. van der Burg. 1999. "Equity in the Finance of Health Care: Some Further International Comparisons." *Journal of Health Economics* 18 (3): 263-90.

Wanless, D. 2001. *Securing Our Future Health: Taking a Long-Term View*. Interim report. London: HM Treasury.

Chapter 5

Social Insurance versus Tax Financing in Health Care: Reflections from Germany

Stefan Greß, Stephanie Maas, and Jürgen Wasem

The health care system in Canada is funded primarily through taxes. The intent of this volume is to explore the advantages and disadvantages of funding through social insurance as opposed to taxation, with a view to determining whether or not Canada should allow a role for social health insurance for health care. Conversely, at the same time, policy-makers and researchers in Germany are exploring the pros and cons of increasing the role of tax-funding in a German system predominantly financed through social insurance.

As a consequence of this trend toward consideration of systems of mixed financing – which is prevalent not only in Canada and Germany – this paper explores trade-offs between policy objectives as well as different institutional approaches in organizing tax funding and social insurance. We address three research questions:

- Question 1: How do social insurance and tax financing compare in *pure* (as opposed to mixed) systems? What are the implications for fairness, financial sustainability, and employment?
- Question 2: How do social insurance and tax financing compare in *mixed* systems? What are the implications for fairness, financial sustainability, efficiency, and employment in Germany?
- Question 3: What are the implications of the findings for Canada?

In section 1, we discuss the pros and cons of tax financing vs. financing by social health insurance contributions. For purposes of analytical clarity, in this section we assume that health care systems are financed by one mode of financing only – either by taxes or by social insurance premiums ("pure" systems). Our rather theoretical approach is useful to identify advantages and disadvantages as well as possible institutional variations of two particular modes of financing.[1] The central message of this section may be surprising: in our model world, designers of health care finance systems can use taxes and social insurance contributions to achieve very similar objectives. Both modes of financing can be fair and financially sustainable and are able to create incentives for employment.

In section 2, we explore mixed models of financing (the real-world plurality of public/private/social health insurance financing). We conclude that the current debate on the future of health care financing in Germany is surprisingly similar to the Canadian one. While in Canada a bigger share of social insurance financing may be an important policy tool to improve the mix of financing, in Germany an increasing share of tax financing may be an important policy tool to the same end. The central message of this section implies that social health insurance financing may be equivalent to tax financing *in theory*. However, Germany's particular version of social health insurance financing is, in our view, inferior to systems like Canada's that rely on tax financing. In particular, the German system is less equitable and provides fewer incentives for employment than the Canadian system.

We conclude by summing up our findings and the implications for Canada. While social insurance probably is not a desirable option for core services of the *Canada Health Act* – at least not in the foreseeable future – our findings may be useful for the design of social insurance schemes of other health care services, for example, prescription drugs, home care, and long term care. In our view, a carefully designed universal social insurance scheme for pharmaceuticals might result in a considerable improvement of the status quo with regard to fairness of financing, financial sustainability, and implications for employment.

1 SOCIAL INSURANCE VS. TAX FUNDING IN PURE SYSTEMS

FAIRNESS

The German and the Canadian societies, like societies in many other OECD countries, consider *fairness or solidarity* as an essential goal of health care financing policies (Wagstaff and van Doorslaer 1992; Wagstaff and van Doorslaer 2000). Fairness or solidarity in this context refers to, at a minimum, at least some form of risk sharing and more generally a redistribution from the healthy to the sick and from the poor to the wealthy. As the commonly used term in Europe is "solidarity," that is the one we will use throughout this paper.

Several dimensions of fairness or solidarity need to be distinguished (van de Ven and Ellis 2000). The most basic dimension of solidarity is ex-post risk solidarity between the healthy and the sick. Risk solidarity is limited to health risks that become apparent after the conclusion of a (private) insurance contract. In other words, subscribers are either not covered for pre-existing risks or must pay higher health insurance premiums. In the absence of regulation, this means that there is a limited redistribution of resources from the healthy toward the sick.

However, with the notable exception of the United States, OECD countries do not rely on private health insurance as the predominant mode of health care financing. Designers of health care financing systems prefer to implement modes of financing that provide an enhanced degree of redistribution. Both social health insurance and national health systems that are based on tax funding provide ex-ante risk solidarity as well as ex-post risk solidarity between the healthy and the sick. Ex-ante solidarity between the healthy and the sick first implies that all health risks are covered, not just those that manifest themselves after a contract has been concluded. Second, since restrictions apply to social health insurance premium rates, health insurers have to refrain from charging higher premiums for high health risks.

Although both tax financed national health systems and social health insurance schemes provide comprehensive risk solidarity between the healthy and the sick, there are important differences between both modes of financing. In national health systems such as the English National Health Service or Canadian medicare, one's coverage is based on residence. There are few opportunities to opt out of the system – except for emigrating. In contrast, social health insurance systems restrict coverage (solidarity) to the members of the risk pool. However, if it is not mandatory to take out social health insurance for the entire population, selection problems will follow, i.e., good risks may try to opt out of the social insurance system. They will either take out private health insurance, if it is available, or fall back on the provision of social assistance in the case of need. As a consequence, fewer good risks will be in the risk pool in order to subsidize bad risks. An effective instrument to neutralize incentives for opportunistic free rider behaviour is to require that all the population take out social health insurance – which of course needs to be monitored.

We have seen that comprehensive ex-post as well as ex-ante risk solidarity between the healthy and the sick are indispensable components of social health insurance. Moreover, income solidarity – solidarity between the rich and the poor – may be a fundamental feature of social health insurance as well, but not necessarily so. If social health insurance calculates community-rated premiums, these premiums are independent of income. As a consequence, social health insurance does not redistribute resources from the rich to the poor. What is more, the consequences of community-rated premiums are regressive, i.e., the higher the income, the smaller the share that is spent on social health insurance premiums. In most OECD countries that use social health insurance as the predominant mode of health care financing, these consequences are not acceptable to policy-makers. Therefore, designers of health care financing systems either implement a system of tax financed and need tested premium subsidies or use income dependent premiums as mode of financing. Income dependent mechanisms vary in the degree of progressivity they involve. At the less progressive end of the spectrum, the contribution rate is the same across income levels. Greater progressivity is achieved in social insurance financing, if the contribution rate is not uniform across all income groups but goes up as income goes up. (For an illustration, see figure 2.)

Thus the implication for the redistribution of income in social health insurance systems very much depends on the mode of premium calculation. Similarly, in tax financed national health systems, the implications for the redistribution of income depend on the design of the tax system. The consequences of taxes as well as of social health insurance premiums on the distribution of income can be regressive, proportional, or progressive. Flat-rate premiums are the most regressive. Direct taxes on income have a proportional effect if the tax rate is uniform across all income categories and across all income groups. The consequences are progressive if the tax rate is not uniform across all income groups but goes up as income goes up.

However, direct taxes are only one important component of general tax revenue. Indirect taxes on consumption (for example, in Canada the GST and PST) are another. The consequences of taxes on consumption on income distribution usually are regressive, i.e., the higher the income, the smaller the share spent on indirect taxes. This is a consequence of the fact that low income groups have a smaller savings rate than high income groups. A popular instrument to attenuate this regressive effect of indirect taxes is to exempt basic consumer goods from indirect taxes.

The most important conclusion of our comparison of the fairness implications of tax financing vs. social insurance financing is that both modes of health care financing can be equivalent if very specific circumstances apply. Both may induce comprehensive risk solidarity, and both may provide income solidarity as well as redistribution toward families. However, universal coverage as an important prerequisite for the establishment of an extensive risk pool is easier to obtain in tax financed systems. Enforcement of universal coverage is less problematic in tax based systems.

Table 1 summarizes our findings:

TABLE 1
Taxes vs. social insurance: fairness

Dimension of solidarity	Social insurance		Tax financing	
	Income-dependent premiums	Community-rated premiums	Taxes on income	Taxes on consumption
Comprehensive risk solidarity (ex-post and ex-ante)	+[a]	+[a]	+	+
Income solidarity	+[b]	-	+[c]	-

Notes: [a] If coverage is mandatory for the entire population. [b] If the contribution rate is uniform across all income categories or the contribution rate increases as income goes up. [c] If the tax rate is uniform across all income categories or the contribution rate increases as income goes up.

FINANCIAL SUSTAINABILITY

As health care expenditures tend to increase at higher growth rates than GDP, designers of health care financing mechanisms strive to create schemes that are financially sustainable. We define financial sustainability as the permanent ability of a society to finance a socially acceptable level of health care services. In our view, financial sustainability is a function of the magnitude of the tax base. In turn, the magnitude of the tax base is a function of the share of the population contributing to the financing system. Moreover, the size of the tax base also depends on the income categories that are taxed.

The tax base in tax financed health care financing systems is usually high by definition. As already discussed, there is virtually no opportunity to opt out of contributing to the system. If the financing system primarily relies on direct taxes, the definition of taxable income is an important parameter for the determination of the size of the tax base. The tax base is highest if the definition of the taxable income is extensive and if there are little differences between gross pre-tax income and taxable income. The latter usually occurs if the tax law allows for extensive opportunities to deduct expenses from gross pre-tax income. As for indirect taxes, there are few opportunities to avoid paying a tax on consumption – apart from avoiding consumption. However, the magnitude of the tax base is determined by the extent of goods and services that are subject to indirect taxes. Some goods and services may be exempt; others may be subject to a reduced tax rate.

In social insurance financing systems that primarily rely on income-dependent premiums, the definition of the income that is subject to the payment of health insurance premiums is also an important parameter for the determination of the size of the base from which premiums are collected. Theoretically, income that is taxable for direct taxes may be equivalent to income that is subject to health insurance premiums. For this purpose some kind of payment mechanism has to be established in order to make sure that health insurers receive resources that have been raised by a variety of income categories (labour, capital, rent, etc.). Since most social insurance financing schemes originate from the tradition of employment-based systems, this is a rather challenging administrative proposition. If social insurance financing systems primarily rely on community-rated premiums, income categories that are subject to premiums are irrelevant, since premium payments are paid out of disposable income, wherever it comes from.

While the definition of the income categories is an important parameter for the size of the revenue base in social insurance financing systems, the size of the population that forms the risk pool is probably even more important. We have seen that opting-out provisions may decrease income solidarity and risk solidarity because high-income/low-risk individuals may choose to opt out of social insurance schemes. Obviously, this kind of adverse selection also has implications for financial sustainability. Financial sustainability is higher if good risks (high-income/good health) are unable to opt out of the social insurance system. Social insurance systems need to be universal and mandatory in order to avoid opting out.

Again, we have found that taxes and social insurance can be equivalent modes of health care financing, but very specific assumptions have to apply if the implications for financial sustainability are to be equivalent. However, so far we have not mentioned one assumption from the realm of political economy. Up to now we have assumed that funding by taxes is as steady as funding from social insurance – which is another prerequisite for financial sustainability. It is safe to say that this assumption is a rather daring one (see "Employment," below). Table 2 summarizes our findings.

EMPLOYMENT

Another important aspect of the design of health care financing schemes is the repercussion on employment. Why are these repercussions important? If there is a direct link between health care expenditures and labour costs, rising health care expenditures directly lead to rising labour costs. Moreover, if there is a direct link, rising health care expenditures increasingly drive a wedge between labour costs of the employer and net wages of the employee. As a consequence, microeconomic labour market theory generally assumes that

TABLE 2
Taxes vs. social insurance: financial sustainability

What is the size of the base from which either taxes or premiums are collected?	Social insurance		Tax financing	
	Income-dependent premiums	Community-rated premiums	Taxes on income	Taxes on consumption
Size of the population	Everybody who has income subject to contributions[a]	Everybody[a]	Everybody who has taxable income	All consumers
Income categories	Income subject to contributions	Disposable income	Taxable income	Disposable Income

Note: [a] If coverage is mandatory for the entire population.

incentives for the employee to work diminish. What is more, incentives for the employer to substitute capital for labour – or to substitute cheaper labour abroad for domestic labour – increase. Therefore, all other things being equal, employment decreases (Sachverständigenrat zur Begutachtung der gesamtwirtschaftlichen Entwicklung 2005).

The macroeconomic consequences of social health insurance, which provides a direct link between rising health care expenditures and labour costs for employment, are less straightforward. Rising health care expenditures are spent on health care services, which in turn provide additional employment. The net employment consequences depend on the productivity of industries. If, for example, employment is lost in the manufacturing industry due to rising labour costs, the net employment effect is probably positive: the manufacturing industry is highly productive and comparatively few jobs are lost due to rising costs of employment. Health care services usually are less productive due to a higher ratio between labour and capital. Nonetheless, if the link between rising health care costs and labour costs is weaker rather than stronger, the positive net employment effect of rising health care costs can possibly be increased; that is, the higher the share of health care costs that is financed directly by employment (e.g., by social health insurance premiums), the less favourable are the employment consequences of rising health care costs (Rürup 2005; Schmähl 2006).

In social health insurance systems with income-dependent premiums, the link between health care expenditures and labour costs is very strong. The more the financing of social insurance depends on income from employment, the stronger the link is. If health care expenditures are increasing, health insurers need to increase income-dependent premiums. Labour costs and the wedge between labour costs and net wages increase straightaway. All other things being equal, employment goes down.

In social health insurance systems with community-rated premiums, the link between health care expenditures and employment is less obvious. Rising premiums will lead automatically not to rising labour costs but to a decrease of disposable income for employees. This in turn will lead to less consumption or less savings of employees, but incentives for employment remain unchanged – at least in the short run. In the long run, rising health insurance premiums might lead to rising wage demands and – if the bargaining position of employees is strong – to rising labour costs for the employer.

Turning now to tax-funded health care financing systems, the strength of the link between health care costs and labour costs is different depending on whether the base is from direct or indirect taxes. The link between health care expenditures and labour costs is very strong in tax-funded systems that rely on direct taxes to finance health care. Again, it is the stronger the more the tax system depends on income from employment as a tax base. If health care expenditures are increasing, governments need to raise direct taxes on income. Again, all other things being equal, employment goes down because the wedge between labour costs and net wages goes up. Consequences on employment will be even more pronounced if taxes on profit are increased as well.

The link between health care expenditures and labour costs is less pronounced in tax-funded systems that rely on indirect taxes to finance health care. If health care expenditures increase, government needs to increase indirect taxes. In the short run, incentives for the demand and supply of labour remain unchanged. Similar to the pattern with community-rated premiums, consumption and individual savings will decrease. An important difference between community-rated premiums and indirect taxes is that an increase of community-rated premiums will be fully mirrored by the decrease in consumption or savings. However, in the case of indirect taxes, competition may prevent producers increasing prices for the full amount of the increase of indirect taxes. In that case, all other things being equal, the increase of indirect taxes will also lead to a decline of profits and to a smaller reduction of consumption and savings.

Again we have found that taxes and social insurance may be equivalent modes of health care financing. Again, very specific assumptions have to apply for the implications for employment to be equivalent between these two modes of financing health care. However, to this point we have assumed that it is politically as feasible to raise social insurance premiums as to raise taxes – whether direct or indirect. It is safe to say that this assumption is also a rather daring one. Table 3 summarizes our findings.

TABLE 3
Taxes vs. social insurance: employment

What happens to labour costs and employment if health care costs increase?	Social insurance		Tax financing	
	Income-dependent premiums	Community-rated premiums	Taxes on income	Taxes on consumption
Labour costs	↑	→	↑a	→
Employment	↓	→/↓	↓	→/↓

Notes: ↑ = up; ↓ = down; → = constant
a If taxes on income increase as health care costs increase (no crowding out of other public expenditures).

2 SOCIAL INSURANCE VS. TAX FUNDING IN GERMANY: A CASE STUDY

Health care in Germany is primarily financed by income-dependent social health insurance premiums (see figure 1). Social health insurance accounts only for 56 percent of total health care financing; a separate social insurance scheme for long-term care accounts for a further 8 percent.

Traditionally, taxes play only a minor role in health care financing. Only 6 percent of all health care expenditures are covered by federal and provincial governments – mostly for public health services and health education. Roughly 9 percent of health care expenditures are covered by private health insurance. This primarily consists of supplementary health insurance (covering things that are not included in the social insurance scheme), private long-term care insurance, and alternative private health insurance (which individuals may buy if they opt out of the SHI scheme). All individuals who purchase alternative private health insurance are required to buy private long-term care insurance. Another 14 percent of health care expenditures are paid out-of-pocket. Finally, another 7 percent are funded by employers – mostly public employers who cover part of the health care costs for civil servants – and other social insurance schemes such as accident insurance that covers accidents at the workplace only.

FAIRNESS

As we have shown in section 1, the specific institutional characteristics are very important for the implications of social health insurance financing on fairness, financial sustainability, and employment. Specifically, the following questions need to be answered to assess the consequences of the health care financing system in Germany:

1. Is coverage in social health insurance mandatory for the entire population? No, it is not. Coverage is mandatory for a subgroup of employees only. Social health insurance in Germany is still basically an employment-based system and targets a specific group of employees only. Interestingly, it is not mandatory that low-income employees be covered. Employees with an annual pre-tax income of up to 4,800 Euros may take out voluntary social health insurance. If they do not do so, there are three possibilities: (i) they are covered by their spouse's plan (SHI covers families for no extra cost); (ii) they buy alternative private health insurance; (iii) they are not insured not at all. Also not included on a mandatory basis are employees with an annual pre-tax income of more than 42,750 Euro. This wealthier group may, however, choose to buy social health insurance *voluntarily*, or may take out private health insurance or simply

FIGURE 1
Sources of health care financing in Germany 2004

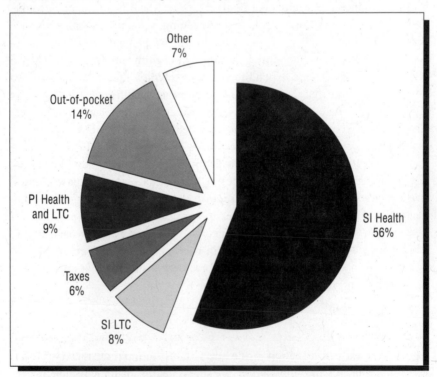

Source: Statistisches Bundesamt 2006.

choose to be uninsured. A third group not included in the mandatory SHI plan are self-employed individuals. The net result of these three exclusions is that only about two-thirds of the populations have compulsory coverage in social health insurance. A further 20 percent are covered in social health insurance on a voluntary basis, and about 10 percent are covered by alternative private health insurance. A small but increasing share of the population – less than 1 percent – has no coverage at all (Greß, Walendzik, and Wasem 2006).

2. Is the contribution rate uniform across all income categories?
No, it is not. The contribution rate is uniform only in the income bracket between 9,600 Euros and 42,750 Euros per year. Employees on average pay a contribution rate of 8 percent, and the employer pays another 7.1 percent. In the income bracket between 0 and 4,800 Euros, employees are not covered mandatorily. They may take out voluntary social health insurance but have to pay a community-rated premium of about 100 Euros per month. Income above the ceiling of 42,750 Euros is not subject to premium payments (see figure 2).

FIGURE 2
Social health insurance premiums of employees as a percentage of pre-tax income

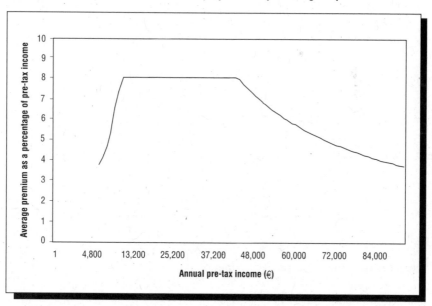

Source: Calculation of the authors based on a contribution rate of 5.1 percent (8 percent to be paid by employees, 7.1 percent to be paid by employers). Below earnings of 4,800 € per annum, individuals need to pay a flat rate premium.

What are the implications for fairness of the German "brand" of social health insurance? Since social health insurance calculates income-dependent premiums independent of health risk, financing by social health insurance entails comprehensive risk solidarity between the healthy and the sick. However, an important caveat applies: redistribution (solidarity) is limited to the members of the risk pool in social health insurance (almost 90 percent of the population). This means that redistribution does not occur from the 10 percent (the wealthiest and generally healthiest) who have opted not to enrol in social health insurance and instead to buy alternative private health insurance.

TABLE 4
Income, morbidity, and consumption of health care services of enrollees in social health insurance and private health insurance

Characteristics	Social health insurance	Private health insurance
Individual gross income (in Euros per year, average)	22,658	38,109
Number of acute and chronic conditions (average)	3.52	2.89
Self-assessed status of bad health (%)	17.9	9.1
Average number of hospital nights during last twelve months	2.21	2.05
Average number of physician visits during last twelve months	6.21	5.1
Share of respondents with continuous consumption of prescription drugs (%)	47.07	41.67

Source: Kriwy and Mielck 2006; Leinert 2006.

Income solidarity in German social health insurance is rather limited as well. As low-risk/high-income individuals are able to opt out of social health insurance, this group is not available for the redistribution of income from high-income groups to low income-groups. Moreover, even within the SHI scheme, progressive income redistribution only occurs within the groups that are mandatorily required to be covered; as figure 2 demonstrates, the wealthier who choose to opt into SHI do not have to pay a progressively higher proportion.[2] Thus premium payments are proportional to income between 9,600 Euros and 42,750 Euros per year. Above that, health care financing in social health insurance is regressive. The reason for the latter is quite straightforward: if financing were proportional to income for high-income employees, incentives to opt out of social health insurance would be even more pronounced.

For the sake of the argument, it is useful to compare the income consequences of social health insurance financing and of tax financing in Germany. So far the share of tax financing is rather small, but both chambers of the German parliament recently have decided to increase the share of tax financing substantially over the next years (see above).

General tax revenue in Germany is comprised of a mix of direct taxes (taxes on income) and indirect taxes (taxes on consumption). Both categories of taxes account for approximately 50 percent of general tax revenue on the federal, provincial, and local levels (Bundesministerium für Finanzen 2006). We have illustrated the consequences of the tax system on income redistribution for income tax (38 percent of general revenue) and federal sales tax (30 percent of general revenue).

Figure 3 illustrates that low-income groups (up to 7,664 Euros per year) do not pay any income tax. After that, income tax as a percentage of total taxable income increases steadily. Thus, the income consequences of the income tax are progressive – income solidarity is high. However, one important limitation applies: the definition of "taxable income" in the German income tax system is less than straightforward. The ability to deduct expenses from gross income and thus the ability to decrease taxable income and in turn to reduce income taxes is distributed rather unevenly across income groups. As a result, the income consequences of income tax are somewhat less progressive than figure 3 implies (Fritzsche et al. 2003). However, revenue from income tax in Germany still provides a higher degree of income solidarity than revenue from income-dependent premiums in social health insurance. This is due also to the fact that individuals who were able to elude income solidarity in social health insurance are unable to get away from paying income tax.

Figure 4 illustrates the fact that the income consequences of the federal sales tax in Germany are regressive. The share of sales tax payments as a percentage of annual disposable income is considerably lower for high-income than low-income groups. While this financial burden is 7.9 percent of disposable income for the 5 percent group of the population with lowest income, it is 5.1 percent for the 5 percent group of the population with highest income (Bach 2005b). This disparity is a consequence of the fact that high-income groups are able to save a higher percentage of disposable income, while low-income groups are often unable to save and may even be forced to incur debt. Reduced sales tax percentages for some consumption goods (food, newspaper, books) are able to somewhat attenuate the regressive income consequences of the sales tax (Fritzsche et al. 2003).

FIGURE 3
Income tax as a percentage of taxable income

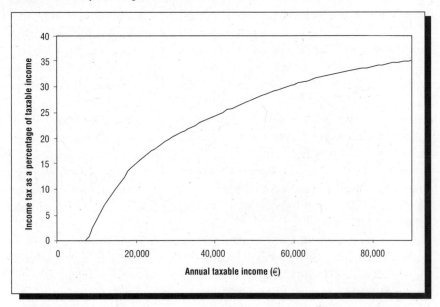

Source: Ministry of Finance, Germany.

FIGURE 4
Federal sales tax as a percentage of disposable income

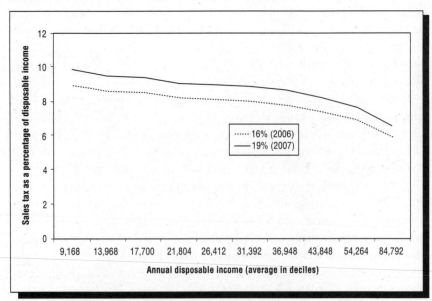

Source: Bach 2005a; Bach 2005b.

It is rather interesting to compare the income consequences of the federal sales tax to the income consequences of social health insurance premiums. Obviously, in low-income groups a sales tax provides less income solidarity than social health insurance. However, the differences are less pronounced for middle-income and high-income groups.

FINANCIAL SUSTAINABILITY

The origin of social health insurance in Germany is employment based (Stone 1980; Greß, Gildemeister, and Wasem 2004). Traditionally, social health insurance was and still is focused on full-time middle-income employees, and it is these groups that are required by law to be enrolled. In contrast, high-income employees and self-employed individuals are not considered to be in need of protection by mandatory coverage. This focus on employment scheme extends to how contributions are assessed. Contributions from those who must enrol in the scheme are assessed on income from employment only. Contributions from individuals who voluntarily opt into the social health insurance scheme are assessed across all income categories including employment income, albeit only up to the income ceiling of 42,750 Euros annually.[3]

As a consequence of this traditional employment-based approach, the financial base of social health insurance is eroding, for a number of reasons (Amelung, Glied, and Topan 2003). First, only 90 percent of the population contribute to the revenue base. About 10 percent of the population do not, since they are not required to enrol in SHI and instead buy private health insurance. The average income of individuals who are able to opt out is much higher than that those who remain in the social health insurance system (see section 2). Thus, adverse selection is a major problem in terms of financial sustainability. Second, the number of full-time employees is decreasing due to structural changes in the labour market. In turn, the number of low-income self-employed individuals and low-income employees is increasing steadily. More importantly, the unemployment rate in Germany is growing constantly as well. Third, the relative share of income from employment compared to other income categories is decreasing. As a result, premium income in social health insurance is growing at a smaller rate than health care expenditures.

Figure 5 illustrates that health care expenditures are growing steadily at a rate higher than growth in GDP. A variety of cost-containment measures since the end of the 1970s have been only partially successful. However, compared to growth rates in other OECD countries, the overall growth rate of health care expenditures in German social health insurance is moderate (OECD 2005). This can be explained by rather strict cost-containment measures in social health insurance. The challenge for long-term financial sustainability in Germany is the slow growth of premium income, which has grown more slowly

FIGURE 5
Health care expenditure and premium income in social health insurance

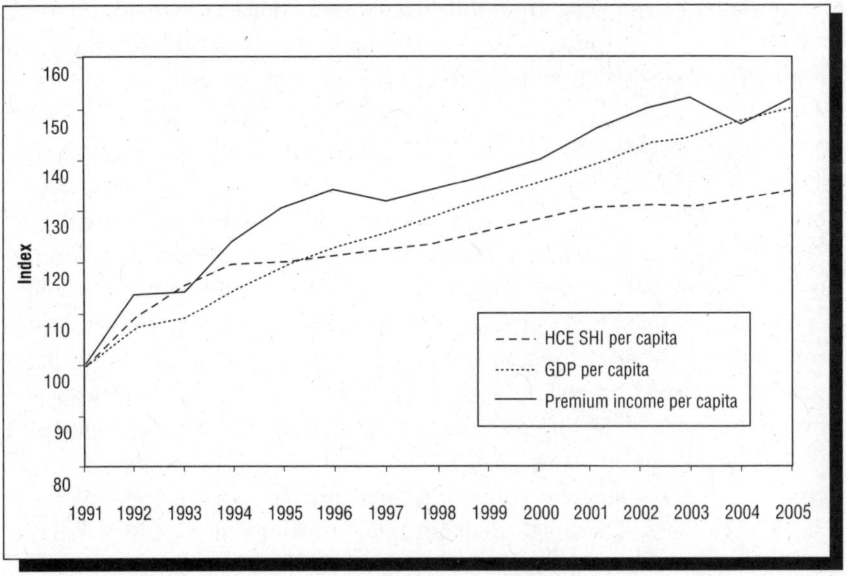

Source: Calculation of the authors, Ministry of Health, Germany.

than GDP during the past ten years. As consequence, income-dependent premiums are rising constantly.

The health policy debate in Germany during recent years has been dominated by proposals of how to broaden the financial base of the social health insurance scheme. One approach – supported by the Social Democrats and the Green Party – advocated a shift toward universal social health insurance. This approach would see the abolition of opting-out provisions, raise the income ceiling for health insurance premiums, and broaden the income categories subject to social health insurance premiums. The second approach – supported by the Christian Democrats – would see the introduction of community-rated premiums in social health insurance and would seek to achieve income solidarity via tax financed and need-tested premium subsidies. Neither of these approaches was implemented with the latest health care reform that came into effect in April 2007. Social Democrats and Christian Democrats have formed a coalition government but were unable to find a compromise that would have substantially increased the financial sustainability of social health insurance. However, the coalition government has decided to increase tax funding of social health insurance. A substantial increase of tax funding will help to improve long-term sustainability of the German system, as everyone pays taxes and not everyone is required to pay social health insurance premiums, the definition of taxable income is broader than "income subject to contributions," and there is no income ceiling.

In terms of a more sustainable health care financing system in Germany, it seems to make sense to raise taxes in order to increase the financial base, which in turn might lead to lower contribution rates – or at least to a more modest growth of contribution rates. However, recent experience in Germany shows that governmental commitment to devoting taxes to the health care system fluctuates (see figure 6).

In 2003 the former government (coalition of Social Democrats and the Green Party) decided to raise taxes for tobacco and in turn increase tax funding of social health insurance – which had been zero before 2004. The health care reform of 2004 earmarked a growing amount of tax money for social health insurance – up to 4.7 billion Euros in 2006.[4] However, the budget consolidation act of the new government reduced tax funding down to zero until 2008. The most recent health care reform in turn increased tax funding – up to 14 billion Euros until 2016. However, it is not clear whether the next government will provide funding for the increase in payments toward social health insurance.

What explains this fluctuation in commitment to increased taxes? An increase of contribution rates in social health insurance is not popular, but when it occurs is mostly attributed to the management by social health insurers of the social health insurance plans. In contrast, an increase in direct or indirect taxes, equally unpopular, will be attributed to politicians who strive for re-election.

FIGURE 6
Tax funding of social health insurance in Germany, 2003–2010

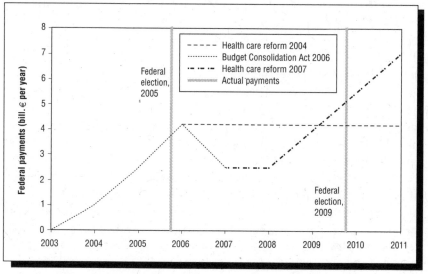

Source: Calculation of the authors.

IMPLICATIONS FOR EMPLOYMENT

For more than 25 years, policy-makers in Germany have tried to control the growth of contribution rates for social health insurance in order to avoid a drain on employment as a consequence of rising health care costs. These attempts have been only partially successful. As we have shown, growth rates of health care expenditures have been modest. Cost-containment measures have increased budgetary pressures on health care providers, primarily outpatient physicians and hospitals. However, premium income of social health insurers has grown much more slowly than health care expenditures. As a result, contribution rates have been growing constantly, from 12.5 percent in the early 1990s to about 15 percent in 2007.

Since social health insurance in Germany is employment based, most of this increase had to be funded by employees and employers. A recent comparative study has found the financial burden on employers of health care related costs (sick pay, costs for health insurance, taxes for health care) was 10.6 percent of total labour costs in Germany. The financial burden on employers in other countries with social insurance health care financing is even higher. In the year 2000 it was 12.5 percent for employers in France and 13.7 percent for employers in the Netherlands (Häussler et al. 2006).[5] However, it is much smaller in the tax financed United Kingdom (6.2 percent). About two thirds of the difference between Germany and the UK are attributable to differences in the financial burden on employers (which takes into account all kinds of taxation on employers, not just payroll taxes) if differences of the level of health care expenditures are accounted for (Häussler et al. 2006). This confirms our supposition that, in contrast to UK-style tax financed systems, employment-based systems place the burden of rising health care expenditure primarily on employers and employees.

This finding has caused considerable political debate over the advantages and disadvantages of increasing the extent to which the German system relies on financing from taxation as opposed to social health insurance premiums. A greater reliance on tax financing would result in health insurers being able to cut or restrain growth in social health insurance premiums. The argument behind these proposals is quite straightforward: a higher share of the financial burden of health care costs will be borne by all taxpayers, and this will decrease the relative financial burden placed upon employees and employers. As a consequence, the supply of labour as well as the demand for labour will go up – employment will increase. A number of simulation studies have analyzed whether this argument is valid empirically (Kaltenborn et al. 2003; Feil and Zika 2005; Meinhardt and Zwiener 2005; Walwei and Zika 2005). Table 5 displays the results of these simulations.

TABLE 5
Employment consequences of a substitution of social insurance funding

Model	Funding by social health insurance premiums	Fiscal spending	Impact on employment (1,000 jobs)
Kaltenborn (2003) I	-10 billion €	+10 billion € (increase of indirect taxes)	+30[a] -20[b]
Kaltenborn (2003) II	-10 billion €	+10 billion € (increase of direct taxes)	+25[a] +20[b]
Kaltenborn (2003) III	-10 billion €	+/- 0 (reduction of public expenditures)	-130[a]
Feil (2005)	-10 billion €	+10 billion € (increase of indirect taxes)	+90[a] +65[b]
Walwei (2005) I	-10 billion €	+10 billion € (increase of indirect taxes)	+129[a] +88[b]
Walwei (2005) II	-10 billion €	+/- 0 (reduction of public expenditures)	-92[a]
Meinhardt (2005) I	-20 billion €	+20 billion € (increase of indirect taxes)	+312[a] +234[b]
Meinhardt (2005) II	-20 billion €	+20 billion € (increase of direct taxes)	+156[a]
Meinhardt (2005) III	-40 billion €	+40 billion € (increase of both direct and indirect taxes, 20 billion € each)	+546[a] +507[b]

Notes: [a] If wages are exogenous. [b] If wages are endogenous.
Source: Kaltenborn et al. 2003; Feil and Zika 2005; Meinhardt and Zwiener 2005; Walwei and Zika 2005.

All models assume that the level of health care expenditures in social health insurance remains constant. However, the models simulate a change in the distribution of funding. The baseline scenario always assumes the 2003 funding model of social health insurance, i.e., social health insurance expenditures are financed by social health insurance premiums only. Six models assume that this share drops by 10 billion Euros (about 6.7 percent of total health care expenditures by social health insurance), two models assume a decrease by 20 billion Euros (13.3 percent), and one model assumes a drop by 40 billion Euros (26.7 percent). In turn, the share of tax funding of social health insurance expenditures increases accordingly.

The findings of the studies displayed in table 5 are consistent. To summarize, a shift from reliance on social health insurance premiums to increased share of tax funding has positive employment consequences. Total labour costs as well the wedge between total labour costs and net wages becomes smaller, because social insurance is not financed by labour only. Because total labour costs go down, incentives to substitute labour for capital go up – demand for labour increases. Because the wedge between total labour costs and net wages becomes smaller, supply of labour increases as well.

Second, the positive employment effect is higher if the increased share of tax funding is financed by increasing *indirect* taxes rather than by increasing direct taxes. This is plausible, because indirect taxes do not distort incentives for the supply of labour. In contrast, income tax in Germany is progressive and lowers incentives for the supply of labour as income goes up.

Third, the results of the simulations are sensitive to a number of crucial assumptions. Probably the most important assumption is whether wages are considered to be exogenous or endogenous. If wages are exogenous, they are independent of changes simulated in the models but are predetermined by other factors. If wages are endogenous, individual or collective bargaining may lead to higher wages as a consequence of the changes simulated in the models – e.g., higher wages as a consequence of higher taxes. Another important assumption concerns the ability of producers to achieve higher prices as a consequence of higher taxes on consumption. The more they are able to do so, the smaller the positive employment effects will be – even more so if wages are considered to be endogenous.

Fourth, positive employment effects may become negative if government refrains from raising taxes entirely and reduces public expenditures in other areas instead (crowding out). If government reduces public consumption, the employment effect is neutral; if it reduces public investment, the employment effect becomes negative (Kaltenborn et al. 2003). This is an important finding because we take it for granted that it is politically more difficult to raise taxes than to have health insurers raise contribution rates. The German government's plan to increasingly fund the system through taxation (14 billion Euros until 2016) may help with sustainability concerns (see "Financial Sustainability," above). However, presently the government is extremely reluctant to raise taxes to fund this proposal – probably because it recently raised the federal sales tax by three percentage points for purposes of fiscal consolidation. As a consequence, the employment effect of this measure might at best be neutral if government decreases public consumption instead (i.e., reduces spending in other areas in order to fund the health care system). It will probably be negative if tax funding for social health insurance crowds out public investment.

Finally, employment consequences are rather modest if only a small share of social health insurance expenditure is financed by tax funding. Employment in the German economy is at about 39 million individuals; unemployment is at about 4 million individuals. The simulations show that only a considerable cut in the share of funding which is financed by social health insurance premiums will lead to substantial job growth. This most certainly will pose a problem politically, because it will in turn take a substantial boost in tax rates to obtain funding to substitute for reductions in social health insurance premiums.

CONCLUSION

In this chapter we have found that funding of health care expenditures by social health insurance premiums and tax funding can be equivalent in terms of *fairness or solidarity*. Two important caveats apply. First, social insurance needs to be universal – which tax funding usually is by definition. Second, only income dependent premiums (premiums are a proportion of income) and a proportional or progressive tax system imply risk solidarity as well as income solidarity. Community-rated premiums imply risk solidarity only.

Financial sustainability of both modes of financing depends on (among others) the number of persons paying taxes or premiums. Legal provisions to voluntarily opt out of the German social health insurance system decrease fairness as well as financial sustainability. Sustainability also depends on the income categories that contribute to social insurance premiums or tax financing. In terms of financial sustainability, community-rated premiums and indirect taxes are preferable to income-dependent premiums and direct taxes. As a consequence, a trade-off may ensue between the fairness and sustainability of policy objectives.

Income-dependent premiums directly link rising health care expenditures and labour costs. Rising labour costs will – all other things being equal – reduce *employment*. The link between community-rated premiums and labour costs is less direct, since rising labour costs as a consequence of rising health care costs will only follow if the bargaining power of employees is high. As a consequence, community-rated premiums are preferable to income-related premiums in terms of implications for employment. Again, a trade-off between the policy objectives' fairness and employment may ensue.

Tax financing and financing by social insurance contributions can be equivalent in theory. However, we have shown that the specific form of social health insurance financing used in Germany is inferior to tax financing. In particular, it is less equitable and provides fewer incentives for employment than tax financing.

Social insurance probably is not a desirable option for core services of the Canada Health Act – at least not in the foreseeable future. However, our findings may be useful for the design of social insurance schemes of non-Medicaid health care services. For non-Medicaid services, the point of departure is different than for services covered by the Canada Health Act. A considerable share of health care expenditures for pharmaceuticals is covered in Canada by private funding – out-of-pocket payments and private health insurance. Private funding is less equitable than social insurance funding (in terms of both redistribution from the healthy to the sick and redistribution from the rich to the poor). A careful design of a universal social insurance scheme for pharmaceuticals (enforcement of universal coverage, calculation of affordable premiums, price regulation, regulation of reimbursement) might thus result in a considerable improvement of the status quo with regard to fairness of financing, financial sustainability, and implications for employment.

NOTES

[1] An important extension of this approach would be to include the interaction of social insurance, taxes, *and* private health insurance.

[2] The figure only shows the income consequences for employees with compulsory coverage and for employees with voluntary coverage above the income ceiling. It can be shown that income consequences for other groups on the labour market (low-income employees, self-employed persons) are even more regressive.

[3] The same rule applies to premium calculation for pensioners.

[4] Total health care expenditures of social health insurance are expected to be about 150 billion Euros in 2007.

[5] According to this study, the financial burden for health care related costs on employers in the US is only slightly lower than in Germany (10.3 percent of total labour costs).

REFERENCES

Amelung, V., S. Glied, and A. Topan. 2003. "Health Care and the Labor Market: Learning from the German Experience." *Journal of Health Politics, Policy and Law* 28: 693-714.

Bach, S. 2005a. "Koalitionsvertrag: Belastungen durch Mehrwertsteuererhöhung werden nur zum Teil durch Senkung der Sozialbeiträge kompensiert." *DIW-Wochenbericht* 72: 705-14.

– 2005b. "Mehrwertsteuerbelastung der privaten Haushalte: Dokumentation des Mehrwertsteuer-Moduls des Konsumsteuer-Mikrosimulationsmodells des DIW Berlin auf Grundlage der Einkommens- und Verbrauchsstichprobe." Data Documentation 10. Deutsches Institut für Wirtschaftsforschung, Berlin. www .bundesfinanzministerium.de/lang_de/DE/Aktuelles/Monatsbericht__des__BMF/ 2006/06/060620agmb005,templateId=raw,property=publicationFile.pdf.

Bundesministerium für Finanzen. 2006. "Struktur und Verteilung der Steuereinnahmen." Monatsbericht des BMF. Juni 2006, www.bundesfinanzministerium.de/lang_de/DE/ Aktuelles/Monatsbericht__des__BMF/2006/06/060620agmb005,templateId= raw,property=publicationFile.pdf.

Feil, M., and G. Zika. 2005. *Mit niedrigen Sozialabgaben aus der Arbeitsmarktkrise? IAB-Kurzbericht 4/2005*. Nürnberg: Institut für Arbeitsmarkt und Berufsforschung.

Fritzsche, B., R. Kambeck, and H.D. von Loeffelhoz. 2003. *Empirische Analyse der effektiven Inzidenz des deutschen Steuersystems. Rheinisch-Westfälisches*. Essen: Instiut für Wirtschaftsforschung.

Greß, S., S. Gildemeister, and J. Wasem. 2004. "The Social Transformation of American Medicine: A Comparative View from Germany." *Journal of Health Politics, Policy and Law* 29: 679-99.

Greß, S., A. Walendzik, and J. Wasem. 2006. "Persons without Health Insurance in Germany: Who Are They and What Can Be Done?" Presentation at the annual conference of the European Public Health Association (EUPHA) in Montreux (Switzerland), November 2006.

Häussler, B., T. Ecker, and M. Schneider. 2006. *Belastung der Arbeitgeber in Deutschland durch gesundheitssystembedingte Kosten im internationalen Vergleich*. Baden-Baden: Nomos.

Kaltenborn, B., S. Koch, U. Kress, U. Walwei, and G. Zika. 2003. "Sozialabgaben und Beschäftigung." *Mitteilungen aus Arbeitmarkt und Berufsforschung* 36: 672-88.

Kriwy, P., and A. Mielck. 2006. "Versicherte der gesetzlichen Krankenversicherung und der privaten Krankenversicherung: Unterschiede in Morbidität und Gesundheitsverhalten." *Das Gesundheitswesen* 68: 281-8.

Leinert, J. 2006. Morbidität als Selektionskriterium. In *Fairer Wettbewerb oder Risikoselektion – Analysen zur gesetzlichen und privaten Krankenversicherung*, edited by K. Jacobs, J. Klauber, and J. Leinert, 67-76. Bonn: Wissenschaftliches Institut der AOK.

Meinhardt, V., and R. Zwiener. 2005. *Gesamtwirtschaftliche Wirkungen einer Steuerfinanzierung versicherungsfremder Leistungen in der Sozialversicherung*. Berlin: Deutsches Institut für Wirtschaftsforschung.

Organization for Economic Cooperation and Development. 2005. *Health at a Glance. OECD Indicators 2005*. Paris: OECD.

Rürup, B. 2005. *Das Verhältnis von Beitragsfinanzierung und Steuerfinanzierung in der sozialen Sicherung*. Gutachten im Auftrag der Hans-Böckler-Stiftung.

Sachverständigenrat zur Begutachtung der gesamtwirtschaftlichen Entwicklung. 2005. Jahresgutachten 2005/06. "Die Chance nutzen – Reformen mutig voranbringen." Wiesbaden: Statistisches Bundesamt.

Schmähl, W. 2006. *Aufgabenadäquate Finanzierung der Sozialversicherung durch Beiträge und Steuern: Begründungen und Wirkungen eines Abbaus der "Fehlfinanzierung" in Deutschland.* ZeS-Arbeitspapier Nr. 5/06. Zentrum für Sozialpolitik der Universität Bremen.

Statistisches Bundesamt. 2006. *Gesundheit: Ausgaben, Krankheitskosten und Personal 2004*. Wiesbaden: Statistisches Bundesamt.

Stone, D. 1980. *The Limits of Professional Power: National Health Care in the Federal Republic of Germany*. Chicago: University of Chicago Press.

van de Ven, W.P.M.M., and R. Ellis. 2000. "Risk Adjustment in Competitive Health Plan Markets." In *Handbook of Health Economics*, edited by A.J. Culyer and J.P. Newhouse, 755-845. Amsterdam: Elsevier North Holland.

Wagstaff, A., and E. van Doorslaer. 1992. "Equity in the Finance of Health Care: Some International Comparisons." *Journal of Health Economics* 11: 361-387.

– 2000. "Equity in Health Care Finance and Delivery." In *Handbook of Health Economics*, edited by A.J. Culyer and J. Newhouse, 1803-57. Amsterdam: Elsevier.

Walwei, U., and G. Zika. 2005. "Arbeitsmarktwirkungen einer Senkung der Sozialabgaben." *Sozialer Fortschritt* 54: 77-90.

Chapter 6

A Competitive Market for Social Health Insurance in Five Countries: Is There a Relation between Funding and Organizing Health Care?

Wynand P.M.M. van de Ven

The central questions of this book are: Is there an appropriate balance between general taxation and social insurance as mechanisms of public finance for health care? How can we best deal with the ongoing quest to provide equity of access, quality of care, and incentives for efficiency within a sustainable funding model? Is there a path forward in social insurance for Canada and what can we learn from the experiences and evidences from other jurisdictions?

Against this background, the goal of this chapter is, first, to explore whether there is a relation between funding and organizing health care, and second, to analyze some recent developments in five countries with a competitive market for social health insurance.

I focus here on five countries with a so-called Bismarck-style mandatory health insurance: Belgium, Germany, Israel, the Netherlands, and Switzerland. From the mid-1990s, citizens in these countries have had a guaranteed periodic choice among risk-bearing health insurers. In the literature this consumer choice of health insurer is associated with the model of managed competition in health care (Enthoven 1988). That is, allocation and prices are in principle determined by the market, but government regulation offers guarantees for solidarity and sets side conditions for efficiency. Government regulation may relate to, for example, adequate risk equalization, consumer protection against quackery and other poor quality of care, adequate consumer information about the quality of both insurers and providers of care, well-defined products, prices related to costs, and guarantees of competition by adequate competition policy. In theory, managed competition is a consistent model in which the competing health insurers act as cost-conscious third-party purchasers of health care on behalf of their enrollees. The model implies competition on the market for health insurance as well as competition on the market for health care provision. Alternatively, health insurers and health care providers may integrate, resulting in a periodic consumer choice of integrated health care financing/delivery organizations such as the health maintenance organizations in the United States. The model of managed competition implies that government allows the *individual* health insurer to be a prudent buyer of care, or to "manage the care." That is, government should not deprive individual health insurers of tools such as *selectively* contracting with health care providers, utilization management, and negotiating with individual providers about price, quality, waiting time, opening hours, and other services. Individual health insurers, rather than government or the collective of all health insurers, should act as the third-party purchasers of care.

Although there are substantial differences between the health systems in the five countries with respect to history, political philosophy and environment, and state administration, a major issue common to these countries is how to make health insurance affordable in a competitive insurance market. To do so, all five countries have implemented a system of risk-adjusted premium subsidies (or risk equalization across risk groups), along with an open enrolment requirement and strict regulation of consumers' premiums to their health insurer. In all five countries the mandatory health insurance covers physician services, hospital care, and prescription drugs.

This chapter deals first with the question of whether there is a relation between funding and organizing health care. Then it turns to a discussion of the experiences of the above-mentioned countries with risk equalization and managing the health care system.

IS THERE A RELATIONSHIP BETWEEN FUNDING AND ORGANIZING HEALTH CARE?

Often the model of managed competition is associated with a social health insurance system and the model of National Health Service (NHS) with general taxes. I argue that there need not be any relation between *funding* and *organizing* health care.

In classifying different models of organizing health care, a crucial question is: who is the third-party purchaser of care? To achieve efficiency in health care, there is a need for a third-party purchaser, an entity who acts as a prudent buyer of care on behalf of the consumer. Because of the information asymmetry between the consumer and the provider of care and because of the moral hazard that results from widespread health insurance coverage, a direct purchasing relation between the consumer and the provider of care generally does not result in an efficient outcome. Logical candidates to fulfil the role of third-party purchaser are government and health insurers. Society's decision about *who* fulfils the role of third-party purchaser largely determines government's role with respect to health care and how to *organize and structure* the health insurance markets. If the role of purchaser is to be fulfilled by government, with central legislation as a tool for managing the care (e.g., in National Health Service systems), or a cartel of health insurers (e.g., in Belgium and Germany), it is hard to think of any rational argument for having a competitive health insurance market with its problems concerning risk rating and risk selection (discussed in the next sections). In that case it can be more efficient to have one national health insurer or an NHS. If the role of purchaser is to be fulfilled by competing risk-bearing insurers who selectively contract with providers, as in the managed competition model in the Netherlands, for example, there is a totally different way of *organizing and structuring* the health care system.

For policy-makers it is important to understand that there need not be a direct relation between organizing health care (e.g., NHS or managed competition) and funding. This can be illustrated by the funding of the managed competition model in the Netherlands, illustrated in figure 1, which consists of the following major components:

- Income-related contributions from consumers to the Risk Equalization Fund (REF);[1]
- Risk-related payments from the REF to the insurers, which in total equal 50 percent of the total revenues of the insurers;
- Direct premiums from the consumers (18 years and older) to the insurers, which in total equal 50 percent of the total revenues of the insurers;
- Government contributions, paid out of general taxes, to the REF for persons younger than 18 years;
- Income-related extra allowances paid out of general taxes. These compensations are dependent not on the chosen insurer but on the national average premium;
- A legal obligation on the part of employers to fully compensate their employees for their income-related contributions. These compensations are taxable income for the employees.

In the Netherlands the political choice has been made to let the direct premiums to the insurers be 50 percent of their total revenues, and the other 50 percent come via the REF.[2] In principle, however, policy-makers could decide to let the great majority of the payments to the insurers go via the REF and/or to fill the REF predominantly out of general taxes.[3] That is, in principle managed competition and predominantly general tax funding can go together. This would be the case, for example, if consumers in the UK had a periodic choice among

FIGURE 1
The financing system in the Netherlands, 2006

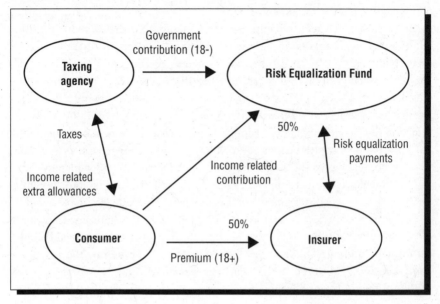

primary care trusts that have financial responsibility for purchasing secondary care. On the other hand, a model with much central top-down government regulation of prices, capacity planning and volume need not be funded out of general taxes but can also be funded by, for example, earmarked payroll taxes, as is the case in social insurance systems such as those in Austria and France and the former Dutch sickness fund insurance (before 2006).

The conclusion, then, is that in principle there need not be a relation between *funding* – i.e., social insurance (which is often associated with earmarked payroll taxes) or general taxes – and *organizing and structuring* the health care system – i.e., managed competition or central planning/regulation.

The amount of cross-subsidies from high income to low income people and from low risk to high risk people that can be achieved under a so-called social insurance system need not be different from that under a general tax system.

In general it is hard to say which form or mixture of funding is most efficient. Probably this also depends on the institutional context. In addition, the actual situation may be a political compromise rather than the most efficient form of funding. For example, in the Netherlands in 2005 the consumer's out-of-pocket premium per person was about €350, and there was no income related extra allowance. In 2006, as a political compromise, this premium was tripled (to about €1,000) and complemented with a costly system of income-related extra allowance.

A FREE COMPETITIVE HEALTH INSURANCE MARKET

A competitive health insurance market creates a great challenge for policy-makers: how to make health insurance affordable for everyone in such a market. In a free competitive insurance market, implicit cross-subsidies in the premiums cannot be sustained because competition minimizes the predictable profits per contract. Consequently, an insurer has to break even, in expectation, on each contract either by adjusting the premium to the consumer's risk (premium differentiation) or by adjusting the accepted risk to the premium (risk selection).

If an insurer will not adjust the premium for a risk factor that is known either to individuals or to insurers, then low risk individuals will choose a competing insurer who offers a lower premium or a contract specifically designed to attract low risk individuals. Consequently the first insurer, left with only high risk individuals, will have to increase the premium. In this way, in the absence of any restrictions on premium rates, a *competitive* health insurance market will tend to result in insurers charging *risk adjusted* premiums that differentiate according to the individual consumer's risk.

Risk adjusted premiums are the norm, not the exception, in competitive markets. If insurers were fully free to set their risk adjusted premiums, competition would result in risk adjusted premiums that could easily differ by a factor of ten or more for demographic risk factors such as age, and by factors of 100 or more once health status is also taken into account.

If the premiums are perfectly risk adjusted, all risk heterogeneity is reflected in them. In practice this is mostly not the case either because of asymmetric information, with the consumer knowing more than the insurer, or because risk rating becomes too costly, technically infeasible, or politically unacceptable. However, the pooling of people with different risks may result in *risk selection*, that is, actions by consumers and insurers to exploit unpriced risk heterogeneity and break pooling arrangements (Newhouse 1996). These actions may have several effects, such as instability in the insurance market, a continuous exit of insurers due to bankruptcy, a welfare loss due to the inability to buy the preferred insurance coverage, and high prices for high risk individuals.

In addition to the equity concerns, there are also efficiency problems. A free health insurance market can only provide protection against *unpredictable* variation of costs in the contract period (usually a year). No insurance is offered that protects risk averse consumers against the financial risk of becoming a high risk in the future. Consequently, consumers cannot equalize the marginal utility of income across different lifetime health profiles, and health insurance can become unaffordable for those who become a high risk. Therefore, a relevant question is: What is the best strategy in a competitive health insurance market to make health insurance affordable for high risk individuals?

HOW CAN HEALTH INSURANCE BE MADE AFFORDABLE IN A COMPETITIVE INSURANCE MARKET?

An effective way to make health insurance affordable is to give the high risk consumers a *premium subsidy* out of a subsidy fund that is filled by mandatory contributions. The subsidies could be related to the level of the premium or to the risk factors on which actuarial premiums in an unregulated competitive market would be based (e.g., age, gender, and health status). Premium related subsidies (e.g., tax deductibility of premiums) reduce the consumer's incentive to shop around for the lowest premium. Thereby they reduce the insurers' incentive for efficiency. In addition, premium related subsidies stimulate consumers to buy more complete insurance than they would have done in the case of no subsidy at the margin, resulting in more moral hazard. The advantage of risk adjusted premium subsidies (i.e., subsidies that are adjusted for the risk factors) over premium related subsidies is that they do not distort competition.

There are at least three ways to organize the subsidy payment flows. According to the first method (Modality A; see figure 2) the subsidy goes directly to the consumer, and the consumer pays the premium partly with the subsidy and partly out-of-pocket. As far as is relevant, consumers pay their contribution to the subsidy fund. For practical reasons an alternative is that the subsidy goes directly to the insurer, and the consumer pays the premium minus the subsidy to the insurer (Modality B). In a competitive market the insurers are forced to reduce the consumer's premium with the per capita subsidy they receive for this consumer. Another alternative is that the consumer pays the "premium minus subsidy plus contribution-to-the-subsidy-fund" to the insurer, while the insurer and the subsidy fund clear the net difference of all the contributions to the subsidy fund and subsidies of the relevant clients (Modality C).

Although at first glance Modality A and Modality C may seem to be quite different, all modalities differ primarily in the way the payment flows are organized. The way that the premium subsidies and the contribution to the subsidy funds are calculated can in principle be the same.

RISK EQUALIZATION

Since the mid-1990s Belgium, Germany, Israel, the Netherlands, and Switzerland have all had systems of risk-adjusted premium subsidies, i.e., risk equalization systems. In addition to cross-subsidies among risk groups, there are also cross-subsidies among income groups. A straightforward and practical way to do this is to make the contributions to the subsidy fund income related and to let risk related cross-subsidies be reflected in the risk-adjusted

FIGURE 2
Three modalities of a subsidy system

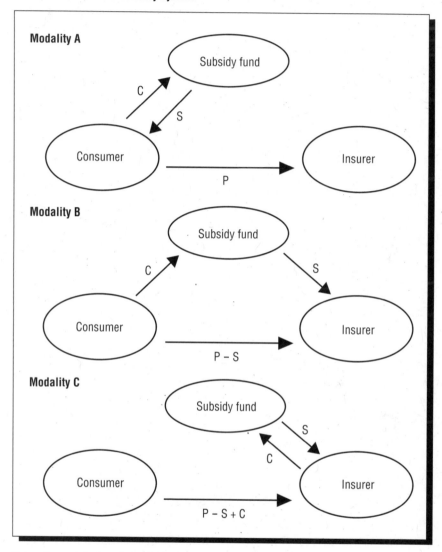

Notes: C = contribution; S = subsidy; P = premium.

premium subsidies. This is the case in Belgium, Israel, and the Netherlands, who have adopted Modality B. From the point of view of the health insurers, this way of organizing subsidies can be seen as an external *equalization system*; the equalization takes place entirely outside the health insurers. An alternative is Modality C, which is applied in Germany and Switzerland. This can be considered a system in which there is an internal equalization *within* each health insurer, complemented with an equalization system *among* health insurers to compensate for differences in risk portfolios among the insurers.

Table 1 provides an overview of the risk adjusters used in 2006 in each of the five countries. All countries use age as a risk adjuster. A major difference among countries is the number and quality of risk adjusters: Israel only uses age, Belgium has a long list, and the Netherlands uses sophisticated health adjusters. Since 2002 some major changes have taken place in the risk equalization system in these countries. (For risk equalization in the year 2000, see van de Ven et al. 2003.)

In Belgium, it has been decided that risk equalization should only be based on factors for which the insurers[4] cannot be held responsible. Policy-makers decided that medical supply should not be included in the risk equalization system, although it was a significant variable in the regressions. Consequently the insurers are held responsible for differences in medical expenditures that are caused by differences in medical supply.

In Germany in 2003 (voluntary) registration in accredited Disease Management Programs (DMPs) was added as an additional risk adjuster. The arguments for such a formula extension relate to both equity and quality: (i) financial inequities between insurers with few and with many chronically ill should be reduced; and (ii) the quality of care for the chronically ill could be improved by the implementation of guidelines of treatment implemented for specific conditions. Government has so far defined four out of seven possible chronic conditions for DMPs to be taken into account in the risk equalization scheme. These conditions are diabetes mellitus, breast cancer, asthma/chronic obstructive pulmonary disease, and congestive heart failure. Guidelines of treatment for these conditions are determined by government on the basis of joint proposals by the medical professions' and health insurers' self-governing corporations. Those insured can voluntarily register in a DMP offered by their health insurer. All insured registered with an accredited DMP are assigned to separate risk groups (cells) in the risk equalization matrix. Almost two million insured have been registered in these programs.

Since its implementation in 1995 the risk equalization system in Israel is based solely on age. In addition health insurers receive a fixed payment for each person who is diagnosed with one of the following "severe diseases": end stage renal failure requiring dialysis, Gauche, Talasemia, Hemophilia, and AIDS. Although there has been a growing dissatisfaction with this formula, no new risk adjusters have been added.

In the Netherlands the following risk factors have been added: Pharmacy-Based Cost Groups (PCGs) in 2002 and Diagnostic Cost Groups (DCGs) and being self-employed (yes/no) in 2004. The R-square of the 2004 model is 0.17, which is a substantial improvement compared with the 0.06 R-square of the 2000 model.

TABLE 1
Risk Equalization System 2006

	Belgium	Germany	Israel	Netherlands	Switzerland
Risk adjusters	Age/gender Disability Invalidity Chronic illness Mortality Employment status Social status Family composition Income Urbanization	Age/gender Disability Registration in a certified disease management program Entitlement for sick-leave payments Income	Age	Age/gender Disability Pharmacy-based cost groups Diagnostic cost groups Being self-employed Urbanization	Age/gender Region
Quality of the Risk Equalization system in 2006	Moderate	Moderate	Low	Fair	Low
Level of ex-post cost compensation	92.5%	4% due to high-cost pooling	5% due to condition-specific risk sharing	47%	0%
Potential profits from risk selection in 2006 [a]	In general low, but can be quite substantial for a small group of "chronic high-cost" insured	Very high	Very high	Fair/high	Very high

Note: [a] The potential profit from risk selection depends on (1) the quality of the risk equalization system (see above, this table), and (2) the extent to which the insurers are retrospectively compensated by cost based (rather than risk based) compensations via mandatory risk sharing arrangements with the Central/Equalization Fund (see above, this table).

On 1 January 2006 the Netherlands government enacted its health insurance act, obliging each person who legally lives or works in the Netherlands to buy individual health insurance with a legally described benefits package from a private insurance company. The previous sickness fund insurance was abolished. The mandatory basic benefits package is legally described in the health insurance act, but there is much room for flexibility in defining the precise entitlements of the insured in the insurance contract (see below). Each year consumers are free to switch insurers.

To organize cross-subsidies, a risk equalization system has been implemented, which is similar to that in the former sickness fund market. In the bylaws of the health insurance act the Netherlands government has made it explicitly clear that risk equalization will be exclusively based on age, gender, and health. In other words, all other risk factors should not be taken into account in the equalization system. For each "basic insurance product," the insurance companies are obliged to accept each applicant ("open enrolment") for the same premium ("community rating per product") per province.[5]

In Switzerland no new risk adjusters have been added to the risk equalization system in the last decade. When implementing the risk equalization system in 1993, the legislator expected that the obligation for health insurers to accept every applicant would reduce the selection problems. The aim was that consumer mobility would eventually lead to a convergence of the risk portfolios of the health insurers in such a way that after 13 years risk equalization would be no longer necessary. In practice this did not occur. In 2004 the national parliament decided to prolong the risk equalization system till 2010.[6]

In summary, since 2000 the risk equalization systems in Belgium, Germany, and the Netherlands have been improved by adding new risk adjusters. In Israel and Switzerland no new risk adjusters have been added. The perspective is that the risk equalization systems might be (further) improved by adding the following new risk adjusters: diagnostic information in Belgium, health based risk adjusters in Germany, gender in Israel, and in the Netherlands, multiple PCGs (rather than only one PCG) per person, multi-year DCGs rather than one-year DCGs, indicators of mental unhealthiness, and indicators of disability and functional restrictions. In Switzerland reform is on the way, which may lead to a law that includes prior hospitalization and pharmaceutical cost groups (PCG) or DCG as adjusters in the equalization formula.

RISK SELECTION

The risk adjusters in all five countries are insufficient to fully compensate insurers for all predictable differences in expenditures among risk groups (see, for example, van de Ven et al., 2004). Therefore in all countries there is an open enrolment requirement, and governments in all five countries impose restrictions on the variation of the premium contributions ("community rating"). Although the intended effect of these restrictions is to create implicit cross-subsidies from low risk to high risk individuals, they also create predictable losses for health insurers on their high risk individuals. In so doing, these restrictions create incentives for selection. By selection I mean actions (not including risk rating premiums) by consumers and health insurers to exploit un-priced risk heterogeneity and break pooling arrangements. Thus, by definition, selection reduces cross-subsidies and threatens affordability.

THE THREAT OF SELECTION

Subtle forms of selection may seriously threaten affordability, efficiency, and quality of care.

First, in the case of large predictable profits resulting from selection, insurers have a disincentive to respond to the preferences of high risk consumers. By high risk (and low risk) consumers is meant those consumers for whom the insurers expect predictable losses (and, respectively, profits), given the risk groups for calculating the premium subsidies and given the restrictions on the variation of the premium contributions. Health insurers may give poor service to the chronically ill and may choose not to contract with providers who have the best reputations for treating chronic illnesses. This in turn can discourage physicians and hospitals from acquiring such a reputation. To the extent that an insurer and its contracted providers of care share financial risk, the providers share the incentive to attract profitable patients and to deter patients who generate predictable losses. As a result of selection, high risk patients may either receive poor care and poor services or pay a very high premium – if they are able and willing to do so – for good care to an insurer that specializes in care for high risk patients (if there is such an insurer). Especially if regulation implies a nation-wide maximum premium contribution (as in Israel, where the premium contribution must be zero for all enrollees), it is suicidal for a health insurer to become known for providing the best care for the chronically ill, because it cannot raise its premium contribution and it will be flooded by individuals who predictably generate more costs than revenues. In sum, selection may threaten good quality care for the chronically ill.

Second, to the extent that some insurers are successful in attracting low risk consumers, these selection activities result in a market segmentation whereby the low risks pay a low premium contribution and the high risks pay a high premium contribution. That is, selection reduces the cross-subsidies and may threaten affordability.

Third, in case of large predictable profits resulting from selection, selection will be more profitable than improving efficiency in health care production.

At least in the short run, when an insurer has limited resources available to invest in cost-reducing activities, it may prefer to invest in selection rather than in improving efficiency. Efficient insurers who do not select applicants, may lose market share to inefficient insurers who do, resulting in a welfare loss to society. So, selection may threaten efficiency.

Fourth, while an individual insurer can gain by selection, selection produces no gains for society as a whole. Thus any resources used for selection represent a welfare loss.

In sum, the restrictions on the variation of the premium contributions that are intended to increase cross-subsidies in the case of imperfect risk equalization instead provide incentives for selection that may threaten quality of care, affordability, and efficiency.

RISK SHARING

Theoretically, the best strategy to reduce selection is good risk equalization. As perfect risk equalization is still a long way off, a second strategy to reduce selection is risk sharing between the subsidy fund (e.g., government) and the insurers. Risk sharing implies that the insurers are retrospectively reimbursed by the subsidy fund for some of their costs of some of their enrollees. Because risk sharing reduces the health insurers' incentives for selection as well as for efficiency, government is confronted with a trade-off between selection and efficiency (van Barneveld et al. 2001).

There appears to be a major difference among the five countries in the level of risk sharing (or ex-post cost compensations) between the subsidy fund and the insurers (see table 1).

In Belgium the insurers retrospectively share more than 90 percent of losses and profits with the subsidy fund, while in Switzerland there is no ex-post risk sharing at all. In Germany in 2002 a high-expenditure pool was introduced to enhance affordability and reduce incentives for selection against very expensive cases. The pool is designed as an outlier risk-sharing arrangement: in 2002, 60 percent of the expenditures above a threshold of €20,450 per insured per year were compensated out of the pool. In 2004 the high-expenditure pool financed €4.6 billion from a total of €126 billion expenditures in the risk equalization system.

In the Netherlands, together with the improvements in the risk equalization system, the insurers' financial risk, i.e., the proportion of efficiency gains or inefficiency losses that on average is reflected in the financial result, increased from 36 percent in 2000 to 53 percent in 2006. This was partly the result of an increase of the "outlier risk sharing" threshold from €4,545 in 2000 to €12,500 in 2006.

EXPECTATIONS ABOUT RISK SELECTION

Hypothetically the extent of risk selection depends on, among other things, the potential profits for insurers from risk selection and the level of competition on the health insurance market. The level of competition influences the incentives for insurers to reduce their expenses, and thereby influences their incentives for risk selection. The potential profits from risk selection depend on, among other things:

1. The quality of the risk equalization system, which we rate as low for Israel and Switzerland, moderate for Belgium and Germany, and fair for the Netherlands (see table 1).
2. The extent to which the insurers are retrospectively compensated by cost based (rather than risk based!) compensations via mandatory risk sharing arrangements with the Central/Equalization Fund: low for Germany, Israel, and Switzerland, high for Belgium, and the Netherlands in between (see table 1). The lower these compensations are, the higher the profits from risk selection in case of imperfect risk equalization.

The potential profits from risk selection can be characterized as very high in Germany, Israel, and Switzerland and fair/high in the Netherlands. In general these profits are low in Belgium (because of the high ex-post cost compensations), but they can be quite substantial for a small group of "chronic high cost" insured, for example, the users of home health care, nursing home care, and psychiatric care.

The higher the level of competition on the insurance market, the higher is the insurers' incentive to reduce costs, and therefore the higher the incentive for risk selection. Table 2 presents some market characteristics of the health insurance market in each of the five countries. Germany and Switzerland have a large number of insurers, making the market very competitive. Belgium and Israel have a small number of health insurers, resulting in a moderate level of competition. In the period before 2005 the Netherlands had a position in between. Since 2006 the health insurance act allows commercial for-profit insurers to enter the social health insurance market, which has made this market highly competitive.

Hypothesizing that the extent of risk selection depends on, among other things, the potential profits for insurers from risk selection (see table 1, last row) and the level of competition of the health insurance market (see table 2, last row), the extent of risk selection can be expected to be very high in Germany and Switzerland, high in the Netherlands, and moderate in Belgium and Israel.

TABLE 2
Level of competition on the social health insurance market in 2006

	Belgium	Germany	Israel	Netherlands	Switzerland
Number of risk-bearing health insurers	6	275	4	33[a]	93[b]
Market share of largest health insurer (at the national level)[c]	45%	36%[d]	55%	20%	18%[e]
Market share of the four largest health insurers (at the national level)	94%	63%	100%	60%	50%[f]
Level of competition/ Incentives for risk selection[g]	Moderate	Very high	Moderate/ fair	High	Very high

Notes: [a] Many of these 33 insurers are part of a larger holding firm. In fact there are only 14 independent funds (year 2006). [b] 23 of these 93 insurers are part of one of the three conglomerates, so in fact there are only 73 independent funds (year 2004). [c] Although regional market shares may be (more) relevant, it is hard to calculate these figures (e.g., what is the relevant geographical market?). [d] All AOKs, which do not compete with each other but have regionally separated markets, are counted as one fund. Largest individual fund: 10 percent market share. [e] 13 percent if a conglomerate is considered as different insurers. [f] Including the three conglomerates. [g] The higher the level of competition in the health insurer market is, the higher are the health insurers' incentives to reduce expenses, e.g., by risk selection.

RISK SELECTION IN PRACTICE

For each of the five countries, is selection a serious problem in practice? Are there indications of the adverse effects of selection? Did any forms of selection arise?

In Belgium some indications of risk selection can be observed. For example, three CEOs of large health insurer associations, in an article in the newspaper *De Standaard* (28 September 2005) entitled "War amongst Health Insurers," accused other insurers and their sales representatives of having aggressive commercial campaigns to unfairly attract new members, sometimes with untrue and misleading information and advertisements. The campaign to attract new enrollees is primarily addressed toward healthy persons, for example, by offering them attractive supplementary health insurance. This is an effective tool for risk selection because the law requires that if the consumer buys supplementary insurance from a health insurer (which the majority does), both the supplementary insurance and the mandatory health insurance must be bought from the same insurer. Since 2000 the number of items included in the supplementary insurance has steadily increased, with rather substantial differences between the different funds. The three CEOs made an appeal to government to make these selection activities impossible.

During the last decade, selection has become a real problem in Germany. Because of price competition, many health insurers hesitated to raise their contribution rates in 2002 and 2003, illegally going into debt. Since 2004 other parameters in addition to price became relevant. Insurers were given the option of reducing the mandatory copayments or giving financial bonuses, for instance, for taking part in preventive programs or for registering in disease management programs.

Since 2000 consumer mobility, measured with price elasticity, has seemed to increase (Schut et al. 2003). The vicious circle of having to raise the contribution rate because of healthy people leaving the large insurers is turning faster and faster. There are indications that the switchers are young and healthy and that they yield predictable profits if risk equalization is based on only age and gender (van Vliet 2006; Berend et al. 2006). The market share of the largest insurers is still decreasing, as healthy people are leaving them. Small insurers are growing fast. Often they also quickly lose members again if they have to raise their contribution rate once their risk structure begins to change toward the mean.

Since 2004, health insurers have been allowed to act as selling agents for private insurance companies for supplemental insurance. There is no real evidence (yet) that this is used as a tool for selection. Andersen and Grabka (2006) conclude that attractive supplemental insurance packages have had an impact on switching. However, the risk profiles of these switchers are unknown. Many of the supplemental insurance contracts offer rebates which the insured lose if they switch insurer for the mandatory insurance.

Health insurers in Israel can provide services directly to their members. This is an effective tool for risk selection. An increasing number of examples indicate the existence of implicit selection activities such as waiting times for particular specialities, accessibility problems to certain clinics, opening of clinics where there is mainly young and healthy population, and advertisements for selected segments of the population. Indications are growing that supplementary insurance is the main area where the health insurers compete and try to attract members. Health insurers constantly innovate and come up with new policies. Although financially managed separately, the revenues from the supplementary insurance become an important source of income.

Until 2004 risk selection was not a serious issue in the Netherlands. However, due to the health insurance act of 2006, things are changing. In autumn of 2005, price competition strongly increased. In the period between 1996 and 2004, competition did not play a major role in premium setting by the former sickness funds (Douve and Schut 2006). In sharp contrast to the previous period, since late 2005 competition now plays a dominant role in insurers' pricing decisions. This increases insurers' incentives for risk selection. At the end of 2005, 18 percent of the population switched to other insurers. In the previous year these figures were around 3 to 4 percent.[7] Although the young, healthy and well educated are overrepresented among the switchers,[8] this observation per se cannot be interpreted as risk selection by the insurers, because age and some indicators of health are included in the risk equalization formula.

Since late 2005, "selection by group insurance" can be observed. According to the health insurance act, insurers are allowed to give a premium rebate to groups of at most 10 percent. On the one hand, insurers give premium rebates to members of a sport club (e.g., football, skating, hockey), to employers, and to self-employed people, but they refuse to give a rebate to unfavourable groups of chronically ill people. In the newspapers insurers clearly state that they do not give a rebate if they fear making high losses on a group.[9] A representative of 19 patient organizations could get a group contract with a premium rebate for only three of the 19 patient organizations. In addition insurers state that they do more for profitable than for unprofitable groups.[10] It can be expected that selection via supplementary insurance will increasingly take place.[11]

In Switzerland, competition among social health insurers was designed to induce the competitors to introduce cost saving models and to improve delivery of health care. However, because the risk equalization formula is based only on age, gender, and region, the incentives for selection are huge. After 10 years of experience, risk selection was revealed to be the most effective strategy measured in gains of market share. Another measure to identify the high risks is to let all applicants fill out a health status declaration, although this form is only permitted for customers who ask for a supplementary insurance contract. Selection via supplementary insurance turns out to be a very powerful tool for risk selection with respect to the health insurer insurance (Paolucci et al. 2005). Also well reported are delayed reimbursements for chronically ill persons, to induce them to leave the insurer.

In sum, based on some market characteristics and the quality of the risk equalization system, we hypothesized the extent of risk selection to be very high in Germany and Switzerland, high in the Netherlands, and moderate in Belgium and Israel. In practice, it turned out that in all five countries there are indications of risk selection. (Appendix 1 provides some anecdotal evidence of selection activities in practice.) In all countries risk selection is increasingly a problem, and indeed this is most severe in Germany and Switzerland. It appears that most switchers are young and healthy. Small new health insurers appear to be the winners and large health insurers the losers.

MANAGED CARE

The rationale of a competitive health insurance market is to stimulate individual insurers to improve efficiency in health care production and to respond to consumers' preferences. In our previous study we concluded that in 2000 in all five countries the conditions for "managed competition," where individual health insurers act as the prudent buyer of care for their members, were by far not fulfilled (van de Ven et al. 2003). An interesting question is thus whether the insurers' tools for managing care have increased in the last years, and whether they have increased their activities to improve efficiency and consumer responsiveness in health care. Table 3 provides an overview of the tools an individual health insurer has to influence its health care expenses for the mandatory social health insurance (year 2006).

In Belgium there is a tendency away from managed care and managed competition toward a cartel of all health insurers. The individual insurers have hardly any tools to manage care and act as a cartel even more than in the past. The government mainly plays a regulatory role. Further, the health insurance market is completely closed for new entrants.

Although in Germany during the last decade individual health insurers were given a little more freedom in contracting with providers, the present framework still is far from what would look like managed competition. Health insurers still form cartels in contracting with hospitals and have to contract with all hospitals listed in a government plan. In the traditional fee-for-service system the contracts are collectively negotiated between the doctors' association and competing health insurers' associations in a region. Nevertheless, some first and very modest steps toward managed care can be observed. Currently there is no active competition policy with respect to health care.

Israel provides a mixed picture. Individual health insurers do have tools for managed care and have the options to form integrated financing/delivery organizations. However, there is limited competition among health insurers, and the situation is more akin to a cartel. There is no active competition policy regarding health insurers, who only compete on copayment and quality.

The Netherlands also provides a mixed picture. With respect to outpatient care, huge progress has been made during the last decade in transforming government regulated cartels into managed competition. Since the very late 1990s there has been an active competition policy, and since 2000 the insurers' tools for managing care have gradually been extended. The 2006 health insurance act provides insurers with several new tools for managing care. The basic benefits package is described in terms of functions of care. That is, the law describes the nature, content and extent of the care, while the insurance contracts determine who delivers the care, where, and under what conditions. This implies that insurers and consumers have ample room for differentiating

TABLE 3
Tools for an individual health insurer to influence its health care expenses for mandatory social health insurance, 2006

	Belgium	Germany	Israel	Netherlands	Switzerland
Is an individual insurer legally allowed to selectively contract with:					
individual providers	No	Only in the special case of "integrated care"	Yes	Yes	Yes
individual hospitals	No	See above	Yes (needs approval)	Yes	Yes
Legal restrictions on prices to be negotiated between an individual insurer and:					
individual providers	Yes	Yes, except in the special case of "integrated care"	No	Yes: maximum prices for most types of providers	No
individual hospitals	Yes	See above	Yes	Yes: ex ante budget per hospital for 90% of expenses; for 10% of free negotiations.	No
Can an individual insurer influence a hospital's infrastructure?	No	In principle, yes; in practice, no	Yes	No	In principle, yes; in practice, no
Is an individual insurer allowed to provide care (like HMOs)?					
Outpatient care	Only pharmacies	No	Yes	Yes	Yes
Inpatient care	No	No	Yes	Yes	Yes

the concrete entitlements in the insurance conditions. Furthermore, consumers can choose between entitlements in kind, reimbursement, or a combination. Also, preferred provider insurance arrangements are possible. Insurers are allowed to selectively contract with all types of health care providers, including hospitals.

In Switzerland since 1990 the law on social health insurance offers the possibility for selective contracting with providers in order to create prepaid Health Maintenance Organizations (HMOs) and Preferred Provider models to contain costs. Within these models, physicians act as gatekeepers and have financial incentives to constrain access to more expensive care such as specialist care or in-patient stay. Despite the real success of the early-day HMOs (Bauer et al. 1998), these models nearly disappeared at the end of the 1990s. Since 2000, more and more physician-owned HMOs are entering the market and replacing most of the old staff models. Since 2005, the market share of managed care is increasing. Ten years of competition in the Swiss social health insurance market under weak risk equalization show growth in selection as well as in managed care activities.

In summary, the managed care activities by individual health insurers in the five countries provide a mixed picture. Mostly government or a cartel of health insurers rather than individual health insurers function as the third-party purchaser of care. In Belgium there is a tendency away from managed care toward a cartel of all health insurers. Germany still has predominantly a bilateral monopoly between health insurers and providers of care, although there is political discussion on whether to have more selective contracting between health insurers and providers. In Israel individual health insurers are increasingly active in managing care. In the Netherlands where individual health insurers have had both more tools and more incentives for managed care activities since 2000, a slight increase in managed care activities can be observed. In Switzerland insurers have had the option to create Managed Care Organizations (MCOs) since 1990. Since 2004 the market share of MCOs has been increasing in Switzerland. Just as in Israel, because of the poor risk equalization system, it is still financially suicidal for a Swiss health insurer to advertise the best care for chronically ill people.

Although developments in the five countries are diverse, there are some weak signals of changes in the direction of managed care. It remains to be seen whether these new developments will continue.

CONCLUSIONS AND DISCUSSION

This chapter has explored the relationship between funding and organizing health care and analyzed some recent developments in five European countries with a competitive market for social health insurance.

We concluded that in principle there need not be a relation between funding (social insurance or general taxes) and organizing and structuring the health care system (managed competition or central planning/regulation). Improving efficiency through central government planning (prices and capacity) or through competition and market incentives can be equally achieved in so-called "social insurance" systems and in "general tax" systems. The amount of cross-subsidies from high income to low income people and from low risk to high risk people that can be achieved under a social insurance system need not be different from that under a general tax system.

We compared the competitive market for social health insurance in five countries with a so-called Bismarck-style mandatory health insurer insurance: Belgium, Germany, Israel, the Netherlands, and Switzerland. In all five countries, citizens now have a periodic choice among risk-bearing health insurers who are responsible for purchasing or providing them with medical care. All five countries have a risk equalization mechanism. Because in all five countries there is strict regulation of consumers' direct premium contributions and because all five have imperfect risk equalization, insurers have financial incentives for risk selection, which may threaten cross-subsidies, efficiency, and quality of care. In practice, in all five countries there are indications of risk selection, which is increasingly a problem. Without substantial improvements in risk equalization, risk selection will likely increase. The issue is particularly serious in Germany and Switzerland. We strongly recommend that policy-makers in these countries give top priority to the improvement of the system of risk equalization. This can best be done by the inclusion of health based adjusters.

Looking at the developments concerning risk equalization and risk selection in these countries, since 2000, two major trends can be observed: risk equalization systems have been improved by adding relevant health based risk adjusters, and in all five countries there is evidence of increasing risk selection becoming a problem. At first glance these two trends seem contradictory, as the improvements in risk equalization are intended to reduce selection. Potential explanations for these seemingly contradictory observations could be as follows (van de Ven and Ellis 2000).

First, in the early stage many players – consumers, insurers' managers, and providers of care, for example – may be unfamiliar with the rules of the game. However, over time they will be better informed and can be expected to react to incentives for risk selection. Secondly, in the early stage the differences among health insurers with respect to benefits packages, premiums, and contracted providers are relatively small. Over time they may increase. Thirdly, risk equalization systems have been implemented in the mandatory social health insurance system. Traditionally, insurers are driven by social motives rather than by financial incentives. However, over time new health insurers and increasing competition can make the market more incentive driven. As soon as one insurer starts with profitable risk selection, the others are forced to copy this strategy. Fourthly, one may argue that selection is not so much of a problem because of medical ethics. However, present ethics may change over time if the entire delivery system becomes more competitive. If these explanations are correct, there is a need to improve the risk equalization system to counteract the upward trend of risk selection over time.

Looking at managed care, there are some weak signals of increasing managed care activities by individual health insurers in all countries except Belgium. A necessary (but not sufficient) condition for managed care is that individual insurers have both the tools and the incentives for managed care. In Israel and Switzerland individual insurers have for a long time had the tools for managed care. However, due to the low quality of the risk equalization system in both countries, the potential profits from risk selection are very high. Probably the returns on investment in risk selection are higher than the returns on investment in managed care. So, at least in the early stage of risk equalization, insurers may concentrate more on risk selection than on managed care.

An interesting observation is that after more than a decade of risk selection in Switzerland, the managed care activities by Swiss health insurers started to increase. An explanation might be that the competition has forced all insurers to copy each other's selection strategy. When all insurers are equally successful in selection, no insurer will gain any further from risk selection (they will only lose when they stop risk selection). At that point the competition forces insurers to invest in other cost-reducing activities such as managed care. However, with imperfect risk equalization, as in Israel and Switzerland, insurers will integrate their managed care activities with their selection activities, which may have adverse effects for society, even if all insurers are equally successful in selection.

The conclusion is that, although the managed competition model is elegant in theory, it is hard to implement fully in practice. Good risk equalization is an essential precondition for reaping the benefits of a competitive health insurance market. Without good risk equalization the disadvantages of a competitive health insurance market may outweigh its advantages.

NOTES

[1] Employers are obliged to withhold this income-related contribution (just as with income tax) from employees' wages and to transfer these contributions to the tax collector. The tax collector transfers these income-related contributions to the risk equalization fund (REF).

[2] In previous years the "income related contribution" in the former sickness fund insurance was reduced from 90 percent (2000) to 78 percent (2003) of the total expenditures. Consequently the consumer's out-of-pocket premium per person of 18+ per year increased from €188 in 2000 to about €350 in 2003 and about €1000 in 2006.

[3] Belgium and Israel have, just as the Netherlands, organized income and risk related *cross-subsidies* in a straightforward way (see section on risk equalization). Switzerland has organized income related cross-subsidies outside the health insurer insurance system by giving premium related subsidies to low income households. In Germany the internal subsidy system has to deal with both income and risk related cross-subsidies.

[4] In Belgium, Germany, and Israel the social health insurers are called the "sickness fund" (just as in the Netherlands until 2006). In this paper I denote them as (health) "insurers."

[5] The Netherlands has 16 million inhabitants and is divided into 12 provinces.

[6] Even if consumer mobility would make the portfolios of all sickness funds identical, the permanent existence of the incentives for selection in the case of no risk equalization form a permanent threat on cross-subsidies, efficiency, and quality of care. Most of the adverse effects that may result from the subtle forms of selection (see section on risk equalization) occur even if all sickness funds are equally successful in selection! This is a sufficient argument to make an adequate risk equalization model permanent and not temporary.

[7] De tussenstand op de zorgverzekeringsmarkt, Monitor Zorgverzekeringsmarkt, De Nederlandse Zorgautoriteit, June 2006, Utrecht.

[8] In the relevant subgroups the percentage of switchers are as follows: young (<44) 20 percent and elderly (>65) 8 percent switchers; healthy 24 percent and unhealthy 11 percent switchers; low-educated 14 percent and high-educated 21 percent switchers (de tussenstand op de zorgverzekeringsmarkt, Monitor Zorgverzekeringsmarkt, De Nederlandse Zorgautoriteit, June 2006, Utrecht).

[9] See, for example, *De Telegraaf*, 7, 9, and 10 January 2006.

[10] NRC Handelsblad, 27 May 2006.

[11] In the transition period of implementing the new health insurance act, in 1 January 2006, "selection via the supplementary insurance" was not an issue because insurers collectively agreed (under pressure of parliament and public opinion) not to refuse applicants on the standard supplementary insurance. Since 1 May 2006 this collective agreement no longer holds.

REFERENCES

Andersen, H.H., and M.M Grabka. 2006. "Kassenwechsel in der GKV 1997–2004. Profile – Trends – Perspektiven." In *Jahrbuch Risikostrukturausgleich 2006*, edited by D. Goepffarth. Berlin: Jahre Kassenwahlfreiheit.

Baur, R., W. Hunger, K. Klaus, and J. Stock. 1998. "Evaluation neuer Formen der Krankenversicherung. Synthesebericht." In *Beiträge zur sozialen Sicherheit*, vol. 1, edited by BSV, Federal Office of Social Insurance. Bern: EDMZ.

Behrend, C., F. Buchner, M. Happich, R. Holle, P. Reitmeir, and J. Wasem. 2006. "Risk-Adjusted Capitation Payments: How Well Do Principal Inpatient Diagnosis-Based Models Work in the German Situation?" *European Journal of Health Economics.*

Douve, R., and F.T. Schut. 2006. *Health Plan Pricing Behaviour and Managed Competition*. CPB Discussion paper no. 61. The Hague.

Enthoven A.C. 1988. "Theory and Practice of Managed Competition in Health Care Finance." In *Lectures in Economics 9*, edited by F. de Vries. Amsterdam: Elsevier.

Newhouse, J.P. 1996. Reimbursing Health Plans and Health Providers: Efficiency in Production versus Selection. *Journal of Economic Literature* 34: 1236-63.

Paolucci, F., F.T Schut, K. Beck, C. van de Voorden, S. Gress, and I. Zmora. 2007. "Supplementary Health Insurance as a Tool for Risk Selection in Mandatory Health Insurance Markets: A Five-Country Comparison." *Health Economics, Policy and Law* 2 (2): 173-92

Schut, F.T., S. Gress, and J. Wasem. 2003. "Consumer Price Sensitivity and Social Health Insurer Choice in Germany and the Netherlands." *International Journal of Health Care Finance and Economics* (3) 117-38.

van Barneveld, E.M., L.M. Lamers, R.C.J.A van Vliet, W.P.M.M van de Ven. 2001. "Risk Sharing as a Supplement to Imperfect Capitation: A Tradeoff between Selection and Efficiency." *Journal of Health Economics* 20 (2): 147-68.

van de Ven W.P.M.M, K. Beck, F. Buchner, et al. 2003. "Risk Adjustment and Risk Selection on the Health Insurance Market in Five European Countries." *Health Policy* 65: 75-98.

van de Ven, W.P.M.M, K. Beck, C. van de Voorde et al. Forthcoming. "Risk Adjustment and Risk Selection on the Health Insurance Market in Five European Countries: Six Years Later." *Health Policy.*

van de Ven, W.P.M.M, R.P. Ellis. 2000. "Risk Adjustment in Competitive Health Plan Markets." In *Handbook of Health Economics*, edited by A.J. Culyer and J.P. Newhouse, 755-845. Amsterdam: Elsevier.

van de Ven, W.P.M.M., R.C.J.A van Vliet, and L.M. Lamers. 2004. "Health-adjusted Premium Subsidies in the Netherlands." *Health Affairs* 23 (3): 45-55.

van Vliet, R.C.J.A. 2006. "Free Choice of Health Plan Combined with Risk-Adjusted Capitation Payments: Are Switchers and New Enrollees Good Risks?" *Health Economics* 15: 763-74.

APPENDIX 1
Anecdotal Evidence of Selection Activities in Practice

The following anecdotal evidence of selection activities in practice, especially in Germany and Switzerland, has been reported:

- Selective advertising (e.g., via the Internet);
- Virtual (Internet) health insurers;
- Offering health insurer insurance via life insurers who make specific selections based on health inquiries;
- Selectively terminating business in unprofitable regions, e.g., by closing offices in high cost areas;
- Group contracts, e.g., employer-related group contracts;
- Limited provider plans such as health maintenance organizations (HMOs) and preferred provider organizations (PPOs);
- Other managed care techniques;
- Offering high rebates in case of a deductible;
- Information given to unprofitable enrollees that they have the right to change health insurer;
- Software programs allowing health insurers to distinguish between profitable and unprofitable insured who are calling them by telephone;
- Turning away applicants on the telephone and ignoring inquiries and phone calls;
- Special bonuses for agents who are successful in getting rid of the most expensive cases by shunting them off to competitors;
- Forming conglomerates of insurers (in Switzerland);
- Health questionnaires;
- Delayed reimbursements for high risk individuals;
- Opening clinics in healthy regions;
- Supplementary health insurance. Most consumers prefer to buy mandatory health insurance and voluntary supplementary insurance from the same health insurer. Because health insurers are allowed to refuse new applicants for supplementary insurance, the voluntary supplementary insurance is an effective tool for risk selection with respect to mandatory health insurance.

Chapter 7

Funding Health Care Services:
The Optimal Balance

Timothy Stoltzfus Jost

The particular contribution of this chapter is to compare social health insurance with alternative funding methods. This is achieved by examining the strengths and weaknesses of each of the approaches generally used to finance health care.

PRIVATE HEALTH CARE FINANCE

PRIVATE OUT-OF-POCKET PAYMENT

Regardless of how health care financing systems are structured, all health care products and services are ultimately paid for by individuals and households (Evans 2004). We pay for health care as consumers when we purchase insurance privately or pay for products and services out-of-pocket. We pay as employees whose wages are reduced to purchase health insurance premiums. We pay as taxpayers through payroll taxes, income taxes, or indirect taxes, which in turn directly fund public insurance programs or indirectly fund tax subsidies for health insurance.

Because individuals and households pay for health care in any event, one could argue that the most efficient approach to health care finance would be simply to pay for all health care out-of-pocket. Surely substantial savings would be possible if we could minimize the considerable administrative costs attributable to insurers, public or private, as well as the inefficiencies caused by taxation. If, moreover, individuals and households purchased products and services out-of-pocket, would they not carefully weigh the value of those health care products and services vis-à-vis other ways of spending their money, and shop around to find the least expensive and highest quality providers? Finally, would not requiring people to pay for health care out-of-pocket eliminate the "moral hazard" that exists when health care is "free" at the point of service to the consumer, i.e., when health care is paid for by a distant government or insurer? Proponents of the "consumer-driven health care" movement in the United States are at this moment vigorously and successfully pressing these arguments in support of a policy agenda of greatly expanding out-of-pocket expenditures for health care (Cannon and Tanner 2005; Cogan et al. 2005; Goodman et al. 2004).

Out-of-pocket private payments for health care in fact play an important role throughout the world. Everywhere there are health care services not covered by public or private insurance, such as over-the-counter drugs or complementary medicine. Most countries also impose cost-sharing obligations for insured services, although these are often limited and not fully imposed on low income patients (Robinson 2002; Rubin and Mendelson 1995). Finally, informal, under-the-table payments for health care providers are the norm in many countries (Lewis 2002).

Despite the apparent benefits of out-of-pocket payments as a mode of finance, no sane health policy advocate would contend that all health care costs should be paid for in this manner. The reason is simple and known to all of us. The distribution of health care costs is enormously skewed. One recent study found that in any given year, 1 percent of the population accounts for 27 percent of health care costs, 5 percent for 55 percent, and 10 percent for nearly 70 percent (Berk and Monheit 2001). By contrast, half of the population consumes virtually no health care services. For most of those households whose costs fall within the highest 5 percent, health care would be simply unaffordable if it had to be paid out-of-pocket from current income (ibid.).[1]

Over time, the distribution of health care costs tends to even out. Many of those whose costs are in the highest 1 percent in any given year die during that year, while others – victims of automobile accidents or operable cancers, for example – return to good health (Roos et al. 1989). Some contend, therefore, that people should save or borrow money to cover high cost years. This is, in fact, the way much of health care used to be financed in the United States before health insurance appeared in the 1930s. Indeed, much of health care is debt financed today in the United States, paid for by credit cards or even through home equity loans (Seifert and Rukavina 2006). Borrowing has its limits, however. Those most in need of health care – the dying, for example – are poor credit risks, and debt financing of health care causes great stress for low income families. The use of medical or health savings accounts (MSAs or HSAs) to accumulate funds for eventual medical needs is a strategy that is being attempted in a number of countries, notably Singapore, South Africa, and China, and is rapidly growing in popularity in the United States (Hanvoravongchai 2002). It is, however, a strategy that has little to offer to low income individuals and families. Many in the United States who currently have health savings accounts are not able to fund them (Government Accountability Office 2006). Finally, and most importantly, many who are chronically ill face high health care expenses month after month, year after year, and many of these high cost individuals have low incomes. Indeed, low income persons tend to on average have particularly poor health (Marmot 2002). It is simply not conceivable that many of these people will be able themselves to cover all of their expenses from saving, borrowing, or current income.

PRIVATE HEALTH INSURANCE

The solution to risk is insurance, and in virtually every country on earth, private insurance is available to cover health care costs. Indeed, even the most vehement advocates of out-of-pocket payments (or user charges, as they are often called) acknowledge that catastrophic coverage is necessary. Private health insurance became widespread in the United States and Canada in the second quarter of the twentieth century in response to rising health care costs. It was available even earlier in Europe. Private health insurance was sponsored initially by guilds or labour, religious, or ethnic organizations as a form of mutual aid, but as it became clear that moral hazard problems were not insurmountable, health insurance was offered first by non-profit and then for-profit insurers as a commercial product (Saltman and Dubois 2004).

Private health insurance allows individuals and families to pool risk with other individuals and families. It effectively shifts resources from the healthy (most of us at any one time) to the sick and injured (few of us at any one time) and thus makes funding for health care available when it is needed. It can also be used to spread risk over time, at least if the insurer is prohibited by contract or law from terminating the contract once the insured becomes ill or injured. Finally, private insurance also often effectively serves as pre-payment, covering routine costs that are both affordable and easily anticipated by most insureds, such as dental checkups, routine primary care, and eyeglasses. This pre-payment function of health insurance is often attributed to tax subsidies, allowing qualified individuals to come out ahead financially by pre-paying for health care through insurance, even after insurer administrative costs are taken into account (Goodman and Musgrave 1992). Even where tax subsidies are not available (as occurs with Medicare supplement policies in the United States and with private health insurance generally in a number of countries), people purchase first-dollar private insurance coverage. The security of knowing that even low cost health care purchases will not need to be driven by personal financial exigencies of the moment (or by national rationing policies in tax financed systems) seems to be of real value to many persons.

PROBLEMS WITH PRIVATE HEALTH CARE FINANCE

Although private health insurance is available almost everywhere, and often offers valuable protection to insureds, it is not viable as a strategy for protecting entire populations. In every developed country, some form of public health insurance (understanding public health insurance in a broad sense as including social health insurance or general-revenue funded health care) is available. In all but one developed country – the United States – private health insurance merely supplements or complements public insurance programs (Maynard and Dixon 2002; Mossialos and Thompson 2002; Jost 2001; Colombo and Tapay 2004).[2] Even in the United States, where private health insurance is the primary strategy for funding the care of working age adults and their families, public health care financing programs (which cover the elderly, the disabled, and poor families) pay for nearly half of all health care. If public employee health benefit programs and tax expenditures to support private health insurance are added, public funds support 60 percent of health care expenditures in the United States (Woolhandler and Himmelstein 2002).

There are a number of reasons why private health insurance cannot cover entire populations. First, if premiums for insurance are actuarially based, private insurance will be simply unaffordable to those who need it most – the chronically ill (Jost 2001). Indeed, persons facing high health care costs may simply be denied health insurance outright. Alternatively, they may only be offered insurance with pre-existing condition exclusions or waiting periods that effectively make coverage illusory for the health problems they face. No rational insurer sells fire insurance to a person whose house is on fire; no responsible private health insurer sells health insurance at affordable rates to a person who is actually suffering from an expensive medical condition or likely soon to be. Recent research from the United States regarding private insurance sold to individuals and families rather than groups (the "non-group" market) demonstrates the difficulty of relying on private health insurance to cover populations (Collins et al. 2006).[3]

Countries that rely on private health insurance to play an important role in health care finance use various strategies to address the incentive that private insurers face to exclude the very people who need insurance the most. Some countries require that premiums be community rated and that enrolment be open to all (Jost 2001). Some outlaw or limit pre-existing condition clauses or waiting periods. Some have laws that limit the ability of insurers to cancel policies or raise rates when insureds incur health care costs. Some countries even create risk reallocation pools to reallocate funds from those insurers who are successful in attracting low risk patients to those who are not (Mossialos and Thompson 2002).

These strategies enjoyed only limited success, however. Regulations that force reallocation of risks through private voluntary insurance create a zero-sum game. For each high-risk insured who pays less because of limitations imposed on risk underwriting, several low risk insureds must pay more. Unless there is a legal mandate requiring all to purchase insurance, low risk persons may well conclude that they are better off not purchasing insurance – i.e., self-insuring. In this context, self-insurance may be a rational choice for a young, healthy individual.

There is, moreover, another problem with relying on private insurance to cover populations. Not only is the distribution of health care costs dramatically skewed, but so in most developed countries is the distribution of wealth. Forty-eight percent of American households have incomes that are equal to or less than 300 percent of the federal poverty level (United States Census 2006) – in 2006, $US29,400 for an individual and $US60,000 for a family of four (Department of Health and Human Services 2006). In 2006, the average cost of an employment-related health insurance policy in the United States was $US4,242 for individual coverage and $US11,480 for family coverage (Kaiser Family Foundation 2006a). Non-group policies are less expensive, at least for younger individuals, but they offer less coverage (they often, for example, do not cover maternity costs) and tend to have much higher deductibles and co-insurance obligations. Premiums for adequate insurance coverage are simply unaffordable to much of the American population. On the other hand, the highest 20 percent of households in the United States earned on average in 2005 $US159,583, while the top 5 percent averaged $US281,155 (United States Census Bureau). The distribution of wealth, as opposed to income, is also highly skewed – in 2001 the top 1 percent of Americans controlled 40 percent of the nation's financial wealth (Domhoff 2006). Distribution of income and wealth is not as dramatically skewed in Canada as in the United States, and per capita health care costs are significantly lower in Canada (Picot and Myles 2005).[4] Nonetheless, even in Canada private health insurance would undoubtedly be unaffordable to many lower income households.

Public insurance permits not only shifting health care costs from the unhealthy to the healthy but also shifting resources from the wealthy to the poor. Because private insurance has limited potential for doing this, at least in the absence of heavy regulation and subsidization, its scope is limited in most countries.[5] In some countries, such as Germany (or, until the 2006 reforms, the Netherlands), private insurance covers those wealthy enough to opt out of social insurance; social insurance covers the rest of the population. In Australia, higher income households are not excluded from public insurance but receive tax subsidies to purchase private insurance for hospital and ancillary care, and face tax penalties if they fail to do so (Healy et al. 2006). In Ireland, public insurance only covers general practitioner services for lower income households, and those with higher income must purchase private insurance or pay out-of-pocket for primary care (Wiley 2005). In countries such as France, private insurance covers out-of-pocket payments (cost-sharing obligations) not covered by social insurance, with public funding of private health insurance for low income households (Sandier et al. 2004). In countries such as the UK, private health insurance allows persons otherwise covered by public insurance to obtain private services more rapidly or conveniently than the publicly covered services to which they are otherwise entitled. Finally, in many countries including Canada, private insurance is available to cover services not covered by public insurance, for example, prescription drugs for certain populations.

Whatever role private insurance plays, it has the potential of contributing to two-tier medicine, with wealthier privately insured households receiving medical care more quickly or in more convenient, comfortable, or attractive settings – and perhaps even receiving higher quality care. Nevertheless, in all developed countries other than the United States, public programs do in the end ensure that the entire population has access to basic health care, and use some form of public financing to shift resources from wealthier to poorer households to make certain that such care is available.

EMPLOYMENT BASED GROUP HEALTH INSURANCE

In the United States, private health insurance has been relatively successful in covering working age households because private insurance has been overwhelmingly employment based group insurance (Glied 2005). Federal and state tax deductions and exclusions have subsidized employment related insurance since the mid-1950s, making it more affordable than individual, non-group insurance. Administrative costs are also much lower for employment related group insurance than for non-group coverage, because insurers are spared the underwriting and marketing costs they face in the non-group market. They also face a lower risk of adverse selection in group health insurance because most employees do not seek employment solely to obtain insurance to cover health problems. Federal law prohibits discrimination in coverage and premiums of employment related insurance either in favour of highly compensated employees or against employees with health problems. Effectively, that is, the law requires community rating and open enrolment within employment related groups, making insurance more available to lower income employees and employees with health issues. Finally, even though economists universally agree that employees pay for employment related health benefits through reduced salaries and wages, employees generally have little idea how much health insurance actually costs and often do not realize that they are effectively paying for their employer's share. It is likely, therefore, that they have been willing to pay more for employment related insurance than they might have paid for individual, non-group coverage.

In recent years, however, the employment related group insurance system in the United States has begun to unravel. The rapidly escalating cost of health care has made it increasingly difficult for employers to fund health insurance by holding down wage increases. Paying for health insurance coverage has been particularly difficult for small employers, who face higher premiums and who often employ lower wage employees. Employers have thus either dropped insurance or, much more often, attempted to pass on cost increases to employees through greater premium or benefit cost sharing. As employees have faced having to pay more out-of-pocket (and often taxable dollars) for health insurance, as well as being offered thinner health benefits with greater cost sharing, many have declined offered coverage. The effect has been a dramatic decline in private coverage in the United States and a concomitant increase in the uninsured (Kaiser Family Foundation 2006a).[6]

PUBLIC HEALTH CARE FINANCE

SOCIAL HEALTH INSURANCE

Most developed countries long ago came to understand the limits of private health insurance for covering populations and turned to public social health insurance or general-revenue funded health care to cover their populations. Social health insurance in Europe began in the late nineteenth century as sickness insurance (Jost 2003). Its primary task was income replacement for employees who were sick or injured, although it also covered the cost of their medical care. It grew up alongside other forms of income replacement insurance such as public pensions and workers' compensation. In part because of its focus on income replacement, this insurance was employment related, funded by employee contributions and often by employer contributions as well. It was usually administered by quasi-public, non-profit sickness funds that resembled earlier mutual aid funds and were often occupationally based. Sickness funds generally purchased services from independent private professionals and institutions. These purchasing arrangements frequently took on corporatist form, i.e., both providers and insurers were organized into corporatist institutions that bargained with each other (Altenstetter and Busse 2005; Busse and Riesberg 2004).

This form of public health insurance came to be known as social health insurance, in contrast to private health insurance or general revenue funded health coverage. It is difficult to define social health insurance precisely because it takes a different form in every country in which it is found. One of the best definitions is that of Norman and Busse: "social health insurance funding occurs when it is legally mandatory to obtain health insurance with a designated (statutory) third-party payer through contributions or premiums not related to risk that are kept separate from other legally mandated taxes or contributions" (2002).

Social health insurance originated in Germany under Bismarck in 1883 and is often referred to as Bismarck-model health insurance. Germany adopted social health insurance for industrial workers in part to stem growing worker support for socialism among this group (Busse and Riesberg 2004). Over time, social insurance spread to cover most of the German population (although the self-employed and civil servants are still in general not incorporated within the system, and higher-income employees can choose not to participate in it). This system also spread eventually to most of central Europe, Austria, Belgium, France, the Netherlands, and Switzerland, as well as Israel. Following the fall of communism, it returned to a number of Eastern European countries as well, including Hungary, the Czech Republic, Slovakia, Croatia, and Estonia (Preker et al. 2002). Public funding that bears many of the characteristics of social insurance is also found in Japan, Korea, and Taiwan. Part A of the US Medicare program also resembles social health insurance insofar as it is funded by payroll contributions and administered by private contractors that in some respects resemble social insurance funds. Finally, social insurance programs cover higher wage employees in many Latin American countries, although private insurance is also common, and lower income employees, agricultural workers, and those who work in the informal sector receive tax funded health care or none at all.

GENERAL REVENUE TAX FUNDED PUBLIC HEALTH INSURANCE

Although social health insurance spread rapidly in the first half of the twentieth century, it faced certain limitations. Because it was employment based and funded through payroll taxes, it did not cover the entire population. By the late 1930s, for example, the British national insurance scheme, founded in 1911, covered only 43 percent of the British population (Allsop 1995). The Germans solved this problem (in part) by paying premiums out of other social insurance funds, such as pension or unemployment compensation funds. Other social insurance countries, as discussed below, infused general revenue tax funds into their social insurance systems.

A number of European countries, however, following the lead of the United Kingdom, moved away from social insurance to general revenue tax funded systems. The British National Health Service was established in 1946 in response to a report of a commission headed by Lord Beveridge, and became one model for tax funded health care systems often identified as the Beveridge model. Tax funded systems spread throughout Europe through the later half of the twentieth century, but, as is true with social insurance countries, each country's system is unique. Tax funded systems now exist in Europe in Sweden, Denmark, Finland, Norway, the UK, Ireland, Greece, Italy, Spain, and Portugal. They are also found in Canada and Australia, where their form has been heavily influenced by federalism. Most public health insurance systems in the United States – Medicaid, Medicare Part B, the Veterans' Administration, and the Indian Health Service – are also general revenue tax funded. Finally, most developing countries have publicly funded hospitals and clinics that provide some health care to those who cannot afford private care.

MIXED FUNDING IN PUBLIC INSURANCE SYSTEMS

Over the twentieth century there was considerable movement of countries from one model to the other. Many of the countries that currently have tax funded programs, including the UK, Denmark, Italy, Norway, Portugal, and Spain, at one time had social insurance funded programs (Saltman and Dubois 2004). On the other hand, as noted above, a number of Eastern European nations have moved in the last decade from tax funded to social insurance models.

Many countries today use a mix of social insurance and tax funding. Social insurance systems almost inevitably receive some general revenue tax funding. It is difficult to stretch employment based funding to cover the entire population. Tax funding is necessary to assure adequate funding for lower income workers and persons not participating in the formal job market (such as the disabled). In Belgium, Israel, Luxembourg, and France, general tax funding plays a significant role in subsidizing the social insurance system (Busse et al. 2004). In some countries, moreover, tax funding covers particular services. In Austria and Switzerland, tax financing funds hospital care (ibid.). In Germany and France, capital investment costs for hospitals are covered by tax financing (by the state governments, or Länder, in Germany) (Henke and Schreyögg 2005). Only in Germany and the Netherlands (prior to the most recent reforms) have wage based contributions – a classic marker of social health insurance – funded more than 60 percent of health care costs. In Austria and Luxembourg, wage based contributions fund less than 50 percent of total health care expenditures, in Belgium less than 40 percent, and in Israel only 25 percent (Busse et al. 2004). Indeed, some countries often described as social health insurance systems (Israel, for example) rely so heavily on general revenue funding that they could be seen as tax financed health services with some social insurance funding, rather than vice versa.

Developed nations with tax funded systems, on the other hand, also often rely to some extent on wage based contributions. Wage based national insurance contributions still fund about one-eighth of the health expenditures in Britain, and indeed were increased by 1 percent in 2002 to enhance NHS funding (European Observatory on Health Care Systems 1999). Finland, Ireland, Italy, Portugal, Spain, and Sweden also fund their health services in part from wage-based contributions (Wagstaff and van Doorslaer 2000). In developing nations, as already noted, social insurance plans for higher income employees and civil servants often exist alongside tax funded systems that take care of most of the population.

Tax financed systems are, however, less likely than social insurance systems to draw on mixed sources of financing. Most tax financed systems rely exclusively on direct or indirect general revenue taxes for funding, often supplemented by private insurance but less often by wage based contributions (Evans 2002). Tax funded systems also are generally administered directly by the government, in contrast to the quasi-independent fund infrastructure characteristic of social insurance countries (even though "government administration" may mean local or regional rather than the national administration).

RELATIVE ADVANTAGES AND DISADVANTAGES OF SOCIAL HEALTH INSURANCE AND TAX FINANCED COVERAGE

One of the greatest advantages of tax funded systems is their broad revenue base. Payroll tax funded systems tax only wages. They do not tax returns on capital such as interest, dividends, and rents. Return on capital constitutes a large and growing portion of the income of developed nations, and in particular constitutes a significant share of the income of the wealthiest members of society (Mossialos and Dixon 2002; Stock et al. 2006). In general, because tax financed systems tax both income and the population more broadly (and because they do not cap income subject to taxation), there is some evidence that they are more progressive than social insurance systems (Wagstaff and van Doorslaer 2000).[7]

Tax funding also gives governments greater control over costs (Evans 2002). In tax funded systems, all revenues flow through the budget of the government (or in federal systems, through the budgets of the national and regional governments). The government can therefore decide how much it will spend in any one year, and that amount, plus any funds spent out-of-pocket or through private insurance, becomes the amount the nation spends on health care. In social insurance systems, particularly those with multiple, semi-autonomous social insurance funds, control over the health care budget is much more difficult to achieve. This is particularly true if funds are allowed to run deficits, spending more than they collect in premiums, as they did for years in France. Administrative costs also tend to be high in social insurance systems (Henke

and Schreyögg 2005). Finally, there is some evidence that the public generally is more accepting of increases in social insurance contributions dedicated
to health care than to across-the-board tax increases (Normand and Busse
2002; Mossialos and Dixon 2002). On average, social insurance countries spend
more of their GDP on health care than do general-revenue tax funded health
care systems, although the issue is complex and other factors (such as the
relative wealth of nations) may explain more variation in health care costs
than does the form of organization of health care finance (Evans 2002; Figueras
et al. 2004).

Social health insurance systems seem also to be more "consumer friendly."
Waiting lists for services, common in tax funded systems, are uncommon in
social insurance countries (Siciliani and Hurst 2003). Social insurance programs rarely limit consumer choice through gatekeeper systems (the
Netherlands has been a prominent exception). This rationing tool is more commonly employed in tax funded systems (Calnan et al. 2006; Busse et al. 2004).
Social insurance programs are more likely to offer free choice of provider.

There is limited evidence of any real differences, however, in access to
health care depending on the method of public health care finance. A recent
Commonwealth Fund survey found that Germans with health problems were
more likely to be able to get an appointment to see a general practitioner on
the same day as they needed help or the next day than were patients in Australia, Canada, the UK, or the US; were less likely to have to go to an emergency
department for a condition that could be seen by a regular doctor if available
than were patients in any of these countries (or New Zealand); and were more
likely to be able to see a specialist in less than a week and to have elective
surgery in less than a month than were patients in Australia, Canada, the UK,
the US, or New Zealand (Schoen et al. 2005).

Social health insurance offers other benefits as well. Social insurance programs have traditionally been operated by quasi-independent, self-governing,
social insurance funds, a tradition that continues in many social insurance
countries. The independence of these funds frees them to some extent from
political interference and permits greater program stability, including funding stability (Mossialos and Dixon 2002; Chinitz et al. 2004). The operation
of these funds is also, at least potentially, more transparent than is the operation of tax funded programs. It is not surprising that many of the countries in
Eastern Europe turned to social insurance with the end of communism.

EXPANDING FUNDING FOR PUBLIC HEALTH INSURANCE

Social insurance is a well-established tradition in the countries in which it
exists; indeed, it has been described as "a way of life" (Saltman 2004). But

social insurance systems are also under serious pressure. All health care systems, whether tax or social insurance funded, are threatened by cost increases. The average annual increase in real health spending per capita for OECD countries between 1993 and 2003 was 3.4 percent (Anderson et al. 2006). The relentless improvement of medical technology, the increased incidence of chronic diseases, the aging of the populations, and many other factors are continually driving these increases (Henke and Schreyögg 2005). In many countries, increases in national productivity have not kept pace with rising health care costs. Health care, therefore, is consuming an ever greater share of the gross domestic product.

In those social insurance countries where health care continues to be funded in part by employer contributions, continual premium increases are perceived as a major barrier to job growth (Stock et al. 2006). Although employer contributions are in theory borne ultimately by employees, in countries with high minimum wages and substantial employer obligations for funding other social insurance programs (such as pensions, workers compensation, or unemployment compensation), hiring additional workers becomes very costly. As capital has become increasingly mobile in a global market, it becomes increasingly difficult to attract new jobs to countries with high labour costs.

Countries that rely on tax funded health care, on the other hand, also face increasing difficulties in raising taxes to cover health care costs, as well as their many other priorities. This is a particular problem in Europe, where the European growth and stability pact that grounds the common currency limits deficit funding (Henke and Schreyögg 2005). Where health care is funded through a federal system as in Canada or the United States Medicaid program, increased health care costs have also led to conflict between federal and regional or local governments. Both tax financed and social insurance programs, therefore, are seeking alternative approaches to funding health care.

Social insurance programs have increasingly turned to general revenue tax funding (Busse et al. 2004). Few tax funded programs have increased payroll tax funding, but examples can be found, such as the increase of national insurance contributions in the UK in 2002. Both social insurance and tax financed countries have also relied more and more on private insurance and out-of-pocket expenditures. Australia, for example, launched a major initiative to expand private insurance coverage in the late 1990s, and some look to expansion of private insurance to take the pressure off Canada's health care system. Some countries, including Germany and the Netherlands and apparently Canada, are also seeking new sources of public revenue for expanding public insurance funding – payroll taxes in general revenue funded countries, general revenue funding in social insurance countries.

The Netherlands, in health care reforms that went into effect in 2006, moved from a system that relied on social insurance for lower and middle income households and private insurance for higher income households to a unitary system that imposes a requirement on all persons to purchase insurance from private "care insurers." The new system is funded in part by income related contributions (in effect, payroll taxes) and in part by premiums payable by the insured, which vary somewhat from insurer to insurer but are not based on income (Ministerie van Volksgezondheid and Welzijn 2005; Greß et al. 2007). Lower income households and children receive supplemental payments from the state to assist in covering the premiums, but no one is exempt from paying something for coverage. To some extent, this resembles the Swiss system in place since 1996, which requires private purchase of community rated insurance, with public assistance for those who cannot afford it (European Observatory on Health Care Systems 2000). A lump sum premium model for health care is also being considered in Germany. The Dutch system introduces a form of managed competition: insurance funds are expected to compete with each other for customers by operating more efficiently (although they must all cover the same services, and a risk-equalization system is supposed to discourage competition based on risk selection). The system also reaches a new revenue source for funding health care.

There is much to be said for a system that relies on a variety of sources of public funding. Payment for a significant portion of health care costs through hypothecated taxes (which could be payroll taxes, but could also be consumption taxes or even earmarked supplemental income taxes) might be more acceptable to the public than a simple increase in general taxes. Part of health care expenditures, however, can also be buried in general revenue accounts, where they would be less visible. If payroll taxes are relied on, supplemental general revenue funding may alleviate pressure on job creation. Supplemental funding from private insurance is also possible, although it usually raises problems of equity and often draws resources away from the public system (Tuohy et al. 2004).

A PRINCIPLED APPROACH TO ALLOCATING HEALTH CARE FUNDING SOURCES

If countries are increasingly drawing on mixed sources for funding health care, are there any principles on the basis of which health care funding sources can be allocated? In fact, in most countries with mixed funding, funds from both sources flow into a common pool and are used to fund all covered services without distinction. In a few social insurance countries, as noted above, hospitals are separately funded by tax funding, in whole or in part. This anomaly is probably attributable to a tradition of public hospitals or a history of funding hospitals at the local level. Separate funding of services from separate sources of funding, however, is very uncommon, except, of course, where non-covered products and services are privately funded.

The most prominent example of intentionally segregating services by source of funding is the Dutch system. In the Netherlands, health care products and services are divided into three compartments (den Exter et al. 2004). As elsewhere, a variety of health care products and services including cosmetic and dental surgery are not covered by the public system and must be paid for out-of-pocket or by private insurance. Most acute care services were traditionally covered by either social or private insurance, but under the new system described above, are covered by mandatory social insurance provided by private insurers, partially financed by payroll taxes and partially funded through premiums (with tax funded assistance for lower income insureds). The most interesting aspect of the Dutch system, however, is the third compartment of services, covered under the Exceptional Medical Expense Act (AWBZ), which are funded by income related contributions and government funds. This segment basically covers long-term care (including long-term hospital care), although covered services are defined in functional terms rather than as specific covered services. These services are separated out because they are the most expensive and the least likely to be affordable from private funds or to be covered by private insurance. These are services for which the social sharing of risk is most important.

The Dutch system, then, provides one principle for separating out particular services for a particular form of funding: extraordinarily expensive services that are least affordable and that are most often needed by those least capable of paying should be funded from sources that provide the widest possible risk spreading – which would generally mean general revenue tax funding. Japan's recently created long-term care insurance program relies in part on general revenue funding, and, although Germany's long-term care insurance program is a social insurance program, it covers the entire population and all must contribute (Creighton, Campbell and Ikegami 2000).

Public funding for extraordinarily expensive services is also the principle advocated by a number of commentators in the United States, who are calling for public reinsurance for high cost cases. Katherine Swartz's recent book, *Reinsuring Health: Why More Middle-Class People Are Uninsured and What Government Can Do* (2006), argues persuasively for this approach. Public funding of reinsurance was also proposed by John Kerry in the 2004 US presidential election campaign. Finally, public funding of high cost care is also consistent with tax financing of hospital care in Austria and Switzerland, though it probably is not the main explanatory factor of those countries' approach.

Another principle represented by the Dutch approach but found in many other systems is the use of private funding (either insurance or out-of-pocket) to fund non-essential products or services such as cosmetic surgery or products or procedures that are scientifically regarded as ineffective. The problem, of course, is defining medically necessary or essential services. The current Canadian approach illustrates the considerable difficulties of making that determination (Flood et al. 2006).

A third principle is that traditional population based public health services should be tax financed. It is difficult to pay for population based services on the individual, fee-for-service basis that characterizes traditional social insurance payment (McKee et al. 2004). Environmental public health measures – providing safe water and proper waste treatment, for example, obviously cannot be paid for by social insurance funds. Arguably, however, services like immunizations that have substantial external benefits should also be tax financed. Finally, collection of most public health data is probably a job ill-suited to social insurance funds and is better done by a tax-financed public agency.

A fourth principle would support paying the most politically powerful providers – those best able to protect themselves in the rough and tumble of public budget politics – out of public funds. To return to another point often made by Robert Evans, every health care cost is someone's income or profit, or in the words of Uwe Reinhardt, paying for health care often amounts to feeding the horses to feed the birds (Reinhardt 1998). In many countries, certainly the United States, Canada, England, and Germany, doctors are the most politically powerful providers. Pharmaceutical companies are often powerful as well. Perhaps their services should be tax funded, as these providers are best able to assure that their services will receive priority in public budgeting processes. More vulnerable services could be funded through hypothecated taxes. Of course, politically powerful providers may well exercise their political power to assure that they are paid for by social insurers rather than by the government and thus protect themselves from budget priority battles and direct government oversight.

A fifth principle, again widely observed, is to pay for frequently purchased, low cost items out of pocket. This saves insurers or the government the cost of processing numerous small bills. One of the most dramatic effects of drug copayments is that they completely exclude from coverage drugs whose costs are below the copayment amount, and thus save both the cost of these drugs and also the cost of processing payments for them. Similarly, over-the-counter drugs and eyeglasses are often not publicly funded. On the other hand, it is important that provision be made for low income individuals or the chronically ill, for whom even small copayments cause financial hardship.

While these principles might be helpful to nations considering diversification of funding sources for determining how best to fund different services, it may well be that devising different funding mechanisms for different services is in the end not advisable. The silo approach to health care funding has been roundly condemned in countries where it exists as contributing to poor coordination of health care services. In Germany, for example, the strict separation between the ambulatory and in-patient sector no doubt contributes to the fact that Germany has high levels of duplication of medical tests and examinations and poor hospital discharge planning (Schoen et al. 2005). Throughout the world there are calls for better coordinated management of chronic diseases. This would seem to argue against having different approaches to funding for different services.

LESSONS FOR CANADA

One of the goals of this book is to explore whether social insurance funding might be useful to expanding publicly funded health care services in Canada, particularly for pharmaceutical and long-term care. It is difficult for me to think of a principle other than political expediency for Canada to fund prescription drugs or long-term care through a social insurance program. If it makes sense for Canada to expand coverage in these areas, however, and it is not politically possible to increase general revenue tax funding, perhaps payroll tax funding would be advisable. Indeed, payroll tax funding is already in place in Quebec for funding pharmaceuticals. Payroll tax funding, however, does not fully capture the essence of traditional social insurance. It is hard to believe that Canada should, or even could, construct the full institutional infrastructure of traditional social insurance programs – i.e., multiple social insurance funds and perhaps corporatist organizations for providers – simply to fund pharmaceutical and long-term care services. Canada has, of course, a private health insurance system in place, and private insurers could potentially be transformed into social insurers, as has in a sense happened in Switzerland, but this would be a very ambitious agenda.

The experience of the recently created United States Medicare drug program might prove instructive for Canada (Kaiser Family Foundation 2006b). The US program is voluntary, with approximately one-quarter funded by premiums and three-quarters from general revenue funds. General revenue funds also provide reinsurance for catastrophic cases. This mixed approach to funding has resulted in a bizarre benefit structure, with a low deductible and initial co-insurance to attract voluntary enrolment of relatively healthy beneficiaries, catastrophic coverage to protect really high cost beneficiaries from financial disaster or lack of medication, and a huge gap in coverage, leaving totally without protection expenses for drugs ranging in cost from $US2,250 to $US5,100. Premiums are subsidized for low income beneficiaries, but many subsidies are only available on application, and many eligible beneficiaries have not applied. The program is administered by competing prescription drug and managed care plans, each of which has its own formularies and negotiates its own prices with drug companies. The government gave up the economic power it would have had as a monopsonistic purchaser in hopes that independent plans would be able to leverage the bargaining power they have from being able to omit drugs from their formularies, something the government itself would have a difficult time doing. It is too early to tell whether the program will succeed or not. It has significantly expanded drug coverage for Medicare beneficiaries, and premiums have been below predicted levels for the first two years of the program. On the other hand, the program has proved to be incredibly complicated, many of those eligible for low income subsidies have not received them, and significant gaps in coverage have proved unpopular. In sum, mixed funding may have expanded program revenues but only at a considerable cost in complexity.

In virtually all developed countries, health care finance continues to be a work in progress. Traditional approaches are increasingly proving inadequate to the job. Countries are looking for additional revenue sources to enhance traditional means of funding health care. In most instances, new sources of revenue have simply been used to supplement traditional sources, often as a way to expand access for those who would otherwise face limits in their access to health care. If countries are to continue to pursue new approaches, however, it is important to consider principled approaches to deciding how different health care services should be funded. The principles described above may prove useful, both to Canada and to other nations, in considering how best to pursue mixed funding for health care services.

NOTES

[1] The top 5 percent of insured Americans paid on average $US17,871 for health care in 1996. This figure would be much higher today.

[2] In many countries, private insurance covers the cost of public insurance cost sharing or of services not covered by public insurance. In some countries, private insurance allows its members to jump the queue and obtain services more quickly than is possible for those who totally rely on public insurance. In a few countries, the wealthy are allowed to opt out of the public insurance system and to purchase private insurance. For discussion of the role of private insurance in various health care systems, see Maynard and Dixon (2002); Mossialos and Thompson (2002); Jost (2001); Colombo and Tapay (2004).

[3] Almost half of surveyed American adults with health problems found it difficult or impossible to find coverage in the individual non-group insurance market.

[4] The income of families in the 90th percentile was about four times the income of families in the 10th percentile in Canada in the late 1990s, compared to a ratio of 5.4

in the United States, although income inequality in Canada is growing, as it is in the United States (Picot and Myles 2005).

[5] The Netherlands and Switzerland rely on private health insurance to cover their entire population, but it is regulated so heavily that it is effectively social health insurance in function, even if it is private insurance in form. See the discussion of these systems below.

[6] In 2000, 69 percent of firms offered health benefits to at least some of their employees. In 2006, 61 percent did. In 2000, 63 percent of workers had health coverage through their employer. In 2006, 59 percent did (Kaiser Family Foundation 2006).

[7] Progressivity depends on a number of factors other than source of revenues, however, as is discussed further in Sherry Glied's chapter in this volume.

REFERENCES

Allsop, J. 1995. *Health Policy and the NHS: Towards 2000,* 2nd ed. London: Longman.

Altenstetter, C., and R. Busse. 2005. "Health Care Reform in Germany: Patchwork Change within Established Governance Structures." *Journal of Health Politics, Policy and Law* 30: 121.

Anderson, G.F., B.K. Frogner, R.A. Johns, and U.E. Reinhardt. 2006. "Health Care Spending and Use of Information Technology in OECD Countries," *Health Affairs* 25: 819.

Berk, M., and A. Monheit. 2001. "The Concentration of Health Care Expenditures Revisited." *Health Affairs* 20: 9.

Busse, R., and A. Riesberg. 2004. *Health Care Systems in Transition: Germany.* Copenhagen: European Observatory on Health Care Systems.

Busse, R., R.B. Saltman, and H.F.W. Dubois. 2004. "Organization and Financing of Social Health Insurance Systems: Current Status and Recent Policy Developments." In *Social Health Insurance Systems in Western Europe,* edited by R.B. Saltman, R. Busse, and J. Figueras, 3. Maidenhead: Open University Press.

Calnan, M., J. Hutten, and H. Tiljak. 2006. "The Challenge of Coordination: The Role of Primary Care Professionals in Promoting Integration across the Interface." In *Primary Care in the Driver Seat,* edited by R. Saltman, A. Rico, and W. Boerma, 85. Buckingham: Open University Press.

Campbell, J.C., and N. Ikegami. 2000. "Long-Term Care Insurance Comes to Japan" *Health Affairs* 19 (3): 31.

Cannon, M.F., and M.D. Tanner. 2005. *Healthy Competition: What's Holding Back Health Care and How to Free It.* Washington: Cato Institute.

Chinitz, D., M. Wismar, and C. Le Pen. 2004. "Governance and (Self-) Regulation in Social Health Insurance Systems." In *Social Health Insurance Systems in Western*

Europe, edited by R.B. Saltman, R. Busse, and J. Figueras, 155. Maidenhead: Open University Press.

Cogan, J.F., R. Hubbard, and D. Kessler. 2005. *Healthy, Wealthy, and Wise: Five Steps to a Better Health Care System*. Jackson, TN: American Enterprise Institute.

Collins, S., J.L. Kriss, K. Davis, M.M. Doty, and A.L. Holmgren. 2006. *Squeezed: Why Rising Exposure to Health Care Costs Threatens the Health and Well Being of America's Families*. New York: Commonwealth Fund.

Colombo, F., and N. Tapay. 2004. *Private Health Insurance in OECD Countries: The Benefits and Costs for Individuals and Health Care Systems*. Paris: OECD.

den Exter, A., H. Hermans, and M. Dosljak. 2004. *Health Care Systems in Transition: Netherlands*. Copenhagen: European Observatory on Health Systems and Policies.

Department of Health and Human Services. 2006. *The 2006 DHHS Federal Poverty Guidelines*. http://aspe.hhs.gov/poverty/06poverty.shtml.

Domhoff, G. 2006. *Wealth, Income and Power*. http://sociology.ucsc.edu/whorulesamerica/power/wealth.html.

European Observatory on Health Care Systems. 1999. *Health Care Systems in Transition: United Kingdom*. Copenhagen: European Observatory on Health Care Systems.

– 2000. *Health Care Systems in Transition: Switzerland*. Copenhagen: European Observatory on Health Care Systems.

Evans, R. 2002. "Financing Health Care: Taxation and the Alternatives." In *Funding Health Care: Options for Europe*, edited by E. Mossialos, A. Dixon, J. Figueras, et al. Buckingham: Open University Press.

– 2004. "Financing Health Care: Options, Consequences, and Objectives." In *The Fiscal Sustainability of Health Care in Canada (The Romanow Papers, Vol. 1)*, edited by. G. Marchildon, T. McIntosh, and P.-G. Forest. Toronto: University of Toronto Press.

Figueras, J., R.B. Saltman, R. Busse, and H.F.W. Dubois 2004. "Patterns and Performance in Social Health Insurance Systems." In *Social Health Insurance Systems in Western Europe*, edited by. R.B. Saltman, R. Busse, and J. Figueras. Maidenhead: Open University Press.

Flood, C., C. Tuohy, and M. Stabile. 2006. *What is In and Out of Medicare? Who Decides?* In *Just Medicare: What's In, What's Out, How We Decide*, edited by C. Flood. Toronto: University of Toronto Press.

Glied, S. 2005. "The Employer-Based Health Insurance System: Mistake or Cornerstone?" In *Policy Challenges in Modern Health Care*, edited by. D. Mechanic, L. Rogut, and D. Colby. New Brunswick, NJ: Rutgers University Press.

Goodman, J., and G. Musgrave. 1992. *Patient Power: Solving America's Health Care Crisis*. Washington: Cato Institute.

Goodman. J., G. Musgrave, and D. Herrick. 2004. *Lives at Risk: Single Payer National Health Insurance around the World*. Lanham, MD: Rowman & Littlefield.

Government Accountability Office. 2006. *Consumer Directed Health Plans: Early Experience with Health Savings Accounts and Eligible Health Plans*. Washington: GAO.

Greß, S., M. Manouguian, and J. Wasem. 2007. *Health Reform in the Netherlands*. CESifo DICE Report 1/2007.

Hanvoravongchai, P. 2002. *Medical Savings Accounts: Lessons Learned from Limited International Experience*. Geneva: World Health Organization.

Healy, J., E. Sharman, and B. Lokuge. 2006. *Health Care Systems in Transition: Australia*. Copenhagen: European Observatory on Health Care Systems.

Henke, K., and J. Schreyögg. 2005. *Towards Sustainable Health Care Systems*. 2nd ed. Geneva: International Social Security Association.

Jost, T. 2001. "Private or Public Approaches to Insuring the Uninsured: Lessons from International Experience with Private Insurance." *New York University Law Review* 76: 419.

– 2003. *Disentitlement: The Threats Facing Our Public Health Care Programs and a Rights-Based Response*. Oxford: Oxford University Press.

Kaiser Family Foundation. 2006a. *Employer Health Benefits, Summary of Findings*. Washington: Kaiser Family Foundation (Health Research and Educational Trust).

– 2006b. *The Medicare Prescription Drug Program Fact Sheet*. http://www.kff.org/medicare/upload/7044-04.pdf.

Lewis, M. 2002. "Informal Health Payments in Central and Eastern Europe and the Former Soviet Union: Issues, Trends and Policy Implications." In *Funding Health Care: Options for Europe*, edited by E. Mossialos, A. Dixon, J. Figueras, et al. Buckingham: Open University Press, at 184.

Marmot, M. 2002. "The Influence of Income on Health: Views of an Epidemiologist." *Health Affairs* 21: 31.

Maynard, A., and A. Dixon. 2002. "Private Health Insurance and Medical Savings Accounts: Theory and Experience." In *Funding Health Care: Options for Europe*, edited by E. Mossialos, E. Mossialos, A. Dixon, J. Figueras, et al., 109. Buckingham: Open University Press.

McKee, M., D.M.J. Delnoij, and H. Brand. 2004. "Prevention and Public Health in Social Insurance." In *Social Health Insurance Systems in Western Europe*, edited by R.B. Saltman, R. Busse, and J. Figueras. Maidenhead: Open University Press.

Ministerie van Volksgezondheid, Welzijn en Sport. 2005. *Health Insurance in the Netherlands: The New Health Insurance System from 2006*. The Hague: Ministerie van Volksgezondheid, Welzijn en Sport.

Mossialos, E., and A. Dixon. 2002. "Funding Health Care: An Introduction." In *Funding Health Care: Options for Europe*, edited by E. Mossialos, A. Dixon, J. Figueras, et al., 1. Buckingham: Open University Press.

Mossialos, E., and S.M. Thompson. 2002. "Voluntary Health Insurance in the European Union." In *Funding Health Care: Options for Europe*, edited by E. Mossialos, A. Dixon, J. Figueras, et al., 128. Buckingham: Open University Press.

Normand, C., and R. Busse. 2002. "Social Health Insurance Financing." In *Funding Health Care: Options for Europe*, edited by A. Dixon, J. Figueras, et al. Buckingham: Open University Press.

Picot, G., and J. Myles. 2005. *Income Inequality and Low Income in Canada: An International Perspective*. Ottawa: Statistics Canada.

Preker, A., M. Jakab, and M. Schneider. 2002. "Health Financing Reforms in Central and Eastern Europe and the Former Soviet Union." In *Funding Health Care: Options for Europe*, edited by E. Mossialos, A. Dixon, J. Figueras, et al., 128. Buckingham: Open University Press.

Reinhardt, U. 1998. "Abstracting from Distributional Effects: This Policy Is Efficient." In *Health, Health Care, and Health Economics: Perspectives on Distribution*, edited by M.L. Barer, T.E. Getzen, and G.L. Stoddert. New York: John Wiley & Sons.

Robinson, R. 2002. "User Charges in Health Care." In *Funding Health Care: Options for Europe*, edited by E. Mossialos, A. Dixon, J. Figueras, et al., 161. Buckingham: Open University Press.

Roos, N., E. Shapiro, and R. Tate. 1989. "Does a Small Minority of Elderly Account for a Majority of Health Care Expenditures: A Sixteen Year Perspective." *Milbank Quarterly* 67: 347.

Rubin, R.J. and D.N. Mendelson. 1995. "A Framework for Cost Sharing Policy Analysis." In *Sharing the Costs of Health: A Multi-Country Perspective*, edited by N. Mattison. Basel, Switzerland: Pharmaceutical Partners for Better Healthcare.

Saltman, R. 2004. "Social Health Insurance in Perspective: The Challenge of Sustaining Stability." In *Social Health Insurance Systems in Western Europe*, edited by R.B. Saltman, R. Busse, and J. Figueras, 3. Maidenhead: Open University Press.

Saltman, R., and H.F.W. Dubois. 2004. "The Historical and Social Base of Social Health Insurance Systems." In *Social Health Insurance Systems in Western Europe*, edited by R.B. Saltman, R. Busse, and J. Figueras. Maidenhead: Open University Press.

Sandier, S., D. Polton, and V. Paris 2004. *Health Care Systems in Transition: France*. Copenhagen: European Observatory on Health Care Systems.

Schoen, C R., P. Osborn, T. Huynh, M. Doty, J. Peugh, and K. Zapert. 2005. "Taking the Pulse of Health Care Systems: Experiences of Patients with Health Problems in Six Countries," *Health Affairs*, Web Exclusive, W5-509, W519.

Seifert, R.W., and M. Rukavina. 2006. "Bankruptcy Is the Tip of a Medical-Debt Iceberg." *Health Affairs*, Web Exclusive.

Siciliani, L., and J. Hurst. 2003. *Explaining Waiting Times Variations for Elective Surgery across OECD Countries*. Paris: Organization for Economic Cooperation and Development.

Stock, S., M. Redaelli, and K.W. Lauterbach. 2006. "The Influence of the Labor Market on German Health Care Reforms." *Health Affairs* 25: 1143.

Swartz, K. 2006. *Reinsuring Health: Why More Middle-Class People Are Uninsured and What Government Can Do*. New York: Russell Sage Foundation 2006.

Tuohy, C., C.M. Flood, and M. Stabile. 2004. "How Does Private Finance Affect Public Health Care Systems? Marshaling the Evidence from OECD Nations." *Journal of Health Politics, Policy and Law* 29: 359.

United States Census. 2006. *Annual Demographic Survey, March Supplement, Table POV01*. http://pubdb3.census.gov/macro/032006/pov/new01_300_01.htm.

United States Census Bureau. *Historical Income Tables, Families, Table H-3*. http://www.census.gov/hhes/www/income/histinc/h03ar.html.

Wagstaff, A., and E. van Doorslaer. 2000. "Equity in Health Care Finance and Delivery." In *Handbook of Health Economics*. Vol. 1B, edited by A.J. Culyer and J.P. Newhouse, 1804. Amsterdam: Elsevier.

Wiley, M. 2005. "The Irish Health System: Developments in Strategy, Structure, Funding and Delivery Since 1980." *Health Economics* 14: S169, S170.

Woolhandler, S., and D.U. Himmelstein. 2002. "Paying for National Health Insurance – and Not Getting It." *Health Affairs* 21: 88.

Chapter 8

The Comparative Dimension of Policy Analysis: Rules of the Game?

Ted Marmor

This essay presumes the importance of the substantive questions posed by the framers of this book: namely, the fiscal pressures on Canadian governmental jurisdictions by past and expected increases in health care costs. First, however, we address one important way to understand and to evaluate policy options in this area of health care finance: the interpretation of cross-national policy studies.

COMPARATIVE STUDIES: ROLES AND RULES OF ENGAGEMENT

Comparative policy commentary has mushroomed in recent decades, in part because technological innovations have speeded up the transfer of information about what is happening abroad. Indeed, few can escape the "bombardment of information about what is happening in other countries" (Klein 1995). The pressing question is whether this augmented informational dispersion is a help or a hindrance to understanding what governments do, why they do it, and with what effects. So, before turning to this chapter's policy question – what can the experiences of other OECD nations with social insurance financing of medical care teach Canadian policy-makers? – let me review what might be called the rules of this cross-national policy analytic game.

There are at least three obvious ways in which policy analysis might be improved by cross-national understanding. One is simply to define more clearly what is on the policy agenda by reference to quite similar or quite different formulations elsewhere. The more similar the problems or policy responses, the more likely one can portray the nuanced formulations of any particular country. The more dissimilar, the more striking the contrast with what one takes for granted in one's own policy setting. This is the gift of perspective, which may or may not bring with it explanatory insight or lesson drawing. This mode is obviously relevant to learning about social insurance financing and trying to gain perspective from those experiences. And the other chapters of this book provide a good deal of detail in this regard, for example, about the Netherlands, Germany, Israel, the United Kingdom, and the United States.

A second approach is to use cross-national inquiry to check on the adequacy of nation-specific accounts. Let's call that a defence against explanatory provincialism. What precedes policy-making in country A includes many things – from legacies of past policy to institutional and temporal features that "seem" decisive. How is one to know how decisive as opposed to simply present? One answer is to look for similar outcomes elsewhere where some of those factors are missing or configured differently. Another is to look for a similar configuration of precedents without a comparable outcome. Here, as we shall see, there are few instances of OECD countries going from predominantly general tax financing to a mixed system, with social insurance sources of revenue added relatively late in the development of public health insurance.

A third and still different approach is to treat cross-national experience as quasi-experiments. Here one hopes to draw lessons about why some policies seem promising and doable, promising and impossible, or doable but not promising. This is obviously at work in the review of experience with medical care costs across the OECD in this book.

Of interest here, however, is not in the broad topic of the promise and perils of cross-national policy studies (Klein, 1991; Marmor, Okma, and Freeman, 2005). Rather, the aim is to offer some illustrations of how comparative understanding can advance the art and craft of policy analysis. This chapter presently turns to the specifics of social insurance financing and comparative lessons for Canada. First, however, the discussion depends on some examples of each of the above comparative approaches, positive or negative.

A useful starting point is to take a misleading cross-national generalization that, upon reflection, helps to clarify differences in how policy problems are in fact posed. A 1995 article on European health reform claimed that "countries everywhere are reforming their health systems." It went on to assert that "what is remarkable about this global movement is that both the diagnosis of the problems and the prescription for them are virtually the same in all health care systems" (Hunter 1995). These globalist claims, it turns out, were mistaken (Jacobs 1998; Marmor 1999). But the process of specifying exactly what counts as health care problems – whether of cost control, poor quality, or fragmented organization of services – turned out to be helpful. The comparative approach first refuted the misleading generalization; it then helped enrich what one imagines is going on when analysts portray national "problems." So, for instance, a British health policy researcher coming to investigate Oregon's experiment in rationing in the decade 1990–2000 would have soon discovered that it was neither restrictive in practice nor a major cost control remedy (Jacobs, Marmor, and Oberlander 1999).

Offering new perspectives on problems and making factual adjustments in national portraits are not to be treated as trivial tasks. They are what apprentice crafters of policy should spend a good deal of time perfecting. That is because all too many comparative studies are caricatures rather than characterizations of policies in action. A striking illustration of that problem is the 2000 World Health Organization (WHO) report on how one might rank health systems across the globe. Not only was the ambition grandiose, but its execution would be best regarded as ridiculous (Williams 2001). The WHO posed good questions about how health systems work: are they fair, responsive, efficient, and so on. But those questions were answered without the faintest attention to the difficulties of describing responsiveness or fairness or efficiency in some universalistic manner. What's more, WHO used as partial evidence the distant opinions of Geneva-based medical personnel to "verify" what takes place in sites as varied as Australia, Oban, or Canada. With comparativists like that, one can easily understand why some funders of research regard comparative policy studies as excuses for boondoggles. But clear mistakes are insufficient justifications for giving up the enterprise.[1]

The most commonly cited advantage of comparative studies, however, is as an antidote to explanatory provincialism. Once again, a health policy example provides a good illustration of how and how not to proceed. There are those in North America who regard universal health insurance as incompatible with American values. They rest their case in part on the belief that Canada has enacted health insurance and the US has not because the two countries' values are sharply different. In short, these comparativists attribute a different outcome to a different political culture in the US. In fact, the measured values of Canada and the United States, while not identical, are quite similar. Indeed, Canada's value distribution is closer to that of the United States than any other modern, rich democracy. As with siblings, differences are there. Actually, the value similarities between British Columbia and Washington State are greater than those between either of those jurisdictions and, say, New Brunswick or New Hampshire on the east coast (Lipset 1990; Inglehart, Nevitte, and Basanez 1996). Similar values are compatible with different outcomes, which in turn draw one's attention to other institutional and strategic factors that distinguish the Canadian from the American experience with financing health care (Maioni 1998; White 1995). One can imagine multiplying examples of such cautionary lessons, but the important point is simply that the lessons are unavailable from national histories alone.

The third category of work is directly relevant to our inquiry. It is worth noting that drawing lessons from the policy experience of other nations is what supports a good deal of the comparative analysis available. The international organizations have this as part of their rationale. WHO, as noted, is firmly in the business of selling "best practices." The OECD regularly produces extensive, hard-to-gather statistical portraits of programs as diverse as disability and pensions, trade flows and the movement of professionals, educational levels and health expenditures. No one can avoid using these efforts, if only because the task of discovering "the facts" in a number of countries is daunting. But the portraiture that emerges requires its own craft review. Does what Germany spends on spas count as health expenditures under public regulation, or should it, as with the United States, be categorized differently? The same words do not mean the same things. And different words may denote similar phenomena. For now it is enough to note that learning about the experience of other nations is a precondition for learning from them. A number of comparative studies fail on the first count and thus necessarily on the second. On the other hand, if one were to look for exemplary instances of cross-national learning, one would turn quite quickly to Japan, Taiwan, and Korea. All have sent first-rate civil servants abroad to find promising models, have worried about the barriers to transplantation, and when using these apparent models, have worked carefully on issues of adaptation, transformation, and implementation.

THE CASE FOR SOCIAL INSURANCE FINANCING: COMPARATIVE PERSPECTIVES

With this background, we turn directly to the comparative questions raised about the experience of other industrial democracies with social insurance financing of medical care and the implications of those findings for Canada. The conference from which this volume emerged proceeded as if the questions were straightforward. So, for example, there were discussions of Germany's long experience with social health insurance, though mention was given to recent reform discussions of proposed deviations from that established financing norm. Likewise, the discussion of the Netherlands noted both the history of social health insurance and its recent (2006) abandonment in favour of mandated, subsidized, and highly regulated private health insurance. In addition, the discussion of Korean experience with its version of social health insurance emphasized both the East Asian importation of German models and the different role that social health insurance plays when small business constitutes a large part of the labour force. Finally, the data presented included quantitative reviews of the cost experiences of OECD nations, arrayed by degree of social insurance versus general tax financing of medical care. That exercise provided few grounds for grand generalizations about cost control and the sources of finance.[2]

Comparative perspectives here are genuinely revealing, but not necessarily as a straightforward response to the Canadian-centric policy problem. First, it is obvious – and well known to the Canadian scholars who set the questions – that OECD nations are everywhere concerned about the cost pressures of modern medical care publicly financed directly or indirectly. Whatever the level of total or public expenditure, the governments of the OECD express dismay at medical care's persistent inflationary pattern. The share of national income devoted to medical care varies between 7 or 8 percent at the low end (Australia, New Zealand) to 11 to 15 percent at the high end (Switzerland, the United States).

What is one to make of that, given that everywhere the language of a cost crisis is commonplace? The short answer is that national communities experience local phenomena, not the results of comparative research. So, if medical care costs are rising, from whatever starting point, the opportunity cost of paying for such increases is felt locally: higher taxes, lower expenditures of other claims on public finance, or both.

The implication of this is important. Canada is really no different in its concerns about either the level of medical expenditures or about the opportunity costs of those expenditures. In this respect, there is comfort in worrying about a real issue of widespread significance. But the cross-national finding generates an equally important caution: namely, that the level of expenditure is less significant than the persistent rate of increase over time for producing political pressure. `

The second, even more important implication of the comparative portraiture is that there are very few instances of other OECD democracies addressing this book's formulation of Canada's problem. In other words, few if any nations with general tax financing of medical care have shifted – or are contemplating shifting – to social insurance financing in part or in whole. Recent changes in the UK in national insurance contributions to the NHS might be considered a counter-example, but that took place in the context of rapid increases in NHS expenditures amidst vibrant economic growth and was not justified as a remedy for crowding out other social expenditures. Moreover, the expansion of the employer-employee "national insurance" tax in the UK did not change eligibility, nor did it operate as a separate administration of funding for the NHS.[3] In short, the formulation of Canada's problem is special, if not unique – in the notion, for example, that Canada's education outlays have suffered in the competition with medical care and might be moderated if social insurance financing were expanded.

Viewed this way, there is no close analogue to this formulation of Canada's issue. That does not mean that comparative evidence has no bearing. Rather, it suggests that what bearing the experiences others have had must be reconceptualized before those experiences inform the issue formulated as Canada's problem. What could those re-conceptualizations reasonably be?

One of them might be to emphasize the very generality of cost control on the agendas of modern democracies. This generalization, as noted, is consistent with widely divergent experience with health expenditures, as the following figures demonstrate:

FIGURES 1, 2, AND 3
Perspectives on OECD health expenditures, 1970–90*

FIGURE 1
Total health care expenditure (as a percentage of GDP) and public share of total health care financing in 1970

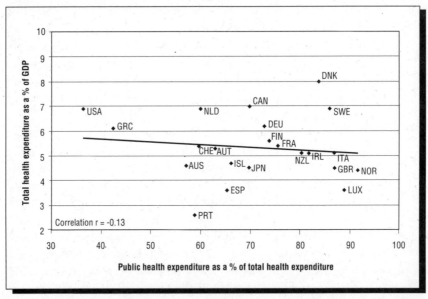

Notes: Belgium: data missing; Denmark: data for 1969 (THE in % of GDP) and 1971 (PHE in % of THE); Netherlands: data for 1972; Switzerland: data from OECD 2002.
Source: OECD 2002; OECD 2004.

---

* Abbreviations are as follows: AUS: Australia; AUT: Austria; BEL: Belgium; CAN: Canada; DNK: Denmark; FIN: Finland; FRA: France; DEU: Germany; GRC: Greece; ISL: Iceland; IRL: Ireland; ITA: Italy; JPN: Japan; LUX: Luxembourg; NDL: Netherlands; NZL: New Zealand; NOR: Norway; PRT: Portugal; ESP: Spain; SWE: Sweden; CHE: Switzerland; GBR: United Kingdom; USA: United States.

FIGURE 2

Total health care expenditure (as a percentage of GDP) and public share of total health care financing in 2000

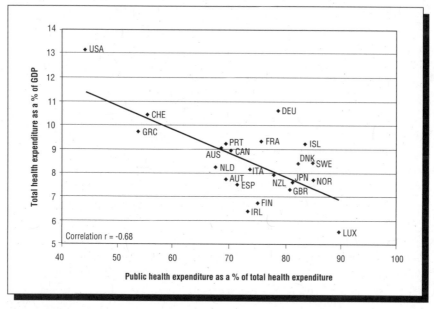

Notes: Belgium: data missing; Netherlands: data for 1997 (PHE in % of THE).
Source: OECD 2004.

FIGURE 3

Public health care financing as a percentage of total health care financing in 1970 and change of total health expenditure as a percentage of GDP from 1970 to 2000

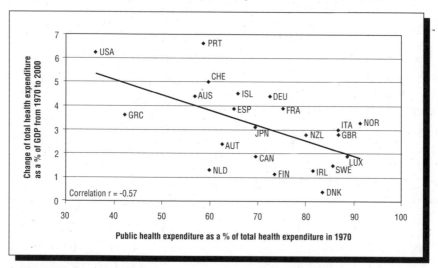

Source: OECD 2004, own calculation.

Given these cross-national facts, the Canadian search for alternative sources of finance is no different from the variety of policy options – for finance, organization, or delivery of care – that marks other policies. The search for a portfolio of responses to the pressures of medical inflation, in other words, is the common, cross-national pattern. In this respect, Canadian analysts can think of any particular policy option – social insurance financing here – as only one of many diverse responses to the persistent pressures of modern medical care's innovations, demands, and costs.

Turning more directly to the question of whether social insurance financing has some advantages other than diversification,[4] let us review the effects attributed to particular sources of financing. The obvious question seems to be whether social insurance financing gives political protection to prudent policy in this area. What that would be is itself a good question. So, let's interpret the question to mean whether social insurance financing provides more (and sustained) support for the public financing of medical care. Posed this way, the question leads some researchers to compare the control of costs across different financing regimes. This is what Sherry Glied has done in her chapter, and she finds the picture is as clear as mud. Among general tax regimes, you have high spending Sweden and low spending UK. Among social insurance regimes, you have high spending Germany and modest spending Netherlands (at least until 2003). The picture does not change substantially if one compares changes over time in rates of cost increases rather than at one time. There are differences in cost control experience between, for example, France and the Netherlands, but both are predominantly social insurance health financing regimes. The source of financing cannot explain their expenditure differences in, for instance, the 1990s.

Making sense of this diversity is easy only if one gives up on the idea that the sources of financing dominate the explanation of what a country spends on medical care. Financial sources may well be *part* of the explanation for a nation's rate of medical inflation, but exactly how much depends upon being able to control for other explanatory factors.

It might be helpful here to illustrate the dangers of drawing inferences from too limited comparative data. A group of German scholars have recently compared the cost experiences of three countries with quite different sources of financing medical care: the US, the UK, and Germany. This research is as yet unpublished, but I have the authors' permission to use their findings and interpretations for present purposes.

Figure 4 presents the cost data for each of these countries, presented along with the OECD average.

The results would surprise no scholar of health policy. Everyone knows that the United States is the highest spender; most know that the United Kingdom's reputation for fiscal restraint is well earned. And Germany's "middle

FIGURE 4
Comparative health care costs: US, UK, Germany, and OECD average

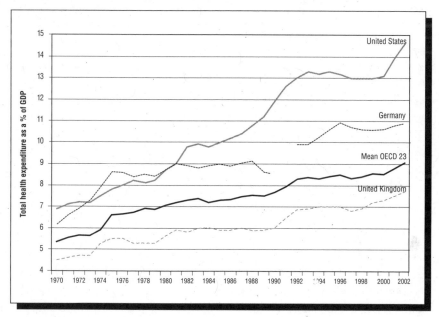

Note: Germany: data until 1990 are for West Germany; data from 1992 onwards are for United Germany.
Source: OECD 2004.

way" is legendary. The question, however, is whether the rankings here reflect some dominant effect of the source of finance or not. The competing hypothesis is that national expenditures reflect multiple causes: governmental structure (unified or fragmented), the degree of common financing, the degree of private health insurance, and ideological commitments to medical care as a merit good. The three-country study represented here cannot sort out the answer. It only provides information that bears on the question. That said, this portraiture – if used to account for comparative differences – illustrates the dangers of drawing lessons too quickly from findings that, however accurate, are insufficient grounds for firm generalizations.

If firm generalizations are unavailable for the precise questions this book was meant initially to address, what useful commentary can one nonetheless add from the search this work prompted? I would venture three suggestions. The first is the importance of distinguishing between the unavoidable pressures of high growth rates of medical expenditure and any close link to modes of financing. That is the cautionary lesson I have drawn from the exercise. The second suggestion is that the role of social insurance financing needs to be understood separately as a potential source of political support as distinct from its contribution (or lack of it) to cost control. The evidence on cost control is far less compelling – and less clear – than what appears possible regarding potential support. (We will turn to that momentarily). The third and last suggestion is that the exercise of casting Canada's circumstances in a comparative light is valuable even if it turns out that adding social insurance financing turns out to be a policy dead end as an anti-inflationary measure. Put another way, the rationale for social insurance financing may itself be transformed by comparative understanding, including most prominently that it has special relevance where older grounds for public finance of collective action have weakened.

Both of these last two themes are linked. If one's diagnosis is that for Canadians the support for medicare is weakened by a fear about fiscal sustainability, the appeal to social insurance financing is in one respect bogus. Canadians pay for medical care in the end, whether it comes out of their left or right pockets. (It is obviously true that how they pay determines the distributional fairness of Canadian medical financing, and I do not mean to treat that topic as trivial.) No public finance expert can fail to note that fiscal stability over time will reflect the state of national income, as well as the legitimacy of claims on it. It is here – the legitimacy basis – that the case for social insurance financing might be made. The grounds for deservingness in social insurance systems include one's own "contribution" to a common pool for an earmarked purpose. It is not simply that one is a citizen, though that provides legitimacy of a different kind. Rather, the central ideas of social insurance provide a sustained, historically important basis for treating benefits enjoyed as deserved and the distribution of those benefits, whether cash or in-kind, as "earned" and therefore expected to be delivered (Marmor and Mashaw 2006).

The process by which social insurance adds to a program's cultural legitimacy is worth exploring at some length here. First of all, social insurance rests on the widespread acceptance of the desirability of protecting workers and their families from dramatic losses of economic status brought on by a set of common risks to labour market participation. For virtually all advanced industrial societies, those risks are taken to include age (both youth and old age), illness, accident, and involuntary unemployment. A strong historical case can be made that, beginning with Otto von Bismarck's social insurance initiatives in the late nineteenth century, the social provision of income protection against these risks has been a fundamental precondition for the flourishing of industrial capitalism. Viewed historically, social insurance is a deeply rooted tradition, the major viable alternative to state socialism.

That social insurance programs have maintained their attractiveness as the appeal of socialism has waned is a testament to their economic sensibleness and their social respectability. That respectability largely arises from a complex ethic of fairness built into social insurance arrangements which has widespread appeal. The explanation for social insurance's durable appeal is roughly as follows:

Social insurance is a political precondition for the maintenance of market capitalism precisely because it insures against risks that private insurance markets deal with poorly or not at all. Private, voluntary insurance is beset by two well-known difficulties: adverse selection (the highest risk people tend to be the biggest demanders of insurance) and moral hazard (the tendency of the insured to incur more than their fair share of losses). When both of these problems are characteristic of an insurance market, insurance rapidly becomes unaffordable – a generally recognized description of markets that insure risks such as illness, accident, disability, or unemployment. If anyone is to be insured at reasonable cost, it is usually necessary to compel everyone, or nearly everyone, to be insured through a publicly mandated program.

Other risks, such as premature death or extended old age, have more modest adverse-selection and moral-hazard problems but encounter other difficulties. One is over-optimism. Another is the inherent difficulty of planning for things like retirement, given the massive uncertainty of individual life expectancies, long-run inflation rates, and the short-run performance of portfolios near or during retirement. Moreover, the simple myopia of Americans in planning for retirement has been demonstrated over multiple generations. Mandatory and near-universal programs of life and survivors' insurance and old-age insurance solve these problems and an additional one as well. Because we are unlikely to allow the aged to die in the streets, or their survivors to languish in poverty, compulsory participation in Social Security-style programs makes everyone a contributor to a common pool. This eliminates free riders and constrains demand for overly generous benefits.

That programs make economic sense does not necessarily make them durable. They must also be understood as fair and socially respectable. Social insurance programs satisfy these conditions through several elements of their common design. First, the risks covered are generally not attributable to the fault of the beneficiary. Providing assistance where misfortune is not the fault of the victim taps into one basic strain of our common understanding of fair arrangements. This sense of fairness is increased by covering most people who are at risk and treating everyone equally as risk bearers. The financing of most social insurance, unlike commercial insurance premiums, does not vary with individual risk. Finally, financing (wholly or in substantial part) by contributions from covered workers makes benefits seem "deserved" or "earned" to most workers. This socially respectable "fairness" pedigree is enhanced by administrative arrangements that do not question morally freighted matters such as family income and assets, household composition, or individual work effort.

Given these characteristic features of social insurance regimes, relative political stability has been their predictable fate. That they cover common risks and have broad coverage of the population means that social insurance programs engage most of the electorate. And because everyone is both a contributor and a potential beneficiary, the politics of social insurance tends to be "us-us" rather than "us-them." Each individual's sense of earned entitlement or deservingness makes it politically costly to renege on promises in social insurance programs.

The social, economic, and political "logic" of social insurance helps explain why these programs represent the largest category of federal non-defence spending and why they have persisted over such a long period in the United States and elsewhere. But as a nation's economy and social order changes, arrangements that fit well in one era can become outdated. A society's underlying sense of "fairness" or "appropriateness" in guarding against risks to loss of labour market income can change as well. In the Canadian context, however, social insurance financing of medicare is a policy option for expanding the bases of political support rather than a source of fiscal magic.

In conclusion, I want to urge this formulation of the chapter argument: to what extent, in the context of Canadian beliefs and values, would medicare stand to gain from an earmarked tax that highlighted the proportional contribution of Canadian workers and their employers? This is not a public finance suggestion; many can think of other sources with various advantages. It is a suggestion of inquiry based on the possibility that Canadians have experienced a weakening of their sense of citizen – as opposed to worker-saver – solidarity. Looked at that way, the social insurance tradition has considerable appeal.

NOTES

[1] There are, of course, other interpretations of the WHO action, however unreliable the precise evaluations of national performance. One such interpretation is that the ranking of countries on the basis of specious data surely would provoke local political interest in gathering and presenting more reliable data about health across the globe. In the case of Australia, for instance, the civil servant in charge of the federal health department did in fact challenge the WHO report; in other capitals outrage did lead to condemnation and the provision of counter-evidence. This was certainly one result of the exercise, and there is reason to believe this aim was in the mind of the WHO study director, Murray. This chapter's author confronted Murray at a conference during the spring of 2001 in London with the inaccuracies and absurdities of this ranking. Murray

responded by invoking the experience of national income accounts. No one, he said, thought GDP measured income perfectly or did so correctly at the outset. But, he went on to add, "we would not want to go back on GDP measures, would we?" The notion that producing junk science energizes better science may have some empirical backing, but it is the weakest possible defence of any particular flawed study.

[2] There are, in contrast, studies of the US, the UK, and Germany that, when arrayed by source of financing, suggest that general tax systems are first in cost control, social health insurance second, and private health financing third (Wendt 2006). The obvious problem with this tripartite analysis is distinguishing among the various causes of each national experience, of which financing of medical care is only one candidate. As a hypothesis, it is worth exploring, but such a finding alone cannot sustain a generalization about causality.

[3] As one of the book's editors, Carolyn Tuohy, has rightly noted, I would say that NHI can be considered "social insurance" only in that it is a payroll tax paid by employers and employees. However, eligibility for health care benefits is not linked to contribution, funds are not earmarked but flow into general revenue, and there is hence no governance structure for the funds separate from the Exchequer. Each of these features of social insurance has, however, recently been proposed and debated in the UK.

[4] Diversification of financial sources for medical care expenditures, it should be emphasized, has been quite common among the industrial democracies over the past three decades. One can interpret that cross-national response as exemplifying the pressures on government budgets – and on sickness funds – from the persistent, common pressure of relative medical inflation. For a discussion of that pressure and its connection to the structure of governmental institutions, see Marmor (1983).

REFERENCES

Hunter, D. 1995. "A New Focus for Dialogue." *European Health Reform: Bulletin of the European Network and Database* 1 (March).

Inglehart, R., N. Nevitte, and M. Basanez. 1996. *The North American Trajectory: Cultural, Economic and Political Ties among the United States, Canada and Mexico.* New York: Aldine de Gruyter.

Jacobs, A. 1998. "Seeing Difference: Market Health Reform in Europe." *Journal of Health Politics, Policy and Law* 23 (1): 1-33.

Jacobs, L., T. Marmor, and J. Oberlander. 1999. "The Oregon Health Plan and the Political Paradox of Rationing: What Advocates and Critic Have Claimed and What Oregon Did." *Journal of Health Politics, Policy and Law* 24 (1): 161-80.

Klein, R. 1991. "Risks and Benefits of Comparative Studies." *Milbank Quarterly* 69 (2): 275-91.

– 1995. "Learning from Others: Shall the Last Be the First?" In *Four Country Conference on Health Care Reforms and Health Care Policies in the United States, Canada, Germany and the Netherlands: Report*, edited by K. Okma. The Hague: Ministry of Health.

Lipset, S.M. 1990. *Continental Divide: The Values and Institutions of the United States and Canada*. New York: Routledge.

Maioni, A. 1998. *Parting at the Crossroads: The Emergence of Health Insurance in the United States and Canada*. Princeton, NJ: Princeton University Press.

Marmor, T. 1983. "The Politics of Medical Inflation." In *Political Analysis and American Medicare Care (Essays)*, edited by T.R. Marmor. Cambridge University Press.

– 1999. "The Rage for Reform: Sense and Nonsense in Health Policy." In *Health Reform: Public Success, Private Failure*, edited by D. Drache and T. Sullivan, 260-72. London: Routledge.

Marmor, T., and J. Mashaw. 2006. "Understanding Social Insurance: Fairness, Affordability, and the 'Modernization' of Social Security and Medicare." *Health Affairs*. www.healthaffairs.org.

Marmor, T., K.G. Okma, and R. Freeman. 2005. *Health Policy, Comparison and Learning*. New Haven: Yale University Press.

White, J. 1995. *Competing Solutions: American Health Care Proposals and International Experience*. Washington: The Brookings Institution.

Williams, A. 2001. "Science or Marketing at WHO? A Commentary on World Health 2000." *Health Economics* 10 (2): 93-100.

World Health Organization. 2000. *The World Health Report 2000, Health Systems: Improving Performance*. Geneva: World Health Organization.

Chapter 9

Challenges and Changes in Pharmacare: Could Social Insurance Be the Answer?

Steve Morgan

The problems encountered in attempting to provide prescribed drugs on an insurance basis have been difficult to resolve in Canada. Excessive patient demand, excessive prescribing, too many repeat prescriptions, the lack of historic plateau or benchmark of use or average prescription price – these are some of the difficulties cited to demonstrate that prepayment for pharmaceuticals is impractical.

> – Royal Commission on Health Services, Canada, 1965

The more things change.... Developing a financing mechanism for prescription drugs in Canada continues, over 40 years after the statement above, to pose a significant dilemma for policy-makers. While the subject of financing per se may conjure up images of tax returns, insurance forms, and complex equations, how countries finance health care says much about their society. Health care financing reflects a complex mix of a nation's values, the interplay between major actors in the society (government, health professionals, and industry, to name a few) and the legacy of past decisions that give rise to institutions and traditions (Tuohy 1999). This book's editors have argued that, through the use of social insurance or other mechanisms of health care financing, we are searching for "the grail" – a mythic object thought to have unusual powers. Indeed, given that the goals of a system for health care financing include equity, efficiency, accountability, sustainability, and more, it would appear that we are indeed in search of something miraculous. A grail is also an object of a prolonged endeavour that is all but unattainable for those who seek it. Canadian "pharmacare" fits both definitions.

This chapter concerns prescription drug financing. It begins with a review of the basic economics of health care financing, outlining differences in the structure and complexity of Canada's systems for financing hospital care and physician services on one hand and pharmaceuticals on the other. It explores the consequences of Canada's multi-payer system of financing. With costs increasing rapidly for all populations, and public liability focused on senior citizens in particular, Canada is poised for significant pharmacare reform in the coming years. In exploring the concept of social insurance for pharmacare, I pay particular attention to the systems needed to ensure that those managing funds for the purchase of pharmaceuticals have the incentives and ability to do so in a way that is efficient, equitable, and accountable. I conclude with (perhaps tentative) support for the idea of a substantive social insurance fund being created for the purchase of pharmaceuticals in Canada.

A SCHEMATIC VIEW OF HEALTH CARE FINANCING

The financing of health care is about putting money into the system; a financing system defines where funds may be drawn from and where they may be pooled. This distinguishes financing from funding: financing concerns the way that revenues are raised and stored in order to pay for health care, while funding concerns how the funds are spent (Mossialos and Dixon 2002). The two steps are interrelated in many ways, but they are nevertheless distinct components of the financial aspects of health care systems.

A definition of "grail" that can be used to illustrate the basics of health care financing systems is "chalice." Think of the Canadian expression of "budgetary silos" as depicting bowls or buckets into and out of which funds for particular programs might flow. Different systems of health care financing reflect differences in the ways by which funds are collected (from whom, at what rates, through which channels). They also reflect differences in the nature of the pooling of funds, and the extent. Because of uncertainty and variability in the need for health care over time and among individuals, all health care systems involve some degree of financial (or risk) pooling. But the nature of the chalices into which funds flow and from which they are drawn can differ significantly. Figure 1 illustrates a stylized view of pools (buckets) of financing available for health care; it shows where funds flow from, where they might be pooled (e.g., through government budgets, social insurance funds, or private insurance), and how the funds ultimately flow through to providers of health care services and goods.

The financial pools created by a health care financing system may be very large, reflecting the pooling of resources across large populations, between many types of service, and/or over long periods of time. They may also be quite small, as in the case where individuals might pool their own resources over time by way of devices such as medical savings accounts. The pools may involve contributions by individuals, employers, governments, or other actors. There may also be a degree of pooling that runs across smaller pools – such as

FIGURE 1
Health care financing as the flow of funds between pools (or buckets)

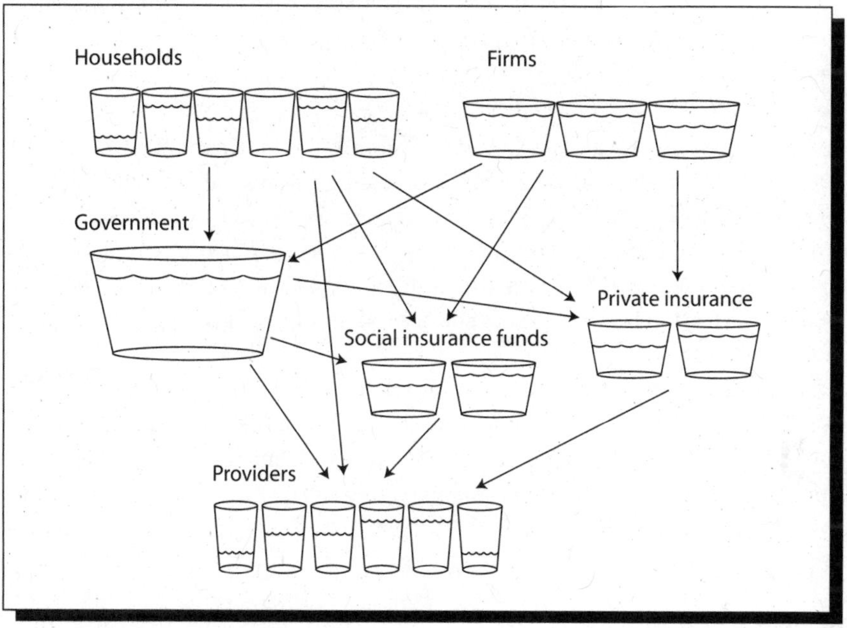

Source: Adapted from Normand and Busse 2002.

when many social insurance funds operating in a given country pool some funds between them. Some pools will be ones from which only contributors can draw; others may allow members of entitled groups to draw upon pooled resources even if they did not contribute.

At the end of the line in the financing process are the recipients of payment, those who provide goods and services for patients. This conjures up the final definition of a grail worth discussing in the context of financing: the trophy, something people compete for and fight over. There will be competition and intense debate over financing policy because every dollar collected is not just a dollar of income taken from the payer, it is a dollar that will go toward services received by an individual (not necessarily the payer) and thereby become a dollar of income to someone working within the system. Since no financing mechanism is truly magical, Robert Evans's law applies (1997): the total amount of money going into the system must equal the total cost of the goods and services provided, which at the same time must equal the total earnings of those providing the goods or services. Therefore, various actors – those who pay, those who get services, and those who get paid – will care greatly about the sources of payment going into the system, the allocations among it, and the payments to providers within it. Because of this, financing policy is intensely political.

FINANCING SCHEMATICS FOR HEALTH CARE SERVICES AND
PHARMACEUTICALS IN CANADA

Following the conclusion of the Royal Commission on Health Services in the mid-1960s, the Canadian government enacted legislation that formed the basis of Canada's public health insurance system. With federal cost sharing and provincial administration, Canada's medicare system has provided universal coverage for medically necessary hospital and physician services in all provinces since 1971. The financing of these services under medicare is illustrated in figure 2.

Figure 2 illustrates the fact that, since the 1970s, 91 percent of hospital care and 98 percent of physician services in Canada have been financed through public revenues (CIHI 2005). The figure shows a very large pool of government funds collected through various taxation mechanisms. It is notable that only a limited amount of revenue collected by government is specifically

FIGURE 2
The financing of medically necessary physician and hospital services in Canada

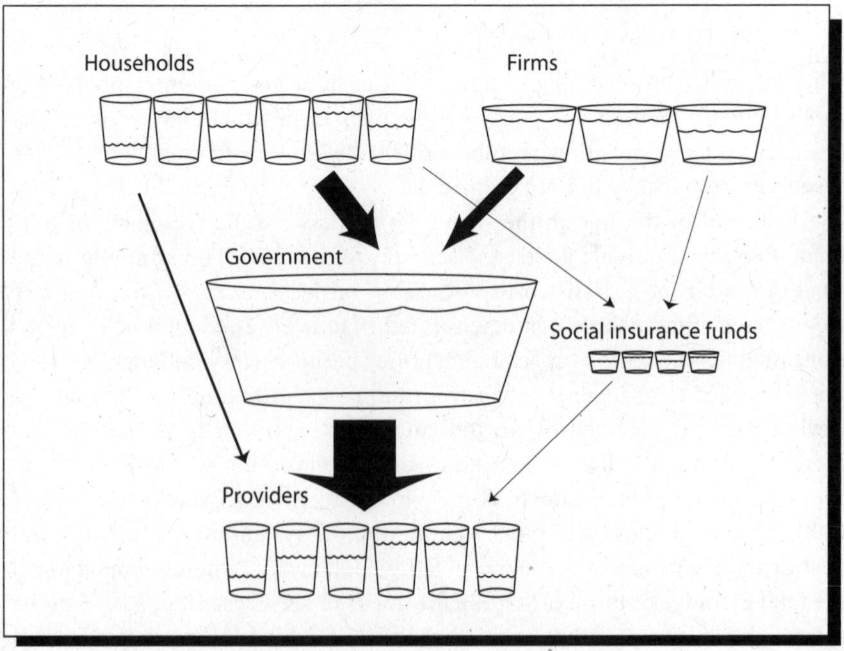

Source: CIHI 2005.

labelled for health care. Moreover, even those sources of government funds that are nominally labelled as health care premiums – levied by a few provincial governments – are effectively added to the enormous pool of general government revenues that is then allocated to health care and other government programs by government. Hence, the government pool of funds is much larger than the total amount needed for health care in any one year.

There is a very limited role for direct payment of physician and hospital services in Canada, and virtually no private insurance for such. Private payments for medical and hospital services include fees charged for private rooms and other hospital amenities and fees for non-insured medical services such as medical examinations for travel and life insurance. Approximately 1 percent of the cost of hospital and physician services in Canada is financed by social insurance mechanisms such as workers' compensation funds that pay for health care required to treat work-related illness or injury.

The financing of pharmaceuticals in Canada differs significantly from that of hospital and physician services. Canada's current system of drug financing is depicted in figure 3. The most obvious difference between figures 2 and 3 is complexity. Whereas there are limited pools and ways in which funds flow to pay for medical and hospital services, there are many channels through which drug purchases are financed, including some that involve pooling and some that do not. Government continues to represent a major source of funds and mechanism for pooling such funds in the pharmaceutical sector: provincial and federal governments financed 37.7 percent of pharmaceutical purchases in 2006 (CIHI 2006). Workers' compensation and the Quebec drug plan financed a combined 3.6 percent of drug expenditures through social insurance mechanisms. A variety of private insurance plans pool funds for the purchase of medicines on behalf of particular populations (e.g., employees of a firm offering expended benefits); they accounted for 32.5 percent of drug expenditures in 2006. Finally, payments made directly by patients for prescribed and non-prescribed medicines accounted for 26.1 percent of drug expenditures in 2006.

Another distinct feature of the pharmaceutical sector illustrated in figure 3 is the relative size of providers. In contrast to the many hundreds of hospitals and thousands of health care professionals providing health care services in Canada, there are relatively few pharmaceutical manufacturers. The volume of funds transferred to pay even for specific pharmaceutical products is often on the order of millions of dollars. Just a few dozen products, with sales exceeding $50 million each, account for nearly half of the pharmaceutical market in Canada (Morgan, McMahon et al. 2005). Such volume of sales per product (and per provider) is important insofar as it relates to the concentration of gains and losses from any changes to pharmaceutical financing. If a financing structure changes the volume and distribution of funds flowing through the system, major stakeholders will be motivated to engage in the debate.

FIGURE 3
The financing of pharmaceuticals in Canada

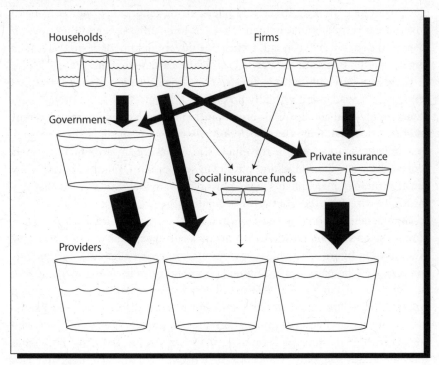

Source: CIHI 2006.

THE EVOLUTION OF PROVINCIAL PHARMACARE PROGRAMS

Prescription drugs consumed outside hospitals are not covered by the Canada Health Act or by any other national legislation that would ensure standards for universal accessibility. While a national pharmacare program was proposed by the Royal Commission on Health Services, the commission recommended the program be deferred until drug costs reached a "plateau," giving policy-makers the predictability thought needed to plan, finance, and implement a pharmacare program (Canada 1965). In the years that followed, public pro-grams for the coverage of prescription drugs evolved independently in each province and territory (Canada 1985; Morgan, Barer et al. 2003).

Governments of the 1960s were more concerned about pharmaceutical pric-ing and marketing practices than with drug financing per se (Canada 1963; Canada 1965; Lang 1974; Temin 1980). The postwar therapeutic revolution had produced considerable numbers of truly effective medicines, but changes in patent law (particularly in the United States) during the late 1950s led to large numbers of imitative ("me-too") drugs being patented and promoted intensely at prices thought to be excessive. Canada responded to the market concerns with a 1969 amendment to the *Patent Act* that allowed any firm to import and sell a patented drug subject to a fixed royalty fee of 4 percent of sales (Lanoszka 2003). Patent holders could not block the licence – hence, it was "compulsory." The policy was designed to encourage price competition between brand and generic suppliers and thereby control the cost of medicine (Canada 1963; Canada 1985).

Most provincial pharmacare programs evolved in the 1970s, a time when prescription drugs were an increasingly common yet still relatively affordable component of health care. Most drugs used outside of the hospital setting in the 1970s were for relatively common, generally time-limited conditions (such as infection), and therefore came at relatively modest cost. Given that most medicines were available at relatively modest cost, and that prices would be kept in check through generic competition, there was little concern that average consumers would be unable to afford the medicines they needed. Moreover, drugs accounted for less than 2 percent of total health spending in Canada in the early 1970s (CIHI 2005), so the idea of designing the drug financing mechanism in a way that would enable a third-party payer to manage expenditures on behalf of patients had not caught on. Indeed, the concept of actively managed drug benefits would not become a major consideration – in Canada and other like countries – until the late 1980s, by which time drugs accounted for 4 percent of health care costs.

The provincial pharmacare policies that evolved in the 1970s were generally motivated by concerns regarding financial burdens on society's most vulnerable members (Grootendorst 2002). General social welfare programs evolved prescription drug benefits on the basis that welfare recipients would be unable to afford even modest drug costs. Similarly, seniors were also covered through a variety of drug subsidy programs, in part because they were expected to have higher than average needs for medicines and lower than average incomes. Consistent with the idea that pharmacare was largely a financial aid program, many early pharmacare programs were offered not by health care ministries but by welfare ministries.

Today, most provinces offer coverage for the elderly and social assistance recipients with relatively modest copayments or deductibles. The provinces of British Columbia, Manitoba, and Saskatchewan, however, have reformed their public drug plans to cover primarily those individuals (regardless of age) who have drug costs exceeding income-based deductibles. Quebec passed a law in 1997 compelling all residents to purchase premium-based drug insurance. Quebec workers are required to purchase insurance through regulated private insurance providers; the unemployed, under-employed, and retired purchase premium-based insurance through a government plan.

POSSIBLE EFFECTS OF CANADA'S PATCHWORK SYSTEM FOR DRUG FINANCING

As a result of the different ways in which drug benefits are provided by provinces, some Canadians have little or no coverage for pharmaceuticals. Nationally, it is estimated that public programs provide coverage for approximately a third of the population and that approximately half of the working-age population participate in private drug insurance plans as part of employment-related groups (Applied Management, Fraser Group et al. 2000). Approximately 10 to 20 percent of the population has no drug coverage of any kind (Canada 1998; Applied Management, Fraser Group et al. 2000).

Of greatest interest in recent years has been the degree to which Canadians might find themselves lacking coverage for catastrophic drug expenses depending on their age and province of residence. The definition of what constitutes "catastrophic" costs is still an unclear matter – more accurately, it has never been subject to disciplined review and specification. Definitions currently in use consider populations to be underinsured for high drug costs if their private payments for prescription drugs exceed 3 to 4 percent of household income (Applied Management, Fraser Group et al. 2000; Canada 2002b; NPS 2006). However, virtually no matter where one draws the line, studies of Canadians' access to coverage against catastrophic drug costs typically point to the same problem: residents of provinces in Atlantic Canada are far more likely to lack coverage for drug costs that would exceed modest percentages of household income than are residents of other provinces (Applied Management, Fraser Group et al. 2000; Coombes et al. 2004).

The multi-payer system of drug financing in Canada also has the effect of making it difficult to manage expenditures. With so many sources of funds being drawn upon, costs increase without much resistance. For, as expenses under private or public drug plans have increased, those managing such plans have sought greater budgets (e.g., through increased premiums for private insurance plans or greater allocations of overall government revenues), shifted increasing costs onto patients (through increased copayments and deductibles), or both. This is in contrast to the degree of control over costs that results from our system of financing medical and hospital services. For services covered under the *Canada Health Act*, government has only the option of increasing the share of government revenues charged; it cannot shift costs onto patients or into the private sector through a parallel private insurance system. As a result, government has greater incentive to manage expenditures on hospitals and physician services. Moreover, because it is a single payer in those markets, government also has greater options for engaging in such management – for example, by exercising buying powers and setting capped budgets, both of which are proven to assist with expenditure control (Barer, Lomas et al. 1996).

Figure 4 illustrates Canadian trends in expenditure on hospitals, physician services, and pharmaceuticals from 1975 to 2006, and then projects these expenditures
from 2007 through to 2017. Figures are reported in inflation-adjusted (year 2006)
dollars per capita so that they have accounted for effects of population growth
and general inflation. Figure 4 shows that drug expenditures in Canada have grown
more rapidly than expenditures on hospitals and physician in recent decades.
Inflation-adjusted expenditure per capita on hospital care in Canada increased by
a total of 51 percent (or 1.4 percent per year) between 1975 and 2006; inflation-
adjusted expenditure per capita on physician services increased by a total of 98
percent (or 2.2 percent per year); and inflation-adjusted expenditure per capita on
pharmaceuticals increased by a total of 338 percent (or 4.9 percent per year).

FIGURE 4
**Canadian expenditure on physicians services, hospitals, and pharmaceuticals,
1975 to 2005, with projections to 2017**

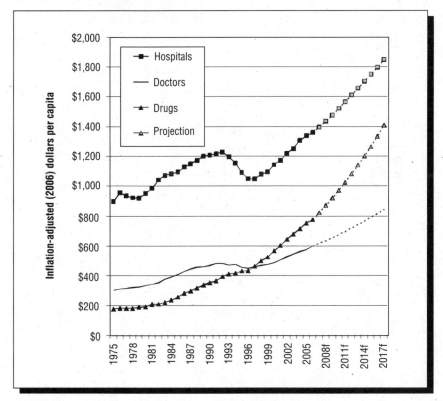

Sources: Expenditure data extracted from CIHI, National Health Expenditures Database.
Projections for 2007 to 2017 based on average annual growth rate over the period of 1995 to
2006 for each component of expenditure.

On average, in 2006, Canadians spent $775 per capita on pharmaceuticals (CIHI 2005; CIHI 2006). This represents over half of what was spent on hospitals ($1,360 per capita), 30 percent more than was spent on physicians ($598 per capita), and nearly twice times what was spent on drugs in 1996 ($432 per capita, in year 2006 dollar terms). If trends of the past decade continue, the level of spending on pharmaceuticals by 2017 will approach spending on hospitals: $1,409 per capita on pharmaceuticals versus $1,850 per capita on hospitals, in year 2006 dollars.

These trends in spending do not come without opportunity cost. A dollar invested in pharmaceutical care is a dollar that is not invested in medical care, hospital care, or other activities. Consider the following thought experiment. Suppose that we, as a nation, were able to freeze drug expenditures for one year, so that in 2008 we spent the same amount on pharmaceuticals that we spent in 2007 and then we allowed drug expenditures to grow at current rates following that one-year freeze. Relative to a world where we did not hold drug spending constant, this one-year freeze would free up roughly $2 billion in spending. The opportunity cost of spending that $2 billion on pharmaceuticals lies in how the funds might otherwise be spent, such as hiring 20,000 new nurses or 10,000 new primary care doctors, per year, every year, forever.

Canada should not necessarily invest in an army of doctors and nurses instead of using pharmaceuticals. We need to consider more carefully the "return on investment" from pharmaceutical care. Is the right drug getting to the right patient at the right price? That is, is the sector itself organized in a technically and allocatively efficient manner? Do the benefits of increased investment in pharmaceuticals surpass those that would be achieved from other investments in the health of the population? That is, is the broader allocation of societal resources for the production of health and well-being technically and allocatively efficient?

It is unclear whether these questions are being asked and acted upon, because our system for financing pharmaceutical purchases is very complex and involves a multiplicity of payers – including direct private payment, private insurance, social insurance, and government financing. Because of the financing system, no payer of pharmaceuticals appears to have sufficient incentive to consider the societal return on investment in pharmaceutical care. Also due to the financing structure, it would appear that no payer has the tools necessary to manage society's investment in pharmaceutical care.

CATALYST FOR CHANGE

Partially due to the current problems caused by Canada's pharmacare system (or lack thereof), reform to the system of drug financing in Canada is underway. While variation in drug coverage in Canada has been one of the motivations behind recent calls for national standards (Canada 1998; Canada 2002a; Canada 2002b), one of the primary catalysts for change is arguably demographics. But contrary to popular perception, the aging of our population does not have a major impact on total drug expenditures in Canada. It is the impact of aging on the private-public split in payments that will likely be the catalyst for pharmacare reform.

Drug expenditures have been growing at a rate of more than 10 percent per year in recent years. Yet, population aging has caused expenditures to grow by just 1 percent per year (Morgan 2006). The remainder of drug expenditure growth (more than 9 percent per year) results from the facts that Canadians of all ages are using more medicines to treat more conditions and that each year Canadians are prescribed newer, more expensive drugs for their treatments. While these trends place pressures on drug benefit programs (in both the private and public sector), they are not the sole motivation for the policy reforms that are underway in some provinces and those that might occur in others in the near future.

The impact of population aging on incentives for pharmacare reform in Canada has more to do with the rapid growth in drug expenditure for people of all ages and with the age of the significant baby boomer generation (Morgan 2005). Although the oldest in this large demographic cohort have now reached 60, it is not a significant financial burden on most provincially run pharmacare programs. This is because, as described above, pharmacare in Canadian provinces arose largely as an assistance program for those with low incomes and, importantly, those over age 65. While the baby boomer generation is below age 65 (the age of pharmacare entitlement in many provinces), they do not represent a burden on public drug plans. This is illustrated in figure 5, which plots the population pyramid for Canada as of 2006. Age 65 is highlighted to show when residents of most provinces become entitled to age-related pharmacare programs; it is at this point that their drug expenses become a major public liability. The population pyramid shows the numbers of males and females of every age in Canada, clearly illustrating the significant boom in the population of Canadians currently in their 40s and 50s, and the much smaller populations of younger ages (the "baby bust"). When the baby boomers turn 65, the influence on public liability for pharmacare benefits will be significant – if provinces retain age-based pharmacare programs.

Foreseeing this pending boom in the ranks of seniors entitled to pharmacare, many provinces will reconsider the tradition model (if they have not done so already). The catalyst for change will come not from ministries of health but from ministries of finance and treasury departments. British Columbia made this relatively explicit when in 2003 the province replaced age-based pharmacare with income-based pharmacare, based in part on concerns that a seniors' drug program would not be sustainable when baby boomers reached the age of entitlement (Morgan and Coombes 2006). A recent pan-Canadian

FIGURE 5
Canada's 2006 population pyramid and the public liability of age-based pharmacare

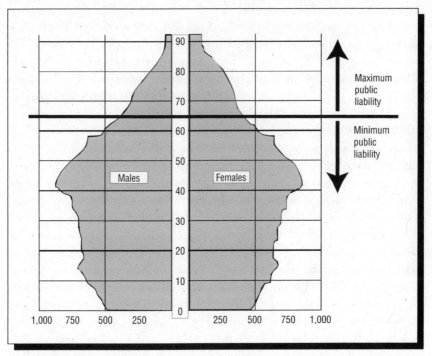

Data source: Statistics Canada.

expression of interest in income based pharmacare – by way of the progress report on Canada's National Pharmaceuticals Strategy (NPS 2006) – suggests that many other provinces (most notably Ontario) may be looking at similar changes. By the look of figure 5, it would appear that such changes are likely to occur *before* 2010.

Regardless of who is calling for pharmacare reform, it is arguably clear that the window of opportunity for policy reform is now open. Now is the time for ministries of health, the public, and, of course, stakeholders to start planning. This is a rare opportunity for the policy research community to assist with planning for solutions that will be desirable, "reasonable," and sustainable for the long-term.

SOCIAL INSURANCE AS A MODEL FOR PHARMACARE

Saskatchewan, Manitoba, and British Columbia have opted for income-based pharmacare programs, and the National Pharmaceuticals Strategy has announced that income-based pharmacare is the leading candidate for a national standard in Canada (NPS 2006). While the pros and cons of income-based pharmacare are sure to be a matter of considerable debate – some of which I have written about elsewhere (Morgan and Willison 2004; Morgan, Evans et al. 2006; Hanley and Morgan 2007) – there are other pharmacare options to consider. One such option is a social insurance program for pharmaceuticals.

Social insurance is a mechanism through which individuals (and usually their employers) are required to contribute standardized rates to a pool of resources that are dedicated to the provision of services and/or financial compensation related to particular types of loss; social insurance funds are usually managed by a body accountable to the contributors and contributions (Rosen 1985; Mossialos and Dixon 2002). The first key ingredient in the definition of social insurance is the requirement of participation. This is the main way in which social insurance differs from a private insurance contract that would be voluntarily undertaken by individuals or groups. The second key ingredient is the dedication of funds toward particular uses related to the social protection being offered. This is the main way in which social insurance differs from government financing of benefits. In the case of government financing, revenue sources are not strictly earmarked for particular uses. Funds might be collected from program-specific fees or levies, but these revenues may simply serve as complements to or substitutes for general revenues that might be drawn upon for provision of benefits.

There are several potential motivations for social insurance, as opposed to free markets or government financing, including paternalism, efficiency, and income distribution (Rosen 1985). These "textbook" motivations for social insurance illustrate a contrast between the use of social insurance for risks related to financial loss (such as social insurance for loss of income) and the use of social insurance as one of many mechanisms aimed at providing equitable access to necessary health care.

Paternalism: The compulsory participation aspect of social insurance is a motivation in the cases where people might not purchase enough insurance in a free market. This can occur due to lack of foresight about risks and losses or because individuals anticipate that government would "bail them out" even if they did not have insurance. Automotive insurance is a market for which compulsory participation would be a motivation for a social insurance financing mechanism.

Administrative and decision-making efficiency: The standard package of insurance benefits is a potentially positive aspect of social insurance when the choice of insurance policies would require considerable cost of gathering and processing information. If it can be assumed that government can do an adequate job of choosing basic benefits related to particular losses, social insurance would save the administrative, marketing, and decision-making costs that sellers and buyers of insurance would otherwise incur in a free market.

Income distribution: Compulsory participation at standardized rates can put social insurance at an advantage over private markets when redistribution of income is one of the goals of the financing system. Through individual self-selection, insurer risk-adjustment, or both, competitive markets will segment by risk status unless regulations require otherwise. When a policy goal is to provide benefits in proportion to need while collecting revenues in ways that are not, then a regulated system of social insurance might be desirable. To achieve this goal, the social insurance funds (pools) into which individuals are obligated to contribute funds must be very large and must include a diverse population base, or the system will need to be highly regulated, with mechanisms of cross-subsidizing differential risks across smaller social insurance funds.

Social insurance for health care might be motivated by many of these considerations. But health care is also distinct in important ways. Many of the distinctions related to health care imply that insurance in this market is not merely a financial instrument used simply to compensate for a financial hardship. Losses in this sector are uniquely personal, non-tradable, and often non-compensable. Financing mechanisms in health care go to pay for care required to assist the ill or to maintain the health of the well. Social insurance mechanisms might achieve this goal in an efficient and equitable fashion, but they would need to be designed in a manner that provides the incentives and ability to manage the care ultimately being delivered. That is, for the goals of health care financing (revenue collection) to be achieved, it may be necessary to consider how that system affects the processes and outcomes of health care funding (payment for services).

WHY ARE PHARMACEUTICALS UNIQUE?

The pharmaceutical sector is in many ways a distinct economic market. To begin with, it is obvious that pharmaceuticals are not ordinary consumer goods. They are potent inputs into the production or maintenance of the health of patients and populations. Given the cost, inconvenience, and potential risks associated with pharmaceutical use, pharmaceuticals derive their societal value from the established effects they have on patient health. However, it is difficult for patients or prescribers to determine these impacts with certainty. A person who feels better or worse after drug consumption cannot know with certainty whether nature, placebo, or the drug was responsible for any change in health status. As a result of the specialized knowledge and skills required for informed drug choices, and the inherent risk involved in making uninformed choices, the legal requirement of a physician's prescription (in most countries) is imposed to ensure that a suitably trained expert acts as an agent for the patient in diagnosing the need for treatment and selecting among treatment options.

Moreover, mechanisms for third party payment of pharmaceutical costs have evolved around the world to promote access to medicines and to reduce both risks and inequities of financial burdens associated with ill health. Owing to such coverage – and to the ways in which physicians are paid for their prescribing services – patients and prescribers seldom bear the full cost of drugs consumed.

These "market imperfections" in the demand for pharmaceuticals create an environment with unique forms of competition. In particular, the lack of price sensitivity among prescribers and patients combined with the difficulty for prescribers and patients to determine the comparative effectiveness of products gives manufacturers incentive to "invent around" existing patents and market similar products. Firms selling imitative patented drugs compete not in terms of price per unit of performance but through intense promotion of minor differences among products.

The pharmaceutical market does not function like an ordinary marketplace of well-informed consumers making welfare-maximizing decisions subject to standard budget constraints. Thus, there is a role for third-party payers to intervene to ensure that demand is made more "rational" through the tailored incentives of reimbursement policy and that the significant market power of large, patent-holding manufacturers is met with a maximal degree of countervailing purchasing power.

LEGITIMACY OF THE THIRD-PARTY AGENT

Legitimacy in social insurance is not a new concept or concern. The evolution of social insurance in Eastern Europe began with the rise of corporations and related labour movements. Workers who joined in solidarity around issues related to their remuneration and conditions of work also perceived common benefit in creating insurance pools for the financial risks associated with illness. Employers could also benefit from having a workforce with ready access to necessary health care. The insurance groups that evolved from this grew into the employment and occupational sickness funds, with considerable influence from the 1883 establishment of statutory sickness funds in Germany by Chancellor Bismarck.

For these early models of social insurance, the natural unit of solidarity and thereby governance (not necessarily "government") was the occupational group. The common visions shared by members of such groups meant that employees (or at least a significant majority of them) would willingly accept the particular constraints imposed by a social insurance mechanism and the *ex ante* distribution created by the pooling involved. Social insurance of this form is a social contract as individuals in a given group are compelled to participate in the insurance scheme. When the rules and governance of the pool are seen to reflect the common will of the members, the imposition of these restrictions is an accepted price for obtaining greater outcomes than those that would be obtained without those limits. This relates to Rousseau's idea that legitimacy of government comes only when government (in this case governance of a social insurance fund) reflects deep, shared principles of membership in the group/society (Rousseau 1968).

In the pharmaceutical sector the collective good from uniting in the collection and management of a pharmaceutical budget goes beyond notions of risk- or income-solidarity. The technical benefits from the creation of a third-party agent must also be taken into consideration. These include the benefits of purchasing power and of decision-making authority as it pertains to setting the limits on what will be covered. Potential purchasing power is maximized by larger groups; the maximum such power for Canada would come from a truly "national" pharmacare program. Coverage decision-making is an increasingly important issue in pharmaceutical policy, and it includes such decisions as what will be covered, for whom, under what circumstances, and on what terms (Garber 2001; Daniels et al. 2003; Neumann 2004). Determining such important terms of coverage for populations contributing to an insurance pool can be a difficult and costly process, which would suggest large and centralized drug systems. However, centralized guidance on drug coverage decisions may serve more localized decision-making by smaller funding groups as well.

A CLEAR AND TRANSPARENT "SOCIAL PHARMACARE FUND"?

What therefore appears to be needed in pharmaceuticals is a clear fund from which resources can be drawn for the purchase of medicines that represent the greatest value to the population's health and to the health care system. The revenues for this fund may be raised through traditional mechanisms of social insurance – levies on employees and employers – though they could be collected through a mix of such mechanisms and the tax mechanisms that fund traditional "pharmacare" programs. But it would be unwise to create a pharmaceutical insurance system that simply aims to cover the costs of drug purchases. Such "insurance" solutions will fail to assist in the management of this important component of health care. What is most important is setting and managing reasonable limits for pooled funds available for pharmacare spending – just as is done by the Pharmaceutical Management Agency of New Zealand, PHARMAC (Braae et al. 1999; Brougham et al. 2002).

The pharmacare fund will require clear and "reasonable" processes for setting the limits on what total amount of pooled revenues are to be spent (the amount of funds raised in the first place). It should, at least in my view, provide benefits to persons based on needs and not age or income; for, among other reasons, incomes will undoubtedly be used to determine contributions to the fund, and one does not want to set up a system that would be seen as a double tax on the wealthy (taxed once in contributions and then again in terms of the income-based reduction in eligibility for subsidy when care is needed). Moreover, the system will require clear evidence-based processes for the allocation of resources toward the purchase of specific drugs for eligible populations. There is now a significant literature on such processes (Daniels 2000; Garber 2001; Daniels et al. 2003; Neumann 2004; Morgan, McMahon et al. 2006), and Canada is working toward models that might be adapted to the broader purpose of managing a social pharmacare fund (McMahon, Morgan et al. 2005).

A well defined and managed social pharmacare fund would not necessarily equate to first-dollar coverage for all pharmaceuticals. It is relatively well established that user charges that apply to both essential and non-essential medicines are likely to reduce the use of both types of drug (Soumerai et al. 1987; Soumerai et al. 1990; Soumerai et al. 1993), and reductions in the use of essential medicines have been shown to increase the use of other health care services, such as emergency departments (Tamblyn et al. 2001). However, some cost-sharing policies – such as generic substitution incentives, reference pricing, or tiered copayments – can be used to provide coverage for (and thereby steer utilization toward) the most cost-effective options while allowing some level of patient choice.

Efficient and reasonable application of cost management policies will require the breaking down of some of the silo mentality that comes from separate budgeting of medical, hospital, and pharmaceutical care. This may mean a limited role for the private insurance industry serving as managers, as might be the case in a social insurance system for pharmaceuticals achieved (as in Quebec) through compulsory participation in private insurance programs. It would be debatable, however, whether private insurance could function as a reasonably legitimate rationing agent for the groups served by the fund – private companies do not pay for other components of the health care system. A public body would have a more direct financial incentive to consider the offsets that might be created by managing the social pharmaceutical fund too aggressively; for example, reducing drug coverage too far could lead to increased hospitalizations or medical service use when patients do not have access to effective drug treatments.

Achieving the right balance between financial tenability and the scale required for the social pharmacare fund to have significant influence on the market will be important. Long run sustainability may require significant short run investment.

DISCUSSION

Owing to the unique nature of pharmaceuticals and the marketplace in which they are bought and sold, third-party payers have potentially important roles that extend well beyond the act of risk pooling or income distribution that is the conventional stuff of social insurance. A third-party payer by way of a clear and accountable fund for pharmaceutical purchases can assist in the management of expenditures and in the setting of fair and transparent limits on coverage. A substantive social insurance fund for pharmaceuticals may therefore play an important role in determining the allocations within pharmacare programs. By defining limits and managing budgets for pharmaceuticals, social insurance can also significantly influence the allocations across components of health care. In cases such as the New Zealand PHARMAC program, savings (or cost overruns) from the drug program are tied directly to finances of other components of health care. This can help to align incentives for the prudent management of total spending and for ensuring that resources available to the social insurance fund for pharmaceuticals are spent on goods that are of benefit to the population – or, at the very least, that the population is not denied cost-effective drug treatments. Given the magnitude of expenditure trends in pharmaceuticals, consideration of these aggregate trade-offs will be important not only to the sustainability of any pharmacare option to be adopted in the coming years but also to the sustainability of Canada's other health care components so closely related to the use of (and related benefits from) pharmaceuticals.

REFERENCES

Applied Management/Fraser Group. 2000. *Canadians' Access to Insurance for Prescription Medicines.* Ottawa: Health Canada.

Barer, M.L., J. Lomas, and C. Sanmartin. 1996. "Re-Minding Our Ps and Qs: Medical Cost Controls in Canada." *Health Affairs (Millwood)* 15 (2): 216-34.

Braae, R., W. McNee, and D. Moore. 1999. "Managing Pharmaceutical Expenditure While Increasing Access: The Pharmaceutical Management Agency (Pharmac) Experience." *PharmacoEconomics* 16 (6): 649-60.

Brougham, M., S. Metcalfe, and W. McNee. 2002. "Our Advice? Get a Budget!" *Healthcare Papers* 3 (1): 83-5; discussion, 87-94.

Canada. Department of Justice. 1963. *Report Concerning the Manufacture, Distribution and Sale of Drugs.* Ottawa: Department of Justice.

Canada. 1965. *Provision, Distribution and Cost of Drugs in Canada: Royal Commission on Health Services.* Ottawa: Queen's Printer.

Canada. 1985. *Report of the Commission of Inquiry on the Pharmaceutical Industry.* Ottawa: Supply and Services Canada.

Canada. 1998. Directions for a Pharmaceutical Policy in Canada. *Canada Health Action: Building on the Legacy.* Vol. 2, *Synthesis Reports and Issues Papers.* Ottawa: National Forum on Health.

Canada. 2002. "Chapter 9: Prescription Drugs." In *Building on Values: The Future of Health Care in Canada – Final Report.* Saskatoon: Commission on the Future of Health Care in Canada.

Canada. 2002. "Expanding Coverage to Include Protection against Catastrophic Prescription Drug Costs. In *The Health of Canadians: The Federal Role.* Vol. 6, *Recommendations for Reform.* Ottawa: Standing Senate Committee on Social Affairs, Science and Technology, 392.

CIHI. 2005. *National Health Expenditure Trends, 1975-2005.* Ottawa: Canadian Institute for Health Information.

– 2006. *Drug Expenditures in Canada, 1985-2005.* Ottawa: Canadian Institute for Health Information.

Coombes, M., S. Morgan, M. Barer, and N. Pagliccia. 2004. "Who's the Fairest of Them All? Which Provincial Pharmacare Model Would Best Protect Canadians against Catastrophic Drug Costs?" *Longwoods Review* 2 (3): 13-26.

Daniels, N. 2000. "Accountability for Reasonableness." *British Medical Journal* 321 (7272): 1300-1.

Daniels, N., J.R. Teagarden, and J. Sabin. 2003 "An Ethical Template for Pharmacy Benefits." *Health Affairs* 22 (1): 125-37.

Evans, R.G. 1997. "Going for the Gold: The Redistributive Agenda behind Market-Based Health Care Reform." *Journal of Health Politics, Policy and Law* 22 (2): 427-65.

Garber, A.M. 2001. "Evidence-Based Coverage Policy." *Health Affairs (Millwood)* 20 (5): 62-82.

Grootendorst, P. 2002. "Beneficiary Cost Sharing under Canadian Provincial Prescription Drug Benefit Programs: History and Assessment." *Canadian Journal of Clinical Pharmacology* 9 (2): 79-99.

Hanley, G., and S. Morgan. 2007. "Chronic Catastrophes: Persistence Prescription Drug Expenditure for Residents of British Columbia." Centre for Health Services and Policy Research Discussion Paper. (Under peer review.)

Lang, R.W. 1974. *The Politics of Drugs: A Comparative Pressure-Group Study of the Canadian Pharmaceutical Manufacturers Association and the Association of the British Pharmaceutical Industry, 1930–1970.* Farnborough, Hants: Saxon House; Lexington, Mass.: Lexington Books.

Lanoszka, A. 2003. "The Global Politics of Intellectual Property Rights and Pharmaceutical Drug Policies in Developing Countries." *International Political Science Review/ Revue internationale de science politique* 24 (2): 181-97.

McMahon, M., S. Morgan, and C. Mitton. 2005. "The Common Drug Review: A NICE Start for Canada?" *Health Policy* 77 (3): 339-51.

Morgan, S., and M. Coombes. 2006. "Income-Based Drug Coverage in British Columbia: Towards an Understanding of the Policy." *Healthcare Policy* 2, Supplement:
6-22.

Morgan, S., R, G. Evans, and L. Yan. 2006. "Income-based Drug Coverage in British
Columbia: Lessons for BC and the Rest of Canada." *Healthcare Policy* 2 (2): 115-
27.

Morgan, S., M. McMahon, J. Lam, D. Mooney, and C. Raymond. 2005. "The Canadian Rx Atlas." Vancouver: Centre for Health Services and Policy Research, 77.

Morgan, S., M. McMahon, C. Mitton, E. Roughead, R. Kirk, P. Kanavos, and D. Menon.
2006. "Centralized Drug Review Processes in Australia, New Zealand, the United
Kingdom, and Canada." *Health Affairs (Millwood)* 25 (2): 337-47.

Morgan, S.G. 2005. "Booming Prescription Drug Expenditure: A Population-Based
Analysis of Age Dynamics." *Medical Care* 43 (10): 996-1008.

Morgan, S.G. 2006. "Prescription Drug Expenditures and Population Demographics."
Health Services Research 41 (2): 411-28.

Morgan, S.G., M.L. Barer, and J. D. Agnew. 2003. "Whither Seniors' Pharmacare:
Lessons from (and for) Canada." *Health Affairs (Millwood)* 22 (3): 49-59.

Morgan, S.G., and D. Willison. 2004. "Post-Romanow Pharmacare: Last-Dollar First ...
First-Dollar Lost?" *HealthcarePapers* 4 (3): 10-20.

Mossialos, E., and A. Dixon, eds. 2002. *Funding Health Care: An Introduction.* European Observatory on Health Care Systems. Buckingham: Open University Press.

Mossialos, E., and A. Dixon, J. Figueras, and J. Kutzin, eds. 2002. *Funding Health
Care: Options for Europe.* European Observatory on Health Care Systems, Buckingham: Open University Press.

Neumann, P.J. 2004. "Evidence-Based and Value-Based Formulary Guidelines." *Health
Affairs (Millwood)* 23 (1): 124-34.

National Pharmaceuticals Strategy Task Force. 2006. *National Pharmaceuticals
Strategy Progress Report.* Ottawa: Health Canada: 50.

Normand, C., and R. Busse. 2002. "Social Health Insurance Funding." In *Funding
Health Care: Options for Europe*, edited by E. Mossialos, A. Dixon, J. Figueras,
and J. Kutzin. Buckingham: Open University Press.

Rosen, H.S. 1985. *Public Finance.* Homewood, Ill.: R.D. Irwin.

Rousseau, J.-J. 1968. *The Social Contract.* Baltimore: Penguin Books.

Soumerai, S.B., J. Avorn, D. Ross-Degnan, and S. Gortmaker. 1987. "Payment Restrictions for Prescription Drugs under Medicaid : Effects on Therapy, Cost, and
Equity." *New England Journal of Medicine* 317 (9): 550-6.

Soumerai, S.B., D. Ross-Degnan, E.E. Fortress, and J. Abelson. 1993. "A Critical
Analysis of Studies of State Drug Reimbursement Policies: Research in Need of
Discipline." *Milbank Quarterly* 71 (2): 217-52.

Soumerai, S.B., D. Ross-Degnan, S. Gortmaker, and J. Avorn. 1990. "Withdrawing
Payment for Nonscientific Drug Therapy: Intended and Unexpected Effects of a

Large-Scale Natural Experiment." *Journal of the American Medical Association* 263 (6): 831-39.

Tamblyn, R., R. Laprise, J.A Hanley, M. Abrahamowicz, S. Scott, N. Mayo, J. Hurley, R. Grad, R., E. Latimer, R. Perreault, P. McLeod, A. Huang, P. Larochelle, and L. Mallet. 2001. "Adverse Events Associated with Prescription Drug Cost-Sharing among Poor and Elderly Persons." *Journal of the American Medical Association* 285 (4): 421-9.

Temin, P. 1980. *Taking Your Medicine: Drug Regulation in the United States.* Cambridge, Mass.: Harvard University Press.

Tuohy, C.J. 1999. *Accidental Logics: The Dynamics of Change in the Health Care Arena in the United States, Britain, and Canada.* New York: Oxford University Press.

Chapter 10

Between the Dream and Sleepwalking: Pragmatic Possibilities for Canada

Terrence Sullivan

GRAILS, PAILS, OR TRAVAILS?

The central challenge of this collection concerns optimal financing methods for health care services in Canada: in particular, the trade-offs among tax based financing, social insurance, and marketplace methods. Our quest to find the grail of appropriate financing methods, as this book's editors suggest, may be challenging. Indeed, as Steve Morgan puts it, perhaps it is more of a search for the right pails in which to sort our funding methods, or even to bail out a leaking boat. It would seem, however, at the end of the reflections in this collection, we still face some significant travails.

The challenge cannot be addressed without understanding the Canadian context. Our principal concern is not really to choose between a tax based, Beveridge style method of finance and payroll financed social insurance funds or Bismarck model of public finance for health care in Canada. (Beveridge was the father of English social policy as Bismarck was the father of German social policy.) Canada's current financing mechanism is largely a Beveridge model with market elements of private purchase. About 30 percent of financing comes from private sources (out of pocket and private insurance; see figure 1). In addition, with our hospital sector being overwhelmingly private, not-for-profit corporations, we have elements of a managed competition within the publicly financed part of our system. Very little of our health care finance is associated with state-mandated social insurance financed by payroll contributions.

The question for Canada posed in this collection is whether to inject a greater measure of social insurance into Canada's predominantly tax based system. Apart from Quebec with its mandatory payroll coverage for pharmaceuticals, the modest revenues from health premiums currently levied through payrolls in several provinces actually find their way into consolidated tax revenue, as

FIGURE 1
Public and private sector shares of total health expenditure

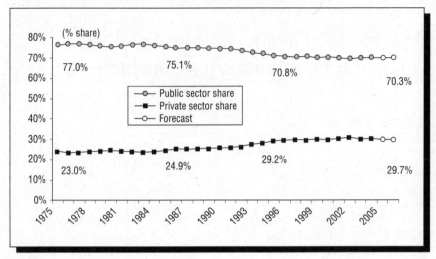

Source: CIHI 2006.

Gunderson and Hyatt point out. Fundamentally, our challenge is to deal with the trade-off inherent in a funding framework that combines a dominant system of taxed based finance with a large market based system of finance. The real boundaries between these two principal methods of health financing, once clear in the early days of Canadian medicare, have grown murky in both the public and the political eye, causing significant distortion in the public debate on solutions (Drache and Sullivan 1999). Moreover, the public debate hopelessly conflates financing and delivery issues, making matters worse.

This confusion exists throughout the Canadian delivery system and in Ontario in particular, where the private market for private payment is largest relative to other provinces (CIHI, 2006).

OUR PROBLEM: THE DREAM AND THE SLEEPWALKERS

Simply stated, in this chapter I argue that two key issues are pivotal to getting us past our current muddled preoccupation with what is public and what is private. The first has to do with sleepwalking and our need to wake up the public. The second concerns how to move toward practical and progressive methods of paying for drugs and community services without sleepwalking our way into an ever more private market financing model for drugs and community services. Tax based methods of financing health care have advantages over other methods of health system financing, as noted in several papers in this collection, although the price of these advantages may be waiting lists. Our tax financing method tends to produce a more equitable and progressive distribution of resources with the net effect that those at the low end of the income continuum with higher health burdens and higher needs are supported more actively by those who contribute the most at higher ends of the income spectrum with the lowest burden of health problems (Sullivan and Mustard 2001). It has also been argued that Beveridge-style systems tend to be slightly less expensive overall, although they are very susceptible to cyclical problems in the economy, as we saw with provincial and federal revenues in the early 1990s in Canada when the denominator shrunk and health spending as a function of GDP rose for the first time to over 10 percent.

The "sustainability" challenge associated with largely tax based financing in our country is not one driven so much by uncontrolled expenditure as it is by a falling tax ceiling. As figure 2 shows, provincial government program spending on health care has been fairly stable, growing very modestly in the last decade from just under 6 percent to about 6.5 percent of GDP currently. This is hardly an uncontrollable situation.

Overall program spending by governments as a fraction of GDP, on the other hand, has been falling, especially in the last 15 years (see figure 3). It is not so much that expenditure control is poor as it is the case that program expenditure across government is shrinking as a function of GDP. This falling program expenditure is responsible for crowding out other areas of public spending in the face of slow growth in health expenditure. The sustainability problem, as noted by Flood, Stabile, and Tuohy in the opening paper, is not one of expenditure control; it is rather one of tax shrinkage. Tax shrinkage

FIGURE 2
Provincial/territorial government health expenditure proportion of Gross Domestic Product, Canada, 1974–1975 to 2006–2007, in current dollars

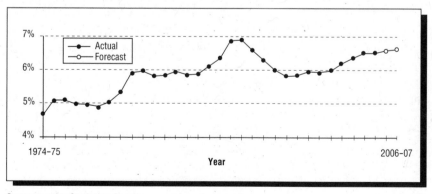

Sources: CIHI; Statistics Canada.

FIGURE 3
Provincial/territorial government expenditure as a proportion of provincial/territorial Gross Domestic Product, Canada, 1992–1993 to 2005–2006

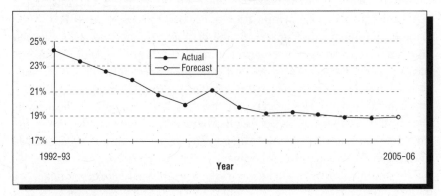

Source: Statistics Canada.

may be good for several things, but it does presage continued problems for the Beveridge-style method of health financing in Canada. Much as we might like tax financing methods for their strong points, governments in Canada are definitely showing a diminished appetite for such methods.

Our delivery system, having grown up on the basis of hospital and physician insurance, provides relatively complete public coverage for hospital and physician services in a fashion that is reasonably comparable across provinces in Canada, thanks in part to equalization transfers within the country. By contrast, Canada provides incomplete and provincially non-comparable public coverage for drugs and community services, and not surprisingly these are the areas where private financing methods are most dominant. But this is not how we *think* about our delivery system, nor is it the way we *behave* when it comes to the question of paying for drugs and community services. Our collective reaction to funding challenges on drugs and community services is to push for the idea that we should have a comprehensive base of such services. This is our reaction, even though our national plan, loosely embodied in the *Canada Health Act*, compels no national standard with respect to drugs or community services. We believe that we *should* have comprehensive coverage for drugs and community services, and we behave with outrage when we don't, despite the fact that we have never had a national public mechanism to ensure (and insure) these latter two areas.

Tommy Douglas introduced medicare in the 1960s, and it has been a great triumph for covering physician and hospital costs. Canadians have always been very attached to Douglas's dream, and for very good reason. Years later, following the Supreme Court decision of *Chaouilli* in 2005, governments and the electorate have been abruptly awakened, like Rip Van Winkel, from a 45 year slumber. Many are now wondering which part of the dream was real and which was not. Yet some among our electorate still believe if we just put our collective heads down, then public coverage for drugs and community services would miraculously appear under our pillows while we slept.

With governments facing a closing tax ceiling, private financing of drugs and community services are issues that are only likely to grow in scale. The awakened but slightly confused Canadian electorate for the most part not only resists private financing and other market mechanisms but behaves as if they are an illegitimate intrusion into our national dream. The unpleasant reality is that these mechanisms have been there since the beginning of the dream. Our governments meanwhile continue to rush around managing public finance of health care as if all will be fine despite downward pressure on taxation. The increased and inevitable fiscal pressure may drive some productivity improvement in health service, but the dream is at risk without a real alternative financing mechanism for drugs and community services.

In our sleepy-eyed state we are especially indignant when this fact intrudes on our public discourse in the area of drugs. Despite political commitments at the level of first or national ministers toward national pharmaceutical care and a national basket of community services, we have seen no effective federal or national mechanism to cover either of these two areas of care.

DRUGS AND COMMUNITY SERVICES: AWAKENING THE ELECTORATE

Although patient concerns about private payment for cancer drugs were prominently portrayed in a *Globe and Mail* series in the fall of 2006, it is clear that overall public concern for drug coverage in Canada is actually quite low, despite that fact that expenditures on drugs are the fastest growing segment of health expenditure, with the most recent ten year average growth rate of close to 9 percent (CIHI 2006). This is presumably because most Canadians have some coverage. Ontario polling data from Ipsos Reid in spring of 2006 in figure 4 show that public concern for drug coverage is quite modest and the public has no burning desire to act on this situation. In separate survey work done in the same year in relation to cancer (Ipsos Reid 2006), funding for cancer drugs fell to the bottom of the list of priority areas for service.

Steve Morgan's chapter presents a compelling demographic story on drug coverage. This demographic shift is also an issue for cancer services. Based on current incidence numbers, we know that roughly 40 percent of the Ontario public will face cancer during their own lifetime and that all of us will be touched by it as the population ages. Cancer is increasingly being managed by a complex multimodal approach to treatment, including increasingly

FIGURE 4
Top priorities for health care spending

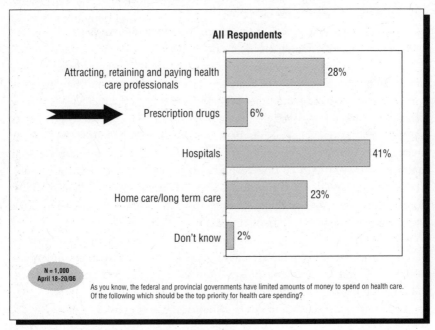

Sources: Courtesy of John Wright (Ipsos Reid 2006).

expensive drugs, many of which confer some survival advantage. The increasing costs of new biologically active agents mean that, if more stringent cost effectiveness considerations are applied to public coverage, more of these drugs will have to be managed by private expenditure or alternatively patients must simply do without. The debate about how stringent cost-effectiveness thresholds should be in cancer drugs is raging internationally with big pharmaceutical companies playing a major role in stimulating the debate (Coleman 2006).

Numerous patients in Canada now face the option of attending a private clinic elsewhere or crossing the border to the US. The recent modest expansion of these private infusion clinics across the country was a first indication of the pressure (Priest 2006). The immediate Canadian challenge is not so much trading off Beveridge for Bismarck; when it comes to drugs and community services, it is the travail of having to pay for it out of our own pockets or private insurance or by borrowing funds, as the case may be. A passive market solution to a comprehensive drug and community service envelope evolves while governments in Canada wring their fiscally constrained hands.

In the area of uncovered cancer drugs in particular, the public has behaved as if all such drugs were covered in the public system. Oral agents have always been a multi-payer environment with provincial drug plans typically covering the elderly and the indigent (as is the case in Ontario), and payroll plans covering a range of family drug benefits. The payment picture for IV drugs is more complex. Cancer Care Ontario recently issued a report and a set of recommendations related to uncovered intravenous cancer drugs in Ontario, suggesting that we needed some mechanism to allow these drugs to be infused in safe environments close to the cancer patients' usual points of care and service in a public hospital (CCO 2006). A reasonable panel of thoughtful practice leaders, having reviewed the evidence for some high profile drugs, has suggested that while the drugs in question may have some significant medical benefit or confer survival advantage, the price of this benefit would not be justifiable for a public scheme. So when the price of a new cancer drug gets up into neighbourhoods of exceeding $100,000 per life year gained, even when it confers, say, a five-month survival advantage, formulary decision panels in Ontario and elsewhere in Canada are recommending against paying. This leaves cancer patients with the painful choice of deciding whether to go to a border city, or a private clinic that operates in Ontario, or go without the drug, as opposed to having an option to pay or seek third-party payment for an intravenous cancer drug in an Ontario hospital.

Of course, the consequence of this growing challenge of expensive new biological agents that do not satisfy cost-effectiveness criteria is not unique to cancer drugs, although cancer, in my view, is foreshadowing the problems to be faced with a new frontier of expensive biological agents. For a number of new intravenous drugs that have medical benefit but may not be cost effective, the alternative is private infusion and private clinics offered by private providers charging fees and mark-ups on the drugs. At least one possible alternative is that public hospitals be allowed to infuse such drugs for payment at the point of care, as opposed to encouraging a fully fledged private infusion system.

AWAKENING PRACTICAL CONSIDERATIONS BY GOVERNMENTS

The popular but not yet realized solution for spotty drug coverage in Canada has been to suggest a national pharmaceutical program. Such a program was proposed by the federal Liberal party in two successive elections without ever being delivered once the party was in power. A national program could be efficient, bargain better prices, and work with one unique evidence-based formulary rather than 14 to 18 distinct, conflicting, and inconsistent formularies, to name a few possible advantages. These advantages were laid out clearly in the Romanow and Kirby reports, including initial costing. But when good ideas are floated and do not emerge at the end of the day, there may be strong reasons why a comprehensive national program is unlikely. In addition to the political obstacles to mounting a new federally sponsored, social spending initiative in our federation, serious questions remain regarding the capacity of the federal bureaucracy to mount such a program. If real provincial consensus were to evolve on the need for a national program, the federal government might easily take over the jurisdiction for drug coverage and create a fantastically popular new program. This is essentially what happened with Employment Insurance some decades earlier. But once again, we must contend with the challenge of a falling tax ceiling.

It may nevertheless be plausible and politically feasible to mount a catastrophic program and provide comparable coverage from coast to coast. As an alternative to one federal program, such a national program could be asymmetrically distributed through reimbursements to provincial governments based on patient claims, or it could work through direct patient claim procedures. In either case a possible federal solution is available for the growing challenges of comparable and fair drug coverage, if it begins with catastrophic coverage.

Having made the plausibility argument, even with a catastrophic program we need to get used to the idea of a mixed model of payment for drugs, including public and private payment and out-of-pocket payment. We desperately need to awaken our policy leaders to the need to create new policy alternatives that take account of this reality without creating barriers for patients who may elect to infuse drugs that are beyond the payment threshold for public plans. It is also worth exploring a new public mechanism to accommodate patients who have a capacity to pay for such drugs. While this may offend those of us who would wish for one payment mechanism for drugs because we wrongly believe that the fundamental tenet of Canadian medicare promises this to us, drugs have and still do exist in the multi-payer environment in Canada. A federal catastrophic program would go some way to level the playing field between provinces and perhaps introduce greater fairness and transparency. But it would not pay for all drugs. With certain possible exceptions related to expensive drugs for rare conditions, a catastrophic plan is unlikely to pay for drugs that are deemed to be cost ineffective. So we will continue to face the challenge of dealing with both oral and IV drugs that have medical benefit but are cost ineffective.

As determinations of cost effectiveness play an increasingly important role in decisions about drug coverage, we clearly require a better federal-provincial harmonization of technology assessment for drugs and devices, which would allow the technical review of both medical benefit and cost effectiveness. While the efforts of the Common Drug Review in Canada have been important, they have to date dealt only with new oral agents. In Ontario, building on the NICE experience in the UK, a complementary and promising "Citizen's Council" is being implemented to provide advice on difficult questions of public value in relation to drug coverage questions arising from the recent provincial

Transparent Drug System for Patients Act (Jeynathan et al. 2006). In addition, an interprovincial experience is underway in Canada to harmonize coverage decisions for all cancer drugs (Ontario 2007).

Drug coverage also looms large in thinking about community services. Once again, there has always been the illusion of public coverage for community services, despite more than a threefold variation in processes of coverage across Canada. While public concern for drugs is low, public concern for the disabled elderly is higher, particularly with the number of patients being moved out of hospital earlier and sicker than in the past.

In the area of financing community services, Michel Clair, chair of the 2000 Quebec Health Review, suggested a very interesting idea at the time, which was to create a new social insurance fund characterized as a "loss of independence" fund. Although widely panned, this Quebec version of Bismarck still merits some exploration. Given that tax financing is under pressure and that we need to preserve the solidaristic elements of our delivery system into the future, then as one alternative to market solutions, does a limited Bismarck fund have something for us to consider? As Morley Gunderson noted in the discussions associated with this volume, an old tax is a good tax. Consider Ontario, for example, which already has a health levy in place that raises in the neighbourhood of $4 billion per year for health services, and these funds are blended into consolidated revenue. While it may upset our finance officials to segregate this fund and create a person-specific fund for disability and potentially even for additional drug coverage, it could be that from the ashes of our provincial health levy a new and progressive supplementary health benefits fund could rise, inspired by Bismarck. A person-specific fund might even be topped up with voluntary contributions to create a viable tiered way of financing uncovered services in a world that pretends that everything is paid for publicly. So this modest proposal is to migrate our existing employer health levy to a person-specific, loss of independence fund that could be used broadly for health care purposes. In principle at least, this payroll-specific fund could be slowly enlarged over time, and there could also be the prospect for voluntary supplementary contributions.

Among the obvious hurdles to this proposal is, first of all, the non-trivial problem of replacing this $4 billion in consolidated revenue. A payroll-driven fund would leave the indigent and the disabled outside of the workforce to be covered by a residual public complementary pool for loss of independence. In addition, of course, the problem of the self-employed surfaces here, but there is really little recourse to the challenge of tax crowding other than to look at all possible mechanisms of supplementary payment including both payroll type funds as well as cash payments. All of these hurdles have remedies, however, and faced with market mechanisms versus payroll mechanisms, Bismarck looks more progressive and promising.

To conclude, the challenge in our jurisdiction is not so much replacing Beveridge with Bismarck as it is to reshape, in a practical public policy environment, any methods to supplement tax funding as a progressive way to pay for health services. The trick is to manage this without political crisis or major concern about the economic viability of other methods. I have suggested in this brief commentary that Canadians and Ontarians will need to embrace the reality that drugs and community services have never been fully publicly covered. They have always had market supplements; and, in the case of drugs, private payroll-financed methods have been in place as the mainstay for most Canadians. Therefore the creation of a federal catastrophic fund makes good sense as a policy option that has been widely supported among officials and policy communities. Currently, however, this option has generated little public enthusiasm because overall concern for the upcoming tsunami of drug costs has been low. Yet, there is also no evidence of public opposition to such a catastrophic fund; it is merely not the top of mind with the electorate. As an alternative, with respect to community services, the creation of a segregated fund for the health sector starting from a migration of the existing employer health levy into a segregated person-specific fund would be a viable way of building additional supplementary funding over the next two to three decades with careful escalation in mandatory and voluntary contributions to match the pressures that are being faced in community services and potentially in areas of supplementary (non-catastrophic) coverage.

At the end of the day, health care must be paid for either from people's private pockets, through private health insurance, through their company payrolls, or through the tax system. Governments in Canada behave as if the tax ceiling is closing in. The growing share of public budgets consumed by health care is a result of program expenditure reductions in other areas, not a result of uncontrolled growth in the health sector. Finding practical solutions must involve at a minimum the expansion of mandatory payroll-related financing methods as well as ways of dealing with those drugs and technologies that may have benefit but simply cannot be dealt with on cost-effectiveness grounds through the public system. In the latter cases, private payment, including private payment for treatment in public institutions, needs in practical terms to be one of the options considered. This awakening from a dream may cause some headaches for the electorate and the elected, but some practical steps are required soon if we are to preserve the dream's most noble features.

REFERENCES

Canadian Institute for Health Information (CIHI). 2006. *National Health Expenditure Data Base*. www.secure.cihi.ca/cihiweb/dispPage.jsp?cw_page=statistics_results_source_nhex_e (accessed 3 January 2007).

Cancer Care Ontario. 2006. *Report of the Provincial Working Group on the Delivery of Oncology Medications for Private Payment in Ontario Hospitals*. www.cancercare.on.ca/documents/Report_on_Unfunded_Cancer_Drugs.pdf.

Coleman, M. 2006. "New Drugs and Survival: Does the Karolinska Report Make Sense?" *CancerWorld* (September-October): 26-35.

Drache, D., and T. Sullivan. 1999. "Health Reform and Market Talk, Rhetoric and Reality." In *Public Success/Private Failure: Market Limits in Health Reform*, edited by D. Drache and T. Sullivan. London: Routledge.

Ipsos-Reid. 2006. Public Opinion Survey Material presented by J. Wright, Senior Vice President, at The Environment for Pharmaceutical Change in Canada: Challenges and Opportunities. Kingbridge Centre, King City, Ontario, 23-25 April 2006.

Jeyanathan, T., I. Dhalla, T. Culyer, W. Levinson, A. Laupacis, D.K. Martin, T. Sullivan, and W.K. Evans. 2006. "Recommendations for Establishing a Citizens' Council to Guide Drug Policy in Ontario." Toronto: Institute for Clinical Evaluative Sciences. www.ices.on.ca/file/Citizens_Council_Report_Nov-06.pdf.

Ontario Ministry of Health and Long-Term Care. 2007. *Ontario Drug Benefits Program*. Toronto. www.health.gov.on.ca/english/providers/program/drugs/oncology_review.html (accessed 18 August 2007).

Priest, L. 2006. "Private Clinics Reflect Need for Drug Policy, Experts Say." *Globe and Mail*, 9 December.

Sullivan, T., and C. Mustard. 2001. "Canada: More Market/More State." In *The Social Economics of Health Care*, edited by J. Davis. New York: Routledge.

Chapter 11

Policy and Politics: A Commentary on the Conference on Social Insurance for Health Care: Economic, Legal, and Political Considerations

Joseph White

The purpose of the conference that inspired this book was to begin discussion among Canadians about social insurance as a way to finance medical care. In their framing chapter, the organizers do not assert that social insurance, as they define it, is necessarily superior to financing from public general revenues. They begin instead from a presumption that social insurance is likely to be superior to private finance of medical care. The basic question, then, is whether social insurance might be a viable alternative, in the Canadian context, to a growing privatization of Canadian medical services.

Privatization, Colleen Flood, Mark Stabile, and Carolyn Tuohy argue, could result from something that is already happening and something that might happen. The ongoing trend is realignment of care practices toward services that are not guaranteed under the *Canada Health Act*. These services, mainly pharmaceuticals and long-term care, are partially funded by provincial programs, but either eligibility is limited (for pharmaceuticals), or access is constrained by supply shortages (nursing homes). As spending shifts toward these services, the public share of Canadian health care expenditures has been slowly declining. Table 1 indicates the result has been a lower public share of health care spending in Canada than in most other rich democracies.[1] This ongoing trend can be seen as a somewhat automatic privatization.[2]

The potential trend is increasing political support for privatization of *Canada Health Act* services. Strong public support for the act's principles has not been paired with effective demands that politicians raise taxes to match increases in the costs of that care. In response to overall budget pressures in the 1990s, provincial governments squeezed public spending tightly (see table 1). Among the results

234   JOSEPH WHITE

TABLE 1
Canadian health care expenditure

	Total as % of GDP	Public as % of GDP	Public as % of total	Public as % of government outlays	Public in Canada $ per capita, in 2000 prices
1960	5.4%	2.3%	42.6%		
1970	7.0	4.9	69.9	13.4	923
1980	7.1	5.4	75.6	12.8	1,331
1990	9.0	6.7	74.5	13.6	1,927
1991	9.7	7.2	74.6	13.7	2,012
1992	10.0	7.4	74.1	13.7	2,052
1993	9.9	7.2	72.7	13.6	2,013
1994	9.5	6.9	72.0	13.6	1,991
1995	9.2	6.5	71.4	13.3	1,934
1996	9.0	6.3	70.9	13.4	1,887
1997	8.9	6.2	70.1	13.9	1,913
1998	9.2	6.5	70.6	14.2	2,047
1999	9.0	6.3	70.0	14.6	2,091
2000	8.9	6.3	70.3	15.1	2,172
2001	9.4	6.6	69.9	15.5	2,290
2002	9.7	6.7	69.6	16.1	2,395
2003	9.9	6.9	70.1	16.7	2,480
2004	9.9e	6.9	69.8e	17.2e	2,539

Note: The final column is expressed in the value of dollars as of the year 2000 in order to control for the effects of overall price inflation.
Source: *OECD Health Data, 2006.*

of this constraint were declining public satisfaction with the Canadian health care system and particularly concern about waiting lists (Donelan et al. 1999, Blendon et al. 2003). Although governments responded by raising spending as a share of GDP after 2000, the organizers of this conference worry that increased costs will again not be matched by increased revenues, and that eventually spending cutbacks will lead to stronger demands to allow private reimbursement for *Canada Health Act* services. The Supreme Court of Canada's decision in the *Chaoulli* case has already encouraged provider interests to campaign for such changes (Lemmens and Archibald 2006).

These pressures could be met with measures to better control the costs of services, or to limit public demand for services. Costs could be better controlled, for example, with tougher payment rules or by refusing to reimburse for low-value treatments. Or demand could be reduced, according to many believers in the merits of increased primary and preventive care, with measures that reduce future need for expensive acute care. There has been plenty of consideration of such measures, however, so this conference was organized to direct attention to another possibility: diversifying the revenue sources for health care, so that constraint on direct public revenues would not require either excessive constraint on services or much greater reliance on private spending.

SOCIAL INSURANCE, PRIVATE INSURANCE, AND GOVERNMENT INSURANCE

While it may seem obvious and logical to Canadians, Canada's method of health care financing, in which the government directly operates insurance for both medical and hospital care, is unique. Most other rich democracies either rely mainly on separate social insurance funds or provide most services directly, without an explicit insurance mechanism. Germany, France, and Japan are examples of social insurance countries. The United Kingdom, Norway, and Sweden are examples of direct provision. A few countries provide insurance funded from general revenues for a portion of the population (Parts B and D of the US Medicare program for the elderly and disabled) or a portion of services (medical services in Australia, "extraordinary" expenses in the Netherlands).[3]

Hence, the question for this conference was whether it makes sense for Canadians to adopt some form of a method with which there is substantial experience. By social insurance, as Flood, Stabile, and Tuohy reported, we mean a system with the following aspects:

- Participation is compulsory: that is, a large portion of the population is required by law to join the system and contribute to its financing.
- Participation is based mainly on employment, with contributions then including payments from both employers and their employees, though they may be augmented with other funds.
- Thus most of the financing of benefits is derived from these dedicated funds.
- These funds are administered by one or more non-profit entities that are formally at arms' length from the government. It is then possible to argue that the revenues and spending are not directly part of government.
- Although the organizers did not emphasize the point, there are always multiple funds, which helps demarcate the separation between government and social insurance.

The most significant differences between social insurance and private insurance or out-of-pocket spending are:

- Mandates ensure that the individuals subject to the mandate will have insurance.
- Contributions based on payroll are much more proportional to income than are the payments in any private system. At best, private insurance will charge flat community rates, which means that poorer people must pay the same amount as wealthier people. At worst, private insurance will also charge families with more members or greater risks more, regardless of their ability to pay. Both patterns may, as in the United States, price some people out of the market.
- Although the managers of the social insurance funds may want to feather their own nests, they are not subject to the demands for profit-making and the formal pressures on managers that apply to managers of private insurers. Put another way, the "discipline of the market" does not apply. Indeed, "carriers are not allowed to go bankrupt and leave subscribers unprotected" (Glaser 1990, 19).
- Historically, competition for enrollees (or to avoid costly enrollees) has been a minor aspect of social insurance systems, while it is one of the basic dynamics of any private market insurance system. The chapters by Wynand van de Ven and Stefan Greß describe efforts to inject competition into a system, yet still have it retain the solidaristic advantages of social insurance. The results remain to be seen.[4]

Compared to private insurance, therefore, social insurance could be seen as having the basic equity and security advantages that are also offered by the *Canada Health Act*. It avoids the merits or demerits of market-based approaches – competition, "choice," people having different coverage according to their different personal utilities or abilities to pay – in favour of the merits or demerits of government coverage: social sharing, simplicity, redistribution, and security.

Why, then, would believers in these goals of the *Canada Health Act* object to social insurance? While public finance analysts often classify social insurance programs with public spending,[5] William A. Glaser (1990) is among those who have argued that there are distinct and important differences between social insurance and paying for health care from government revenues. The most obvious difference, and a potential reason for objection within the Canadian context, is that, at least formally, social insurance seems to violate the standard of "public administration." This issue was not, however, raised during the conference, and Professor Tuohy commented afterwards that it would likely not be a problem because a "non-profit authority accountable to the provincial government and subject to provincial audit" would probably be considered sufficient. The governance issues nevertheless would have to be addressed, but it is more likely that social insurance arrangements would be controversial because of their substantial reliance on payroll contributions and the fact that revenues are dedicated specifically to medical care costs. These topics were major themes in the conference discussion.

For *payroll contributions*, one key controversy is whether they are "regressive" and thus unfair compared to public insurance. The second is whether levies specifically on payroll have particularly undesirable economic effects. For *dedicated* (or *"earmarked"*) *revenues*, one key issue is whether this is a good way for governments to make budgeting decisions, as a matter of democratic or public finance principle. The other issue is whether earmarked financing has any predictable effect on levels of spending or security of financing, and, if such an effect exists, whether it is desirable. For *separate management*, the basic issues involve how to ensure that the governance structure serves public purposes.

The next three sections of this commentary consider each of these issues in turn. The final section will turn from policy to politics.

PAYROLL CONTRIBUTIONS

REDISTRIBUTION

The first issue about payroll contributions is their distributional effect. The framing paper echoes a common assumption that financing by general tax revenues "is usually progressive," while payroll contributions are regressive. Yet scholars of the welfare state have long observed that the progressivity of income tax rate schedules may be largely offset by preferential treatment of capital and by large consumption taxes, such as VAT or GST. Moreover, tax-welfare backlashes are less likely if revenues are less visible, which suggests that it is easier to support more generous social provision with more "regressive" taxes such as sales taxes (less visible) than with more "progressive" taxes like a graduated income tax (more visible). Harold Wilensky describes the pressures for tax revolts in nations with particularly visible tax burdens (such as high reliance on income taxes or, in an extreme case, Margaret Thatcher's poll tax). He adds, "Now contrast the countries that get away with expensive programs, however variable their efficiency: their financing of social programs rests heavily on indirect taxes such as the VAT or sales taxes, together with social security contributions of employers or employees" (Wilensky 2002, 384).

Hence concerns about lesser redistribution within a social insurance approach may be misguided for two reasons. First, finance from general revenues may not be much more redistributive. Second, social insurance financing may enable more robust programs, and so more redistribution on the spending side.

Wilensky's work has explained ways in which systems are not so progressive. There is reason to believe that systems have become even less progressive over the past two decades, for income tax rates have generally fallen while consumption tax rates have risen (Heady 2002). But there are serious disagreements among experts about how to measure progressivity (Norregaard 1990), as a result of which I could find no recent comparative measures beyond a study of direct taxes alone (Verbist 2004). That study confirms Wilensky's observation that high tax capacity is associated with lower progressivity, even without considering consumption taxes.[6]

However, in a major study of the progressivity of health care financing regimes as of around 1990, Wagstaff et al. (1999) compared 13 OECD countries, though not Canada. The data did not show a large or even consistent difference between the distributional effects of general revenue and social insurance financing. On balance, the authors concluded, health care finance in ten tax-financed systems was "proportional or mildly progressive" (ibid., 288). Mildly means very mildly: the most progressive overall system, the UK, had a Kakwani index of 0.051 (on a scale from -2, extremely regressive, to +1, extremely progressive). In contrast, finance in two of the social insurance countries (Germany and the Netherlands) was regressive, but in the third social insurance country, France, it was progressive. Overall, even the public component of health care finance did not deviate strongly from proportionality. Thus, among the countries in which health care was predominantly financed through public means, the Kakwani index of tax incidence for the public share ranged from -0.1003 (Netherlands in 1990) to 0.1112 (France in 1989).[7]

General revenues were not very progressive partly because indirect taxes are not. In addition, not all income taxes are progressive: much of health care in Denmark and Sweden is funded by local flat income taxes. The difference between France and the Netherlands "makes sense," the authors report, because, "in contrast to the Dutch scheme, the French scheme includes high earners as well as low earners; furthermore, pensioners and the unemployed, who are more likely than not to be in the bottom income groups, are virtually exempt from contributions (contribution rates are a mere 1 percent for these groups) (Wagstaff et al. 1999, 284).

In short, social insurance per se is not always less progressive than general revenue finance. General revenues can be proportional (the local income tax in Sweden) or regressive (almost all consumption taxes). The incidence of social insurance taxes depends not only on flat rates but also on exclusions and discounts (whether high income people pay on a lower share of income, or low income people have income excluded or taxed at lower rates).

Moreover, the marginal differences in redistribution on the revenue side are likely to be much less significant than the effects of finance methods on the spending side. As Sherry Glied discusses in this volume, the key question is progressivity of the system as a whole. Proportional payment for medical care is in itself a dramatic redistribution from the norm in a market, in which people with the same needs must pay the same amounts. If a family with a $30,000 income receives the same health care as does a family with a $90,000 income, while each pays the same proportion of income in taxes, the former family is getting three times as much value for money. If slightly less progressive finance allows a society to cover more of health care through social sharing, and less according to market awards, then the overall result for lower income citizens may well be better than if they paid a bit less in taxes and received less in coverage.

On balance, therefore, people who define equity as redistribution have no good reason to object to a social insurance form of health care finance, even though it is likely to rely predominantly on payroll contributions.

EFFECTS ON THE ECONOMY

There is more reason for concern that raising money specifically from a tax on wages, split between payments by employers and by employees, could reduce employment.

As Gunderson and Hyatt explain in their chapter, economists tend to promote two contradictory ideas. The first is that employers can determine their total payment for labour, that contributions toward the costs of benefits are simply part of that total, and so higher payments for benefits must be balanced out by lower cash wages. If this is true, health care spending should have no effects on the costs of hiring. The second view is that social insurance contributions by employers are in essence taxes on employment: in order to hire a person, the employer must pay not only what that person is worth (his or her wage) but a tax to the state in the form of the health care (or pension, or some other) percentage. The second view could not be true if those payments were simply traded for wage reductions.

Gunderson and Hyatt make the useful point that, even if you believe most of the cost would be paid by the employees, some portion might not, and there could be a lag, such that higher payroll contributions would only be incorporated into lower wages over a period of years. At least small lags must occur if wage bargaining does not happen at the same time as contributions are determined, so any contribution increases cannot be countered by immediate wage reduction. That does not tell us, however, either what portion of any social insurance charges would be "extra" from the standpoint of an employer or to what extent that could be sufficient to cause a reduction in employment.[8]

Although Gunderson and Hyatt provide estimated effects, I have to admit to scepticism about any macroeconomic analysis. Not only will results depend on many assumptions but it seems highly unlikely that effects would be linear. Rather, if a company is to respond by shifting jobs out of Ontario, there is likely to be a cut point below which the transaction costs of the transition are not worth the shift, and above which they are.

Moreover, any effects should depend greatly upon the sector and so particular labour and product markets involved. Assume a new social insurance program for pharmaceutical costs required that employers and employees each pay 2 percent of payroll on wages up to some maximum. At most that is a 2 percent increase for the employer. If it chooses to shed a proportional share of its labour, then management must either be willing to forego the sales that those workers would have enabled, find efficiencies that enable it to increase production with the reduced work force (in which case they might have shed the workers anyway), or produce with workers elsewhere. It is highly unlikely that this extra cost would be significant relative to the difference between wage levels in Ontario and in any Asian country. So the real question is whether such marginal extra costs would have much influence on decisions to manufacture in Ontario as opposed to, say, Ohio or Alberta.

The comparison to the United States will depend on whether the company pays health benefits in the US. If it does, any Canadian financing arrangements will seem a comparative bargain. The comparison within Canada would depend on whether any new social insurance approach is provincial or nationwide, and on whether the social insurance is for a service (say, pharmaceuticals) that was previously being substantially funded by employers anyway. If social insurance arrangements shift the visible burden of pharmaceutical costs from employers to employees, that might be a political problem, but it would certainly not inhibit employment.

This analysis suggests that the economic effects of any new required payroll contributions will depend on what the contributions cover. If they were to replace current *Canada Health Act* financing, these contributions could be large enough to potentially influence hiring decisions, at least in the short run. If they cover only a smaller portion of total costs – pharmaceuticals or long-term care – the effects would have to be quite modest. If there is some offset from reduction of wages, the effects would be even more modest. If new arrangements replace coverage that is largely paid by employers now, they should have no effect or even a positive one.

We should also remember that any financing can be accused of distorting the economy. Income taxes are said to depress incentives to earn and invest; budget deficits are said to reduce savings. Moreover, payroll taxes can and likely would be only part of the financing for any Canadian social insurance; proportional contributions could be assessed, for example, on pension benefits. Hence not all of the costs of any system would influence employment.

On balance, the economic effects of payroll contributions are unlikely to be positive. But, within the range that might be involved for services outside of the *Canada Health Act*, they seem unlikely to have much effect on employ-ment. Any effects on employment in Ontario would be limited further if other provinces adopted similar financing.

TRUST FUNDS AND DEDICATED FINANCING, OR EARMARKING

The second important distinction between social insurance and general rev-enue finance is that social insurance dedicates or earmarks some flow of funds to a particular spending purpose. The accounting may be set up, in American language, as a "trust fund," with special reports on whether funds are ad-equate to pay for program costs (Patashnik 2000).

EARMARKING IN PRINCIPLE

Earmarking of funds is roundly criticized in traditional public finance theory, on the grounds that it reduces decision-makers' flexibility to allocate resources efficiently. Eric Patashnik (2000, 22) summarizes this view: "Dedicating rev-enue for specific uses prevents policymakers from maximizing social welfare by directing revenues where they are needed most." As Musgrave and Musgrave (1973, 197) put it, earmarking "introduces rigidities" into public budgeting.

When a program has earmarked funds, it is hard to justify claims that it should be cut in order to pay for something else, and that is why earmarking reduces flexibility. That is also, of course, the point of earmarking: it solidi-fies government's commitment to a program, at least up to the amount of the earmarked revenues. Moreover, earmarking can clarify the link between taxes and spending, and so reduce some of the pathologies of public budgeting.

A basic budgeting dilemma is that inconsistent individual preferences may have no consistent solution. Consider what may happen when a government's budget is balanced, health care spending is funded by general revenues, and health care spending rises faster than revenues. Aside from cutting back on health care, there are three possible responses: to (i) increase revenues to pay for the health care; (ii) cut other spending to pay for the health care; or (iii) allow a (growing) budget deficit.

Now imagine that taxpayers would be willing to pay more for health care. They still might not accept a tax increase, for the following reasons. Some might prefer cutting defence to paying more in taxes. Some might prefer cut-ting education. Some might prefer to cut support for the poor. Some might prefer cutting rural programs, others urban programs. If a majority prefers cutting other programs, tax hikes might not pass. But there might be no ma-jority for cutting any particular program, so the deficit could increase by default.

The standard public finance view essentially posits a single rational actor making trade-offs. As soon as you allow for inconsistent preferences among the voters who actually get to decide, the process becomes a lot less responsible. In contrast, by limiting options, dedicated funding forces more direct decisions: if voters want more health care, they should be willing to pay for it.[9]

This argument is not perfect, but on the whole it convinces me that dedicated finance can work in principle. It seems particularly appropriate for health care, which is likely to be the kind of commitment that governments would change only rarely.

EARMARKING HEALTH CARE REVENUES IN PRACTICE

What, then, is the effect of dedicated revenues on level of spending? This topic was discussed extensively in the conference.[10] Although Sherry Glied described her analysis as the effect of social insurance on "efficiency," it was actually about costs. Wynand van de Ven, Stefan Greß, and others also commented, all agreeing that the form of finance has no direct relationship to the level of costs. This is true because most of the important cost control options, such as how to pay physicians, have no necessary relationship to how the money is collected.[11]

Although Glied's analysis was interesting and suggestive, its somewhat scattered results may be partially a result of its methods. Too many other factors are relevant for any statistical analysis to be reliable, given the small number of cases. Moreover, systems' relative results during one period may be a reaction to their contrary results in another period.[12] Both our discussions and other information do allow some reasonable, if not statistically verifiable, conclusions. To draw them, however, we must recognize two distinctions. First, the social insurance/general revenue finance distinction tends to be correlated with a difference in form of budgeting, and that difference can have effects for cost control that would be mistaken for an advantage for general revenue finance. So we should distinguish among those types of budgeting. Second, in order to understand the effects of dedicated finance on spending, we need to distinguish between two kinds of budget situations.

The two forms of budgeting are bureau budgeting and entitlement budgeting (White 1998). Governments usually organize programs by creating a bureau and promising the voters that the bureau will provide some good thing. This government bureau then is budgeted by allocating inputs of money and staff each year. In entitlement programs, by contrast, the government promises to either pay cash benefits (as for pensions) or to reimburse the costs of services purchased on the market (as in health insurance programs).

In health care, this is basically the difference between Beveridge (bureau) and Bismarck (entitlement) systems. All Beveridge systems, however, are financed by general revenues, while many entitlement systems are financed through social insurance. Any statistical comparisons will be sensitive to the years and countries selected, and the comparisons in this conference did not find a clear difference. Nevertheless, other things being equal, one should expect it to be easier to control the costs of Beveridge systems because bureau budgeting is easier to control than entitlement budgeting.[13] This then would look like an advantage for general revenue finance.

Overall budget conditions should also have a systematic effect. Professor Glied's analysis of different periods of time showed no clear pattern of advantage for one financing method over the other, but that is because they should have different cost control effects under different conditions. In our discussions, one participant pointed out that Canada and Sweden, which have general revenue systems, were able to drive costs down for periods of time in ways that no social insurance system managed. Professor Glied replied that in the 1980s, however, Germany was the cost control leader. This is true, but Germany led in the 1980s not by driving costs down but by stabilizing costs while they rose in other systems.

This pattern makes sense if you consider how the dynamics of other spending and of total revenues can affect health care budgeting in a general revenue system. During conditions of what Eugene Steuerle calls "easy financing," such as in the United States during most of the period from the late 1950s through about 1979, higher spending on some programs could be enabled by both an automatic increase in general revenues (through "bracket creep," which allowed politicians to "cut" taxes without revenues in fact declining), and a secular decline in some spending, mainly defence (Patashnik 2000). Similar dynamics (especially of progressive income taxes) existed for many years in other countries as well. In these situations, dedicated financing should be more constraining, because increased spending requires a visible decision to raise the earmarked taxes. During tough budget times, however – characterized by pressures on general revenues and competition from other needs – dedicated revenues should relatively protect health spending, by insulating it from budgetary competition. Concern about government deficits, for example, would not justify cutting a program that "pays for itself."

From these perspectives, one would predict that the general revenue systems of Canada or Sweden should have been more able to actually cut spending under conditions of serious budget constraint, both because of the greater pressure for trade-offs and because cuts to bureaus (in Canada this means hospital budgets), unlike entitlement cuts, do not have immediate visible consequences (though they became visible within a few years; see Donelan et al. 1999). In contrast, at least after the recession of the early 1980s, Germany's dedicated financing should have posed the cost control question more acutely than did the general revenue financing in many other countries.

Hence general revenue financing should be better if spending cutbacks are desired. Yet dedicated financing could be a bit better for restraining increases, at least during good times. Moreover, by making the option of increasing revenues more obvious, earmarked funding can bring choices more closely in line with public preferences by allowing direct decisions about how much health care to pay for. To put this another way, it should be easier to increase revenues as needed, if desired, with dedicated finance than with general revenue financing.

These distinctions appear relevant for considering social insurance financing for pharmaceuticals or long-term care in particular. In each case the agenda includes how to get the public to decide how much of each it is willing to pay for. The cost control agenda, given the growing needs, is more likely to be a matter of restraining growth than of cutting from the current base. In the case of long-term care, there is some reason for pre-funding, which, as Keith Banting reported during the conference, has been done with pensions and is inconceivable without earmarked funds. In the case of pharmaceuticals, the benefit is inherently an entitlement; no system provides it in bureau form.

From the perspectives of both budgeting principle and the ability to relate costs to income, therefore, I conclude that some form of dedicated funding, especially for services that are not covered under the *Canada Health Act*, is at least no less appropriate than general revenue finance and may be superior.

(OSTENSIBLY) SEPARATE MANAGEMENT

As Professors Flood, Stabile, and Tuohy report, social insurance per se involves some sort of governance structure that is at least nominally separate from government. Professors van de Ven and Greß address the issue in part, but focus mainly on how to make funds compete, if that is what policy-makers desire, while keeping them from competing through risk selection. They agree that this is hard, though Greß is more optimistic, and I am more pessimistic than either.[14] Yet there are many other relevant issues, and Canadian policy-makers might benefit from investigating the normal situation in which social insurance funds have not been expected to compete.

Canada's Ministry of Health generally wants social insurance funds to control expenses but also to take the blame for cost controls and to deal with the angry providers. Fund managers want the government to force providers into cost control deals and, by the way, take the blame – or kick in extra money from general revenues – or both.[15] However it plays out, this relationship is essentially a form of "stewardship," in which the government structures health care finance by statute (Glaser calls it "statutory health insurance") and then seeks to influence the system more or less indirectly, depending on whether it can live with the results of less interference.

Provincial governments might see some advantages from a social insurance structure. Yet it may not be so easy to hide behind the social insurance curtain and pull the strings, especially in a country where, as Ted Marmor argues, direct government control of insurance is the norm. Policy-makers would need to decide, for example, who should have authority to determine prices for pharmaceuticals or to create formularies.

The governance issues may be more problematic than reliance mainly on payroll taxes or the earmarking of funds. Nevertheless, they have been managed in enough other places that there ought to be a way to manage them in Canada. Overall, I would conclude that social insurance in principle is a perfectly reasonable way to finance some of Canada's health care. Policy-makers should be willing to consider the approach, particularly for those services not currently under the *Canada Health Act*.

POLITICAL CONSIDERATIONS

Whether such proposals make sense, given the political situation in Ontario or in Canada more generally, is an entirely different question. The political question is basically who will perceive gains and who will perceive losses from any specific proposal.

There are good reasons for scepticism of any social insurance proposal for pharmaceuticals. Proponents of such policies face a miniature version of the obstacles to national health insurance initiatives in the United States. Most people already have coverage, and from their perspective this coverage is largely paid by somebody else. Employers appear to pay for most workers, and government appears to pay for pensioners and lower income workers. The fact that a portion of lower paid workers is left out seems unlikely to be enough to get the rest of the voters to support a reform that demands more visible payment from them for something they are already receiving.

On the other hand, Steve Morgan makes a powerful argument that, as the baby boomers retire, there will be a major cost-shift from employers' budgets to government budgets, because governments largely pay for pharmaceuticals for the elderly. Moreover, as costs per capita rise, employers are likely to reduce the benefits they voluntarily provide, which would create pressure for a larger government role. Either effect would lead to a larger increase in government spending than in total pharmaceutical spending. Government spending is what premiers and finance ministers worry about, and so they will have strong incentives to look for an out. According to Morgan's account, there is room for much more successful cost control, both through stricter price controls and refusing to pay more for copycat drugs. So there are five possibilities – slashing current pharmaceutical benefits, higher spending funded by deficits, higher spending financed by cutting other programs or raising general taxes, stricter cost control, and alternative financing – all of which are likely to be unpopular. The result cannot be predicted with any confidence.

Turning to long-term care (LTC), we should remember that both Germany and Japan enacted new long-term care entitlements financed through social insurance, despite macroeconomic concerns, during the 1990s. The two systems appear to be imperfect but fairly successful both as policy and politics. If arrangements to pay for nursing homes and home help are patchy and unreliable in any given province in Canada, if the need is likely to increase over time, if the province is already paying for substantial (but insufficient) services from general revenues, and if policy-makers can even make a fairly familiar argument for pre-funding, some sort of LTC social insurance initiative could seem attractive. Whether the voters perceive the same need is questionable; participants in the conference reported that voters appear unconcerned.

From the perspective of provincial premiers or finance ministers, any new social insurance arrangements for either pharmaceuticals or LTC would be attractive if they freed up some of the revenues the provinces currently spend for those services. This suggests that provinces could provide some general revenue subsidies to new social insurance funds, yet still perhaps free up new resources to improve access to *Canada Health Act* services, therefore reducing pressure to privatize those services. It would be easier for provincial leaders to justify this kind of budgetary manoeuvre – which after all would still involve mandating new payments from many citizens – if they could claim that the federal government provided incentives for them to do so. For instance, the federal government, making the kinds of arguments that were used to sell pre-funding of pensions, could declare a coming long-term care crisis and offer supplementary funds to provinces that create social insurance plans for LTC.

I will not pretend to judge the prospects of such manoeuvres. Whenever politicians seek to reallocate visible costs among citizens, they take major risks. But they will take risks also if they try to cut medical benefits for their citizens. Social insurance is a perfectly reasonable way to finance health care, and far superior to relying on private finance. There is good reason to consider creating funds for some portion of those services not included in the *Canada Health Act*. Whether that consideration will turn into policies will depend on political circumstances, and political entrepreneurship, in the future.

NOTES

[1] According to OECD data, the public sector paid for 70.1 percent of Canadian health care in 2003. This was toward the low end of a list of 21 countries that seem most comparable in terms of levels of economic development (Australia, Austria, Belgium, Canada, Finland, France, Germany, Iceland, Ireland, Italy, Japan, Luxembourg, the Netherlands, New Zealand, Norway, Portugal, Spain, Sweden, Switzerland, United Kingdom, United States). With one exception (Spain), the countries that were lower – Australia, the Netherlands, Spain, Switzerland, and United States – are well known for the role of private insurance in their systems. Austria, Belgium, and Portugal all had public shares within three percentage points of Canada's. The other 12 countries all had public shares at least five percentage points higher. Over the decade from 1993 to 2003, the Canadian public share fell, but slowly: by 2.6 points. The public share rose in 11 of the countries; it fell by more than in Canada only in Spain, the Netherlands, and Austria. These data are subject to many caveats about reliability, as the OECD analysts report (data taken from *OECD Health Data, 2006*).

[2] This form of privatization is not quite "automatic," because it depends on provincial decisions about coverage of these services, so on provincial choices. In fact, data provided later in the conference by Professor Greg Marchildon showed that much of the increase in provincial spending has gone for services that are not covered under the *Canada Health Act*. Thus governments have chosen to limit the proportion of these services that will shift to the private sector.

[3] For further description of this difference see White (2001); it is often referred to as the difference between Bismarck (social insurance) and Beveridge (direct provision) systems. Neither type is likely to be entirely pure, but the distinction is worthwhile for reasons described below.

[4] Glaser (1990) provides the authoritative description of these dynamics over time in many countries.

[5] For example, OECD Health Data 2006 has only two categories, "public" and "private" expenditure, and classifies social insurance as public expenditure.

[6] In addition to searching plausible websites (OECD, IMF) and journals, I consulted with Professor Sven Steinmo of the University of Colorado, who works in this area, and he agreed that both definitional arguments and the pure difficulty of the work meant no recent studies of overall progressivity cross-nationally that he knew of. For a good explanation of the trends in tax policy in OECD nations, see Steinmo (2002).

[7] The figures cited here use the later result for countries for which the authors report two results. The US and Switzerland are the two countries in the sample for which finance at the time of study was not predominantly "public" in the study's sense. Ironically, because poor people in those countries were disproportionate beneficiaries of public funds, their public spending was measured as more progressive. But their total spending is the most regressive in the data. This is another indication

that the share of spending that is covered in the public sector matters more than the "progressivity" of the public sector revenues.

[8] Discussion at the conference included statements that the "big three" American automakers have much better margins on vehicles manufactured in Canada because their health care costs per vehicle are on average much less. A business reporter for the *Globe and Mail* told me in personal conversation on the day before the conference that the difference is about $800 per vehicle. This would only be relevant if the automakers are *not* paying that extra $800 in wages to Canadian workers. This is actually a marvellous test of the economists' theory, since you have the same employers and the same unions on both sides of the border, and the result does not confirm the "there is a fixed amount of compensation and it is just allocated between wages and benefits" hypothesis.

[9] This is an idealized account because there may be spending on a program that is not coming from the earmarked funds, which will confuse the relationship. Patashnik (2000) explains how this has been a factor in the funding of airport construction in the US. But there is still a distinct difference between the visibililty of financing choices for programs with dedicated funding and programs funded from the general fund.

[10] It also has been debated by policy-makers, for example at the time the US enacted its Medicare program. For a summary of the contrasting views at the time, see Patashnik 2000, 97-8.

[11] See White (1999) for an extensive discussion of this point; there are associations between, for example, high socialization of finance and coordination of payment; but they are not necessary associations. Van de Ven's argument was essentially that methods that I argue are not likely to work very well – forms of "managed competition" – also can be implemented within both social insurance and general revenue financing approaches

[12] I would expect, for example, that the spending increases in the UK and Canada in the first decade of the twenty-first century would make general revenue systems seem relatively generous at present; yet in each case those increases are a reaction to the previous strong constraint in those systems.

[13] For the full argument see White (1998). It is easier for politicians to deny the effect of bureau spending restraint, displacing blame for any service shortages on the "bureaucrats." They can also delay maintenance on bureau facilities. In contrast, controlling entitlement spending requires either explicitly cutting payments to providers who, unlike bureaucrats, are powerful interest groups, or explicitly constraining promises to the voting beneficiaries.

[14] Compared to Professor van de Ven, I am more impressed by the overall negative experience to date.

[15] I see this as being especially the logic for many years in Germany, where both fund managers and providers received "guidance" as to the amount of premium increase that would be allowed, if any.

REFERENCES

Blendon, R., C. Schoen, C. DesRosches, R. Osborn, and K. Zapert. 2003. "Common Concerns amid Diverse Systems: Health Care Experiences in Five Countries." *Health Affairs* 22 (3): 106-21.

Donelan, K., R.J. Blendon, C. Schoen, K. Davis, and K. Binns. 1999. "The Cost of Health System Change: Public Discontent in Five Nations." *Health Affairs* 18 (3): 206-16.

Flood, C.M., K. Roach, and L. Sossin, eds. 2006. *Access to Care, Access to Justice: The Legal Debate over Private Health Insurance in Canada.* Toronto: University of Toronto Press.

Glaser, W.A. 1990. *Health Insurance in Practice.* San Francisco: Jossey-Bass.

Heady, C. 2002. "The Truth about Tax Burdens." *OECD Observer* (24 October 2006). http://www.oecdobserver.org/news/printpage.php/aid/651/The_truth_about_tax_burdens.

Lemmens, T. and T.Archibald. 2006. "The CMA's Chaoulli Motion and the Myth of Promoting Fair Access to Health Care." In *Access to Care, Access to Justice: The Legal Debate over Private Health Insurance in Canada,* edited by Flood et al., 323-46. Toronto: University of Toronto Press.

Musgrave, R.A., and P.B. Musgrave. 1973. *Public Finance in Theory and Practice.* New York: McGraw-Hill.

Norregaard, J. 1990. Progressivity of Income Tax Systems. *OECD Economic Studies* 15 (autumn): 83-110.

OECD. 2006. *Health Data 2006 database.*

Patashnik, E.M. 2000. *Putting Trust in the U.S. Budget: Federal Trust Funds and the Politics of Commitment.* New York: Cambridge University Press.

Steinmo, S. 2002. The Evolution of Policy Ideas: Tax Policy in the Twentieth Century. *British Journal of Politics and International Relations* 5 (2): 206-36.

Verbist, G. 2004. "Redistributive Effect and Progressivity of Taxes: An International Comparison across the EU Using EUROMOD." *EUROMOD Working Paper* No. M5/04, October.

Wagstaff, A., E. van Doorslaer, and H. van der Burg. 1999. "Equity in the Finance of Health Care: Some Further International Comparisons." *Journal of Health Economics* 18 (3): 263-90.

White, J. 1998. "Entitlement Budgeting vs. Bureau Budgeting." *Public Administration Review* 58 (6).

– 1999. Targets and Systems of Health Care Cost Control." *Journal of Health Politics, Policy and Law* 24 (4).

– 2001. National Health Care/Insurance Systems. *International Encyclopedia of the Social and Behavioral Sciences.* Vol. 15. 4th ed. Amsterdam: Elsevier.

Wilensky, H.L. 2002. *Rich Democracies: Political Economy, Public Policy, and Performance.* Berkeley: University of California Press.

Chapter 12

Conclusion

Colleen M. Flood, Mark Stabile, and Carolyn Hughes Tuohy

The preceding essays from scholars around the world have probed the possibility of implementing some element of social insurance funding in the Canadian health care system. We have done so through an examination of other jurisdictions, through theory and evidence on health care financing, and through evidence from other social programs. In our view, five dimensions emerge as important to consider in evaluating the advantages and disadvantages of providing a greater role for social health insurance in Canada's health care system. These dimensions are equity and universality, efficiency and employment, sustainability (which includes tax tolerance/willingness to pay), wait times, and effective administration. We address each of these in turn below.

EQUITY AND UNIVERSALITY

Canadians have reaffirmed their desire for a universal and equitable health care system time and again. We expect that health care will be available for everyone, regardless of ability to pay. Despite the importance we place on this value, most provinces still lack universal coverage for prescription medication and long-term care, and while many individuals have private coverage to make up this gap, a sizable number of Canadians (approximately 10 percent) have no coverage, and another 10 percent are significantly underinsured (Health Canada, 2000).

Our explorations of the advantages and disadvantages of social health insurance highlight several important considerations for ensuring both universality and equity in financing Canadian health care. First, all models of public health care finance considered in this volume, including general tax revenue financing and social insurance financing, can both achieve universal coverage and be more or less progressive or regressive depending on how they are structured. That said, in practice it appears that general tax financing is usually more progressive than social insurance financing across countries with different financing structures and even within countries with elements of both general revenue financing and social insurance financing (Wagstaff et al. 1999). The income tax system in most countries (which is often a large source of revenue for health care) is generally more progressive than either payroll taxes or social insurance premiums. This may be related, in part, to the closer connection made in social insurance models between individual costs and benefits, or may be due to the administrative ease in progressively scaling income tax rates versus premiums that are shared by employers and employees and, in some cases, paid directly to insurers.

Despite the fact that general taxation is slightly more progressive, it is important to note that if progressive redistribution were the primary goal, one would need to look beyond just health care finance. As Glied points out in her chapter, another dollar spent on health care is likely less progressive than a dollar spent on social assistance or public education. In general this is because health care utilization is higher among the elderly, and older people of higher socio-economic status tend to live longer and therefore use more care. Conversely, social assistance is generally focused on low socio-economic status individuals. Public education falls somewhere between these two. In light of this a more practical goal for health care finance, harkening back to our introductory chapter, is to balance progressivity, efficiency, and sustainability. Certainly, we do not discount the importance of ensuring progressivity, but insisting that each additional dollar of finance must be as progressively raised as the last risks upsetting the goals of efficiency and sustainability and potentially ignores a broader progressivity agenda in government spending. Thus, there is no reason in our view not to explore from an equity perspective the potential for a greater role for social health insurance in the health care system, particularly if it allows for other taxation dollars to be spent on other critical areas such as education and social welfare.

Both general tax finance and social insurance financing can be used to improve on the universality of coverage outside hospital and doctor services in Canada. Canadian provinces already vary in the mechanisms they use to finance prescription drug coverage. Most provinces use general tax financing to cover some or all of the population. One – Quebec – uses a combination of a contributory public plan, general tax financing, and regulated private health insurance to achieve universal coverage (more on this later). All provincial plans incorporate deductibles and copayments into the financing structure. These payments can, and in some cases do, vary by ability to pay.

Introducing social insurance models into this mix would, however, impose some design complications not currently imposed by the general tax revenue models. In particular, any new financing model not based on general tax revenues would need to consider how to best collect funding from the elderly.

Given the demographics of Canadian society, and particularly given the pattern of use and expenditures on drugs for the elderly, social health insurance could not be sustainable if the elderly were not required to make any contribution to costs. Per capita drug expenditures increase sharply after age 65, peaking in the 80-84 age category and then declining for those 85 and older (Canadian Institute for Health Information 2005, Appendix E; Morgan 2006).[1] Presuming that beneficiaries should continue to pay for benefits past retirement, should the employment relationship remain the primary collection mechanism, or should payments be made directly to the government? Similar contribution issues would apply to dependents and the unemployed. Any proposal for introducing a greater component of social insurance into the system would have to tackle this issue and incorporate a fair level of contribution on the part of the elderly to ensure the new program's sustainability. Since other jurisdictions have also wrestled with this issue, it may be possible to learn from abroad in developing the Canadian approach.

EFFICIENCY AND EMPLOYMENT

In their chapters, Glied, Gunderson and Hyatt, Mintz, and White all examine the efficiency of social insurance financing versus tax financing. Most authors, for the purposes of their analysis, have assumed that systems are financed entirely through tax revenues or entirely through social insurance. On balance, the research in this volume suggests that as a single source of finance, general tax financing from a combination of sources including both income and consumption taxes is preferable from an efficiency perspective, given the disincentive effects of taxes on labour (the contributions required by employers and employees may be viewed in substance, some argue, as a tax on labour) and Canada's historical reliance on general revenue to finance social spending. However, in practice, jurisdictions are not restricted to a single source of finance. With multiple financing options available to choose from, it is neither clear that it is efficient to rely on a single source, nor that the marginal dollar should come from the largest source of financing.

One key concern noted by Gunderson and Hyatt (chapter 4) is that a payroll tax (for in their view this is what social insurance contributions effectively amount to) may have a negative effect on employment. Joe White disagrees (chapter 11), but assuming that Gunderson and Hyatt are correct, it is worth considering how the magnitude of the problem might vary depending on the characteristics of different sectors of the health care system. Consider, for example, financing prescription drugs through a social insurance system. While prescription drug insurance is not universal in Canada, it is the norm for the employed population. Approximately two-thirds of full-time workers have supplemental private health insurance, including drug coverage, through their employment relationship (Stabile 2001). Financing for this supplemental private insurance is similar to social health insurance in that it is usually split between employer and employee contributions. These contributions include amounts to cross-subsidize risk across the population. Few, if any, include amounts to cross-subsidize by ability to pay; in other words, private health insurance is less progressive than either general tax finance or social health insurance. Shifting to a social insurance contribution that includes greater progressivity of financing would mean that contributions by employers and employees would need to increase in order to cross-subsidize lower income individuals. This could then lead to a reduction in employment, as noted by Gunderson and Hyatt. On the other hand, it might also be the case that some cost efficiencies may be gained through larger purchasers and reduced administrative costs.

Importantly, the overall increase in contributions will be a function of the net increase in costs, if any. Therefore, any employment effects for the majority of the working population already paying contributions for supplemental insurance will also be on the net increase in contributions. It seems likely then that in this sector the employment effect of universalizing employment based drug coverage will likely be small. However, for the minority of individuals and employers not currently paying for supplemental coverage, there will be a larger increase in taxes or premiums paid and a correspondingly larger potential employment effect.

It is nonetheless important to keep in mind several mitigating factors. First, the employment effects of requiring increased contribution from employers and employees need to be considered not in isolation but relative to the effects of raising equivalent revenue through general taxation. Any increase to general income tax rates to finance health care costs would also presumably result in reduced labour supply. Second, Gunderson and Hyatt's hypotheses presume that employees would not value the increased health benefits at their full cost, or would not associate the increased cost with any individual or public benefit. If employees do value the benefits at the full (or greater than full) cost, then presumably the trade-off of wages for increased public services would be completely passed on to workers in terms of lower wages and there would no employment effects.

SUSTAINABILITY: TAX TOLERANCE/ WILLINGNESS TO PAY

Harking back to our introduction and the question of whether a health care system can expand on all frontiers of quality, accessibility, and sustainability, we turn now to examine whether social health insurance finance may not offer a more sustainable model of funding. (We refer here to political, not actuarial sustainability.) One of the assumptions driving the recent consideration of more diversified sources of public finance in both tax based and social insurance systems is that taxpayers and contributors to social insurance respectively are at or approaching the limits of their tolerance for rate increases. Hence policy-makers in tax based systems are beginning to consider whether there is room to introduce or increase social insurance contributions, while those in social insurance systems look for tax room to increase revenues.

The possibility that there is an increased "willingness to pay" as a result of introducing a component of social insurance funding into tax based systems was certainly something that animated us to bring together scholars to debate the advantages of social health insurance. Ted Marmor in his contribution picks up on this point and speculates that social insurance "has special relevance where older grounds for public finance of collective action have weakened." He argues that social insurance provides a different base of legitimacy: the "grounds for deservingness" in a social insurance system include not only one's status as a citizen but also "one's own 'contribution' to a common pool for an earmarked purpose." The central ideas of social insurance, he states, "provide a sustained, historically important basis for treating benefits enjoyed as deserved and the distribution of those benefits – whether cash or in-kind – as 'earned' and therefore expected to be delivered."

Joe White proposes another reason why the electorate, at least in theory, might be more amenable to the introduction or increase in social insurance contribution than in general taxes. Tax increases confront the classic problem of inconsistent preferences among voters. That is, Voter A may want to see an increase in spending on Program A, but believes it should be financed not by raising taxes but by cutting Program B. Voter B, on the other hand, wants spending on Program B increased by cutting Program A, not by raising taxes. Aggregated across all voters, these preferences defeat any proposed increases in general taxation. On the other hand, social insurance contributions are clearly targeted to certain programs and not others. Social insurance funds, to be sure, can be supplemented in various ways from general revenues. Given their ultimate accountability for the results, governments may be drawn into such subsidization on occasion. Nonetheless, the existence of a separate fund, established on a self-sustaining basis, creates an additional political and accounting buffer to reallocation. And as we argue in the final section of this paper, a formulaic approach to the adjustment of social insurance contributions over time can reduce the likelihood of government intervention.

In Canada, the pervasiveness of tax reduction agendas (or at least the aversion to tax increases) by federal and provincial governments of all partisan stripes in the past decade suggests that governments have been responding to either or both of the dynamics described by Marmor and White – a weakening of citizen solidarity or a rational calculus of the relationship between taxation and expenditure. Health care, however, may be one important exception to these general trends. In public opinion polls, expenditures on health care typically win in pair-wise comparisons of preference with most other areas of expenditure or with tax cuts. Hence social insurance contributions dedicated to health care could be more attractive than increases in general taxation.

Empirical evidence on this question is limited. Unfortunately for our purposes, no polling has been done in Canada on the specific question of social insurance for health care, and there is limited political experience with social insurance options. There is, however, considerable evidence regarding public attitudes toward taxation for health care. The annual Pollara Health Care in Canada survey has tracked public opinion regarding tax increases for health care since 1998. In these surveys, reallocating funding from other areas of government spending to health consistently receives stronger support than tax increases, even if those taxes are income related and/or the revenues are earmarked for health care. Responses, however, are somewhat volatile and dependent on the framing of the question. In 2002 and 2003, respondents were asked whether they would pay more, either through taxes or out of pocket, to maintain the current level of service. In 2002 a majority (56 percent) indicated such a willingness to pay; in the following year the proportion fell to 47 percent. Asked whether they would be willing to pay more to *improve* the range of services covered or the timeliness of care, respondents indicated greater willingness: 69 percent in 2002 and 60 percent in 2003 (Pollara 2003). In 2006 the options were framed differently: forced to choose one option for increasing funds for health care, 33 percent supported reallocation from other programs as compared with 18 percent who supported earmarked taxes for health care (Pollara 2006). While these results do not relate to social insurance per se, they suggest that the introduction of a social insurance component into Canadian health care would need to be carefully framed: to be related clearly to increased benefits, at least for a substantial proportion of the population, and constituted separate and apart from the funding of other programs.

(On the latter point, a rough bird's-eye view of European health systems suggests that there may be a link between levels of public spending on health and the design of financing arrangements. The top ten OECD nations in terms of public health spending as a proportion of GDP in 2005 are either social insurance countries – France, Germany, Iceland, Austria and Belgium – or the tax financed but highly decentralized Nordic countries – Norway, Denmark, and Sweden, in all of which health care revenues are raised largely at the level of the counties, whose principal responsibility is health care.[2] Only one of the top ten public spenders, tiny Iceland, with a population of 290,000, has a centrally financed and administered public health insurance regime. On its face, this pattern seems to suggest that assigning responsibility for raising health care revenues to a public agency other than the central government is associated with greater willingness to pay on the part of the citizenry. While intriguing, this hypothesis needs much more careful investigation to take account of the range of other historical, political, and economic factors at play.)

Apart from polling data, there is also limited and mixed evidence of Canadians' willingness to support increased taxes for health through the political process. Several provinces levy taxes that are labelled as health premiums, although the funds flow to general revenue and account for only a small proportion of total provincial health spending. Contrasting experience in Quebec and Ontario with the introduction of health premiums in the recent past suggests how politically delicate this measure can be.

In the 2004 provincial budget the Ontario government introduced a "health premium" to be paid by individuals on an income related scale.[3] The premium bore little resemblance to a social insurance contribution. As the government acknowledged, it was in fact a tax.[4] Although the impetus for the tax was indeed the rising share of health care in the provincial budget, the revenue it generated flowed to the Consolidated Revenue Fund, and receiving health care benefits was not contingent on payment of the premium. Indeed, asked to report on expenditures made possible by the new revenue, the government listed a number of environmental initiatives that, while addressing the social determinants of health, clearly did not fall into the category of "health care." The measure was greeted by a storm of public protest which did not abate, particularly since the premier had clearly aligned himself with the "no tax increase" agenda in the 2003 provincial election. Public ire was exacerbated by the fact that several services such as physiotherapy were partially or fully delisted in the same 2004 budget. The health premium was made an issue by the opposition parties in the 2007 Ontario election; it was clear that lingering public discontent remained. Although the campaign overall turned in favour of the Liberals, who were returned with a majority government, the experience with the health premium may well make future Ontario governments leery of earmarked taxes per se for health care. In fact, however, this case gives us limited information about the political feasibility of social insurance, which would differ markedly from the health premium as a separate contributory fund linked to specific benefits.

The Ontario experience contrasts with that of Quebec, where the Parti Québécois government introduced premiums for public drug coverage in 1996. The new framework was designed to fill the gaps between employer based plans of drug coverage and existing public programs for the elderly and those on public assistance, to ensure universal coverage for prescription drugs outside hospitals. The changes involved mandating individuals to have such coverage: those eligible for coverage under a private group plan (typically employer based) were required to register, while all others were required to enrol in the public plan. The framework also involved some further regulation of employer based plans, requiring them to cover dependents, include all drugs on the government formulary, and have deductibles and copayments no higher than the government plan. The expansion of public coverage was to be financed in part through income scaled premiums (waived entirely for social assistance recipients and low income seniors) collected through the income tax system, copayments, and deductibles for the new public plan, as well as (in a highly controversial measure) the introduction of income scaled deductibles and copayments for recipients of existing public coverage for the elderly and welfare recipients. The plan was generally supported by medical associations and private insurers, although the latter criticized some of its features (Canadian Life and Health Insurance Association 2000). Advocates for seniors and welfare recipients attacked the plan for its imposition of user charges. Escalating costs for pharmaceuticals exceeded initial cost projections for the program, and because the government was not willing to pass these costs on with fully proportionate increases in premiums, the share of costs covered by premium revenue declined quite rapidly from 25 percent to 20 percent over the first five years (Forget 2002). Nonetheless, the plan has become a fixture of the Quebec health insurance system. Although the Liberals denounced the plan when in opposition, they retained it upon assuming office in 2003.

In contrast to Ontario, the Quebec plan had some of the features of European style social health insurance. A separate Drug Plan Account was established in the government's books to receive revenues from contributions, whether paid by subscribers or on their behalf by government from the Consolidated Revenue Fund. Contributions were tied to benefits – a dimension that was emphasized by the fact that, while coverage was compulsory, individuals could chose between employer based plans and the public plan. And like some systems of social insurance for health care elsewhere, the Quebec framework incorporated both regulated private insurance and public insurance to achieve universal coverage. However, several features of the program – the facts that subscriber contributions covered only about one-fifth of the costs of the public program and that it was administered by the Quebec public health insurance board, the Régie de l'assurance maladie du Québec (RAMQ), and heavily subsidized from general revenue – mean that it is essentially a general government program with a social insurance "flavour."

How would the introduction of a more fully fledged version of social insurance for a component of health care financing fare in the Canadian political context? Some interesting insight can potentially be gained from another arena in which social insurance currently exists in Canada: namely, public pensions. In that case, the public appears to be more tolerant of increases in contributions. In 1997, in the context of increasing concern about the future viability of the Canada Pension Plan (CPP), reforms were introduced that increased payroll based contribution rates (shared equally by employers and employees) from 5.6 percent to 9.90 percent (a more than 75 percent increase) over the 1997–2003 period, and also provided for an automatic increase in contribution rates in the future depending on regular analyses of the future viability of the plan by the CPP chief actuary.

Public opinion polling at the time found that support for raising premiums garnered by far the strongest support among the available options for dealing with the potential gap between future funding and demand, in a context in which reallocation from other areas of government spending was *not* seen as an option, given the separate administration of the CPP (Mendelsohn 2002).[5] These reforms were negotiated through the federal-provincial governance mechanisms of the CPP and did not become a significant political issue.

A number of dimensions of pension policy in Canada may help to explain the public acceptability of these contribution increases. The CPP forms part of a framework that also incorporates private employment-based pensions, private tax-sheltered savings, and old-age benefits funded through general taxation. Hence the burden of funding for retirement and old-age benefits is shared across these sources of finance. As Béland and Myles have pointed out (2002), this has allowed payroll-based CPP contributions (both employer and employee) to be relatively modest in international perspective,[6] and therefore increases do not cause the same alarm about employment effects as has been the case in other nations.[7] Furthermore, by raising the rates for the contributory portion of pension funding, government appealed to the "worker-saver" basis of solidarity highlighted by Marmor, at a time when a tax-cutting agenda was asking less from "citizens."

These characteristics are also exhibited to some degree in the Quebec pharmacare case. There as well, premiums were related to a public plan that was one component of a broader framework incorporating private employment-based insurance and a fully tax-supported plan for low income beneficiaries. Pomey and her colleagues argue that these very characteristics of the Quebec "public/private partnership" are what account for its success as a political compromise (Pomey et al. 2007).

Clearly, the design of any new social insurance component introduced into the Canadian funding mix for health care, and its relationship to existing components of the system, would be crucial to its public acceptability. It would need to be no less generous in its benefits than any component of the public or private coverage that it replaced or changed, although it could require a greater individual contribution. Public opinion polls, as well as the contrasting experiences with the Ontario health premium, Quebec pharmacare, and the CPP, suggest that there is more tolerance for contribution increases that are associated with increased benefits (or at least with the avoidance of benefit reductions) than with those that are simply devoted to maintaining the status quo or, even worse, are also accompanied by benefit reductions. The Quebec and CPP cases additionally suggest that these conditions are more likely to be met where contribution increases are tied to a plan that forms one component of a balanced framework incorporating other modes of public and private finance as well and building on existing institutions (e.g., the presence of private health insurance to which employers and employees already contribute and in which some risk-pooling occurs).

As with the other criteria for assessing the potential of social insurance in the Canadian context, the key to success in political acceptability appears to lie in a well-designed diversification of funding sources. That may limit the role of social insurance to those areas of the health system in which private insurance can also play a significant role without negative feedback effects on the public sector. We return to this point below.

WAIT TIMES

Just as the prospect that a dose of social health insurance might assist in insuring the sustainability of the public system (through engendering greater willingness to pay) animated our initial interest in social health insurance, so did the issue of wait times. The puzzle was how European social health insurance countries, which spend approximately the same level of GDP on health care as Canada (although somewhat more than most tax financed countries), appear less afflicted with the problem of wait times. Siciliani and Hurst (2004)[8] found that waiting times are a serious health policy issue in the twelve countries involved in the OECD Waiting Times project: Australia, Canada, Denmark, Finland, Ireland, Italy, the Netherlands, New Zealand, Norway, Spain, Sweden, and United Kingdom. Of these countries, only the Netherlands is a "social health insurance" country, and it seems that there the magnitude of the wait times problem was relatively small and has now been virtually eliminated. Siciliani and Hurst found wait times to be of little policy concern in a second group of countries: Austria, Belgium, France, Germany, Japan, Luxembourg, Switzerland, and the United States. Again, all these countries apart from the US either operate social health insurance systems or have universal, heavily regulated private health insurance schemes (Switzerland).

That at least some European countries do not appear to struggle with wait times and lists of the magnitude experienced in Canada has not gone unnoticed. Brian Day, the president of the Canadian Medical Association, has argued that, following in the footsteps of countries such as France, Switzerland, and Germany, Canada should allow private health insurance for medically necessary hospital and physician services. Similarly, John Carpay of the Canadian

Constitutional Foundation states, "With parallel private and public system operating side by side, Austria, Belgium, France, Germany, Japan, Luxembourg and Switzerland all have no waiting lists in their public health care systems" (Carpay 2007). Their prescription for wait times in medicare, however, assumes the key difference between Canada and these European countries is the existence of "parallel" private health insurance. In truth, the key difference is that these European countries are run on a social health insurance model (or in the case of Switzerland, on a universal, regulated private health insurance model) and not a tax funded model. Countries that are run on a tax funded model and allow a parallel private health insurance tier (as would be the case in Canada if Day and Carpay are successful in their advocacy) include countries like Ireland, the UK, and New Zealand – all of which have long struggled with wait times.

None of our contributors directly addressed the puzzle of why European countries with social health insurance systems seem to largely avoid difficulties with wait times. Part of the reason may be that there is no systematic, yearly, internationally comparable collection of wait time data. Even amongst jurisdictions where wait times have been identified as a policy issue, a uniform definition has been elusive, and thus comparable data are difficult to obtain. Furthermore, a growing body of research suggests that wait times per se are not an appropriate indicator of the effectiveness of a health care system, especially if the length of waiting is not linked with some measure of necessity of treatment. Nonetheless, wait times remain a significant political issue. Within the Canadian system the seeming failure on the part of governments to eliminate them is leading Canadians to question the very structure of the public system. There are increasing calls for privatization so that those with resources can buy their way to the front of queues; a number of court challenges have arisen (*Chaoulli*), and more are emerging (see Flood and Xavier 2007) with the intent of overthrowing regulations preventing the flourishing of a parallel private insurance sector. So, in short, the existence of long wait times imperils the political sustainability of Canada's public system.

There is no shortage of innovative approaches to the issue of wait times around the world. Examples include tying funding for hospitals and other providers to wait time targets; sub-contracting with private hospitals and clinics; publishing wait time information about hospitals and providers and allowing dollars to "follow the patient" as they seek out providers with low wait times; setting in place wait time targets or guarantees and then paying for patients to go out of the jurisdiction if these are not met; centralizing wait lists; and better controlling prioritization on the wait list and who gets on. Approaches loosely fall into two categories: demand side management (trying to control and mediate the demand for services for which there are wait times) and supply side management (trying to more efficiently organize the system to meet demand). Yet, apart from these myriad approaches – none of which has yet to emerge as the cure-all – is there something in the method of financing that contributes to either ensuring that wait lists don't manifest or, if they do, to ensuring they are attended to?

Siciliani and Hurst (2004) compared nations that identified wait times as an issue (recall that all but one of these 12 countries is tax financed) with nations that either have reported low wait times or do not identify wait times as an issue in their health care system (recall that these are primarily systems funded through social health insurance). They found that "countries which do not report waiting times, on average spend more in health care, have higher capacity (measured in terms of acute care beds and doctors), and implement more frequently forms of activity-based funding for hospitals and fee-for-service systems for doctors (as opposed to salary)." In the Canadian system we seem to have some of the attributes associated with countries that do not experience wait times. For example, unlike other tax financed countries, we spend similar amounts on health care to European countries, and we pay our physicians on a fee-for-service basis. Nonetheless wait times remain a problem. Applying Siciliani and Hurst's analysis to wait times in Canada seems to be linked to relatively lower numbers of physicians per capita and hospital beds per capita and the fact that our hospitals are not funded primarily on an activity basis. With respect to numbers of physicians per 100,000, there is a particularly appreciable difference, and Canada can be clearly catalogued with tax financed countries that record low levels of physicians. Canada, the UK, and New Zealand have, respectively, 2.1, 2.3, and 2.2 physicians per 100,000 population (2004 OECD figures); in contrast, Germany, the Netherlands, and France have, respectively, 3.4, 3.6, and 3.4 physicians per 100,000.

The Canadian system, unlike a number of other tax financed systems, does not employ its physicians on a salary basis. This may explain in part why Canada does not seem to exhibit as great a control over total health care spending as other tax financed countries like the UK and New Zealand. But if social health insurance systems have greater capacity than that within the Canadian system (more doctors, more hospital beds) yet spend similar amounts as percentage of GDP on health care, do they pay their health professionals less, and if so, how do they achieve this? Unfortunately, it is difficult to draw any conclusions from the patchy international comparative data that exist on remuneration of health professionals; in particular, data on reimbursement for specialists are not available.

If it were true that social health insurance systems are better able to support great capacity by negotiating prices/tariffs/reimbursements with their health providers and/or driving higher productivity, then in turn one must ask what it is within the structure of social health insurance that makes this possible. Hypothetically it may be a function of larger numbers. In countries like Canada

with relatively low numbers of physicians, the profession might have additional bargaining power because of the perceived shortage. Earlier empirical
work (e.g., Barer and Stoddart 1991) found a correlation between numbers of
physicians and total health care spending (particularly in fee-for-service payment systems) but little relation between increasing numbers of physicians
and improved health care outcomes. It may be time to revisit this analysis in
the context of differential bargaining power that exists as a result of different
financial/institutional arrangements and concerns about timeliness of treatment (which at the time of this early analysis was not a significant issue).
Hypothetically, it may be that having more doctors, at least in social health
insurance systems, reduces their relative bargaining power, meaning that more
doctors are working for less, possibly improving overall productivity and reducing waiting times. This merits further exploration.

Another possibility is that in centrally managed tax financed systems it is
easier for governments to more tightly control spending on health care and
inputs into the health care system (the number of physicians trained, etc.). We
have written before on the significant and lingering effects on the Canadian
health care system of governmental reductions in spending in the early and
mid-1990s (Tuohy et al. 2004). Since that time, investments have been re-
stored, but this cyclical approach to investments in health care can have lasting
and negative impact. In contrast, social health insurance systems do not seem
to suffer from the same roller-coaster of finance; the payment system is separate and discrete and thus somewhat immune from government's fiscal angst.
Moreover, in social health insurance systems, as employers make contributions, there may be more willingness to pay to ensure shorter wait times so
that employees are more quickly able to return to work.

Another explanatory factor might be *who* bargains with physicians. Despite the advent of regionalization from coast to coast in Canada (most recently
in Ontario), responsibility for bargaining with physicians lies within the hands
of government. This process is a highly politicized one (Flood et al. 2006). In
contrast, in social health insurance countries an alliance of social health insurers and private health insurers generally negotiates in concert with the health
professions. Government is the backdrop for this negotiation but not the major player (although as we note below under "separate administration," if things
are not going well, it seems that even in social health insurance countries
participants will attempt to draw in the government).

A further issue is whether or not key provider groups are more or less content with remuneration negotiations in social health insurance countries as
opposed to tax financed countries. Is, for example, labour strife less frequent
in social health insurance countries? The Canadian system seems to have been
profoundly shaped by a series of labour disputes (Kravitz and Shapiro 1992;
Thompson and Salmon 2006). The history of these encounters may have left

bitterness on both sides that impedes evidence-based policy choices on the part of government and colours providers' perceptions of how they are valued. When we look at the experience in Europe, there too are examples of strikes (2003 in Germany, 2004 in France). To substantively compare SHI countries and tax financed countries would take a much more systematic review than is possible here. We will have to leave this issue with many questions to be resolved and research to be conducted.

In sum, social health insurance countries do not seem to have a significant problem with wait lists; Canada and other tax financed countries frequently do. Potential explanations include the possibility that shifting bargaining away from central governments to arms' length agencies like non-profit sickness funds changes the dynamic of bargaining power; that social health insurance systems are much less susceptible to the fiscal flux that occurs when governments directly control the pipeline of funds for the system; and/or that in social health insurance models there is more willingness to pay because of the connection to the employment base and the desire to shorten wait times to get employees back to work. However, much of this is speculation, and untangling of cause and effect is presently difficult because of a lack of comparable international data. These issues certainly warrant further exploration, particularly as advocates for greater privatization within the Canadian system point to European social health insurance countries in extolling the benefits of private health insurance. At this point, given the many areas of exploration that require the further and systematic research identified above and the reservations expressed by a number of the contributors to this volume, we are not in a position to make any substantive recommendations vis-à-vis the employment of social health insurance financing as a cure to problems of wait times in the Canadian system. Instead, we limit ourselves to considering adapting aspects of social health insurance into the prescription drug sector for the reasons discussed in other sections of this chapter.

EFFECTIVE ADMINISTRATION

Many OECD nations relying on general taxation to fund health care have been moving toward more decentralized management models, often through regional and local structures for the allocation and management of health budgets. As long as health care funding is drawn from the consolidated revenue of the general government, however, regional (and in turn local) agencies are dependent upon the central budget process for their overall budgets. This means that health care demands on government revenue are decoupled from management. In turn, as Glied points out, the health care budget is then determined within the politics of the general provincial budgetary process by the power of stakeholders and the public salience of health care. Given the influence of both of these factors, the result is often that health care crowds out other priorities for public spending – some of which may be more important in achieving equitable outcomes, including health outcomes.

One of the key purported advantages of social insurance systems is that they link the revenue base for health care with resource allocation and system management in dedicated agencies at some remove from the central government.[9] There are two broad models for making this link: organizing social insurers as monopolists along industry and/or regional lines (as was historically done), or allowing social insurers to compete with each other and/or with private health insurers within a nation-wide market (as recent reforms have done in Germany and the Netherlands). In theory, this should discipline decision-making on both sides of this equation. Decisions to raise revenue for health care (or not) must be supported by indicating how those funds will be spent (or not). Decisions to spend funds must identify a source of funding within the existing revenue base or accept responsibility for raising contribution rates.

These administrative and managerial advantages of social insurance, while important, should not be exaggerated. In practice, the budgetary process of social insurance is not immune to broad politics. Joe White's observations in this regard are worth quoting at some length:

> The Ministry of Health generally wants social insurance funds to control expenses but also to take the blame for cost controls and to deal with the angry providers. Fund managers want the government to force providers into cost control deals and, by the way, take the blame – or kick in extra money from general revenues – or both [as has been the case in Germany for many years]. However it plays out, this relationship is essentially a form of "stewardship," in which the government structures health care finance by statute (Glaser calls it "statutory health insurance") and then seeks to influence the system more or less indirectly, depending on whether it can live with the results of less interference.

Indeed, in the Canadian context, the political ability and willingness of provincial governments to refrain from interference would remain to be seen. Experience with regionalization in Canada, and in other nations such as the UK, suggests that central governments still "own" the results of decision-making about spending public funds in a tax based system. Hence, in both Canada and Britain, regionalization regimes have cycled through numerous iterations. A social insurance model, given its separate revenue base, would provide greater political distance from the central government. In the Canadian case, however, any social insurance component would be introduced into a system accustomed to direct government control of the health budget (as Marmor and

White have pointed out), and the central government would continue to have direct responsibility for large swaths of the system. In such circumstances we should temper our expectations as to how much political distance a separate revenue base per se may provide: it may shield neither the provincial government from blame nor the social insurance agency from political interference.

There may be at least one way of introducing social insurance into the current system that would establish an appropriate degree of political distance. Establishing social insurance for out-of-hospital pharmaceuticals would introduce it into a context that is currently dominated by private insurance, not a universal government plan. Within this frame a considerable degree of independence for the social insurance body would appear to align it organizationally with the private insurers who also populate the arena. In the end, however, the provincial government would remain ultimately accountable for the performance of social insurers – an outcome not to be decried.

One final concern about the effects of separate administration of social insurance remains to be addressed. Arguably, having one component of the public system managed separately from the others would exacerbate the already considerable problems of integration. Currently, within provincial ministries of health, the pharmaceutical budget is managed separately from the physician budget, which in turn is managed separately from the hospital budget, etc. Segregating the responsibility for drug coverage (or any other component of the system such as long-term care) could further entrench a "silo" for that component. However, there is no empirical example of a pure and comprehensive social insurance system: as White reminds us, all systems wrestle with integrating administration and governance across different components, and there is potential for cross-national learning in this regard.

MOVING FORWARD

In the end the decision of whether or not to introduce a component of social insurance into the financing arrangements for Canadian health care comes down to judgments about trade-offs across multiple objectives. The principal reason to consider such a move is to create a diversified base of public funding. Both theory and evidence suggest that the optimum may lie in a combination of sources of finance rather than in reliance on any one pure model. The particular optimal combination for Canada, as for any system, must be consonant with the nation's history and core values.

The contributors to this volume offer multiple reasons to be cautious about introducing a dimension of social insurance into the funding mix for health care in Canada, and it behooves us to keep these cautions in mind as we think about diversifying the revenue base. In our view the sector that is least vulnerable to the pitfalls of which we were warned is that of pharmaceuticals outside hospitals. While it is possible that experience and institutional evolution over time will make it possible to consider extending the social insurance model to some other sectors such as long-term care or even physician and hospital services, we can make no judgments in advance on the merits of doing so; we confine ourselves here to a consideration of how this might work in the pharmaceutical sector.

For several of the reasons discussed in the previous section, it makes most sense to introduce social insurance into a sector in which there is not currently universal coverage and in which private insurance is well established. In the pharmaceutical sector, private insurance currently covers more than half of drug expenditures. We therefore propose that *a new contributory public program be established covering out-of-hospital pharmaceuticals*. This new social insurance plan would sit alongside the private plans and thus accord with the existing institutional architecture of the system. Social insurance premiums would have a clear rationale in a sector in which many people are accustomed to paying private insurance premiums. Because social insurance would allow for the extension of coverage to the entire population, it would demonstrably provide increased benefits, not simply replace existing coverage. Furthermore, moving in this direction would also entail the regulation of private insurance in order to integrate both private and social insurance into a comprehensive framework, and would thus improve equity in the private insurance market. We further propose that existing public programs of prescription drug coverage be migrated to this model. Attempting to achieve progressivity through an age-based approach to public subsidy no longer makes sense when old age cannot be used as a proxy for low income. British Columbia has already recognized this fact in its adoption of subsidies based on income alone. Eligibility for coverage in the new public program should be expanded to the entire population under the conditions we outline in the following points.

The devil of such a proposal is in the details: the design of the program has important implications for its economic and political feasibility, and some difficult trade-offs must be made. A blueprint for moving forward and providing prescription drug coverage through a social insurance type model that would include payments on the part of both individuals and firms would need to meet five important principles. These principles have their genesis in the research contained in this volume but also consider the practical realities of Canadian health care financing. Taken together they outline a model for funding prescription drug coverage that achieves incremental diversification of financing sources and increased access to health care without large-scale disruption of the current market for supplementary health insurance. The model addresses the fastest growing component of provincial health care budgets and the largest growth area for health care technology. As such, it allows for some relief of the growing pressure on health ministry budgets, improving the sustainability of the tax financed components of health care.

The principles for expanding drug coverage and diversifying funding through a greater reliance on social insurance type mechanisms are as follows:

1. *Include private insurance companies as partners in achieving universal coverage.* The framework we envisage would include the regulation of private insurers, requiring them to cover a basic formulary of drugs and to establish a "community rate" for premiums, common to all members of the insured group.

    Canadian policy-makers have been wary of incorporating private insurance formally into the framework of health care financing other than through tax deductions for premiums. This caution is understandable: given their international ambit and the large pools of capital that they control, private insurance firms are potentially very significant political and economic actors, and increasing their role changes the dynamics of the health care arena. Nonetheless, in the particular case of prescription drug insurance, there are good reasons for embracing private insurers as partners. First and most obviously, private insurance is currently well established in this sector. This in itself would not be a reason to maintain it: after all, public insurance for the bulk of physician and hospital services replaced private insurance in the 1950s and 1960s. But second and more important, in the prescription drug sector, unlike the physician and hospital services sectors, allowing social and private insurance to exist side by side would not have negative consequences for the supply of publicly funded services. The covered basket of out-of-hospital drugs would be accessed by patients at the same pharmacies from the same stock, whether they were paid for by social or private insurance.

    Supplementary coverage for drugs not covered in the basic plan would undoubtedly be offered by private insurers as well. Again, in contrast to the physician and hospital services sectors, this is not likely to feed back negatively on public coverage. Whereas there is the potential in the case of physician and hospital services for supplementary services to be bundled with publicly funded services as a condition of access, this is not likely to be the case for prescription drugs.

2. *Include both individual and employer mandates.* In order to ensure broad risk pooling and avoid problems of adverse selection and cream-skimming, enrolment must be compulsory. This can be achieved through an individual mandate alone, as Quebec has done. We believe, however, that an employer mandate is necessary as well. Presenting a policy reform as a shared responsibility of employers, individuals, and government (through tax credits or other mechanism of subsidy as discussed in the following

paragraph) may enhance the likelihood of its political acceptability, as we observed in the case of CPP reforms in the 1990s.

3. *Include a mechanism to progressively finance insurance coverage so that insurance is truly accessible.* Various options are available to achieve progressive financing in a social insurance type model. Two options include a progressive and refundable tax credit and an arms-length funding pool that redistributes funds to insurers. Contributions as well as credits could be administered through payroll systems for those with employment based private insurance. It may also make sense to administer contributions as well as credits through the income tax system for those in the new public plan. This would avoid cash-flow problems created by lags between contribution payments and tax refunds, but it would also diminish the perceived separation of social insurance contributions from taxes. There are no doubt several other options worth considering. Each of these presents implementation issues that will need to be overcome. Any progressivity measure will require a substantial amount of revenue and should likely be considered in the context of revising the current tax deductibility of health insurance premiums, which regressively helps finance private insurance.

4. *Ensure arm's-length administration with dedicated and isolated funding from a combination of employee and employer payments.* Establishing the social insurer as a separate scheduled agency is critical to the success of this proposal. It is also important that the financing of the plan be from a separate fund, not simply through an accounting arrangement that leaves a more permeable boundary with the Consolidated Revenue Fund. The agency would incorporate the current Ontario Public Drugs Programs Branch of the Ministry of Health and Long-Term Care and would be structured as a not-for-profit insurance corporation. The Ministry would be responsible for the regulation of private insurers.

5. *Begin a transition toward a more formulaic financing of comprehensive retirement benefit coverage that might include income replacement, prescription medication coverage, and long-term care financing.* The one area in which a social insurance model is well established in Canada is that of public pensions, which has been put on a sustainable basis through provisions for formulaic adjustments that in the normal course of events do not require government intervention. Government action is required only if policy-makers choose to make changes to the program to avoid or mitigate the effects of the formula. This makes sense in an area in which future requirements (in this case income replacement) are fairly predictable. Much of the need for health care, on the other hand, is unpredictable – hence the need for risk pooling through insurance. Even among the elderly, utilization of physician and hospital services is highly concentrated in a relatively small proportion of high users. A study using Manitoba

data showed that almost three-quarters of physician and hospital services expenditure for those 65 and older is concentrated in the top 10 percent of users of the system.[10] However, certain other health care sectors, such as long-term care and prescription drugs, are more akin to the pension world in the predictability of expenditures over the life course. In contrast to the high concentration of physician and hospital expenses within a small proportion of the elderly population, in British Columbia data presented by Steve Morgan at our conference, the top 10 percent of consumers of prescription drugs in the 65 and older population accounted for less than 40 percent of expenditures. For this reason, it makes sense to structure the way we finance prescription drugs as more akin to the way we finance pensions, through a contributory regime over the life course of individuals. Formulaic increases in contributions over time would also allow for a phasing in of the program, which as noted below is critical to its political acceptability. A default funding mechanism, moreover, makes it more likely that government will preserve the sustainability of the program over time, since it will not have to take the political risk of acting explicitly to increase contribution rates or reduce benefits as necessary.

Interestingly, a recent report by the Commonwealth Fund recommends a combination of public and private insurance as a way of achieving universal health insurance coverage in the United States. As noted above, the prescription drug sector is the one area in which the pattern of health care finance in Canada is most similar to that which currently characterizes the broad pattern in the US – marked by widespread employer based coverage, public programs for the elderly and the poor, and an uninsured segment of the population. For reasons similar to those advanced in this chapter, the authors of the Commonwealth Fund report view the adoption of individual and employer mandates, a new contributory public program, and a regulatory regime for private insurance as the most feasible route to universal coverage in the American context (Collins et al. 2007). Our proposal for the prescription drug sector in Ontario is similar to that of the Commonwealth Fund in these core respects.

Several hurdles must be overcome in the design of a model such as we propose. These issues are tricky but resolvable through well-formulated public policy. We list some of these issues here for consideration:

1. Changing health care entitlements in Canada is always politically difficult. While we believe that the proposed changes increase accessibility and enhance equity and sustainability, some groups of individuals may stand to lose from this proposal. Communicating the goals and necessity of such a transition will be crucial.

2. There are several new drugs on the market that may not be deemed appropriate for funding by either arm's-length public insurers or private insurers. Individuals may not agree with these decisions and may wish to purchase drugs privately in the event that they are not covered by their insurance package. Insurance companies may even wish to offer supplemental packages for high cost, low incidence drugs. In our view, allowing private purchase or supplemental insurance specifically limited to prescription drugs will not undermine the proposed plan and may ease transition issues. However, this may be politically contested.

3. The assignment of responsibility for establishing the common formulary and negotiating prices with pharmaceutical firms needs careful consideration. This role is currently performed by government. In a regime in which the payment function is shifted to an arm's-length social insurance agency, it may make sense to shift the formulary-setting and negotiation function as well, in order to keep incentives aligned. The further question is then whether private insurers should also be brought into the formulary-setting and negotiation process, since they would be subject to the common formulary. Experience in Europe in these respects is varied and evolving (Willison et al. 2002).

4. While there is not extensive evidence of cream-skimming in the current private prescription drug market, care should be taken to ensure that moving to a social insurance type financing model for prescription drugs does not open the door for cream-skimming by private insurers. Employer mandates can go some distance toward mitigating this danger, since insurers would have to risk-select entire groups and not individuals. But as van de Ven reports in this volume, risk selection continues to be a problem to varying degrees in the five countries he studied with managed competition regimes, even though regulations and risk adjustment mechanisms of varying levels of sophistication have been put in place to prevent it. Hard-won experience in these and other jurisdictions, while not yet fully successful, can be a guide in this endeavour.

5. We have not specifically addressed the issue of whether public and private insurers should compete with each other, or whether they should serve different segments of the population. Competition between public and private insurers under a regulatory umbrella is increasingly common in Europe. The recent Commonwealth Fund report cited above recommends instituting competition between public and private insurers in one segment of the market.[11] Managing any such competition would create further administrative and regulatory complexities, since it would exacerbate the potential for cream-skimming. Nonetheless, offering choice may well be more politically attractive (unless it proves too confusing) and in theory could drive insurers to greater efficiencies. This is an area in which further

experience with current reforms in Europe could provide some guidance as noted above.

6. The short-run transition from the existing financing system to a new system will require special attention. Up-front funding to ease transition will be necessary, along with grandfathering of populations who have not had the opportunity to plan for such changes.

7. We have not addressed the issue of deductibles, copayments, and premium scaling. In principle the model we present does not dictate any one particular design or level of such payments: a variety of options is possible, provided that access to important drug therapies is not adversely affected.

Facing the range of objectives, issues, and trade-offs outlined in this volume, policy-makers confront a daunting but inevitable task in seeking to put in place a financing structure that will maintain and enhance the quality, accessibility, and sustainability of Canada's health care system. Nonetheless, we believe that a way forward lies in diversifying the sources of public finance in Canada by introducing a well designed program of social insurance for out-of-hospital pharmaceuticals within a regulatory framework that incorporates private employer-based insurance as well. The insights and analysis in this volume point both to the promise and the potential pitfalls of such a program, and can provide the basis for its careful design.

NOTES

[1] Per capita drug expenditures in the 80–84 age category were seven times those in the 60–64 category in 2002 (CIHI 2006).

[2] The 2005 OECD Economic Survey of Sweden noted, "Because the counties are responsible for little apart from health care it is also like having 21 earmarked health taxes ... This means that it is hard to trade off health spending against other demands on the public purse" (OECD 2005, 129).

[3] Ontario had levied a flat-rate premium until 1989. Two other provinces, Alberta and British Columbia, continue to levy premiums, which flow into general revenue. Premium revenue has accounted for a decreasing proportion of total provincial health spending in both of those provinces over time, and in the mid-2000s it amounted to about 11–13 percent of the health budget in each province.

[4] Chen and Mintz estimated that the premium would raise effective marginal tax rates on average by one percentage point (Chen and Mintz 2004).

[5] Support for premium increases was 47 percent, as compared with 13 percent for raising the retirement age, 9 percent for lowering benefits, and 24 percent for all other options.

[6] At 5.6 percent before the reforms, Canadian rates were less than half the 12.4 percent rate in the US.

[7] See also Weaver (2004) for an argument regarding the multi-faceted nature of the reforms as a political compromise.

[8] See also Luigi Siciliani and Jeremy Hurst, (I) *Tackling Excessive Waiting Times for Elective Surgery: A Comparison of Policies in 12 OECD Countries*, available at http://www.oecd.org/dataoecd/24/32/5162353.pdf (annexes 1, 2, and 3 available at http://www.oecd.org/dataoecd/24/35/5163379.pdf) and (II) *Explaining Waiting Times Variations for Elective Surgery across OECD Countries* (2003) (available at http://www.oecd.org/dataoecd/31/10/17256025.pdf)

[9] Tax-based systems can link revenue raising and system management at a level below the central government, as is the case in Sweden in which local councils have both responsibilities. But this simply means that the competition between health care and other spending priorities is driven down to the local level.

[10] Calculated from Forget, Deber, and Roos (2002), Table 1.

[11] The Fund recommends the establishment of "health exchanges" that would offer a choice of private and public group plans to small businesses and to individuals without access to employer-based plans or existing public programs (Collins et al. 2007).

REFERENCES

Barer, M.L., and G.L. Stoddart. 1991. *Toward Integrated Medical Resource Policies for Canada*. Vancouver: University of British Columbia Centre for Health Services and Policy Research.

Béland, D., and J. Myles. 2003. "Stasis amidst Change: Canadian Pension Reform in an Age of Retrenchment." Research Paper no. 111, Program for Research on Social and Economic Dimensions of an Aging Population. Hamilton: McMaster University. http://socserv2.mcmaster.ca/sedap.

Canadian Institute for Health Information. 2005. *Provincial and Territorial Government Health Expenditure by Age Group, Sex and Major Category: Recent and Future Growth Rates*. http://secure.cihi.ca/cihiweb/products/Provterrhealthexpend2005_e.pdf.

Canadian Life and Health Insurance Association. 2000. "Submission Concerning the Report on the Evaluation of the General Drug Insurance Plan." Presented to the Social Affairs Commission, Quebec City, February 2000.

Carpay, J. 2007. "Suing the Government for the Right to See and Live." *National Post*, 7 September.

Chen, D., and J.M. Mintz. 2004. "Ontario's Fiscal Competitiveness in 2004." Paper prepared for the Institute for Competitiveness and Prosperity. http://204.15.35.174/images/uploads/ChenMintzReport_241104.pdf.

Collins, S.R., C. Schoen, K. Davis, A.K. Gauthier, and S.C. Schoenbaum. 2007. *A Roadmap to Health Insurance for All: Principles for Reform.* New York: Commonwealth Fund. (October 2007.) http://www.commonwealthfund.org/publications/publications_show.htm?doc_id=514761.

Flood, C., M. Stabile, and C. Tuohy. 2006. "What Is In and Out of Medicare? Who Decides?" In *Just Medicare*, edited by C.M. Flood, 15-41. Toronto: University of Toronto Press.

Flood, C.M., and S. Xavier. 2008 forthcoming. "Health Care Rights in Canada: The *Chaoulli* Legacy." *Journal of Law and Medicine* (spring).

Forget, C.E. 2002. "The Quebec Experience: Lessons to Be Learned." Institute for Research on Public Policy Conference toward a National Strategy on Drug Insurance: Challenges and Priorities, Toronto, 23 September. http://www.irpp.org/fasttrak/index.htm.

Forget, E.L., R. Deber, and L.L. Roos. 2002. "Medical Savings Accounts: Will They Reduce Costs?" *Canadian Medical Association Journal* 167(2):143-7.

Health Canada. 2000. *Canadians' Access to Insurance for Prescription Medications.* http://www.hc-sc.gc.ca/hcs-sss/pharma/acces/pubs/index_e.html.

Kravitz, R., and M.F. Sharpiro. 1992. "Duration and Intensity of Striking among Participants in the Ontario, Canada Doctors' Strike." *Medical Care* 30 (8): 737-43.

Mendelsohn, Matthew. 2002. *Canada's Social Contract: Evidence from Public Opinion.* Discussion paper no. P/01. Ottawa: Canadian Policy Research Networks.

Morgan, Steven G. 2006. "Prescription Drug Expenditures and Population Demographics." *Health Services Research* 41 (2): 411-28.

OECD. 2005. *Economic Survey of Sweden 2005: Improving Quality and Value for Money in Healthcare.* Issue 9 (e-book). OECD Publishing.

Pollara. 2003. *Health Care in Canada Survey Retrospective, 1998-2003.* Toronto: Pollara. http://www.mediresource.com/e/pages/hcc_survey/pdf/HCiC_1998-2003_retro.pdf

– 2006. *Health Care in Canada Survey 2006.* Toronto: Pollara. http://www.mediresource.com/e/pages/hcc_survey/pdf/2006_hcic_ppt.pdf

Pomey, M.-P., P.-G. Forest, H.A. Palley, and E. Martin. 2007. "Public/Private Partnerships for Prescription Drug Coverage: Policy Formulation and Outcomes in Quebec's Universal Drug Insurance Programs, with Comparisons to the Medicare Prescription Drug Program in the United States." *Millbank Quarterly* 85 (3): 469-98

Siciliani, L., and J. Hurst. 2004. "Explaining Waiting Times Variations for Elective Surgery across OECD Countries." Working paper. Paris: OECD. http://www.oecd.org/dataoecd/15/52/35028282.pdf

Stabile, M. 2001. "Private Insurance Subsidies and Public Health Care Markets: Evidence from Canada." *Canadian Journal of Economics* 34(4): 921-942.

Tuohy, Carolyn Hughes. 2006. "Quality, Accessibility, Sustainability: Can We Have All Three in Health Care?" Paper presented at the Health Law and Policy Seminar, Faculty of Law and Department of Health Policy, Evaluation and Management, University of Toronto (February 2).

Tuohy, C.H., C. Flood, and M. Stabile. 2004. "How Does Private Finance Affect Public Health Care Systems? Marshalling the Evidence from OECD Nations." *Journal of Health Politics, Policy and Law* 29 (3): 359-96.

Wagstaff, A., E. van Doorslaer, and H. van der Burg. 1999. "Equity in the Finance of Health Care: Some Further International Comparisons." *Journal of Health Economics* 18 (3): 263-90.

Weaver, K. 2003. "Cutting Old-Age Pensions." In *The Government Taketh Away: The Politics of Pain in the United States and Canada*, edited by Kent Weaver and Leslie Pal, 41-70. Georgetown: Georgetown University Press.

Thompson, S.L., and J.W. Salmon. 2006. "Strikes by Physicians: A Historical Perspective toward an Ethical Evaluation." *International Journal of Health Services* 36(2): 331-54.

Willison, D., M. Wiktorowicz, P. Grootendorst, B. O'Brien, M. Levine, R. Deber, and J. Hurley. 2002. "International Trends in Managing Drug Plans: Lessons for Canada." Montreal: Institute for Research on Public Policy. http://www.irpp.org/events/archive/sep02/willison.pdf.

Index

Accessibility, 1, 5, 12, 13-18, 57, 139,
  143, 144, 148, 149-50, 153, 165-68,
  172-73, 176, 179, 195, 205, 268-72
Accountability, 19, 59, 63, 71, 74, 85,
  199-200
Adverse selection, 19, 61, 62, 64, 163-69,
  195, 268
Age, 39, 42, 42, 141, 143, 146-47, 205,
  214, 245, 253, 272
  Aging population, 3, 7, 8, 25, 44, 52,
    72, 91, 100, 107, 110, 174, 200, 209-
    10, 225-27
  Baby boomers, 25, 91, 96, 209-10, 272
  Working age population, 20, 75, 107,
    109, 168, 206
Alberta, 1, 6, 26, 59, 80-84, 86, 92, 272
Arm's-length management. *See* Not-for-
  profit agency
Australia, 2, 3, 12, 14, 17-18, 24, 28-31,
  39, 40, 65, 67, 69-70, 92, 167, 173,
  174, 189, 196, 235, 247, 260
Austria, 3, 31, 32, 64, 65, 67, 69, 92, 142,
  170, 171, 176, 247, 256, 260

Belgium, 3, 32, 31, 64, 65, 67, 69-70, 92,
  139-60, 170, 171, 247, 256, 260
Beveridge approach. *See* General taxation
Bismarck approach. *See* Mandatory
  contributions, Payroll funds, Social
  insurance, Universal coverage
Bonus payments, 61, 62, 153
British Columbia, 59, 80-84, 92, 187,
  205, 209, 210-11, 267, 272
Budgets, budgeting, 6, 91, 206, 215, 242-
  43, 245, 257, 264-65
Bureau. *See* General taxation
Bypass surgery, 26

Canada, 4-9, 11, 29-31
  and Diversification of funding base, 19,
    21, 24-25, 59-85, 91-111, 174, 177-
    79, 188-96, 210-12, 221-230, 233-48,
    251-272
  Canadian funding model, 7-9, 13, 17,
    24, 59-60, 62-63, 69-70, 92, 94, 107,
    115, 117, 177, 189, 194, 200-03, 221-
    22, 233-35
  Distinguishing characteristics of
    system, 14, 60, 235
  Health care share of GDP, 11, 18, 30,
    54, 190-91, 223-24
  Mortality, 47-51
  Pharmaceuticals, 7-9, 23-25, 26, 136,
    177-79, 199-216, 225-30, 252-53,
    257-59, 266-72
  Political considerations, 8, 22, 233-48,
    254-60
  Private coverage, 8, 38-40, 60, 64-70,
    136, 165, 167, 174, 178, 206, 268
  Progressivity, 41, 47
  Providers of health care, 177, 202, 206-
    07, 262-64
  Spending levels, 18, 49-52, 56, 71-72,
    91, 185, 190-91, 205-08, 233-34
  Two-tier system, 13-16, 247, 260-61, 264
  Usage of health care services, 47, 99
  Wait times, 13-14, 17, 173, 260-64
  Canada Health Act, 7, 24, 116, 135, 204,
    206, 224, 233-34, 236, 240, 244-46,
    247
Canada/Quebec Pension Plan, 20, 62, 92-
  97, 98-100, 102, 108, 259-60
Canadian Community Health Survey
  2000, 47, 49, 51, 87
Cancer treatment, 6, 19, 23, 225-29

Capitation, 41, 42
Cataract surgery, 6
Catastrophic risk/costs, 8, 23, 60, 64, 104,
    178, 206, 228-30
Centralized/decentralized systems, 5, 21,
    42, 139-60, 214, 256-57, 263, 264-66,
    273
Chaoulli decision, 1, 7, 224, 234, 261
Chronic illness, 146-49, 154, 157, 165,
    166, 174, 178
Community services, 23, 222, 224-28
Community-rated premiums, 117-20,
    121, 122, 125, 130, 135, 136, 148,
    166, 168, 175
Competition, 21, 22, 41, 42, 71, 212, 236,
    271-72
  Managed competition, 139-60, 175,
    221-22, 246, 264-65
Compliance, 93, 100, 107
Copayment. *See* Cost-sharing
Cost/benefit comparison, 19
Costs, 18, 47. *See also* Spending
  Growth of, 1, 6, 7, 11, 16, 31, 32, 37,
    44, 57, 64-66, 71-72, 91-92, 110, 119,
    129-30, 132, 135, 136, 169, 185, 189,
    200, 225-27, 241
  Pressure on, 4, 6, 17-18, 91-92, 173-74
Cost-sharing, 22, 64, 164, 168
  Coinsurance, 42, 70, 76-77, 78, 95, 167,
    178
  Copayments, 7, 8, 12-13, 15, 37, 40, 42,
    62, 70, 76-77, 78, 99, 153, 177, 205,
    206, 215, 252, 258, 272
  Deductibles, 39, 60, 62, 70, 75, 95, 99,
    167, 178, 205, 206, 252, 258, 272
Croatia, 170
Cross-jurisdictional comparison, 4, 16,
    22, 185-97, 266
Cross-subsidization, 3, 15, 21, 93, 94,
    100, 103, 108, 142, 144-48, 149-60,
    212, 254
Czech Republic, 3, 170

Deductible. *See* Cost-sharing
Delivery of health care, 11, 19, 42, 159,
    222. *See also* Providers of health care
    services, System structure
Demographic factors, 18, 25, 39, 44, 49-
    53, 143, 208-10, 225, 253. *See also*
    Age

Denmark, 2, 31, 40, 55, 64, 65, 68, 69-70,
    72, 171, 238, 256, 260
Dental care, 60, 176
Diagnostic services, 6, 15, 49
Direct line of sight. *See* Transparency
Diversification of funding base, 4, 5, 70-
    74, 235, 260, 266-72. *See also*
    Funding mix
Drug therapies. *See* Cancer treatment,
    Pharmaceuticals
Drugs. *See* Pharmaceuticals
Duplicate system. *See* Two-tier system

Earmarked funds, 93-97, 142, 196, 211,
    237, 241-44, 248, 255, 256-57
  Disadvantages of, 241-44
Eastern Europe, 171, 213
Education, 20, 189. *See also* Trade-offs
Efficiency, 11, 19, 20, 22, 37, 41-46, 56,
    57, 59-85, 92, 100, 101, 103, 139-40,
    149-50, 155, 158, 175, 187, 199, 208,
    211, 253-54
Elasticity, 34, 38-39, 78-79, 86, 153
Elderly, seniors. *See* Age, Aging
    populations
Elective procedures, 6, 52, 173
Emergency services, 6, 76, 173, 215
Employment, 20, 105, 174, 180, 239,
    252, 253-54
  Employment-based systems, 4-5, 25,
    39, 43, 72-73, 109, 119-20, 124, 129,
    132, 141, 169-80, 213-14, 235, 268-
    69
  Employment status, 3, 38, 107, 252
  Implications for, 5, 72-73, 100, 105,
    108, 116, 120-23, 132-35, 168-69,
    175, 196, 239, 259
  Labour-management agreements, 24
  Levels and investment, 71, 105, 108,
    239
Entitlement. *See* Social insurance
Equity, 19, 56, 59-85, 100, 143, 199-200,
    251-53. *See also* Fairness,
    Accessibility
  Horizontal, 63, 93
  Intergenerational transfer, 57, 73, 93,
    94, 96-97, 100, 103, 107, 108-09
  Over life cycle, 46-52
  Vertical, 63, 93
Estonia, 170

Experience rating, 60, 62, 94-95, 99, 104, 109

Experience-related premiums. *See* Premiums, usage-based

Fairness, 37, 42, 53-55, 116-19, 123-29, 136, 187, 194-96, 215, 223, 228. *See also* Accessibility, Age, Income, Payroll taxes, Premiums, income-related, Progressive/Regressive, Redistribution
  Income fairness, 2, 118, 120, 126-27, 130, 135, 214
  Risk fairness, 2, 20, 118, 120, 135, 142, 214

Federal government, Canada, 59, 80, 227-30, 255-56

Financing. *See* Funding

Finland, 2, 31, 40, 55, 171, 172, 247, 260

First-dollar coverage. *See* Universal coverage

Fiscal constraint (Canada, 1990s), 17

Formularies, 178, 227, 245, 269, 271

France, 3, 4, 12-13, 14, 15, 16, 18, 24, 30, 31, 40, 55, 64, 65, 67, 69, 92, 142, 168, 170, 171-72, 192, 235, 238, 247, 256, 260, 262

Funding, 37, 41-46, 64-68, 139-60, 199-216, 233. *See also* Pharmaceuticals, funding of
  as proportion of GDP, 11, 14, 18, 30, 37, 54-55, 173, 190, 191, 223-24, 233-34, 260, 262
  as proportion of total public spending, 1, 11, 43, 71, 91, 189, 223-24, 233-34
  Public as proportion of health spending, 189-92, 222, 223-24, 247

Funding sources, 200-03, 233-47
  Dominant, 64-70, 92, 115-36, 221-22
  Funding choices and fairness, 46-52, 199-200
  Funding mix (public-private), 11-13, 17-18, 20, 22, 31-34, 38-40, 43-46, 56, 64-70, 74, 76, 92, 100, 107-08, 115, 139-60, 173-80, 191-93, 197, 209
  General revenues, 64, 74, 76, 92, 115, 170-71, 174-75
  Payroll taxes, 64, 91-111, 115
  Private insurance, 64, 69
  User fees, 70

Gatekeepers, 157, 173

General revenue/taxation financing, 2, 3, 12, 20, 24-25, 37-57, 59-60, 62, 67-70, 71-72, 106, 107, 141, 170-71, 174-75, 178, 202-03, 211, 229, 242-43, 251-52, 253

Germany, 3, 4, 12, 15, 17, 18, 20-21, 28, 30, 31, 38, 40, 42, 54-55, 64, 65, 67, 69-70, 92, 106, 115-36, 139-62, 167, 170, 171, 173, 177-78, 187, 192-93, 197, 235, 243, 246, 256, 260, 262, 265

Greece, 3, 16, 31, 64, 65, 67, 69, 171

Group-based system. *See* Social insurance (Bismarck)

Health maintenance organizations, 140, 157

Health care costs. *See* Costs, Spending

Health care services, 63, 199

Health care system,
  Demand for, 15
  Inputs, 11, 41
  Outcomes, 11,
  Public confidence in, 28, 29
  Rationing in, 165, 173, 187, 215, 234-35. *See also* Wait times
  Satisfaction with, 110, 233-34
  Structure of, 19, 42, 139-60, 172-73, 264-66

High-risk behaviour, 61, 62-63

High-risk individuals, 61, 62, 63, 142, 143, 144, 149, 164, 166, 195

Home care, 4, 7, 19, 116, 151

Hospital services, 47, 49, 52, 60, 64, 76-80, 86, 140, 202, 206-08, 224, 261

Hungary, 3, 170

Iceland, 40, 55, 247, 256, 260

Incentive-based funding, 92-94, 97, 154, 158-59

Income, 12, 46-47, 50-52, 214, 236. *See also* Low income, Redistribution
  Fairness, 3, 21
  Income-based contributions, 160, 176, 210-12, 214-15, 257
  Levels, 8, 22, 47

Information, informed demand, 11, 139-40, 153

Insurance
  Employment based, 168-69
  Insurers, 140-60, 163

Reinsurance, 178
Private. *See* Private insurance
Public. *See* General taxation, Social
    insurance
Switchers, 153-54, 160
Integrated delivery, 42, 140
Integrated funding, 11-13
Intergenerational transfers. *See* Equity
Ireland, 2, 12, 14, 31, 40, 55, 65, 67, 69-
    70, 167-68, 171, 172, 247, 260, 261
Israel, 21, 139-60, 170, 171
Italy, 2, 12, 14, 30, 31, 40, 65, 67, 69-70,
    170, 172, 247, 260

Japan, 3, 24, 30, 31, 32, 40, 55, 64, 65,
    67, 69, 170, 187, 235, 246, 247, 260
Joint replacement, 6, 15, 47, 52

Korea, 3, 40, 170, 187

Labour market. *See* Employment
Life expectancy, 47-48, 50-52
Long-term care, 4, 7, 19, 39, 60, 116, 123,
    151, 176, 178, 233, 240, 244, 246, 251
Low income, 1-2, 22, 39, 42, 46, 47, 56,
    59-60, 74, 75, 106, 124, 129, 160,
    164, 168, 170, 174-75, 179, 205, 227.
    See also Catastrophic risk, Income
Luxembourg, 3, 16, 65, 67, 79, 92, 171,
    247, 260

Macroeconomic effects, 24, 98, 121, 239-
    41, 246
Managed care, 155-59, 178
Mandatory contributions, 2, 38, 136, 167,
    211-12, 215
Mandatory coverage, 117, 120, 129, 139-
    60, 205, 221, 235. *See also* Universal
    coverage
Manitoba, 80-84, 92, 205, 210-11, 269-70
Market approach, 42, 139-60, 221, 236
Medicare
    Canada, 1, 4, 24-25, 117, 194, 202, 222,
        224, 228
    U.S., 3, 24, 38, 47-49, 92, 100, 165,
        170-71, 178-79, 235, 248
Mexico, 3, 40, 86
Monopsony, 9, 42, 107, 178-79
Moral hazard, 19, 59, 61, 62, 64, 71, 104,
    144, 163-69, 195

Mortality, 47-51, 56

Needs testing, 118, 130. *See also* Income
Netherlands, 3, 12, 14, 15, 18, 21, 24, 30,
    31, 40, 55, 65, 67, 69-70, 73, 92, 132,
    139-60, 167, 174, 192, 235, 238, 247,
    260, 262, 265
    2006 reforms, 25, 142-42, 148, 150,
        151, 153-57, 167, 170, 171, 174-75,
        176, 180, 188,
    Exceptional Medical Expense Act, 24,
        176, 235
New Brunswick, 80-84
Newfoundland, 80-84, 92
New Zealand, 2, 12, 17-18, 28-31, 40, 55, 64,
    66, 68, 69-70, 92, 189, 247, 260, 261, 262
    Pharmaceutical Management Agency of
        New Zealand, 23, 214, 216
Non-essential services, 21, 176-77, 203
Northwest Territories, 92, 104
Norway, 2, 24, 31, 64, 68, 69-70, 171,
    235, 247, 256
Not-for-profit agency, 1, 22, 25, 173, 213-
    16, 235-37, 244-45, 264, 269, 271
Nova Scotia, 8, 80-84

OECD countries, 1, 3, 17-18, 31-34, 37,
    39-40, 43, 47, 54, 60, 64, 69-70, 86,
    92, 117-18, 129, 174, 185, 188, 192-
    93, 238, 256
Ontario, 2, 6, 8, 26, 59, 80-84, 86, 92,
    210, 228-29, 240, 257-58, 269-70, 272
Optical services, 60, 177
Opting out, 117, 119, 126-27, 129, 167,
    170. *See also* Mandatory
    contributions, Universal coverage
Organizing health care. *See* Health care
    system, Structure of
Out-of-pocket expenditures. *See* User fees

Parallel systems. *See* Two-tier system
Payroll taxes, 19-20, 38, 64, 67-70, 72-
    73, 91-111, 130, 132, 142, 163, 170,
    172, 174-75, 176, 178, 227-30, 236-
    41, 253. *See also* Earmarked fund
Pensions, 47-48, 174, 258-59, 270
Pharmaceuticals, 4, 8, 19, 22-24, 25, 60,
    62, 116, 136, 140, 199-216, 221, 222-
    27, 233, 244-46, 251, 257-58. *See
    also* Catastrophic Risk

Access to, 1, 16, 168, 233, 271
and Demographic factors, 205
Essential/non-essential, 9, 215
Expensive, 42, 110, 209, 225-28, 271
Funding of, 102, 136, 178, 203-16, 224-27, 240, 253-54, 266-72
Generic, 205, 215
Infused, 8, 23, 227-29
In-hospital, 8, 227
Out-of-hospital, 7-8, 22-23, 24, 205, 257-58, 266-72
Over-the-counter, 164, 177
Price sensitivity, 2, 23, 42, 204-08
Provincial policies on, 8, 62, 203-16, 221-30, 252
Spending on, 110, 205, 206-08
Physician services, 60, 64, 76-80, 86, 140, 157, 202, 206-08, 224, 261
Poland, 3
Political acceptability, 7, 17, 20, 93, 103, 108, 109, 229-30, 233-48, 258-61, 273. See also Willingness to pay
Political considerations, 7, 22, 24, 25, 28-29, 43, 71-73, 91, 95, 101, 135, 141-42, 177, 178, 202, 224-27, 233-48, 265-66, 262-72
Portugal, 2, 31, 64, 68, 69-70, 171, 172, 247
Premiums, 47, 126-27, 141, 270, 272. See also Community-rated premiums
Income-related, 59, 76-83, 92-97, 118, 119, 123, 125, 127, 129-30, 135, 141
Risk-adjusted, 3, 42, 60, 140, 143
Subsidization of, 21, 62, 118, 130, 140, 143, 144-48
Usage-based, 59, 61
Preventive care, 234-35
Prince Edward Island, 80-84
Private clinics, 8, 227, 261
Private insurance, 1, 3, 8, 12, 16, 18, 22, 38-39, 62, 64, 67-68, 74, 75, 86, 102, 123, 129, 165-70, 172, 174-75, 176-77, 178-79, 188, 203, 206, 221, 235-37, 258, 264-65, 266, 268-72. See also Cross-subsidization
Commercial, 3, 17
Cream-skimming, 3, 268, 271
History of, 165
Regulation of, 3, 7, 102, 117, 267-68
Voluntary, 3, 124-25
Private provision, 67-70, 163-69, 233-37

Belgium, 64
Canada, 13-16, 40, 60, 64, 75, 136, 168, 224-27
France, 14-16, 40, 64
Germany, 42, 64, 123, 129, 167
Japan, 64
Netherlands, 40, 42, 141, 167, 176-77, 188
New Zealand, 14-15, 64
Switzerland, 40, 64, 260-61
United Kingdom, 168
United States, 40, 64, 168-69
Privatization, 12, 13, 17, 206, 233-35, 246, 247, 264
Progressive/Regressive, 37-57, 74, 106, 117-18, 126-27, 172, 180, 223, 236-37, 247, 251-52. See also Redistribution
Providers of health care services, 43, 63, 71, 107, 140, 145, 149, 155-59, 163, 177, 199-200, 234, 262-64. See also Hospital services, Physician services
Choice of, 149, 173
General practitioner, 47, 49, 51, 52, 168, 173
Monopoly power, 41
Specialist, 47, 49, 52, 56, 76-80, 173
Provincial drug programs, 226-30, 254
Provincial governments, 6, 9, 59, 62, 80, 85, 86, 91, 203, 227-30, 235, 255-56, 265-66
Public attitudes. See Political considerations
Public insurance. See Financing

Quality of care, 5, 6, 9, 10, 12, 13, 14-15, 139, 149-50, 158, 168
Quality of insurers, 139-40
Quality of health care providers, 139-40, 163
Quebec, 8, 39, 80-84, 92, 97, 203, 205, 215, 221, 229, 253, 257-58, 268
Queue jumping. See Wait times

Redistribution, 2, 3, 4, 8, 37, 43, 46, 50-52, 56, 94, 116-18, 126-27, 167, 168, 211-12, 236, 237-39
Regionalization, 11, 172, 264-66
Regressive models, 126, 140-60, 194-96, 211. See also Progressive risk
Adjustment/Equalization, 3, 21, 62, 139, 140, 141-42, 144-60, 175, 212, 269

Fairness, 20-21, 116-19

Rating, 3, 140, 149

Selection, 21, 43, 140, 143, 148-54, 175, 212, 246, 270-72

Risk-adjusted payments, 42, 43

Risk pooling, 8, 15, 22, 60, 117-18, 120, 126, 165, 200, 268, 269

Risk-sharing incentives, 59-62

Royal Commission on Health Services, Canada, 202, 204

Saskatchewan, 80-84, 205, 210-11

Segregated fund, 229. *See also* Not-for-profit agency

Self-employed individuals, 73, 125, 129, 146-47, 154, 170, 229

Self-financing, 95

Self-insurance, 12

Sickness funds. *See* Social insurance

Slovak Republic, 3

Social insurance, 18, 37, 72-73, 93-97, 101, 109, 139-60, 169-80, 203, 223-24, 229-30, 233, 246, 247, 251-52, 260-64. *See also* Mandatory contributions, Universal coverage

and Accessibility, 7, 37-57, 72, 139

and Fairness, 116-19

and Pharmaceuticals, 210-15, 252, 257-60, 264, 266

and Private insurance, 102, 136, 169-70, 235-37

Comparison with other models, 37-57, 115-36, 163-80, 185-97, 221-25, 235-37, 244-45, 247, 253-54, 256-60, 264-66

Definition of, 2, 170, 235

Historical evolution of, 21, 169-72, 213-14

Not-for-profit, 38-40

Payroll taxes, 72-73, 91-111, 170

Segregated fund, 229

Sickness Funds, 101, 107, 142, 154, 160, 169, 213

Solidarity. *See* Fairness

Spain, 2, 12, 14, 31, 40, 55, 64, 66, 68, 69-70, 171, 172, 247, 260

Specialists. *See* Providers of health care services

Spending, health care, 49-53, 54, 102, 205, 206-08, 223, 225-27, 244, 248, 262-63

and Funding, 31-34, 102

Levels, 4-5. *See also* Costs

Per capita, 6, 43-44, 174, 206-08, 245

Spending smarter. *See* Efficiency

Statutory insurance coverage. *See* Universal care, Mandatory insurance

Supplemental health insurance, 8, 123, 152-54, 162, 229-30, 253-54, 271

Sustainability, 1-30, 73-74, 93, 115-16, 119-20, 129-32, 134, 135, 139, 194, 199, 223, 254-60, 271-72

Balance among factors, 9-12, 17-19

Definition, 9

Sweden, 2, 16, 24, 30, 31, 40, 55, 64, 66, 68, 69-70, 106, 171, 172, 192, 235, 238, 243, 247, 256, 260, 272

Switzerland, 3, 21, 40, 54-55, 64, 66, 68, 69-70, 139-60, 170, 171, 175, 176, 178, 180, 189, 247, 260

Taiwan, 170, 189

Tax treatment, 39, 105

Taxation, 19-20, 38-40, 59, 71-73, 74-85, 103, 117-18, 124, 163, 172, 226-30, 237-39, 243, 253. *See also* Payroll taxes, Willingness to pay

Consumption, 38, 39, 109, 110, 118, 119, 121, 131, 163, 175, 237, 238, 253

Hypothecated, 175, 177

Trade-offs, 6, 9-10, 19, 20, 41, 43, 53, 54, 56, 71, 99, 115, 189, 221-22, 230, 241, 243, 252, 253, 256, 264-65, 266, 267

Transparency, 43, 57, 72, 85, 93, 99, 101-02, 108, 228

Turkey, 3,

Two-tier system, 7, 13-16, 99, 168, 206, 260-61

Unemployment insurance, 62, 93, 95-96, 97, 98-100, 102, 104, 106, 108, 174, 228

Uninsured people, 39, 61

United Kingdom, 2, 12, 14, 17, 24, 28-31, 40, 42, 43, 44-45, 52, 54-55, 66, 68, 69, 72, 132, 141, 170-72, 173, 174, 177, 189, 192-93, 197, 228, 235, 238, 247, 260, 261, 262, 265

National Health Service, 117, 140, 170-71, 189

United States, 3, 4, 8, 17, 28-31, 40, 42,
    43, 44-45, 52, 54-55, 62, 64, 66, 68,
    69-70, 92, 95, 117, 132, 139, 140,
    164-65, 166, 168, 173, 176, 177, 178,
    187, 189, 192-93, 197, 226, 235, 240,
    245, 247, 260, 270
Universal care, 2, 7, 13, 20
Universal coverage, 18, 102, 117, 120,
    121, 124-25, 130, 165, 214-15, 251-
    53, 257-58, 260-72. *See also*
    Mandatory contributions
Usage/consumption of health care
    services, 17-18, 22, 38-41, 47, 52, 74,
    101-02, 108, 126, 269
User fees, user-pay system, 22, 38-40, 42,
    59-85, 123, 136, 142, 155, 163-65,

172, 174, 176-77, 203, 221, 235-37.
    See also Cost sharing

Voluntary contributions, *See* Private
    insurance

Wait times, 1, 4, 6-7, 12, 13, 16, 17-18,
    63, 153, 173, 223, 234-35, 256, 260-
    64
Willingness to pay, 7, 24, 43, 91, 102,
    189, 193, 226, 228, 252, 254-60, 273
Workers' Compensation, 20, 62, 93, 94-
    95, 97, 98-100, 102, 104, 108, 123,
    169, 174, 203
Working poor. *See* Low-income
World Health Organization, 187, 196

Contributors

COLLEEN M. FLOOD is a Canada Research Chair in Health Law and Policy and Scientific Director of the Canadian Institutes for Health Research, Institute of Health Services and Policy Research. She is also Associate Professor of Law at the University of Toronto, cross-appointed to the Department of Health Policy, Management and Evaluation and the School of Public Policy. Her primary area of scholarship is in comparative health care policy, public/private financing of health care systems, health care reform, and accountability and governance issues. She is the author and editor of five books, including *International Health Care Reform: A Legal, Economic and Political Analysis* (Routledge, 2000), co-editor of *Access to Care, Access to Justice: The Legal Debate over Private Health Insurance in Canada* (UTP, 2005), editor of *Just Medicare: What's In, What's Out, How We Decide* (UTP, 2006), co-editor of *Canadian Health Law and Policy* (3rd ed.) (Butterworths, 2007), and co-editor of *Administrative Law in Context* (Emond Montgomery, 2008).

SHERRY GLIED is Professor and Chair of the Department of Health Policy and Management of Columbia University's Mailman School of Public Health. In 1992–93 she served as a Senior Economist for health care and labor market policy to the President's Council of Economic Advisers. She was a participant in President Clinton's Health Care Task Force and headed working groups on global budgets and on the economic impacts of the health plan. She has written articles and reports on women's health insurance, child health insurance expansions, Medicaid managed care, and the role of insurance in hospital care in the U.S. She is author of a book on health care reform, *Chronic Condition* (Harvard University Press, 1998) and co-author of *Better but Not Well: Mental Health Policy in the US Since 1950* (Johns Hopkins University Press, 2006). She is a past recipient of a Robert Wood Johnson Investigator Award through which she has been studying the US employer-based health insurance system. A member of the MacArthur Foundation's Network on Mental Health Policy, of the IOM, the board of Academy Health, the National Academy of Social Insurance, and a research associate of the National Bureau of Economic Research, she served as Chair of the Academy Health Annual Research

Meeting in 2004. Dr. Glied was 2004 winner of Research! America's Eugene Garfield Economic Impact of Health Research Award. She is a senior associate editor of *Health Services Research*, associate editor of the *Journal of Health Politics, Policy, and Law* and a member of the editorial board of the *Milbank Quarterly* and the *Annual Review of Public Health*.

STEFAN GRESS is an economist by training and currently Associate Professor for health services research and health economics at the Department of Health Sciences at the University of Applied Sciences in Fulda, Germany. He was formerly a researcher at the Center of Social Policy at Bremen University and Assistant Professor at the University of Greifswald and at the University of Duisburg-Essen. His main areas of research are health systems design, health policy, and health insurance. He has published in international peer-reviewed journals on topics such as competition and consumer mobility in social health insurance, the definition of benefits packages, the relationship between health insurance and professional autonomy of health care providers, and the regulation of pharmaceutical markets.

MORLEY GUNDERSON holds the Canadian Imperial Bank of Commerce Chair in Youth Employment at the University of Toronto, where he is a Professor at the Centre for Industrial Relations and Human Resources (Director from 1985–97) and the Department of Economics. He is also a Research Associate of the Institute for Policy Analysis, the Centre for International Studies, and the Institute for Human Development, Life Course and Aging, all at the University of Toronto. He has been a Visiting Scholar at various institutions including the International Institute for Labour Research in Geneva, Switzerland (1977–78), and Stanford University. Dr. Gunderson is on the editorial board of the *Journal of Labor Research* and the *International Journal of Manpower,* and is co-editor of the *Labour Arbitration Yearbook*. In 2002 he was awarded the Industrial Relations Research Association Excellence in Education Award in Labour Economics and in 2003 the Gérard Dion Award for Outstanding Contributions to the Field of Industrial Relations.

DOUGLAS HYATT is Professor of Business Economics at the Rotman School of Management and the Institute for Policy Analysis, University of Toronto. He was the Director of Research for two Royal Commissions on Workers' Compensation in Canada. His research interests include workers' compensation system finance, disability policy, and the impacts of experience rating on workplace health and safety.

TIMOTHY STOLTZFUS JOST holds the Robert L. Willett Family Professorship of Law at the Washington and Lee University School of Law. He is a co-author of a casebook, *Health Law*, used widely throughout the United States in teaching health law, and of a treatise and hornbook by the same name. He is also the author of *Health Care at Risk: A Critique of the Consumer-Driven Movement, Health Care Coverage Determinations: An International Comparative Study; Disentitlement? The Threats Facing our Public Health-Care Programs and a Rights-Based Response*, and *Readings in Comparative Health Law and Bioethics*. He has written numerous articles and book chapters on health care regulation and comparative health law and policy, and has lectured on health law topics throughout the world.

STEPHANIE MAAS is a graduate of the course Medical Management at the University of Duisburg-Essen in Germany. During her studies she worked as a student assistant at the Institute of Health Care Management at the University of Duisburg-Essen. Since her graduation she works as a graduate assistant at the Institute. Her main fields of research are health policy and health insurance. She assists in the publication of national and international research reports and articles.

TED MARMOR teaches in Yale's law and management schools and political science department. His books include *The Politics of Medicare* (1973, 2000), *America's Misunderstood Welfare State*, co-authored with Mashaw and Harvey (1992), *Understanding Health Care Reform* (1994), and *Fads and Fashions in Medical Care Management* (2004). Former editor of the *Journal of Health Politics, Policy and Law* (1980–85), former policy advisor to Mondale (1983–84), he is a fellow of the Institute of Medicine, the National Academy of Social Insurance, and emeritus fellow of the Canadian Institute of Advanced Research (1987–93).

JACK M. MINTZ is the Palmer Chair of Public Policy at the University of Calgary (formerly Professor of Business Economics at the Rotman School of Management, University of Toronto). He is a member of the boards of Brookfield Asset Management, CHC Helicopter Corporation, Imperial Oil Limited, Ontario Financing Authority, the Royal Ontario Museum Foundation, Sylvia Ostry Foundation, Member, National Statistics Council, Statistics Canada, and Board of Management, International Institute of Public Finance. He was recently named as the 27th most influential tax expert in the world by the U.K. magazine *Tax Business*. He is Founding Editor-in-Chief of *International Tax and Public Finance*, published from 1994 to 2001. Dr. Mintz has consulted widely with the World Bank, the International Monetary Fund, the Organisation for Economic Co-operation and Development, the governments of Canada, Alberta, New Brunswick, Ontario, and Saskatchewan, and various businesses and non-profit organizations. He has published more than 180 books and articles in the fields of public economics and fiscal federalism. In 2002, his *Most Favored Nation: A Framework for Smart Economic Policy* was winner of the Purvis Prize for best book in economic policy and runner-up for Donner Prize in public policy.

STEVE MORGAN is a health economist from the University of British Columbia. He is Assistant Professor in the Department of Health Care and Epidemiology and Faculty at the Centre for Health Services and Policy Research. He is dedicated to research, teaching, and knowledge translation activities that have academic credibility and policy relevance. He studies health care financing, pharmacare policy, and processes for promoting evidence-based decision-making. His work seeks to identify policies that balance equitable access to necessary care with the need to control costs while providing incentive for valued innovation. He has conducted post-doctoral training at UBC and at McMaster University's Centre for Health Economics and Policy Analysis. He holds career awards from the Canadian Institutes of Health Research and the Michael Smith Foundation for Health Research, and is one of the Canadian alumni of the Harkness International Fellowships in Health Care Policy.

MARK STABILE is Associate Professor of Business Economics and Public Policy and the Director of the School of Public Policy and Governance at the University of Toronto. He is also a Faculty Research Fellow at the National Bureau of Economic Research, Cambridge Massachusetts and a fellow at the Rimini Centre for Economic Analysis, Italy. From 2003–05 he was the Senior Policy Advisor to the Ontario Minister of Finance where he worked on health, education, and tax policy. His recent work focuses on the economics of child health and development, the public/private mix in the financing of health care, and tax policy and health insurance. He has advised the Senate of Canada, Health Canada, and the Ontario Ministry of Health, among others, on health care reform.

TERRENCE SULLIVAN has been with Cancer Care Ontario since July 2001. He was from 1993 to 2001 the President of the Institute for Work & Health (IWH), a private not-for-profit institute affiliated with the University of Toronto which he developed into North America's leading research center on work related injury. He has played senior roles in the Ontario Ministries of Health, Cabinet Office and Intergovernmental Affairs. He served as Assistant Deputy Minister, Constitutional Affairs and Federal Provincial Relations, during the Charlottetown negotiations and served two successive First Ministers of Ontario as Executive Director of the Premier's Council on Health Strategy, including a period as Deputy Minister (1991). A behavioral scientist, he is the author/editor/co-editor of six recent books and numerous papers on occupational health, health policy and cancer control. He holds faculty appointments in the Department of Health Policy Management and Evaluation and the Department of Public Health Sciences at the University of Toronto.

ANDREY TARASOV is currently with the Transfer Pricing practice at Ernst & Young LLP in Toronto, Canada. When working on the contribution on this volume, he was Research Associate at the International Tax Program, Institute of International Business, Rotman School of Management, University of Toronto. He is an economist by training and has research interests in taxation, public policy, and corporate finance.

CAROLYN HUGHES TUOHY is Professor Emeritus of Political Science and Senior Fellow at the School of Public Policy and Governance, University of Toronto. Her area of research and teaching interest is in comparative public policy with an emphasis on social policy. She has recently served in senior academic leadership roles at the University of Toronto, including Vice-President, Policy Development, Associate Provost and Vice-President, Government and Institutional Relations. She is a Fellow of the Royal Society of Canada and a member of the boards of directors of the Institute for Clinical Evaluative Sciences and the Institute for Work and Health. Her most recent book is *Accidental Logics: The Dynamics of Change in the Health Care Arena in the United States, Britain, and Canada* (Oxford University Press, 1999). She is also author of *Policy and Politics in Canada: Institutionalized Ambivalence* (Temple University Press 1992), a treatment of Canadian public policy in comparative perspective. She has written numerous journal articles and book chapters in the areas of health and social policy, professional regulation, and comparative approaches in public policy.

WYNAND P.M.M. VAN DE VEN completed his thesis "Studies in Health Insurance and Econometrics" at Leiden University. Since 1986 he has been professor of Health Insurance at the Erasmus University Rotterdam. His teaching and research focus on managed competition in health care, competitive health insurance market, risk selection, moral hazard, risk equalization, managed care, and priority choices in health care. He has experience as a governor and adviser of insurance companies, political parties, government, research institute, hospitals, and other health care organizations. He has served as a member of many advisory committees and the editorial board of scientific journals. As a consultant for the World Bank and the World Health Organization, he has studied health care systems in Chile, Ireland, Israel, New Zealand, Poland, Russia, South Africa, and Sweden. He is a founding father of the European Risk Adjustment Network. His previous positions are Programme Director of the Master Health Economics, Policy and Law at Erasmus

University and Chair of the iHEA Jury-Committee for the annual Arrow Award for best paper in health economics.

JUERGEN WASEM holds the Alfried Krupp von Bohlen und Halbach Endowed Chair for Health Services Management at the University of Duisburg-Essen, Germany. Previously he was Professor at the Universities of Greifswald (1999–2003) and Munich (1997–99) and the University of Applied Sciences in Cologne (1994–97). He worked at the Max-Planck-Institute for the Study of Societies and at the Federal Ministry of Health. His research interests are in health insurance, cost effectiveness analysis and comparative health systems research. In the German health care system he holds a number of arbitrary positions, including chairperson of the committee to establish the federal fee schedule for GPs in social health insurance.

JOSEPH WHITE is Professor and Chair of Political Science, Luxenberg Family Professor of Public Policy, and Director of the Center for Policy Studies at Case Western Reserve University. He was previously Associate Professor of Health Systems Management in the School of Public Health and Tropical Medicine of Tulane University, and Research Associate and then Senior Fellow in Governmental Studies at the Brookings Institution. His research interests and publications have focused on federal budgeting policy and politics, health care finance in both the United States and other countries, Social Security and Medicare. He is co-author of *The Deficit and the Public Interest: The Search for Responsible Budgeting in the 1980s* (University of California Press and The Russell Sage Foundation, 1989 and 1991) and author of *Competing Solutions: American Health Care Proposals and International Experience* (Brookings, 1995), and *False Alarm: Why the Greatest Threat to Social Security and Medicare Is the Campaign to "Save" Them* (Johns Hopkins University Press, 2001, 2003).

Queen's Policy Studies
Recent Publications

The Queen's Policy Studies Series is dedicated to the exploration of major public policy issues that confront governments and society in Canada and other nations.

Our books are available from good bookstores everywhere, including the Queen's University bookstore (http://www.campusbookstore.com/). McGill-Queen's University Press is the exclusive world representative and distributor of books in the series. A full catalogue and ordering information may be found on their web site (http://mqup.mcgill.ca/).

School of Policy Studies

Canada in NORAD, 1957–2007: A History, Joseph T. Jockel, 2007
Paper ISBN 978-1-55339-134-0 Cloth ISBN 978-1-55339-135-7

Canadian Public-Sector Financial Management, Andrew Graham, 2007
Paper ISBN 978-1-55339-120-3 Cloth ISBN 978-1-55339-121-0

Emerging Approaches to Chronic Disease Management in Primary Health Care,
John Dorland and Mary Ann McColl (eds.), 2007
Paper ISBN 978-1-55339-130-2 Cloth ISBN 978-1-55339-131-9

Fulfilling Potential, Creating Success: Perspectives on Human Capital Development,
Garnett Picot, Ron Saunders and Arthur Sweetman (eds.), 2007
Paper ISBN 978-1-55339-127-2 Cloth ISBN 978-1-55339-128-9

Reinventing Canadian Defence Procurement: A View from the Inside, Alan S. Williams, 2006
Paper ISBN 0-9781693-0-1 (Published in association with Breakout Educational Network)

SARS in Context: Memory, History, Policy, Jacalyn Duffin and Arthur Sweetman (eds.), 2006
Paper ISBN 978-0-7735-3194-9 Cloth ISBN 978-0-7735-3193-2
(Published in association with McGill-Queen's University Press)

Dreamland: How Canada's Pretend Foreign Policy has Undermined Sovereignty, Roy Rempel, 2006
Paper ISBN 1-55339-118-7 Cloth ISBN 1-55339-119-5
(Published in association with Breakout Educational Network)

Canadian and Mexican Security in the New North America: Challenges and Prospects,
Jordi Díez (ed.), 2006   Paper ISBN 978-1-55339-123-4 Cloth ISBN 978-1-55339-122-7

Global Networks and Local Linkages: The Paradox of Cluster Development in an Open Economy, David A. Wolfe and Matthew Lucas (eds.), 2005
Paper ISBN 1-55339-047-4 Cloth ISBN 1-55339-048-2

Choice of Force: Special Operations for Canada, David Last and Bernd Horn (eds.), 2005
Paper ISBN 1-55339-044-X Cloth ISBN 1-55339-045-8

Force of Choice: Perspectives on Special Operations, Bernd Horn, J. Paul de B. Taillon, and
David Last (eds.), 2004   Paper ISBN 1-55339-042-3 Cloth 1-55339-043-1

New Missions, Old Problems, Douglas L. Bland, David Last, Franklin Pinch, and Alan Okros
(eds.), 2004   Paper ISBN 1-55339-034-2 Cloth 1-55339-035-0

The North American Democratic Peace: Absence of War and Security Institution-Building in Canada-US Relations, 1867-1958, Stéphane Roussel, 2004
Paper ISBN 0-88911-937-6 Cloth 0-88911-932-2

Implementing Primary Care Reform: Barriers and Facilitators, Ruth Wilson, S.E.D. Shortt and John Dorland (eds.), 2004   Paper ISBN 1-55339-040-7 Cloth 1-55339-041-5

Social and Cultural Change, David Last, Franklin Pinch, Douglas L. Bland, and Alan Okros (eds.), 2004   Paper ISBN 1-55339-032-6 Cloth 1-55339-033-4

Clusters in a Cold Climate: Innovation Dynamics in a Diverse Economy, David A. Wolfe and Matthew Lucas (eds.), 2004   Paper ISBN 1-55339-038-5 Cloth 1-55339-039-3

Canada Without Armed Forces? Douglas L. Bland (ed.), 2004
Paper ISBN 1-55339-036-9 Cloth 1-55339-037-7

Campaigns for International Security: Canada's Defence Policy at the Turn of the Century, Douglas L. Bland and Sean M. Maloney, 2004
Paper ISBN 0-88911-962-7 Cloth 0-88911-964-3

Understanding Innovation in Canadian Industry, Fred Gault (ed.), 2003
Paper ISBN 1-55339-030-X Cloth 1-55339-031-8

Delicate Dances: Public Policy and the Nonprofit Sector, Kathy L. Brock (ed.), 2003
Paper ISBN 0-88911-953-8 Cloth 0-88911-955-4

Beyond the National Divide: Regional Dimensions of Industrial Relations, Mark Thompson, Joseph B. Rose and Anthony E. Smith (eds.), 2003
Paper ISBN 0-88911-963-5 Cloth 0-88911-965-1

The Nonprofit Sector in Interesting Times: Case Studies in a Changing Sector, Kathy L. Brock and Keith G. Banting (eds.), 2003
Paper ISBN 0-88911-941-4 Cloth 0-88911-943-0

Clusters Old and New: The Transition to a Knowledge Economy in Canada's Regions, David A. Wolfe (ed.), 2003   Paper ISBN 0-88911-959-7 Cloth 0-88911-961-9

The e-Connected World: Risks and Opportunities, Stephen Coleman (ed.), 2003
Paper ISBN 0-88911-945-7 Cloth 0-88911-947-3

Knowledge Clusters and Regional Innovation: Economic Development in Canada, J. Adam Holbrook and David A. Wolfe (eds.), 2002
Paper ISBN 0-88911-919-8 Cloth 0-88911-917-1

Lessons of Everyday Law/Le droit du quotidien, Roderick Alexander Macdonald, 2002
Paper ISBN 0-88911-915-5 Cloth 0-88911-913-9

Improving Connections Between Governments and Nonprofit and Voluntary Organizations: Public Policy and the Third Sector, Kathy L. Brock (ed.), 2002
Paper ISBN 0-88911-899-X Cloth 0-88911-907-4

Governing Food: Science, Safety and Trade, Peter W.B. Phillips and Robert Wolfe (eds.), 2001
Paper ISBN 0-88911-897-3 Cloth 0-88911-903-1

The Nonprofit Sector and Government in a New Century, Kathy L. Brock and Keith G. Banting (eds.), 2001   Paper ISBN 0-88911-901-5 Cloth 0-88911-905-8

The Dynamics of Decentralization: Canadian Federalism and British Devolution, Trevor C. Salmon and Michael Keating (eds.), 2001   ISBN 0-88911-895-7

Institute of Intergovernmental Relations

Comparing Federal Systems, Third Edition, Ronald L. Watts, 2008 ISBN 978-1-55339-188-3

Canada: The State of the Federation 2005: Quebec and Canada in the New Century – New Dynamics, New Opportunities, vol. 19, Michael Murphy (ed.), 2007
Paper ISBN 978-1-55339-018-3 Cloth ISBN 978-1-55339-017-6

Spheres of Governance: Comparative Studies of Cities in Multilevel Governance Systems, Harvey Lazar and Christian Leuprecht (eds.), 2007
Paper ISBN 978-1-55339-019-0 Cloth ISBN 978-1-55339-129-6

Canada: The State of the Federation 2004, vol. 18, *Municipal-Federal-Provincial Relations in Canada*, Robert Young and Christian Leuprecht (eds.), 2006
Paper ISBN 1-55339-015-6 Cloth ISBN 1-55339-016-4

Canadian Fiscal Arrangements: What Works, What Might Work Better, Harvey Lazar (ed.), 2005
Paper ISBN 1-55339-012-1 Cloth ISBN 1-55339-013-X

Canada: The State of the Federation 2003, vol. 17, *Reconfiguring Aboriginal-State Relations*, Michael Murphy (ed.), 2005   Paper ISBN 1-55339-010-5 Cloth ISBN 1-55339-011-3

Canada: The State of the Federation 2002, vol. 16, *Reconsidering the Institutions of Canadian Federalism*, J. Peter Meekison, Hamish Telford and Harvey Lazar (eds.), 2004
Paper ISBN 1-55339-009-1 Cloth ISBN 1-55339-008-3

Federalism and Labour Market Policy: Comparing Different Governance and Employment Strategies, Alain Noël (ed.), 2004   Paper ISBN 1-55339-006-7 Cloth ISBN 1-55339-007-5

The Impact of Global and Regional Integration on Federal Systems: A Comparative Analysis, Harvey Lazar, Hamish Telford and Ronald L. Watts (eds.), 2003
Paper ISBN 1-55339-002-4 Cloth ISBN 1-55339-003-2

Canada: The State of the Federation 2001, vol. 15, *Canadian Political Culture(s) in Transition*, Hamish Telford and Harvey Lazar (eds.), 2002
Paper ISBN 0-88911-863-9 Cloth ISBN 0-88911-851-5

Federalism, Democracy and Disability Policy in Canada, Alan Puttee (ed.), 2002
Paper ISBN 0-88911-855-8 Cloth ISBN 1-55339-001-6, ISBN 0-88911-845-0 (set)

Comparaison des régimes fédéraux, 2ᵉ éd., Ronald L. Watts, 2002   ISBN 1-55339-005-9

Health Policy and Federalism: A Comparative Perspective on Multi-Level Governance, Keith G. Banting and Stan Corbett (eds.), 2001
Paper ISBN 0-88911-859-0 Cloth ISBN 1-55339-000-8, ISBN 0-88911-845-0 (set)

Disability and Federalism: Comparing Different Approaches to Full Participation, David Cameron and Fraser Valentine (eds.), 2001
Paper ISBN 0-88911-857-4 Cloth ISBN 0-88911-867-1, ISBN 0-88911-845-0 (set)

Federalism, Democracy and Health Policy in Canada, Duane Adams (ed.), 2001
Paper ISBN 0-88911-853-1 Cloth ISBN 0-88911-865-5, ISBN 0-88911-845-0 (set)

John Deutsch Institute for the Study of Economic Policy

The 2006 Federal Budget: Rethinking Fiscal Priorities, Charles M. Beach, Michael Smart and Thomas A. Wilson (eds.), 2007
Paper ISBN 978-1-55339-125-8 Cloth ISBN 978-1-55339-126-6

Health Services Restructuring in Canada: New Evidence and New Directions,
Charles M. Beach, Richard P. Chaykowksi, Sam Shortt, France St-Hilaire and Arthur
Sweetman (eds.), 2006   Paper ISBN 978-1-55339-076-3 Cloth ISBN 978-1-55339-075-6

A Challenge for Higher Education in Ontario, Charles M. Beach (ed.), 2005
Paper ISBN 1-55339-074-1 Cloth ISBN 1-55339-073-3

Current Directions in Financial Regulation, Frank Milne and Edwin H. Neave (eds.),
Policy Forum Series no. 40, 2005   Paper ISBN 1-55339-072-5 Cloth ISBN 1-55339-071-7

Higher Education in Canada, Charles M. Beach, Robin W. Boadway and R. Marvin McInnis
(eds.), 2005   Paper ISBN 1-55339-070-9 Cloth ISBN 1-55339-069-5

Financial Services and Public Policy, Christopher Waddell (ed.), 2004
Paper ISBN 1-55339-068-7 Cloth ISBN 1-55339-067-9

The 2003 Federal Budget: Conflicting Tensions, Charles M. Beach and Thomas A. Wilson
(eds.), Policy Forum Series no. 39, 2004
Paper ISBN 0-88911-958-9 Cloth ISBN 0-88911-956-2

Canadian Immigration Policy for the 21st Century, Charles M. Beach, Alan G. Green and
Jeffrey G. Reitz (eds.), 2003   Paper ISBN 0-88911-954-6 Cloth ISBN 0-88911-952-X

Framing Financial Structure in an Information Environment, Thomas J. Courchene and
Edwin H. Neave (eds.), Policy Forum Series no. 38, 2003
Paper ISBN 0-88911-950-3 Cloth ISBN 0-88911-948-1

*Towards Evidence-Based Policy for Canadian Education/Vers des politiques canadiennes
d'éducation fondées sur la recherche,* Patrice de Broucker and/et Arthur Sweetman (eds./
dirs.), 2002   Paper ISBN 0-88911-946-5 Cloth ISBN 0-88911-944-9

*Money, Markets and Mobility: Celebrating the Ideas of Robert A. Mundell, Nobel Laureate
in Economic Sciences,* Thomas J. Courchene (ed.), 2002
Paper ISBN 0-88911-820-5 Cloth ISBN 0-88911-818-3

The State of Economics in Canada: Festschrift in Honour of David Slater, Patrick Grady and
Andrew Sharpe (eds.), 2001   Paper ISBN 0-88911-942-2 Cloth ISBN 0-88911-940-6

The 2000 Federal Budget: Retrospect and Prospect, Paul A.R. Hobson and
Thomas A. Wilson (eds.), 2001   Policy Forum Series no. 37, 2001
Paper ISBN 0-88911-816-7 Cloth ISBN 0-88911-814-0

Our publications may be purchased at leading bookstores, including the Queen's
University Bookstore
(http://www.campusbookstore.com/), or can be ordered online from: McGill-
Queen's University Press, at
http://mqup.mcgill.ca/ordering.php

For more information about new and backlist titles from Queen's Policy Studies,
visit the McGill-Queen's
University Press web site at:
http://mqup.mcgill.ca/